UFOs
AND
UFOLOGY

UFOs
AND
UFOLOGY

THE FIRST 50 YEARS

PAUL DEVEREUX
AND
PETER BROOKESMITH

with additional material by
Montague Keen and Nigel Watson

Facts On File, Inc.

First published in the UK 1997 by Blandford
a Cassell imprint
Cassell plc, Wellington House,
125 Strand, London WC2R OBB

Overall text copyright © 1997 Paul Devereux
& Peter Brookesmith

Additional text copyright © 1977: Nigel Watson in final part
of Chapter 3; Montague Keen in final part of Chapter 6

Illustrative material copyright as specifically credited and
identified.

Facts on File
11 Penn Plaza
New York, NY 10001

A Cataloging-in-Publication Data entry for this title is available
from Facts on File

Facts On File books are available at special discounts when
purchased in bulk quantities for businesses, associations, institutions
or sales promotions. Please call our Special Sales Department in
New York at (212) 967–8800 or (800) 322–8755.

You can find Facts On File on the World Wide Web at
http://www.factsonfile.com

ISBN:0–8160–3800–7

Designed by Richard Carr
Jacket design Jamie Tanner

10 9 8 7 6 5 4 3 2 1

This book is printed on acid-free paper.

Printed by Dah Hua Printing Press Co., Hong Kong

ACKNOWLEDGMENTS

Paul Devereux would like to thank John Derr, Charla
Devereux, Greg Long, Paul Fuller, Hal Puthoff, Dennis
Stacy, Erling Strand, David Whitley, the International
Consciousness Research Laboratories (ICRL), and
everyone else who has so generously assisted with information, permissions, pictures, field research or general
support.

Peter Brookesmith would like to thank David
Quickenden, Bob Rickard, Paul Sieveking and John
Rimmer for the initial opportunities to develop in print
some of the reflections on ufology and "alien abductions"
presented here; and for information, assistance and
encouragement of various kinds, Christopher Allen; Sue
Blackmore; Rebecca Keith; Philip J. Klass; Errol Bruce
Knapp; Peter Merlin; Sarah Reason; Barbara Skew; and
Ed Stewart.

Both authors are grateful to Montague Keen and Nigel
Watson for their contributions to this work, to Rob Irving
for his assistance, and to their editors at Blandford Press
in London, Stuart Booth and Antonia Maxwell.

Photographs have been credited at point of use. Although
attempts have been made to contact all copyright holders
where known, should there be any unintentional or
unavoidable omissions, authentic copyright holders are
asked to accept the authors' apologies and are invited to
contact the publishers.

Contents

The Riddle of Ufology

I T IS NOW half a century since news of 'flying saucers' first hit the world's headlines, and we still await what many people consider the definitive expression of extra-terrestrial contact: the landing of an other-worldly spaceship on the White House lawn. And if not a landing by relatively peaceable ETs, then at least the vapourizing of the White House itself by more truculent aliens, as digitally realized on our cinema screens in the film *Independence Day*.

As it happens, the appearance of this blockbuster sci-fi movie in 1996 coincided with what popular journalism took as the next best thing to a UFO landing – the opportunity to use the long-savoured headline screaming that there was proof of life on Mars. The more sober reality was that NASA scientists had discovered fossils of bacteria-like organisms, no bigger than one-hundredth the diameter of a human hair, inside a meteorite. The creatures' age was reckoned at about 3.6 billion years. The meteorite was a rock that had been blasted off the Red Planet by the impact of a comet 16 million years ago, and had finally crashed to Earth thousands of years in the past. The consensus was that life on Mars had never developed far and was long gone – if, indeed, further investigation confirmed that it had been there at all, for not all who examined the rock containing the alleged fossils were convinced that it held any evidence of biological activity at all.

In a visually dramatic scene from the Hollywood blockbuster film *Independence Day*, the aliens in a giant craft destroy the White House with fearsome beam weaponry. Today's ufology tends to be paranoid and this scene perhaps provides a cathartic moment for those who complain about government conspiracies.
20th Century Fox (courtesy Kobal)

This meteoric rock from Mars contained features that some scientists considered to be residue from micro-organisms. *NASA*

But scientific caution has no more been the favourite currency of politicians than it has of journalists: US President Bill Clinton welcomed the discovery and announced that he was convening a scientific summit later in the year to 'discuss how America should pursue answers to the scientific questions raised by this finding'. Reporters besieged astronomers with questions about extra-terrestrial life. Radio astronomers, whose programmes to detect alien signals emerging from the depths of space had been languishing due to government budget cuts, found themselves featured in front-page news

stories. Journalists illustrated their articles with stills from *Independence Day*, along with antique depictions of alien invasions inspired by H.G. Wells' *War of the Worlds*.

In addition to journalists, politicians, and scientists with a research programme to maintain, another group of people greatly energized by the news of the weeny worms from Mars were ufologists. Consideration of this group brings us to the central focus of this book.

As flying saucers graduated into the more serious-sounding Unidentified Flying Objects, or UFOs, they attracted a broad penumbra of human interest which has become known as 'ufology'. The dictionary tells us that an 'ology' is a 'science or branch of knowledge', but ufology has shown itself to be a wide-spectrum phenomenon incorporating genuine inquiry and a measure of scholarship at one extreme, and gullibility, cultism and varieties of religious fervour at the other, with various shades of misinformation, intellectual laziness, beliefs, opinions and notions crowding together in between. In fact, the greater the fantasy element they

Topographic features in the Cydonia region of Mars, photographed from a space probe. Are they really pyramids, ruined cities and a vast sculpture of a face, or natural features that simply look at a distance like those things? *NASA*

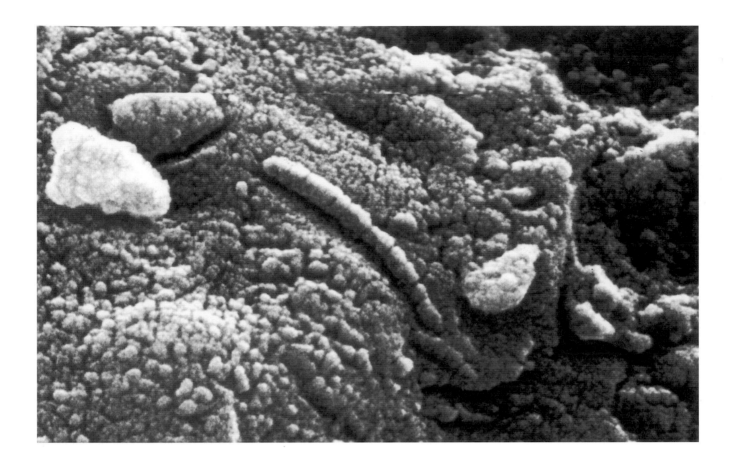

This high-resolution scanning electron microscope image shows an unusual tube-like structural form that is less than 1/100th the width of a human hair in size found in meteorite ALH84001, a meteorite believed to be of Martian origin. This structure will be the subject of future investigations that could substantiate whether or not it is fossil evidence of primitive life on Mars 3.6 billion years ago. NASA

contain, the more easily disseminated do ufological ideas become: like most fringe subjects, ufology feeds a desperate spiritual hunger and need for release from mundanity felt by vast numbers of people within modern Westernized societies.

The news of the Martian proto-bugs revealed this perfectly, for ufologists were, by and large, almost ecstatic – to judge from exchanges on the Internet, a new and sensitive barometer of what interests ufologists today. Subscriber lists, newsgroups and Web pages were suddenly filled with news of the 'discovery' from Mars. Most of those who took part in the discussions seemed convinced that the finding was evidence for their belief that extra-terrestrials had been visiting Earth for at least 50 years, and possibly for centuries. Detached observers could be forgiven for smiling a trifle wryly – not at the possibility that life exists, or has existed, on other planets in the Universe, but at the touching readiness with which a large proportion of those who call themselves ufologists turned a tentative scientific finding into grist for their personal convictions.

The maybe microscopic Martians also provided a fillip for Enterprise Mission, a group that has spent years trying to convince the world that NASA photographs of the Cydonia region of Mars show a mile-wide sculpture of a human face, ruined cities and other artefacts. According to the notion's apologists, these are more than half a million years old, and are the relics of extra-terrestrial activity on Mars. (Earlier in the summer of 1996, the group had announced their discovery of huge crystalline structures on the Moon. NASA, they said, had been covering up the truth for decades. As evidence for their claim they produced a number of photographs taken on the Moon by astronauts on the Apollo 12 mission. The astronauts denied seeing any such thing, which to Enterprise Mission was simply confirmation of a cover-up.) These people, too, fall within the scope of the term 'ufologists'.

In fact, it is now realized that it is profoundly unlikely that any complex life forms could have evolved on Mars, because studies by scientists such as Helmut Lammer of

the Space Research Institute in Austria show that Mars suffered early, strong loss of atmospheric mass due to its small size and gravitational pull, so there was simply insufficient time for an Earth-like biosphere to form. Undeterred, some ufologists promote modified versions of the Ancient Martians idea, invoking such notions as the Prior Colonization Hypothesis, in which it is supposed that a culture that was not indigenous to Mars made the Cydonia features. A special version of this is the Previous Technical Civilization Hypothesis, which proposes that in the prehistory of our race such a civilization had developed, gone to Mars and left the Cydonia features as a message for the future. Such beliefs receive extra spins from claims that the great Neolithic monuments of the Avebury complex – and even Glastonbury Abbey – in southern England display the same geometrical relationships to one another as do the objects on Mars.

In any of these scenarios, of course, the presence of possible bacteria inside an incomprehensibly ancient Martian rock has no relevance – but such logic does not often deter the dedicated ufologist. It is equally difficult to see what Enterprise Mission or other Cydonia *aficionados* have in common with proponents of the belief that extra-terrestrial aliens have abducted huge numbers of Earthlings (mainly citizens of the US, it would appear) and are exploiting them in a programme of forced inter-

The south-west quadrant of the world's largest prehistoric stone circle at Avebury in England. Some enthusiasts claim that the geometry of the layout of the features of this vast Neolithic complex is a scaled down version of that found in the Cydonia region of Mars.
Paul Devereux

breeding, to produce alien-human hybrids – except, of course, that these abductionists are called 'ufologists' and they believe that UFOs are extra-terrestrial craft.

There is no doubt that the overwhelming majority of those interested in UFOs implicitly accept the extra-terrestrial hypothesis (ETH): the slightly self-contradictory notion that 'Unidentified' Flying Objects are identifiable as alien spacecraft. This primary conviction, however, often acts merely as a springboard to a greater array of beliefs. While some maintain that the aliens are demons full of evil intent, others see them as gods from the heavens. Some claim that the government – any government – has known about the alien visitors for decades, and produce what they believe are ultra-top-secret documents to bolster their case. Others think governments are covering up nothing but their own ignorance and confusion as to what UFOs actually are. Some think that aliens need to eat human flesh in order to survive; others maintain that they feed off raw cattle flesh. UFOs may be capable of faster-than-light travel, or may hop through hyperspace, or may have travelled through time. The aliens themselves have been reported to resemble (among other things) golden-haired angelic types of human, horrible hairy trolls, robots, dwarves, giants, and the increasingly familiar 'grays' – small, bald, sexless creatures with huge, black, mesmerizing eyes.

It is thus clear that the ETH is not a single hypothesis, and, taken together, its many different forms fail to gel into a coherent whole – unlike the theories and data of a scientific discipline such as physics. For each of these ideas there is at least one 'ufologist' stoutly defending it, and sometimes a whole host of them.

Yet there are many others who are intrigued by UFO reports (and even claims of abductions by aliens) who believe none of these things. They call themselves ufologists, too. They range from those who think UFOs are somehow used as a means of social control, to those who think they reflect social and mass-psychological conditions and mechanisms. A few even think UFOs are airborne life forms. Others prefer to regard them as materializations – the product of human psychic powers. However, there are some who, although they have published articles in UFO magazines and lectured at conferences about UFOs, reject the ETH and do not describe or even think of themselves as ufologists. Yet, by the very nature of their involvement they labour beneath the wide umbrella of ufology. And then there are the critics of ufology who are neither accorded the title of 'ufologist' nor adopt it: out-and-out skeptics who explain UFO reports as entirely the product of misperceptions, hoaxes, human errors and (sometimes arcane) psychological processes. Yet again, even these skeptics are, willy-nilly, 'ufologists' insofar as they comment on and interpret UFO reports, and make judgements on general trends in ufology.

So, the 'ology' of UFOs does encompass certain valuable areas of knowledge and displays flashes of scientific and scholarly thinking, but many claim that it is not in itself a true branch of knowledge or science. Perhaps it is best to think of it as a kind of riddle. Like any good riddle, it has several mutating aspects. What is the UFO at the heart of ufology – a physically objective phenomenon, or a mirage? What is ufology itself – an equivalent mirage, or a body of knowledge, however disparate and incoherent, that is truly struggling towards the definition of an objective phenomenon? Are there really aliens visiting us, and if so, are they from outer or inner space, from extra-terrestrial sources or from the depths of the human psyche? Is ufology an unperceived result of a clash between two unknowns – some exotic terrestrial phenomenon and poorly understood mechanisms of the human mind? Or is it what the literal-minded ufologists claim it to be – the simple cataloguing of extra-terrestrial craft and entitities?

It is time to take stock, and the advent of the half-centenary of the subject gives us that opportunity. This book does not set out to provide an endless list of detailed case histories of UFO encounters, or exhaustive arguments for one ufological persuasion over another. We have deliberately used broad brushstrokes to paint in the main patterns within ufology. Or, to use another metaphor, we want to see the wood rather than the trees. In so doing, however, we will nevertheless encounter some of the latest information in ufology, parts of it hardly known even among ufological enthusiasts. This is a UFO book for adults, for mature minds, and by the end of our exercise the reader will have decided whether ufology is literally the study of real alien craft, or a passing show of the fads, fancies, fears and dreams of a lonely species – a godless techno-culture's surrogate for religion. Or something in between.

In the final pages of this book, we will indicate some of our own views, but first we have a fascinating journey to undertake through five decades (and more) of the unknown – an unknown that includes the mysteries of human nature and consciousness, as well as strange things seen in our skies and weird beings encountered in remote places.

Paul Devereux and *Peter Brookesmith*

1

The Saucers Fly In

THE DAWNING OF UFOLOGY

A
S IT DRONED eastwards at just over 9000ft (2770m), Kenneth Arnold's Callair aircraft seemed but a speck against the vast surroundings of the Cascade Mountains in the north-western US. Arnold may have thought that all he was doing on that bright and crystal-clear afternoon of 24 June 1947 was looking for a downed plane lost somewhere amid the north–south range of snow-capped volcanoes, but he was in fact flying into a particularly bizarre chapter of history. To many people, Arnold was the man who saw the world's first UFOs, but the facts – the whole story of strange things seen in the sky – give the lie to that superficial impression.

Thomas Sandby and his eighteenth-century colleagues would certainly have challenged it. Sandby was a famous watercolourist and a founder member of the Royal Academy. Along with other artistic and scientific luminaries of the day, he was being royally entertained at Windsor Castle, Berkshire, England. The date was 18 August 1783. As the evening was warm and the sky quite clear, after dinner the distinguished party strolled out onto the castle terrace. Their attention was caught by a remarkable phenomenon to the north-east, as described by one of Sandby's fellow guests, Tiberius Cavallo, in the *Philosophical Transactions* of 1784:

Snow-capped Mount Adams in the Cascade range, viewed from the Yakima Indian Reservation, close to where Kenneth Arnold first touched down after his historic flight, and where there was a huge outbreak of strange lights in the 1970s, as described in Chapter 10. *Paul Devereux*

I suddenly saw appear an oblong cloud moving more or less parallel to the horizon. Under this cloud could be seen a luminous object which soon became spherical, brilliantly lit, which came to a halt. It was then about 9.45pm. This strange sphere seemed at first to be pale blue in colour, but its luminosity increased and soon it set off again towards the east. Then the object changed direction and moved parallel to the horizon before disappearing to the south-east. I watched it for half a minute, and the light it gave out was prodigious; it lit up everything on the ground. Before it vanished it changed its shape, became oblong, and at the same time as a sort of trail appeared, it seemed to separate into two small bodies. Scarcely two minutes later the sound of an explosion was heard.

Sandby estimated the apparent size of the object to be half that of the Moon, but its light was 'much more vivid'. Like Cavallo, he observed that as the object progressed through the sky it 'grew more oblong', and then 'divided and formed a long train of small luminous bodies each having a tail'. It is fortunate that this phenomenon had a number of high-calibre witnesses, including the scientific elite of the day, and that Thomas Sandby was there to record it visually. Not only did he make a painting of the object, but he and his brother Paul also made a series of aquatints, one of which is reproduced here. It is the closest we can come to a photograph of an Unidentified Flying Object by a witness prior to the invention of the camera as we know it.

The 'meteor' of 18 August 1783. Leading scientists and artists of the day viewed the phenomenon from the north-east corner of the Terrace at Windsor Castle in this aquatint by Thomas and Paul Sandby.
Reproduced courtesy of the Trustees of the British Museum

Sandby's 'train of small luminous bodies' was somewhat similar in appearance to what Kenneth Arnold encountered in the Cascades. The searching pilot was startled by 'a tremendous flash... in the sky' that lit up the plane's cockpit. He looked urgently all around his airspace, but no other craft was nearby. Then the flash occurred again: Arnold described it as being 'almost like an arc light'. This time he saw that it came from the direction of a group of objects to the north of Mount Rainier, chief peak of the Cascades, in the area of Mount Baker. 'I saw a chain of peculiar aircraft approaching Mount Rainier very rapidly,' he recalled in 1977. He went on:

They seemed to fly in an echelon formation. However, in looking at them against the sky and against the snow of Mount Rainier as they approached, I just couldn't discern any tails on them, and I had never seen an aircraft without a tail! These were fairly large-sized and there were nine of them.

Arnold initially assumed they were some kind of military craft, but was puzzled by their non-standard flying formation and the fact that each object was independent and moved in its own rhythm. Arnold was fascinated at the way they 'fluttered and sailed, tipping their wings alternately and emitting those very bright blue-white flashes from their surfaces'. In a 1952 account, he commented that at the time he took it that the flashes were reflections off what he assumed were the objects' highly polished surfaces. At first sighting, the chain of glittering objects was about 100 miles (160km) from Arnold's position, but their flight path eventually crossed at what the pilot figured was about 23 miles (37km) in front of him, and at about the same altitude. The amazed airman was able to clock the time it took the objects to cover the 50 miles (80km) from Mount Rainier to Mount Adams in the south. Although he had yet to work out their speed, Arnold knew that they were flying faster than any military plane he knew of (his final calculations gave the formation's speed as around 1300mph/2080km/h).

Between Rainier and Adams is a plateau called Goat Ridge, and knowing the length of this he was able to estimate the extent of the brilliant objects' formation at 5 miles (8km). As he peered at them, he felt he was looking at objects each about 100ft (30m) in diameter. When they tipped one way they flashed and appeared round; when they levelled off they seemed very thin. Not only did they

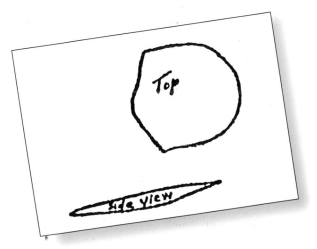

Kenneth Arnold's own sketches of the objects he saw in the Cascades.

not have tail fins – they didn't have wings either! On even keener scrutiny, Arnold made out their shapes as tadpole-like, although the last object was fluttering and jerking so much more even than the others that he couldn't really make out its form at all. 'I thought if there were human beings in them,' Arnold remarked wryly, 'they would have been made into hamburger.' The nine shining objects hugged the terrain, and weaved in and out of the Cascade's jagged peaks and protrusions.

Experiencing an 'eerie feeling', Arnold made directly for his original destination, the airfield at Yakima, on the eastern side of the mountain range. In effect, when he landed there at four o'clock on that Tuesday afternoon, the scrabble to solve the enigma of UFOs began the current phase we now call ufology – but human beings had been making that attempt long, long before Arnold made his eventful flight.

Thomas Sandby was clearly fascinated by what he had seen at Windsor, as evidenced by the number of artistic depictions made of his sighting, but he lived at a time we call the Age of Reason, when the attempt to make a rational, scientific observation of nature, and to identify its laws, had succeeded in its escape from the tight confines of dark, religious dogmatism. It was as if the human intellect, losing its balance one way, had pulled itself over excessively in the other direction in order to correct its wobble. The New Rationalists wanted the Universe to work with the precision and regularity of a machine. In such a world view, then even more than now, there wasn't much room for inexplicable phenomena, and the great scientific institution, the Royal Society, concluded its study of the Windsor object (which in fact was seen over a much wider area than Windsor) by labelling it a 'meteor' – even though many witnesses reported that it was initially stationary, and changed direction and shape when it moved. The unhelpful designation is further highlighted in this account of the 'awful meteor' by Dr William Cooper, Fellow of the Royal Society and Archdeacon of York, who witnessed it from another location:

...singularly striking [were] the sulphurous vapours on every side... a brilliant tremulous light... seemed stationary; but in a short time it burst from its position... It passed directly over our heads with a buzzing noise, seemingly at a height of 60 yards... At last this wonderful meteor divided into several glowing balls of fire, the chief part still remaining in its full splendour... During its progress, the whole of the atmosphere... was illuminated with the most beautifully vivid light. The horses shrunk with fear; and people on the road [were] consternated.

Another 'meteor' sighting was made at Hatton Garden, London, by Sir John Staveley and reported in the *Journal of Natural History and Philosophy and Chemistry* for 10 August 1809. 'I saw many meteors near the corner of a black cloud from which lights were emitted,' wrote Staveley. 'It was as though patches of blinding light were dancing and passing across the cloud.' One of the meteors attained the size and brightness of Venus, he claimed, but he could see 'no body' in the light. He observed this remarkable black cloud, with its lights leaving and re-entering it 'at countless points', for nearly an hour.

¤ DRAGONFIRE

Meteors aside, during the centuries leading up to the Age of Reason one of the favourite explanations for strange lights seen in the sky was that they were dragons. Even the 1783 objects were referred to by some people as *draco volans*, the 'flying dragon'.

Such an interpretation was given to a phenomenon encountered at the English coastal town of Christchurch, Dorset, by a group of French clergy, who in the year 1113 were travelling through south-west England performing miraculous healings with the supposed relics of the Virgin. The account of their travels, written by Herman of Laon, describes a dragon which had come out of the waters of Christchurch Bay (through which runs a geological fault line) 'breathing fire out of its nostrils'. The thing was 'incredibly long and had five heads, from which it breathed sulphurous flames; it was flying around from place to place, and setting fire to houses one by one...'.

A fire-breathing dragon from *Mundus Subterraneus* by Athanasius Kircher, Amsterdam 1678. *Fortean Picture Library*

(It also destroyed a ship in the bay, supposedly containing the local dean, but that could have been a bit of propaganda inserted by the holy men!)

Similarly, the *Anglo Saxon Chronicle* records for the year 793 'exceptional flashes of lightning, and fiery dragons' seen flying in the air over Northumbria in north-east England. Sixteenth-century Swiss scholar Conrad Wolffart chronicled the report of an immense blazing globe seen over Brittany, France, in 457, from which hung a ball of fire that looked like a dragon and emitted beams of light. And so on – accounting for mysterious lights in the sky as fiery dragons was commonplace for many centuries in Europe and across the world.

The *draco volans* interpretation of strange lights in the sky was nevertheless the subject of scholarly challenge, starting at least in the thirteenth century when Albertus Magnus wrote:

> *Some people say they have seen dragons flying in the air and breathing sheets of fire. This I think impossible, unless they mean vapours of the sort described in the book Of Meteors, which are called dragons. These have been shown to burn in the air, to move and give off smoke, and sometimes (rolled into a ball) to fall into water and hiss as white-hot iron would; sometimes again the vapour rises in conditions of wind from the water, breaks out in the air, and burns plants or anything else that it touches. Because it ascends and descends in this way, and because of the cloud of smoke which drifts out on either side like wings, ignorant people take it to be an animal flying and breathing out fire.*
>
> Translation from the Latin by Jeremy Harte

Thomas Hill likewise stated in 1590 that the skyborne, luminous so-called dragon was actually 'a fume kindled' that gave the accidental appearance of the mythical creature. But the belief that strange aerial phenomena were dragons lingered a long time: as late as 1792, for instance, a Scottish pastor recorded in his diary for November that 'many of the country people observed very uncommon phenomena in the air (which they call dragons) of a red fiery colour, appearing in the north and flying rapidly towards the east...'.

¤ SIGNS IN THE HEAVENS

Another popular explanation for unidentified flying objects prior to the Age of Reason was that such things were portents or divine signs. Among the better-known examples of this interpretation is the 'frightful spectacle' that took place at Nuremberg in April 1561, recorded in a contemporary woodcut and broadsheet. Black, blue and deep red objects taking various forms – spheres, crosses, cylinders – clustered in the sky. This was seen by witnesses as an aerial battle, and some objects apparently fell to the ground, dissolving into smoke or steam.

The Nuremberg Broadsheet, 1561.

Similar events seemingly took place over Basel, Switzerland, in 1566, and these were also recorded in a broadsheet of the day. At sunrise and sunset on 17 and 18 July, the sun altered in apparent size and colour, and red globes (seen by some as tears of blood shed by the sun) appeared in the sky; on 7 August, around sunrise, numerous large black orbs were seen chasing through the heavens, and some of these turned red and fiery before vanishing. (It seems that these types of phenomena were not totally unique in Switzerland, for Wolffart noted that 'burning torches, fiery darts, flying fire' were often seen in the skies over Switzerland in 1104.) Two glowing wheels were seen over Hamburg in November 1697, and in his *Historia Francorum* St Gregory, Bishop of Tours, recorded numerous strange lights, golden globes and other aerial phenomena in Europe which he ascribed to signs from heaven.

These sorts of phenomena did not occur only in Europe. In Japan, for example, strange fireballs were frequently seen flying over Kyoto during May 1606. One appeared as a spinning ball of fire, looking rather like a red wheel. This hovered near the Nijo Castle and had many witnesses who considered it a portent. Japan was no stranger to such omens: in August 989, for example, three brilliantly luminous, spherical objects were seen which later merged together.

As bizarre and medieval as these accounts may sound to us, if we strip them of their 'portent' contexts and contemporary connotations, it can be seen that people within the modern age of ufology have reported similar phenomena. For example, 'flying crosses' were a major class of reported UFO in 1967, and accounts of spheres or discs of light merging together is not all that uncommon in the modern literature. Black UFOs, sometimes but not always changing colour, are also reported from time to time: Paul Devereux and a fellow witness saw a round, perfectly black object in eastern England in the summer of 1967, for instance. Even though it was a sunny afternoon, and the object was several yards in diameter, it was so utterly black, with no reflections on it at all, that for all one could tell it could have been a globe, a disc on edge or even a hole in the fabric of space-time sucking in photons. It flew just above tree-top height, and seemed to be pacing the car in which the witnesses were travelling. Suddenly it vanished, only to reappear moments later half a mile (0.8km) further away. Finally, it soared up into the glare of the sky and was lost to sight.

The Basel Broadsheet, 1566.

⌘ FLYING SHAMANS AND WANDERING SPIRITS

There were also other, less well-known cultural ways of identifying Unidentified Flying Objects. The Saami people of Lappland considered mystery lights arcing through their night-time skies to be the disembodied spirits of shamans flying around; similarly, the Penobscot Indians of Maine considered flying lights to be shamans out and about taking part in night battles. To this day, rural people in certain parts of the Valley of Mexico think of the balls of light that haunt their areas as night-flying witches (while people in Mexico City refer to UFOs). In 1895, when Mary Kingsley saw a purple ball of light glide over the waters of Lake Ncovi in Gabon, Africa, and then sink – still glowing – beneath the surface, the local people told her that such a light was *aku* – devil. Similar lights seen over the waters of certain Scottish lochs were so well known that they were given the Gaelic term *gealbhan*. To Chinese Buddhists, large orange or gold lights regularly seen floating around the peaks of sacred mountains such as Wutaishan and Omei were 'Bodhisattva Lights', while white spheres of light that often appeared in the vicinity of Changkat Asah, a hill in Malaysia, were called *pennangal* by the natives, and thought to be the spectral heads of women who had died in childbirth. A group of these lights was witnessed in 1895 by Sir George Maxwell, a government official at Tanjong Malim.

There are hints in some traditions of dangers associated with getting too close to such strange phenomena. The Wintu Indians of California refer to mystery lights as 'spirit eaters'; the people living around Darjeeling in north-east India refer to the *chota-admis*, which are conceived of as the lanterns of supernatural little men, and to approach them is said to incur illness or even death. Modern ufology has numerous reports indicating that close encounters with UFOs can result in burns or strange illnesses, not to mention mental disorders.

There is virtually no end to the range of interpretations given to UFOs by early, traditional and remote peoples. We do not have to accept those interpretations, but we should not assume that 'primitive' peoples simply invented or imagined phenomena that occurred in their environment. In many regards, traditional peoples were – and are – far more sensitive to their surroundings than are modern Westerners. The Ayamara Indians of the Andes, for example, are acutely aware of meteorological phenomena in their high-altitude terrain, and have different words for the various kinds of natural lights they see – meteors, lightning, and so forth. Anthropologist Gary Urton reports that they reserve the term *sullaje* for a particular kind of mysterious light phenomenon which they see on the mountains that does not relate to normal meteorological effects.

Some of today's ufologists who ascribe to the mainstream extra-terrestrial hypothesis (ETH) dismiss these early and traditional accounts of UFOs, saying that they are different to 'real' UFOs, which they consider to be craft. In fact, most modern UFO reports do deal simply

Rural folk in the country around Mount Popocatapetl, Mexico, tell a British TV crew about the mysterious lights they see at night, and which they think to be the flying spirits of witches or magicians. *Paul Devereux*

with 'lights in the sky' (LITS), and even some 'close encounter' accounts describe light forms that are indistinguishable from the reported appearance of some of these non-Western UFOs.

☿ SKY CRAFT

There are a few early accounts of 'craft' in the European historical literature, such as the story recorded by the English chronicler Gervase of Tilbury concerning the churchgoers of Gravesend, Kent, England. They emerged from their church one Sunday in 1211 to see a strange ship in the sky. It dangled an anchor, which caught on a tombstone in the churchyard. An occupant of the ship leaped down towards the anchor, making motions as if swimming in the air. The bishop ordered members of the congregation to give up their attempts to snatch the sky-sailor, and he rejoined his fellows back in the ship. They cut the anchor free and sailed out of view. According to the ninth-century manuscript *Liber contra insulam vulgi opinionem*, there was also a belief in France that there was 'a certain region' called Magonia, apparently situated in or beyond the sky, from which ships sailed in the clouds. Medieval fairs sometimes exhibited people who were said to have fallen from these Magonian vessels.

But it is only when we come to Western accounts in more modern times – the decades leading up to the commencement of what we might call the Ufological Age – that the 'vessel- or machine-in-the-sky' interpretation begins to dominate. Luminous phenomena seen in the skies over Nebraska during the middle decades of the nineteenth century gave rise to a local folk ballad that merges the old dragon imagery with the emerging vision of the machine-in-the-sky:

'Twas on a dark night in '66
When we was layin' steel
We seen a flyin' engine
Without no wing or wheel
It came a-roarin' in the sky
With lights along the side
And scales like a serpent's hide.

Out with the old, in with the new. Researchers Jerome Clark and Marcello Truzzi have noted a remarkably similar description that came out of Chile around the same time. In 1868, the *Zoologist* printed this eyewitness description from a Chilean newspaper:

On its body, elongated like a serpent we could see only brilliant scales, which clashed together with a metallic sound as the strange animal turned its body in flight.

The Mysterious Flying Light That Hovered Over St. Mary's College, Oakland, and Then Started for San Francisco. It Is Exactly Like That Described by Sacramentans, and Similar to the Cut Published a Few Days Ago in "The Call" From a Description Furnished by One Who Saw It.

An engraving from the *San Francisco Call*, November 1896.

In 1891, two workmen in Indiana reported seeing a cylindrical object 20ft (6m) long, which they described as looking like 'a headless monster... propelled by fin-like attachments', in the early-morning hours of 5 September.

This, and the earlier Nebraskan and Chilean reports, seem to have been the harbingers of a wave of sightings that broke out across North America between 1896 and 1897, in which the aerial vessel or machine finally broke through as the dominant interpretation. The wave started with a series of reports of mystery 'hot air balloons' from people in the US and Canada. These took the form of illuminated and black round objects. Then, in the early evening of 17 November 1896, hundreds of people reported an 'electric arc lamp' passing over Sacramento, California. A dark shape was seen looming behind it. Some people claimed to hear music emanating from the object, and others even stated that voices could be heard. Nine days later, an object resembling 'a great black cigar', 100ft (30m) long and with a triangular tail, was seen travelling 'at tremendous speed' through the night sky over Oakland, California, and a great many similar reports came from numerous parts of the state throughout the rest of the month. By February 1897, wandering aerial lights were again seen in the night skies of Nebraska, prompting a local newspaper to comment that the 'now famous California airship inventor is in our vicinity'. One light 'buzzed' a group of people leaving a prayer meeting, and was described as a winged, cone-shaped object with one headlight and three smaller lights studding each side. Soon, reports of the mystery 'airship' were coming from vast areas of the central US, ranging from the Dakotas and Texas to Tennesee in the east. There were even claims of contact with the airship's occupants. Descriptions of these aeronauts ranged from them being 'hideous' creatures and 'Martians' to normal-looking fellows in overalls.

It is now known that this 'wave' of sightings was aided and abetted by downright hoaxing. Some of these were instigated by local newspapers inventing tall tales. On 28 April 1897, for instance, the *Houston Post* published an account of a supposed incident near Sioux City, Iowa, in the preceding month, in which a man was caught by an anchor from a mystery aerial vehicle and dragged for 30ft (10m). After ten minutes a man in uniform slid down the rope, cut the anchor free and climbed back to the craft, which then flew off. This report was, of course, a reworking of the twelfth-century story of the skyship over the church in Gravesend, England (see above).

Some hoaxes came from other quarters, however. One of these involved Kansas rancher Alexander

Hamilton, who claimed he and fellow witnesses saw a giant cigar-shaped object with six 'strange' beings in it hovering over a corral, trying to rope a calf. The bawling animal became trapped in the fence, so Hamilton and his friends freed it, and it then rose slowly with the airship and disappeared to the north-west. The next day, so newspaper reports relate, Hamilton found the animal's butchered remains in a neighbour's pasture. This tale foreshadowed modern cases of mutilated animals in areas of reported UFO activity, but it seems it was also a lie. In 1976, an elderly Kansas woman came forward to state that she had heard Hamilton boast to his wife about the story he had made up, and that the man belonged to a local liars' club.

This wave of sightings also brought something else to the fore that we will encounter elsewhere in this book: the ambiguous role played by the media in the sociology of mysterious phenomena reports. This case occurred before the advent of radio or TV, but it did coincide with the advent of the telegraph. 'Telegraph lines linked the entire country and news could spread at electric speed – and so could hoaxes,' American folklorist Thomas E. Bullard noted in an article in 1988. 'An estimate of 3000 reports of phantom airships during 1996–7 is no exaggeration. This wave reached the dimensions it did with the help of communications and the media as well as expectations and hopes, but the actual substance of the wave is these reports.' So, although only newspapers were involved, they were able not only to instigate and perpetuate hoaxes, but could transform separate incidents, which were widely spaced geographically, into a single and sustained focus of attention for the public at large, thus creating the sociological effect of a single event with various facets and a single explanation. The media therefore make possible the public perception of a 'wave' of incidents (see Chapter 4). This can be the news of an actual situation, but it can also be an artefact, a created impression in the mass mind of a society. And this is infinitely easier today, with the help of modern communications and media forms.

It seems, however, that *something* odd may have been happening in the skies of the US during those winter months. But was it an airship? While airship technology was much in the news in Europe and America over this period of time, and there was a strong sense that humanity was on the verge of controlled flight, it is as certain as it can be that there was no airship in the US then capable of the performances credited to it, if there was one at all. No convincing proof of such a vehicle was ever forthcoming. The histories of flight state categori-

cally that the first airship to fly was a few years later, in Europe. The first airship recorded as flying in the US was in 1904.

We have already seen that mystery tubular objects observed in the skies have been recorded since at least medieval times, and 'cylinders' and 'cigar-shaped' objects are commonplace in modern ufological reports. It may be that the American 'airships' of the 1890s were simply the contemporary interpretation of such still-unexplained phenomena, compounded by large-scale hoaxing, suggestibility and confabulation (involuntary invention of non-existent details).

Whatever they were, they made their appearance again in 1909, but this time over many parts of the world, from Britain and Scandinavia to New Zealand – countries which did not possess airships at that time (Britain's first airship, the *Beta*, made its maiden flight in 1910). In the early hours of 23 March 1909, a policeman in Peterborough, England, saw an oblong object with a powerful searchlight pass over the city, emitting a buzzing sound. Similar reports came from all around the country over the following several weeks. There were accounts of

A contemporary depiction of the object seen flying at 1200 feet over Peterborough, England, in March 1909.

the craft conducting high-speed manoeuvres, and on 18 May in South Wales a man claimed an encounter with the occupants of a landed airship. They 'jabbered furiously' in 'a strange lingo' and took off for Cardiff, where other witnesses reported seeing an airship pass over at about the same time. In New England, too, during this same year, strange airships were reported.

In 1910, people reported dirigibles over Alabama and Tennessee (where the object was nicknamed the 'Chattanooga Chugger' because of the sound it purportedly made), and in August of that year a 'long black object' passed among the skyscrapers of Manhattan on two nights, as thousands of New Yorkers watched in amazement. The vague shape of the object was illuminated from many lighted windows in the surrounding tall buildings, and some claimed it had the appearance of a biplane, but the available descriptions are not clear. None of the 36 licensed pilots in the US at that time was flying in New York on the nights in question.

From October 1912 to March 1913, just prior to World War I, large airship-like objects and lights in the sky were seen over Britain, Holland, France and Germany. Some of the estimated speeds of these objects were higher than those attainable by any of the few airships then flying. There was widespread and worried speculation in Britain that the mystery craft and lights were German spy airships. The Germans viewed them with puzzlement too, however. For instance, a burning airship was seen to crash into the forest near Lake Schwielow, but searches of the area revealed no wreckage. There were even exotic encounters: according to one report, a number of beings 4ft (1.2m) tall were reported as being seen near a landed, cigar-shaped craft with lighted portholes in Hamburg in June 1914. When disturbed, the 'dwarves' ran inside the vessel and took off.

While Britain was at war with Germany, any unexplained object or light was naturally cause for concern. Released Navy papers reveal that the military investigated a curious floating light seen moving across parts of Dartmoor, Devon, on intermittent evenings over a six-month period in 1915. It was feared that a German spy was signalling from the high moor to ships in the English Channel, but investigators from the Naval Intelligence Department found the light to be a brilliant white orb that rose from the ground near a disused tin mine and drifted across the ground for hundreds of feet before going out. It could last anything from two to over 20 minutes at each appearance. Not a spy, but a mystery nonetheless.

The years between the two World Wars were punctuated by a variety of reported strange phenomena. One of the most celebrated was the appearance of a brilliant pearly disc in the sky above a vast crowd at Fatima, Portugal, in 1917. The object was so bright that some of the witnesses feared it was the sun falling. Because of an intriguing and complex social context, this phenomenon was viewed as a spiritual manifestation rather than as a craft. But the machines in the sky didn't stay away for long: in 1922, experienced seafaring witnesses saw what appeared to be a plane fall with extraordinary slowness into the sea off Barmouth, Wales (a location associated with a wave of unusual light phenomena some years earlier – see Chapter 10). No wreckage was found, and there were no reports of missing aircraft. Near San Francisco, early in 1927, writer Ella Young saw 'a cigar-shaped craft shoot out of a cloud beyond the bay'. It moved rapidly across the sky towards Mount Tamalpais. It was slender in shape, yellow in colour, and seemed to contract and elongate as it moved at speed.

In the 1930s, hundreds of reports of gray, unmarked aircraft came out of Scandinavia. These were single-winged flying machines with multiple engines, and they often appeared in bad weather conditions when people would not normally risk flying. They would cut their engines and circle low above the ground without power, and would sometimes scan the ground with powerful searchlight beams. The nature and source of these weird craft were never established – and the Swedes lost two aircraft in vain attempts to investigate the 'ghost planes'.

Kenneth Arnold's sighting was by no means the only incident concerning UFOs in the 1940s. Allied fliers in both the European and the Pacific theatres of war reported strange glowing objects that 'buzzed' their planes. An Associated Press report of January 1944 gave the account of an encounter with these objects, as provided by an airman called Donald Meiers. He described red balls of fire flying along just beyond the aircraft's wingtips, a row of three balls of fire flying ahead of the plane, and 'a group of about 15 lights which appear off in the distance – like a Christmas tree up in the air – and flicker on and off'. Other fliers described seeing silver balls over Germany, and 'red balls of fire' the size of basketballs over the Pacific. These strange objects were interpreted as enemy weapons ('foo fighters', after the French word *feu* – fire), used either psychologically to generate alarm and despondency in Allied aircrews or to interfere with electrical systems on their aircraft, or otherwise as reconnaissance drones – but it was later found that German and Japanese pilots had also seen the orange and red light forms and were as mystified as the Allies.

'Foo fighters' photographed during World War Two.
Fortean Picture Library

After the war, mystery machines returned to Swedish skies, only this time they weren't 'ghost planes' but 'ghost rockets'. Almost 1000 reports of the objects were made during 1946. These were mainly seen as light phenomena at night – 'the bombs are like fireballs with long luminous tails', as one report put it in the *New York Times* – but as cigar-shaped, metallic-looking objects in daylight. Some 'rockets' were seen to crash into lakes with great explosions, but detailed searches failed to reveal any wreckage. There was popular speculation that the rockets represented experiments by the Russians with captured German V-weapons, but this did not hold up to enquiry. The sightings continued in fits and starts into 1948.

¤ THE SAUCERY STARTS

We can see that through history each society interpreted UFOs in terms that related to its own system of knowledge, circumstances, beliefs, outlook and times. Sometimes, various interpretations could coexist within any given society, but there would be an overriding or predominant explanation – dragons, shamans, airships or whatever. As Arnold climbed down from his plane at Yakima field, therefore, we would expect that now, in 1947, a technological interpretation was likely.

Arnold was taken seriously when he told other pilots there about his experience, for not only was he a respected businessman, he was also a licensed air-rescue pilot and a deputy US Marshal. One of his listeners suggested that Arnold had seen 'some of those guided missiles from Moses Lake'. Although he had never heard of a missile base at the lake, Arnold agreed at the time that it was probably the answer. After refuelling his plane, he flew on to Pendleton, Oregon, as one leg on his way back to his home state of Idaho. News of his sighting travelled ahead of him, and there was a group of people waiting for him when he landed at Pendleton. 'When I got out of the plane no one said anything,' he recalled, 'they just stood around and looked at me... but before very long it seemed everybody around the airfield was listening to the story of my experience.'

He wanted to report his sighting to the FBI office in Pendleton, but it was closed, so he talked to journalists at the *East Oregonian*. One of them, Bill Becquette, asked how the objects flew. 'Well, they flew erratic,' Arnold replied, 'like a saucer if you skip it across water.' Becquette misinterpeted or fudged this description, and referred to Arnold's objects as 'saucer-like' in his Associated Press despatch, and some unknown sub-editor used the phrase 'flying saucers' in a headline.

The flying saucers had arrived.

It was not the first time 'saucer' had been used descriptively for a purported UFO. In 1878, farmer John

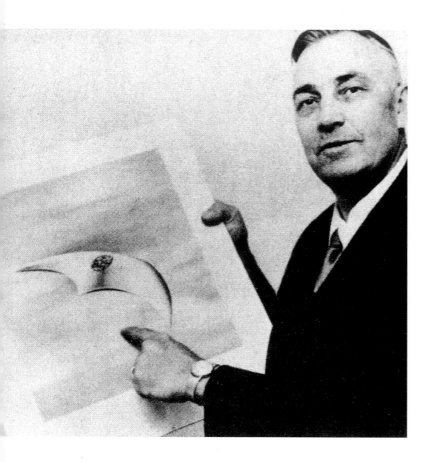

Kenneth Arnold with an artist's impression of one of his Cascades objects. Clearly, it is not a disc or 'saucer' shape. *Fortean Picture Library*

Martin described seeing a large, dark shape, perhaps a balloon, travelling 'at a wonderful speed' in the sky near Denison, Texas. 'When it was overhead,' a newspaper of the day reported, 'it was the size of a large saucer and evidently at a great height.' And at Christchurch, New Zealand, in August 1944, a nurse reportedly observed an object that looked like an 'upturned saucer'. She claimed that she looked through a rectangular window in the saucer-like object and saw short, humanoid figures. Within a few moments, the saucer shot straight upwards.

Arnold's flying objects were only one example of similar sightings reported by others in the weeks, days and hours leading up to his own. In April 1947, a 'disc with a cupola' about 100ft (30m) across was seen in the valley of the River Clarry, France. In the same month, a meteorologist and his staff reported seeing a flat-bottomed silver disc with a domed top crossing the sky above their weather bureau in Richmond, Virginia. In May, similar objects were sighted over Oklahoma, Colorado, Tennessee, Georgia and New Jersey. Only ten days before Arnold's sighting, one Richard Rankin

claimed to have seen a triangular formation of ten 'saucers' from a plane travelling over Bakersfield, California. Eight discs, each 'the size of a house', were seen near Spokane, Washington on 21 June. And on the morning of the fateful day itself, Fred Johnson, a prospector at large within the Cascade Mountains, claimed to have seen several 'round, metallic-looking discs', each about 30ft (10m) in diameter, pass about 1000ft (300m) above him. For the minute or so that he was looking at them, the prospector's compass spun madly. He grabbed a telescope and through it caught what must have been a rather shaky glimpse of one of the discs. He felt that it had tails or fins – unlike Arnold, who specifically felt that his objects did not have protrusions.

So, Arnold actually came quite late on the scene, and a ufological researcher today would probably file his account as a fairly humdrum report. In that case, why did it prove such a key event? Simply because of time, place and the media. Arnold was the right sort of witness, in the right country, at the right time, and his story was delivered in person directly to the press. The US had the resources, the science and the national temperament for exploiting the huge advances in all kinds of technology, including telecommunications, forced by the exigencies of the war. While a shattered Europe started the slow process of repairing itself, and the Russian bear toiled in secret, the US emerged from World War II as the most powerful nation on Earth, physically undamaged, and brash with it. Science was the new god, and Germany had paved the way to the stars with its fearsome V-weapons. Peenemunde, the Nazi rocket base, was plundered for its scientists and rocket engineers by both Russia and the US: the revolutionary developments of aerospace technology we see today were initiated immediately after the war. Space travel was to become a reality. In the US in particular, this was foreshadowed by an increase in published science fiction, which in the 1940s and 1950s grew into a major genre. Before Arnold's sighting there was already a strongly growing sci-fi awareness in the US through the agency of pulp magazines like *Amazing Stories*. The sky was the limit, both metaphorically and technologically. But there was a downside to all this. The war had scarred the Western mind, and there were great political and military fears concerning Russia – the term 'Iron Curtain' had been coined by Winston Churchill in 1946. How technically advanced were the Russians? What secret weaponry were they developing? Did they have the ability to invade us?

The motor of the American psyche was therefore fuelled with a complex and volatile mix of aerospace

Kenneth Arnold did not describe the objects he saw as 'saucers' or even 'discs', but as 'tadpole shaped' or 'boomerang shaped'. The saucer image originated with the fudged *report* of Arnold's sighting, not the sighting itself. Ray Palmer, who had been editor of the pulp sci-fi journal *Amazing Stories*, undoubt- edly helped to cement this image in the public's mind. An illustration in a 1946 issue of that magazine showed disc-like craft, and in 1948 he had Arnold write an article, 'The Truth About Flying Saucers', in his new magazine, *Fate*. The cover showed a wildly sensationalized picture of the pilot's encounter, depicting giant flying saucers emerging from the clouds. Palmer went on to persuaded Arnold to co-write a book with him, which was published in 1952 as *The Coming of the Saucers* and re-used the *Fate* illustration on its cover.

But were there genuine prece- dents for discoid UFOs? Ufologists assumed so for many years with the oft-quoted account supposedly translated from the Latin of William of Newburgh's *Chronicle*, telling of a 'flat, round, shining, silvery object' that flew over Byland Abbey in Yorkshire, England, in 1290 – but this has turned out to be a scholarly hoax. Undeterred, some

The COMING of the SAUCERS

$2.50

By Kenneth Arnold & Ray Palmer

ufologists point to descriptions of military flying machines called 'vimanas' in ancient Indian writings like the *Mahabharata*, and these are shown in popular Indian illustrations today in the form of saucer-like craft. Ufologists also mention the account in Pliny the Elder's *Historia Naturalis* of 'a burning shield scattering sparks' that ran across a sunset sky, but this could have been an exceptionally brilliant meteor. Seemingly metallic discs seen in 329BC while Alexander and his army were crossing into India were similarly described as 'shining silver shields'. And in 1926, artist and explorer Nicholas Roerich saw 'a huge oval moving at great speed' high above his expeditionary party in Mongolia. Before it disappeared into the blue yonder, he caught a glimpse of it in his binoculars. It was 'quite distinctly an oval form with shiny surface, one side of which was bril- liant from the sun'. Also, there were apparently a number of disc sightings immediately prior to Arnold's encounter.

So, discoid 'flying saucers' seem to have appeared occasionally prior to 1947, but their dramatically increased incidence after the fudged report of Arnold's sighting can only raise questions.

---

technology news and visions, science fantasy, and dark fears of foreign military invasion. All that was needed was a spark to ignite it all, and the 1947 UFO wave provided that spark. Although the wave was occurring elsewhere in the world too, that it was happening in America was the key factor. It was only a matter of months for one report or another to engage actively with the cogs of the mass media – the pseudopodia of the American consciousness in particular, and of the Western collective mind in general. It happened to be Arnold's account. The image of 'flying saucers' gave the mass media what it needed: a colourful yet simple handle.

Arnold's story went out on the news wires, and that night he was besieged by reporters and press agencies 'of

every conceivable description'. Letters, telegrams and phonecalls flooded in. Marshal McLuhan's 'global village' was already coming into being, and Arnold's story leapt oceans. The man himself was staggered. 'Before the night was over I had long-distance calls from London, England, from religious groups, from people who thought the end of the world was coming!' What Arnold had seen in the depths of the Cascade Mountains was flashed around the nation and the world. 'In total,' Arnold later estimated, 'I received something like ten thousand letters from all over the world. So many people came to visit me that for almost three years our home was like Grand Central Station.' In a special but real sense, we all saw Kenneth Arnold's flying saucers. It was the first truly mass media UFO sighting.

After being pinned down at Pendleton for three days, Arnold could take no more and flew back to his home in Boise, Idaho. He had convinced himself that he had seen robot-controlled guided missiles, but shortly after arriving home he had a conversation with Dave Johnson, aviation editor of the *Idaho Statesman*. To Arnold's concern, it soon became clear that this informed man did not think that the Cascades objects could be examples of any new craft being developed by the US. For the first time, Arnold began to feel that he had witnessed something totally inexplicable. He was soon being questioned by military intelligence officers, and became convinced that neither they nor anyone else knew what the things were.

Although the response to Arnold's sighting was considerable, it reflected the general confusion of the time. The extra-terrestrial link was made quickly. Arnold recalled that only four days after his sighting a woman rushed into the room, took one look at him and then ran out shouting: 'There's the man who saw men from Mars!' On 4 July, a news report quoted a rumour that Arnold's objects might be spaceships from other planets. The next day, another news item repeated a meteorologist's speculation that the objects might be 'signals from Mars'. The day after that, an Associated Press report mentioned Charles Fort, a researcher into unexplained phenomena and events (see later chapters), and quoted R.L. Farnsworth, a Fortean and president of the US Rocket Society, as saying, 'I wouldn't even be surprised if the flying saucers were remote-controlled eyes from Mars'. In another news item shortly afterwards, another Fortean, R. DeWitt Miller, opined that the Cascades objects could be vehicles from other planets or even from other dimensions. Despite such an extra-terrestrial 'buzz' being in the air, however, only two witnesses of over 800 sightings in 1947 felt that they were seeing alien craft, and general public opinion remained conservative. The first Gallup poll to canvass opinion on the nature of UFOs (itself indicative of the impact the subject had made) found that 77 per cent of those questioned either simply did not know what the saucers were, or considered them to be a US secret weapon, imagination, misperceptions or hoaxes. An extra-terrestrial explanation didn't even register: it was still some years away from becoming enshrined as the dominant belief.

Equally conflicting ideas about the saucers occurred at official levels. An Air Intelligence report, dated 10 December 1948, decided they were probably Soviet in origin; another report, dated only three days later, made for Project Sign (which eventually became Project Blue Book – see Chapter 7) by James E. Lipp, thoughtfully considered the possibility that extra-terrestrials were involved.

Arnold wrote up a report for the Air Force, which became one of the first cases studied by Project Sign. It was analysed by the Project's consultant, J. Allen Hynek, then a professor in astronomy but later the world's premier ufological researcher. Arnold did not get the answers and explanations from officials for which he had hoped. Indeed, it became increasingly clear to virtually everyone that not only did the saucers not belong to the US, but they probably were not the weaponry of foreign powers either. They were unexplained.

Although official opinion was divided and confused, everyone agreed that the term 'flying saucer' made the whole business seem more ridiculous than it need, and so in the late 1940s the Air Force introduced what they intended to be a neutral term: 'Unidentified Flying Objects'. Some critics, however, felt that this nonetheless implied that the objects under study were intelligently guided craft.

Out of the confusion, the dominant interpretation which emerged within the more sensational parts of the media, and a growing section of the public, was that the things seen in the sky were extra-terrestrial craft. It appears that this perception was boosted by the appearance of an article by Donald Keyhoe, a former intelligence officer, in *True* magazine in 1950. Entitled 'Flying Saucers Are Real', in it Keyhoe made a strong case (which is not the same as saying it was accurate, informed or true – see Chapter 2) for considering the saucers to be one of a range of vehicles belonging to an extra-terrestrial race. He considered these beings to have a technology over two centuries in advance of our own, and to be observing us.

'The *True* article was one of the most widely discussed magazine articles of its time,' American researcher Martin Kottmeyer reports. 'It was discussed by prominent newsmen like Walter Winchell and Frank Edwards. The article was expanded into a book bearing the same title later that year.' Subsequent bestselling books by Keyhoe and others further cemented the extra-terrestrial approach. Such publications, together with movies about space visitors and lurid stories from people who claimed that they had contacted space beings or had gone for rides in the saucers, led increasingly large sections of the 1950s American public to assume an alien origin for UFOs, or, at the very least, to be aware of that as being an acceptable explanation. Ufology settled into its shadow-world realm between reality and fantasy.

Kenneth Arnold never did believe in the ETH. He spent thousands of dollars conducting research on UFOs until his death in 1984, and had some further sightings.

He became convinced that UFOs were living creatures: 'groups and masses of living organisms that are as much part of our atmosphere and space as the life we find in the depths of our oceans... they have a natural ability to change their densities at will.' He was not entirely alone in this approach. The eminent psychologist C.G. Jung floated the possibility as one of his ideas about the nature of UFOs, and biologist Ivan T. Sanderson also raised the idea of space creatures in popular books, citing the so-called Wassilko-Serecki Hypothesis which proposed that there were life forms indigenous to space that fed off pure energy. Trevor James Constable believed UFOs to be atmospheric creatures – he called them 'critters' – that were very subtle or 'etheric' most of the time but could be captured on infra-red film. He published dozens of such pictures showing cavorting amoeba-like shapes to back up his claims.

But just what *did* Arnold see? He wrote various versions of his sighting over the years, and changed some details, including his estimates of the distance at which he first saw the nine glittering objects. This, of course, changed determination of their size and speed, although no one has ever doubted that Arnold was honest and credible, and did see something unusual. One thing was certain: the objects were initially too far away for the 'tremendous flash' that first attracted Arnold's attention to be accounted for by reflections from their surfaces – a point that Hynek made in his assessment of the Arnold sighting. Is it possible that the flash was some kind of large-scale light effect accompanying the appearance of the flying objects? And could the glittering effect produced by the objects themselves have been light emissions rather than reflections? We may never know, but essentially all that Arnold actually perceived were nine bright objects of a boomerang or tadpole shape flying erratically. Later, we will look at other explanations than 'craft' (whether human or extra-terrestrial). While it could be that Arnold saw metallic craft, we shall see that all that glisters in daylight does not necessarily have to be metal.

The real point is that the 'flying saucers' sighting that gave birth to ufology remains something of an unknown quantity, and ufology itself continues to be a mirage, for, as we have seen, many explanations for UFOs can be offered. The ETH is just one of several possibilities. It may be true. It may be that we have evolved technologically to such a state that we can at last understand what these strange flying objects really are. But it also has to be said that the evidence for the ETH as it has emerged through 50 years of ufology is contradictory, confused and lacking in any hard proof, while time has shown that

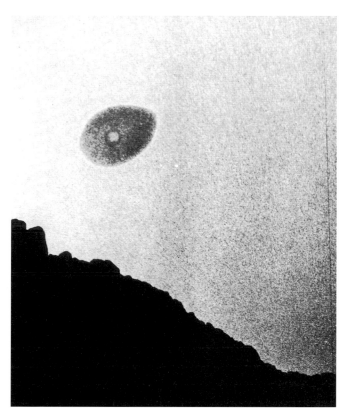

This picture was taken on 17 May, 1958, by Trevor James Constable, using high speed infrared film in a Leica G camera without a filter. At the bottom left of the picture is a ridge adjoining Giant Rock, California. The photograph was shot 'in first light of dawn', and the 'UFO' or 'critter' was not visible to the naked eye. See Constable's book, *The Cosmic Pulse of Life*. Critics point out that Constable's pictures look like a mix of lens flares, processing marks, and folds on negatives. *Trevor James Constable*

much claimed evidence has been inadequate or false for one reason or another. It may be that in believing in the ETH we are as trapped in our contemporary world view as those who were sure they were seeing flying fiery dragons, or shamans out on nocturnal jaunts. The ferocity with which the ETH is sometimes defended seems to support such an observation. Of one thing we can be quite certain: the label 'UFO' unquestionably covers many different things, and maybe (it is no stronger than that) some of them come from outer space. There are psychological, perceptual, geophysical, astronomical and many other kinds of UFO. In among them all, there may or may not be alien craft.

As we shall see in the following chapters, ufology is really a parade of ideas, feeding always off insufficient evidence for any one theory to clinch the argument. The 'U' in UFO stands for Unidentified now just as surely as it did when the term was coined nearly 50 years ago.

Who's There?

CLOSE ENCOUNTERS OF ALL KINDS

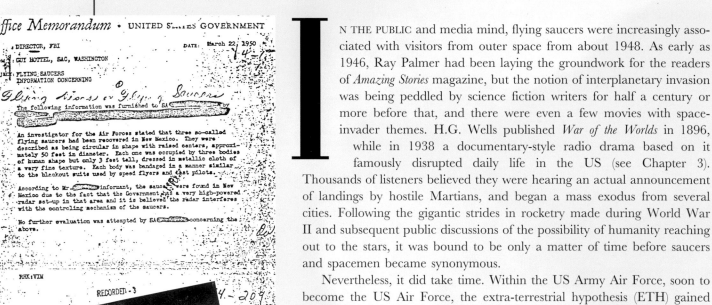

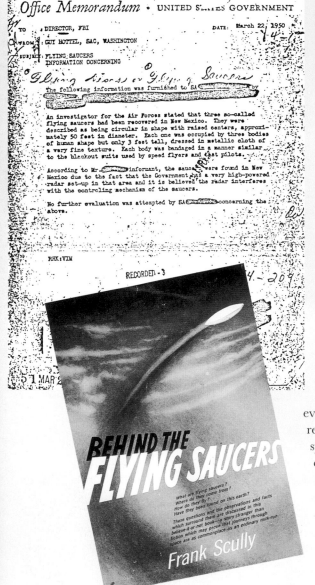

I N THE PUBLIC and media mind, flying saucers were increasingly associated with visitors from outer space from about 1948. As early as 1946, Ray Palmer had been laying the groundwork for the readers of *Amazing Stories* magazine, but the notion of interplanetary invasion was being peddled by science fiction writers for half a century or more before that, and there were even a few movies with space-invader themes. H.G. Wells published *War of the Worlds* in 1896, while in 1938 a documentary-style radio drama based on it famously disrupted daily life in the US (see Chapter 3). Thousands of listeners believed they were hearing an actual announcement of landings by hostile Martians, and began a mass exodus from several cities. Following the gigantic strides in rocketry made during World War II and subsequent public discussions of the possibility of humanity reaching out to the stars, it was bound to be only a matter of time before saucers and spacemen became synonymous.

Nevertheless, it did take time. Within the US Army Air Force, soon to become the US Air Force, the extra-terrestrial hypothesis (ETH) gained ground among a minority in the Technical Intelligence Division only after studies of the reported manoeuvres of the saucers led to the conclusion that no Earthly material – including flesh and bone – could withstand the stresses involved. But in October 1948, a secret *Estimate of the Situation* prepared by the USAF's UFO investigation group, Project Sign, was ordered to be burned by the USAF Chief of Staff, General Hoyt Vandenburg, because its argument for the ETH was rejected as lacking in evidence. Almost exactly a year later, showbusiness columnist Frank Scully reported in *Weekly Variety* that the US government had recovered an alien spaceship that had come to ground in the desert near Aztec, New Mexico. The craft contained 16 dead occupants, exactly like humans apart from being only between 36in (90cm) and 42in (107cm) tall and having perfect teeth. Scully turned his story into a bestselling book published in 1950. The tale was to

Frank Scully's 1950 best seller seemed to offer proof that aliens were visiting Earth, but the FBI were watching his chief informant, who was claiming to be able to detect oil and gold with a gadget based on technology found in a crashed flying saucer. *Fortean Picture Library* be roundly debunked in 1952 – Scully had been thoroughly hoaxed by two con-men and had believed a Hollywood promo scam that tied in with their story – but at the time it seemed to confirm the racy claims published the same year by Donald Keyhoe (see Chapter 1).

Keyhoe, a former US Marine Corps officer who was earning a living as a writer for pulp magazines, became convinced after a convivial lunch with one of his editors that flying saucers were from outer space and that this grand truth was being deliberately kept from the public by the US government. He splashed his thesis across the pages of *True* magazine in January 1950, and published an expanded version as *The Flying Saucers Are Real* in June that year. Keyhoe quoted Air Force statements that did not exist, invented history where necessary, cited pseudo-science as fact, and played fast and loose with what evidence he did have; but all that passed his audience by, for they were far less knowledgeable about the subject than they would be today.

The same year, in *The Riddle of the Flying Saucers*, British author Gerald Heard – whose previous books had consisted mostly of popular theology – speculated on the physical nature of the ufonauts, but could hardly offer much first-hand evidence: 'Maybe, after all, it is good that we cannot see them, for we can better judge them... by their acts,' he wrote. But after producing a specious parade of misinformation and dubious logic, he was drawn to the conclusion that the ufonauts were tiny bee-like insects from Mars. If on nothing else, Scully, Keyhoe and Heard agreed that the flying saucers were intelligently controlled and at the very least were conducting a surveillance of Earth. But if flying saucers existed – and there was surprisingly general agreement

Gerald Heard reasoned that UFO occupants were insect-like – an idea that still surfaces from time to time in rumours that the US Government has a secret cache of dead aliens and the remains of crashed saucers. *Fortean Picture Library*

on that – it seemed reasonable to suppose that there was someone or something inside them. Thus the stage was set for someone, somewhere, sooner or later, to meet an alien.

¤ ALIEN OR ANGEL?

People had been claiming to meet 'men from Mars' and sundry other planets of our solar system since the eighteenth century – even if the most distinguished of them, the Swedish philosopher Emanuel Swedenborg, had to take himself to those worlds in his 'astral body' in order to do so. In the years after Kenneth Arnold's crucial experience (see Chapter 1), the first person to gain wide recognition for his claim of a meeting with an off-world entity was George Adamski. Born in Poland in 1891 and arriving with his parents in the US as a child, by the 1930s Adamski had become a minor celebrity on the Californian occult circuit. He taught the usual blend of diluted Eastern 'philosophy' with a dash of Theosophy, and set up a monastery for his 'Royal Order of Tibet'. According to two former followers, his inspiration for opening the monastery was less mystic devotion than a loophole in the Prohibition Law, which allowed religious orders to make wine for ritual purposes. Adamski said he made 'enough wine for all of southern California', and a 'fortune' besides. Prohibition ended in 1933, and by the mid-1940s Adamski was making ends meet with a four-seat hamburger stand and home-made observatory on the slopes of Mount Palomar, some miles from the world's largest optical telescope. He claimed to have taken his first photograph of a UFO in October 1946, but did not begin to lecture on flying saucers until 1949. In 1950, *Fate* magazine published his UFO pictures.

Then, according to his later account, on Thursday 20 November 1952 Adamski (then aged 62), his secretary Mrs Lucy McKinnis and the proprietor of Palomar Gardens, Mrs Alice K. Wells, met up with four others to go into the desert in the hope of seeing a UFO land. Adamski gives no reason for having chosen this day rather than another, but admits to following a

George Adamski and one of his flying saucer pictures. Variations on terrestrial artefacts have been suggested as the basis of his 'UFO', from a chicken feeder to a wine cooler. Some suggest the saucer was made from a cut-down sola topi (pith helmet) and ping-pong balls.
Fortean Picture Library

hunch as to where they should start their vigil: about 11 miles (18km) down the highway from Desert Center towards Parker, Arizona. The group was richly rewarded.

After a stroll and a light lunch, the party sat scanning the sky. The only thing of note was the passage of a two-engine plane apparently on a routine flight. Then they saw 'a gigantic cigar-shaped silvery ship, without wings or appendages of any kind'. Adamski felt that the ship had come specifically for him, and on another hunch demanded to be taken down the road – they were next to a well-travelled highway, which would discourage a landing.

With Lucy McKinnis at the wheel and Al Bailey accompanying, Adamski was driven off the highway onto a dirt road. After half a mile (0.8km) or so they stopped. Fearing the presence of his companions would deter the aliens, Adamski sent them back to their original parking spot, to watch from there. As they left, a number of aircraft – presumably fighters – roared into sight and tried to circle the huge craft above. In response, the ship 'turned its nose upward and shot out into space'.

Before five minutes was up, Adamski saw a flash in the sky and 'almost instantly a beautiful craft appeared to be

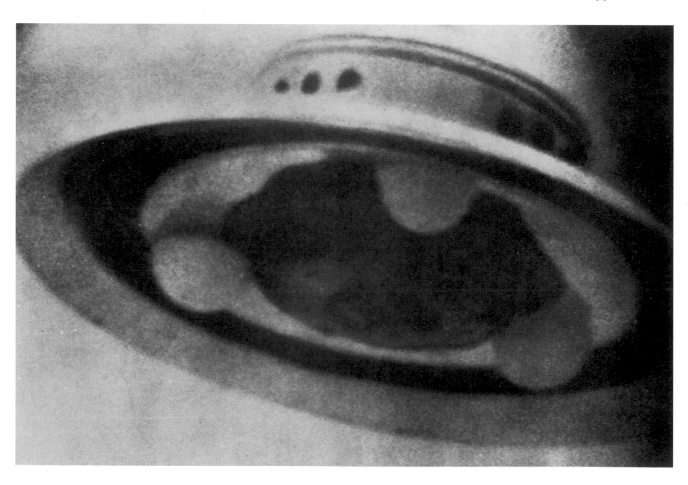

drifting through a saddle between two of the mountain peaks'. It settled on a ridge, and Adamski took photographs. Then it lifted and flew back across the saddle, as two more aircraft came into sight, circled, and flew on. Apparently the saucer had evaded them. After some minutes, Adamski realized that a man was beckoning to him from the opening of a ravine about 450yd (415m) away. Wondering who this was, Adamski made his way towards the figure. Only when he was within arm's length of the man did Adamski realize that he was looking at a visitor from another world.

'The beauty of his form surpassed anything I had ever seen,' he wrote later. The man was about 5ft 6in (1.7m) tall, weighed about 135lb (60kg), and appeared – in Earthly terms – to be about 28 years old. He had shoulder-length, sandy-coloured wavy hair 'glistening more beautifully than any woman's I have ever seen'. His skin was the colour of a suntanned Caucasian's. His face was round and he had an extremely high forehead, 'calm, gray-green eyes' that slanted slightly at the corners, high cheekbones and a 'finely chiselled' nose. He seemed to be beardless. The alien was wearing a single-piece, finely woven chocolate-brown suit with no visible fasteners or pockets, but with a broad waistband and close-fitting, high collar. His shoes were ox-blood red and had blunt toes. Adamski thought the outfit was a uniform of some kind.

His attempts to speak to the creature failed, but by concentrating his efforts he succeeded in communicating using a mixture of hand signals and telepathy. The first thing the alien told Adamski in this manner was that he was from the planet Venus. The Venusians were there, he said, because they were concerned about radiation from atomic explosions: too many of these would destroy the whole of the Earth.

The saucer had been launched from within the atmosphere by the giant 'mother ship' that Adamski had seen earlier. The craft was powered by 'magnetism'. The spaceman observed that Venusians lived according to the laws of the Creator and not the laws of materialism as Earthmen did. People from the other planets in the solar system – all of which were inhabited – and from other systems too were visiting Earth, and there were numbers of aliens living in our midst already. For this reason, the Venusian refused to be photographed, lest his features became recognizable.

Adamski was then allowed to approach the saucer hovering nearby, but was not permitted inside it. After this, the Venusian climbed aboard his craft, and it glided silently away. By an amazing stroke of good fortune, one of Adamski's companions had some plaster of Paris about him, and took a cast of the Venusian's footprints.

The first account of this astonishing tryst appeared in a Phoenix newspaper four days later, but when Adamski's full-length account appeared as part of *Flying Saucers Have Landed*, written with Desmond Leslie, the humble burger-bar philosopher became a world celebrity. Having captured public attention, Adamski published a sequel in 1955. *Inside The Spaceships* tells how, in the months after his meeting in the desert, he met other Venusians who were living in Los Angeles. He visited one of their 'mother ships', where he met similarly human-like natives of Mars and Saturn. The aliens also took him on a trip to view the far side of the Moon. Through the ship's viewing instruments he saw a pleasant Alpine scene: snowy mountains with timbered slopes, lakes and rivers, and a bustling city where vehicles floated through the streets. After a feast of vegetarian food, Adamski was shown similar scenes beamed from Venus. The natives, he was told, had a normal lifespan of 1000 Earth years, thanks to their healthy diet and the protection that their planet's cloud cover gave them from the Sun's rays. (The extraordinarily long lives of space people is a recurring theme in other contactees' accounts.)

When confronted by the photographs taken by the Soviet Luna 3 space probe of the far side of the Moon in October 1959, Adamski retorted that the Russians had retouched the pictures to deceive the US space scientists. Contactees who came forward with their stories in Adamski's wake may have suffered from a similar confusion between reality and fantasy.

⌘ UTOPIAS IN SPACE

On 4 July 1950, Daniel Fry approached a landed saucer near White Sands Proving Grounds, New Mexico, and heard a voice say: 'Better not touch the hull, pal, it's still hot.' The voice came from an extra-terrestrial entity calling itself A-lan, at the time 900 miles (1440km) above the Earth's surface in a 'mother ship'. Fry was invited aboard the landed, remotely controlled saucer and was given a ride to New York and back that took only half an hour. A-lan gave Fry the mission to publish the off-worlders' stupifyingly original message to mankind: 'Understanding is the key to peace and happiness.' A-lan said that his people were descended from an Earthly super-race who, having survived a nuclear conflagration, had migrated into space 30,000 years before. They had settled on Mars, then taken to living in space. Their

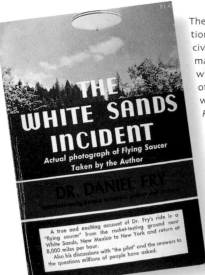

The cover of Daniel Fry's book of revelations concerning an ancient space-faring civilization that had settled on Mars. Like many contactees, Fry backed his claims with a string of almost plausible photos of UFOs – but not one of the aliens whom he contacted so many times.
Fortean Picture Library

mother ship had been their home for generations. Further communications with A-lan were purely by telepathy, although Fry kept producing photographs and films of 'Martian' UFOs until at least the mid-1960s. He is said to have taken a polygraph test on live television, but 'flunked it flat'.

In July 1952, Truman Bethurum was asleep in a truck on State Highway 91, 70 miles (112km) west of Las Vegas, Nevada, and was awoken by the voices of eight small beings with olive skins and dark hair, grouped around the cab. He got out of the truck, to see a saucer 300ft (90m) wide hovering soundlessly a few feet above the ground. He asked the aliens where their home was, and they answered: 'Our homes are our castles in a faraway land.' He was taken aboard the UFO, where he met its stunningly beautiful captain, Aura Rhanes. She spoke perfect English, in rhyming couplets. She explained that her ship came from the planet Clarion, which was permanently hidden from Earth behind the Moon. She said that all the planets in the solar system had an atmosphere like that of the Earth. Clarion was free of disease, crime and politicians, and appeared to have a matriarchal society.

Over the next three months, Aura Rhanes had ten further meetings with Bethurum. Sometimes she materialized in his bedroom, which distressed his wife so much that in due course she apparently cited Rhanes as a co-respondent in her divorce petition. Bethurum was promised a visit to Clarion, but Aura and her spacecraft failed to show up at the agreed time and place. Bethurum set eyes on Aura Rhanes one more time, in a restaurant in Glendale, Nevada, but when he spoke to her she claimed not to know him.

Orfeo Angelucci said he had his first message from aliens, who called themselves 'Space Brothers', on 24 May 1952, through a video link from a UFO parked in a field near Los Angeles. They warned him (as others had warned Adamski) that 'material advancement' was threatening humanity's evolution. The aliens maintained that they did not need spacecraft, but manifested flying saucers – which could travel at the speed of light – so that humanity could perceive them. 'The speed of light is the speed of truth,' they said, somewhat obscurely. In July 1952 Angelucci came upon a UFO parked under a freeway, and stepped in. It took off, and he was given a discourse on the Space Brothers' philosophy, which ended with a musical rendition of the Lord's Prayer and a white beam of light shining from above, in whose glow Angelucci 'knew the mystery of life'. In the course of many subsequent encounters and saucer rides, Angelucci visited the aliens' (unnamed) planet, met Jesus of Nazareth (who told him He was an alien, and that 'This is the beginning of the New Age'), and was informed that in a previous life he had been a Space Brother himself, named Neptune. Angelucci was also told that unless humanity changed its ways and learned to co-operate together, a major catastrophe would strike the Earth in 1986.

In April 1953, Dino Kraspedon was visited at his home in São Paulo, Brazil, by the captain of a flying saucer from Jupiter, whom he had first met in the mountains near Paranã the previous November. Many further meetings took place: the pair discussed celestial mechanics, theology, UFO propulsion and other matters. Kraspedon was warned that a second sun would join the solar system, and of the dangers of the nuclear age. 'Dino Kraspedon' was an alias for Aladino Felix. He apparently made a series of predictions in the mid-1960s; the last prophesied an outbreak of robberies, bombings and murders in Brazil – which indeed occurred. Police finally arrested the perpetrators on 22 August 1968. Their leader was Aladino Felix. He claimed the aliens would free him and avenge his arrest – but for some reason, they abandoned him to his Earthly fate in jail.

On 27 December 1954, Elizabeth Klarer was alarmed when she briefly saw the attractive occupant of a saucer 55ft (17m) wide that was hovering over a hill near her farmhouse in the Drakensberg Mountains, South Africa. On 7 April 1956 (then aged 46), she visited the hill again and found the same handsome humanoid, dressed in a cream-coloured suit, beside his UFO. It seems to have been a case of love at second sight. 'Not afraid this time?' he asked in perfect English, and she replied, 'I have known your face within my heart all my life.' 'I am not from any place on this planet called Earth,' he whispered with his lips in her hair. His name was Akon and his home the planet Meton, near Alpha Centauri. Klarer took a trip with him in his craft, which was powered by 'natural forces', and discussed life on his planet and music in particular. When Klarer became pregnant as a result of later meetings with Akon, he took her to Meton, where their son Ayling was born. Metonites were vegetarian, and the planet was free from war, disease, politics and money. Klarer stayed there for only four months because she had difficulty breathing the atmosphere. Her last contact with Akon was in 1963, when he visited her in South Africa with their son.

In the earliest reports of Klarer's 1956 meeting with Akon, published within months of the event in *Flying Saucer Review*, she maintains that her alien lover was a Venusian, was with another crew member, and was wearing a 'dark-brown' suit (like Adamski's contact). She also makes a point of saying: '...the tall, soft-spoken Venusian told me that the air I had been enjoying so much in the craft was Venusian air!' These statements contradict her account in her book *Beyond The Light Barrier*, published in 1977.

Howard Menger claimed his contact with the 'Space People' began when he was eight, in 1932, and involved a curvaceous blonde whom he met in a wood. More contacts came during World War II. In August 1956, a flurry of UFO sightings around his New

Jersey home led to another series of contacts. Menger's Space People were from Venus, Mars and Saturn. They had apparently contributed to Aztec civilization, and gave him a model of a 'free energy motor' (a perpetual-motion machine), which has been photographed but has never been seen working. Menger also made a long-playing record of music he had learned from the aliens. He returned from visiting the Moon in their company with specimens of lunar potatoes, which had five times more protein than terrestrial varieties. However, they have since remained in the custody of the US government, to whom Menger had handed them. He was much concerned with nutrition, and devoted 63 pages of his book about his contacts to dietary matters. Like Orfeo Angelucci, Menger was told he had been a Space Person living on Saturn in a former life. His second wife, Constance Weber, claimed to be a Venusian, where she was known as Marla.

In the early 1960s, Howard Menger recanted his contactee tales, claiming that the CIA and the Pentagon had enlisted him in an experiment to test reactions to accounts of extra-terrestrial contact. To reinforce his story, they had provided him with faked films of UFO sightings. Then, in 1967, he retracted his 'confession', and returned to his original theme: 'What most people don't want to hear, a message of love and understanding.'

Buck Nelson, a semi-literate farmer from the Ozark Mountains of America, was supposedly contacted in April 1955 and other occasions by 'Little Bucky' of Venus - and his dog. On trips to Venus and Mars, Nelson noted with approval that their peoples were racially segregated. Nelson also sold Venusian dog hair to those suitably impressed. *Fortean Picture Library*

Howard Menger, who once recorded an album of music composed by aliens, at the piano, on which rests a portrait of his allegedly Venusian wife. While helping female aliens to integrate with Earthly ways, Menger made the (then) startling discovery that they had no use for such items of apparel as brassières. *Fortean Picture Library*

¤ REALMS OF THE IMPOSSIBLE

J. Allen Hynek's comment that contactees are frequently 'pseudo-religious fanatics... bringing us regular messages from the 'space men' with singularly little content', if harsh, is partly true, for several were deeply immersed in occult lore or fringe religions long before they put their platitudinous ethics into the mouths of their alien visitors. Most seem to have had mundane, if incredible, relations with their alleged contacts, and their claims about the cosmos are more amusing than dangerous. For instance, in the 1950s, the planets of the solar system from which these tall, blond, handsome voyagers claimed to come were already known or suspected to be uniformly uninhabitable. And, if the laws of celestial mechanics have any meaning at all, it is impossible that a planet (the alleged 'Clarion') could remain permanently out of sight and undetected 'behind the Sun' in the same orbit as the Earth. Such a body would in any case be detectable by its effects on the orbits of other planets.

It is both striking and strange that the contactees publicly supported one another, although their stories about life on the other planets of the solar system rarely agreed with one another. Rodney Stark, in the 1950s a reporter who spent much time with the contactees, maintained that out of public hearing they 'even called their followers "marks"' – 'mark' being the term applied to the target or victim of a con-trick. It seems astonishing that anyone believed any of them.

Today, very few ufologists do. There still exists an Adamski Foundation – it even boasts a 'Space Research Division' – and from time to time it surfaces to defend Adamski's good name. Invariably citing other ufologists, rather than hard-nosed scientists, in its support, it never mentions the work of science fiction that Adamski wrote, which bore such a remarkable resemblance to his later tales of trips to other planets, or the lies he was caught in, or the numerous denunciations of his photographs. But the other contactees of the era have faded into the history books, their stories overshadowed by far more startling claims whose significance, and truth, is still being debated today.

It was not always so. The UK's *Flying Saucer Review* (known as the *FSR*) supported Adamski from its beginning: its then editor, Waveny Girvan, had bought the rights to Adamski's first book. *FSR*'s most revered editor, Charles Bowen, was never convinced that Adamski was a hoaxer; its current editor seems to have difficulty accepting that hoaxers exist at all. As late as 1983, Lou Zinsstag, an old Adamski fan, and Timothy Good, soon to gain fame as one of the leading proponents of a 'government cover-up' of UFO secrets, published a sympathetic biography. In the US, the leading ufologist of the day, Donald Keyhoe, director of the National Investigations Committee on Aerial Phenomena (NICAP), was unimpressed, and actually fired an employee of NICAP who had presented Adamski with a complimentary membership card. Keyhoe, the then thriving Civilian Saucer Intelligence of New York (CSI), and his rivals Jim and Coral Lorenzen of the Aerial Phenomena Research Organization (APRO) did not merely find the contactees' claims ridiculous: they feared that they would distract public and, more important, official attention from what they believed was a genuine and disturbing phenomenon.

Both the CSI and APRO – but not NICAP – were, however, prepared to believe accounts of aliens who emerged from flying saucers and who, by and large, kept their mouths shut but did things that explorers on a strange planet might do – such as take soil samples, or appear to mend the engine, or occasionally attack a witness. Such reports were being filed from the early 1950s until the end of the 1980s.

In passing, we may note that these reports tend to cast some doubt on the hypothesis that ufonauts are representatives of a highly advanced extra-terrestrial civilization. A handful of trips to the Moon and one unmanned landing on Mars sufficed to provide backward humanity with reams of information about our nearest planetary neighbours. So why do aliens, with their supposedly superior technology and intelligence, need to take so many more soil samples, and to persist in taking them over and over again for several decades? And why, even more often, do the aliens seem to have landed for no better reason than to take a quick gander at the witnesses (or their livestock) before flying away? Don't these creatures watch television? We wonder, for that matter, why the entities are so disparate in appearance – from dwarves in diving suits to begoggled females in luminous clothes, with a few birds and reptiles thrown in – and attempt to communicate in so many different ways: by drawings, sign language, telepathy, and 'speech' that ranges from barking noises to the most liquidly melodious sounds. The craft they travel in show almost as much variety. We can see these inconsistencies even in a handful of reports, from the earliest to the most recent.

¤ VARIOUS, BEAUTIFUL AND NEW

As already noted, it was reasonable to assume that if UFOs were actual extra-terrestrial craft, they would have occupants – especially as people often reported that they had windows, which were presumably for the convenience of some kind of crew. And hardly had Kenneth Arnold drawn breath after his epoch-making sighting in the Cascade Mountains than there were three alleged meetings with occupants of flying discs: one in Tennessee, reported in a Nashville newspaper on 9 July 1947, one in Brazil on 23 July 1947, and one in Italy on 14 August 1947. At least, that is how it seems today, and those persuaded that UFOs are from outer space probably find some comfort in the idea. But that is not how it seemed at the time. There were no ufologists to classify and label the reports, and according to available records there was no organized military effort anywhere in the world to investigate them either. In the summer of 1947, few people even thought of the newly discovered 'flying saucers' as extra-terrestrial.

In veteran commentator Jerome Clark's opinion, the report from Tennessee has the hallmarks of a spoof, referring as it does to 'little men, all heads and arms and legs, and glowing like fireflies' who landed, communicated in sign language, and promptly flew away.

In Italy, artist and writer Rapuzzi Johannis was staying on the lower slopes of the Carnico del Col Gentile (in the foothills of the Austrian Alps) looking for fossils. At the time, he knew nothing about flying saucers, and the Italian press had not 'even started to talk about them'. He came in sight of a 'large lenticular object of a vivid red colour', about 30ft (10m) wide, partly embedded in a rock cleft on a river bank, about 55yd (50m) away. It had a 'low central cupola with no apertures' (so not even windows are a consistent feature of crewed flying discs) with an antenna on top. Johannis decided to investigate, then saw two 'boys' whom, he soon realized as they approached, were 'dwarves, the like of which I had never seen nor even imagined'. About 3ft (90cm) tall, they wore dark blue overalls with vivid red belts and collars, and brown, tight-fitting caps 'like an alpinist's bonnet'. Their skin was 'an earthy green'. Their heads were oversized, their eyes 'enormous, protruding, and round', and they had very long, straight noses. Their hands were claw-like, each with two opposed sets of four fingers.

Johannis shouted and waved at them – an action they seemed to take as hostile, as one used a device on his belt that, with a puff of smoke, laid Johannis out flat and paralysed him. The creatures got into the craft, which shortly afterwards 'shot straight out from the rock and rose into the air'. Johannis rested, then staggered back to his lodgings and went to bed.

The account of this encounter was first published only in 1964. The Brazilian event was mentioned in two São Paulo newspapers in August 1947, but languished unnoticed for 14 years before it surfaced in the ufological literature. These early cases – like the far more celebrated and despised Roswell incident of July 1947 (see Chapter 9) – have acquired significance

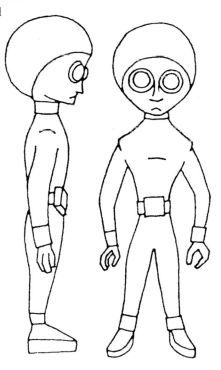

Sketches by Italian artist and science fiction author Rapuzzi Johannis of the ufonauts he said he encountered in 1947. His account, first published in 1964, nonetheless contains one of the earliest images of 'baby-like' aliens. *Fortean Picture Library*

only in retrospect. By the time the Italian encounter was revealed, there was no lack of such cases in the public domain on which a hoaxer could draw for inspiration – and Johannis was a popular author of science fiction stories. And, unlike 99 per cent of other encounter witnesses, he reports seeing the little green men so often mocked by skeptics and media alike. But what of the Brazilian event?

José C. Higgins was a survey worker from Baurú, São Paolo. At work in the countryside, he heard a piercing, high-pitched whistle and saw a gray-white, rimmed disc, 150ft (45m) wide, land on curved metallic legs. His co-workers fled, and Higgins found himself facing three entities, 7ft (2m) tall, dressed in 'transparent suits covering head and body, and inflated like rubber bags', with metal boxes on their backs. Under the suits they wore brightly coloured clothes. The three creatures themselves were identical, with 'huge round eyes, huge round bald heads, no eyebrows, no beards, and legs longer in proportion than ours'. Higgins found them 'strangely beautiful'. At some point in the encounter, Higgins observed that they avoided bright sunlight. They surrounded him, and one pointed a metal tube at him. Thinking they were going to lure him on board their craft, Higgins managed to hide in a thicket. From there he watched the creatures gambol about for half an hour with amazing agility, tossing huge stones. They then re-entered the craft, which took off towards the north.

From one point of view there are blatant science fiction elements in this story, while the game with stones reeks of a tall tale. From a symbolic point of view, on the other hand, there are intriguing features: huge heads (indicating enormous intelligence) combined with the appearance and behaviour of playful, innocent, 'noble savages'. The images are provocative, even if the event was only partly imagined. But that is not how it was greeted by ufologists, particularly APRO and *FSR*. Anticipating his later 'diabolic' interpretation of UFO phenomena, *FSR*'s Gordon Creighton managed to connect the case to the ancient Greek mythic figure Cyclops, and opined that there 'remain a host of jokers in our pack... Surely someone, somewhere, is having a wonderful game with us! ...We dream of a logical Universe; what if it isn't logical at all, but a vast surrealist nightmare?'

These 'close encounters of the third kind' (CE-IIIs), as J. Allen Hynek was to dub them (see Chapter 4), have a curious aura of pointlessness, better suited to a brief surviving scene from a longer, lost narrative than the rational behaviour of spacefaring scientists. In the 1990s, one branch of ufology would see them as just that:

episodes in a mythic drama that was yet to be completed. The very futility of CE-IIIs was the prime clue to their lack of objective reality. This kind of 'psychosocial' analysis brings loud snorts of derision from those dedicated to the ETH, and even from devotees of still more exotic ideas – that ufonauts are time travellers, or coexist with us on Earth but in some 'parallel universe'.

Yet they cannot explain such curious aspects of the phenomenon without flying in the face of Occam's razor (the principle that explanatory causes, especially hypotheses, should be kept to an absolute minimum in any theory) and resorting to yet more, and increasingly unsustainable, hypotheses. Charles Bowen, for example, speculated that aliens were not only extra-dimensional beings 'from universes parallel with ours but with a different time stream', but (perhaps using something akin to laser technology) they also 'projected' hallucinations into witnesses' minds, although he confessed (in private, at least) that he could not explain the purpose of the exercise.

¤ HERE BE GIANTS

The alien presences most often – but still not exclusively – reported today from the US are small, gray, skinny, naked, ostensibly sexless creatures with enormous black eyes and huge bald heads. Two reports from Russia in the summer and autumn of 1989 confirmed rumours that a wave of sightings involving spherical UFOs with very different occupants indeed was occurring west of the Urals.

According to the news agency TASS, in July a milkmaid and other witnesses had seen two orange globes land near the city of Perm on the Volga. Unusually tall entities, who, unlike many Western alien visitors, had *small* heads, had emerged. One of the mysterious globes was photographed. In October, TASS reported that a spherical UFO had landed in a park in a suburb of Voronezh, 300 miles (480km) south of Moscow, and afterwards witnesses had seen two giant aliens, also with disproportionately small heads, nearby. With them was a small robot-like creature. Witnesses were said to have suffered panic attacks for several days following the sighting. Scientists who investigated the site shortly afterwards found what they regarded as traces of a landing: a depression 60ft (18m) wide and four deep dents in the grass.

Perm and Voronezh are roughly 700 miles (1100km) apart, and that the sightings were so similar is intriguing. However, details are scant, and the Perm photographs are of low quality. And it may be significant, in tracing a link between these distant events, that giants figure strongly in Russian folklore. Imagination, or perhaps an altered state of consciousness that gave the imagination free rein, may have played a large part in both reports.

We mentioned the alleged visitations of alien 'grays' (which actually has to be spelled 'grays', for in its present incarnation it is an American invention) not only by way of contrast to the Russian reports, but also in order to pick up the historical thread and the theme of hindsight. In the 1950s, close encounters of the third kind were embraced first (in the US) by APRO – whose declared belief was that 'saucer phenomena... are in fact interplanetary vehicles', and contact 'with the beings operating them shall be strived [sic] for' and (in Britain) in the early 1960s by *FSR*, which decided that 'occupant cases' were the key to the UFO enigma. We should note too that the French wave of 1954, which featured numerous accounts of UFO landings and associated entities, also generated enormous interest in this aspect of the phenomenon. But it was later shown to be largely a social and political phenomenon, involving a huge proportion of practical jokes, dirty tricks and settling of old scores through exploitation and with the connivance of the press (see Chapter 4). In the US, Donald Keyhoe and NICAP rejected close encounter reports until 1969.

From then until the early 1980s, ufology was, not to put too fine a point on it, a shambles. All manner of hypotheses, wild ideas and theories competed for precedence in the wake of the stunning blow delivered by the dismissive Condon report (see Chapter 7) to the ETH and the flying saucer belief system. And then came abductions, widely popularized as a *general* UFO experience by Budd Hopkins in his 1981 book *Missing Time*. These were already well established by then as a facet of ufology by the experience of Betty and Barney Hill (see Chapter 11), which John Fuller had recounted in his *Interrupted Journey* of 1966, but Hopkins' book put abductions into the centre of ufological debate, while reports of CE-IIIs were published far less frequently. And here that ever more indispensable item of ufological furniture, hindsight,

came into play yet again. By the early 1990s, Hopkins' associate David Jacobs was suggesting that the CE-III was a screen memory or psychological cover for an abduction event by the 'grays'. How curious, then, that the CE-III witnesses rarely, if ever, describe these entities in their reports.

Abductions are by no means pleasant experiences. From the cosmic saviours and kindly helpmeets reported by the contactees, ufology had moved through the inconsequential absurdities of the CE-IIIs to the grim programme of human manipulation allegedly being conducted by little gray aliens and their cohorts. Either the UFO experience was evolving, just like the world in which it occurred, or the aliens were indeed acting out a 'surrealistic nightmare' and humanity was its victim. Ufologists, unlike the scientists whom they so often claim to emulate, had no consensus of theory, hypothesis or even data by which to judge any of the encounter experiences, and were as divided as the witnesses as to the meaning of it all.

'Michelin Man' aliens and their un-saucer-like craft witnessed on the Île de Réunion in the Indian Ocean in July 1968. Reports of this type of alien go back to the 1920s, while reports of 'giants' emerging from UFOs span the whole history and geography of ufology. Not everyone meets 'grays'! *Mary Evans Picture Library*

3

Before Our Eyes

UFOS LAND ON THE SILVER SCREEN

OVER THE DECADES, ufology has displayed a close interrelationship with the media industry. Without a single alien nut and bolt coming into the public domain, the reality of UFOs has been established in millions of minds purely through the agency of books, magazines, newspapers, radio, TV and the cinema. This crucial connection is a key to understanding much about ufology.

We have noted, for instance, that Kenneth Arnold's sighting in the Cascades (see Chapter 1) was essentially a mass media event, which allowed his experience to be telegraphed into the seething psychosocial cauldron following World War II, which had been unlike any previous conflict. Global war had now established itself as a reality, as a perpetual threat in which all people were at risk – at least theoretically – even when going about their humdrum lives far from any front line. Nuclear energy had been released in the most awesome weaponry, and threw its mushroom-shaped shadow over the post-war years. Russia, with its alien system of Communism, was perceived as a rising threat, a great fearsome bear stalking the wilds beyond the pale of the Western mind – a boundary conceived of as an Iron Curtain.

Put simply, the collective mind of the West in the post-war period was effectively in a state of trauma. There was even a contemporary phrase that to some extent recognized this: 'war nerves'. People lived on the edge of abysses containing possible terrors, which superimposed themselves on the recent memories of war, when inhumanity had reached depths beyond nightmares. Yet at the same time, technology had undergone unprecedented development in the war years, and so, as God was now dead, a brave new world of technology and science was looked to as a way of elevating humanity out of its dark, organic fears. The clean, bright light of this technological dawn was reflected in the beaming chrome and whitewall tyres of the new, welcoming era.

America was now the pressure-cooker of the Western culture, and it was there that the extremes, positive and negative, were to show. In the late 1940s and into the next decade, the fear of Communism and of invasion was endemic. The CIA was formed. McCarthyism raised its dark and frowning head. The need for military superiority and security was paramount: Reds might indeed be under the beds of the West! The media event of Arnold's sighting became a prominent part of this volatile mass psychology because it was needed. If it had not been Arnold, it would have been someone else. And it had to be in the US. Machines in the sky. Russia. Extra-terrestrials. Invasion. Fear of invasion from the Red Planet Mars (or from anywhere else) and Reds under the beds were interchangeable motifs. As we shall see, the early post-war sci-fi movies demonstrated this clearly.

Myths are public dreams, the mythographer Joseph Campbell has told us, and dreams are private myths. And he might have said the same for those dark dreams we call nightmares. Long ago, in tribal times, we sat around open fires and our mythic tales were told by an elder as we gazed dreamily into the mesmerizing embers. Beyond the flicker of firelight, at the edge of the village, was the dark night, the womb of the mysterious and the unknown. But things are very different in our culture. We live more inside our heads than human beings did in the past; we inhabit a more abstract world. The world itself has become a global village; the dark night now has its metaphor in the blackness of outer space, and it is there that we locate the source of the aliens that haunt us and where only our astronauts venture (with video cameras). The deep, dark contents of our subconscious mind are projected onto that endless night of space rather than the velvet Earthly night around us, which is banished at each dawn. Indeed, the remarkable 1956 movie *The Forbidden Planet* actually used a human's subconscious mind as the rampaging alien.

But we have traded the soft flicker of firelight for the more mechanical glow of the cinema or TV screen. We sit in darkened places and watch our collective desires and fears, our tribal myths, conjured before our eyes. Our collective unconscious cultural mind is reflected back at us through an externalized mythologizing process with which we have a symbiotic relationship: the film-makers display what they sense as the psychological undercurrents within the culture, add their own creative spins and emphases, and present that to the collective conscious mind of the culture. This material then cycles through the culture, forming part of its psychic fabric. A kind of feedback loop is set up that has never before existed on such an all-consuming scale.

By observing this process, we can form some idea of the inner workings of the collective psyche of our times. In the post-World War II period, the formative years of ufology, cinema was more influential and important than TV. As we will learn, in those faraway days the images of our cultural consciousness on the screens showed aliens as metaphors for Russians and the Cold War, among other things. TV started to become more prominent in the 1960s, and out of the psychedelic decade came televisual myths such as *Star Trek*, which seamlessly blended technological sci-fi, extra-terrestrials and powerful social and spiritual themes on the canvas of deep space. Translated to the Big Screen, the later *Star Trek* movies still had the capacity to ask some noteworthy questions. In *Star Trek IV*, for example, the extra-terrestrial spaceship comes to Earth not to land on the White House lawn (an expected action which is just a cultural assumption we make – especially if we are American) but to contact the most intelligent creatures on the planet, which turn out in the movie to be the whales: a melding of ecology, spirituality and ET sci-fi, as well as a humorous poke at our instinctive anthropocentrism. In similar vein, the *Star Wars* movie series invoked otherworldly-wise elders in another galaxy long ago and far away, drawing on the insight of Joseph Campbell to ensure use of authentic mythic archetypes. This successful formula was grafted onto techno-action sci-fi to make it palatable to a modern, cinema-going audience.

The ultimate cinematic shaman, Steven Spielberg, presented his culture with a lovable extra-terrestrial who got on better with kids than adults in *E.T.*, and a hopeful, enhancing meeting with a superior and benign extra-terrestrial civilization in *Close Encounters of the Third Kind*. In scenes that amazed and stunned movie-goers worldwide, these god-surrogates arrived on earth in a vast, phantasmagoric craft that one film reviewer perceptively noted looked like the descent of the New Jerusalem. The massive international success of this movie effectively made humanity's meeting with the alien a cinematic experience. The film paid conscious homage to ufology by containing a cameo appearance of arch-ufologist J. Allen Hynek, the man who had categorized a range of 'close encounters' as part of the varieties of human interaction with reported UFOs (see Chapter 4), and based the character played by Francois Truffaut on real-life ufologist, Jacques Vallée.

Close Encounters also hardened the image of the extra-terrestrial in the mass mind as a being with a wasted body and a large head containing huge, slanted eyes, all

The alien mother ship descends to Devil's Tower in the culminating scene from Spielberg's *Close Encounters of the Third Kind*.
Columbia Pictures (courtesy Kobal)

glistening black and without pupils – the classic 'gray'. This creature born of ufology has invaded not only our cinema and TV screens, but posters, book jackets and mass-circulation magazines.

Nevertheless, in the shadowy corners of the silver screen there still lurked the alien who embodied our darkest fears, as is well expressed in the devil-like extra-terrestrial in the *Alien* series of movies. This trend of alien-as-nightmare is resurfacing once again as the first 50 years of ufology draws to a close, on the cusp of a new millennium rendered uncertain by ecological doubts and a faltering 'New World Order'. TV's hugely popular *The X-Files* appeals to those who suspect government cover-ups, and creates an atmosphere of ill-defined but sinister alien presence. The struggle between our rational and dark sides is well played out episode by episode. New TV series such as *Dark Skies* continue these themes, drawing in associated issues such as crop circles and emphasizing the conspiracy element.

What is effectively a summary of the major current ufological themes is provided by *Independence Day*, probably the silver screen's last giant offering of ufology's half-century. As the Earth faces the approach of enormous

and hostile spaceships, UFO conspiracy theory, the Roswell crash, abductions and the mysteries of the military-restricted zone of Area 51 in Nevada, are all brought into the film's scenario. The deep suspicion of government held in some sectors of American society is given a digitized catharsis in the alien zapping of the White House, and mollified by the cinematic revelation that the US President himself was kept in the dark about the aliens of Roswell by a sinister CIA. The film also tells more than its story, for 50 years on we see that the UFO is still a propaganda vehicle for movie-makers, although this time the concern is not the Russians and the Cold War. The film makes use of superb computerized technical wizardry to package hints of ecological awareness and over-obvious political correctness in the service of a vision of a *Pax Americana*, the core of the New World Order. With open reference to the Gulf War, the US leads the Allies against the aliens. After a stirring July 4 speech in which he states that Independence Day will no longer be seen as just an American holiday but will become relevant to all humanity, the US President, a veteran of the Gulf War, himself leads the squadron of jet fighters that make the first effective strike against the alien craft, after a black airman and a Jewish computer nerd insert a computer virus into the workings of the giant Mother Ship (a cybernetic nod towards the biological virus that did away with the Martians in H.G. Wells'

War of the Worlds). A good old boy from the American West is the one who, at the cost of his life, delivers the final *coup de grace* to the craft being attacked by the President's squadron. Key US domestic and foreign policy themes are thus played out before the dazzled eyes of the whole cinema-going world. The film reveals the main currents of popular ufology to be primarily of American creation, as much now as in the beginning five decades ago.

In this manner, ufological themes, whether true or false, are brought into mainstream cultural awareness and given currency. The boundaries between fact and fiction become blurred something that happens with increasing frequency in a society where real-life events can become TV soap operas within months; where mass-circulation tabloids can publish photographs of real-life politicians apparently conversing with aliens; where even the concept of 'faction' can arise. Most of us live in a limbo world of manipulated information. Into this world come TV documentaries purportedly showing the post-mortem of an extra-terrestrial being, with conflicting claims as to its authenticity (see Chapter 9). How are we to know what is really real?

UFOs, ufology and the media industry have come a long way together, and after 50 years it is almost impossible to tell them apart. Perhaps they were always one and the same phenomenon. Nigel Watson is a researcher who has made a special study of this process, and for the remainder of this chapter we have invited him to provide a summary of his findings.

¤ ALIENS IN A CINEMA NEAR YOU

Flying saucers and their alien pilots provide powerful and flexible symbols for film-makers to play with. As early as 1903, with his *A Trip to the Moon*, George Melies realized that audiences enjoyed seeing wonderful inventions, space travel, dancing girls and plenty of special effects. Actual alien invasion came in the guise of the comic film *When the Man in the Moon Seeks a Wife* (Percy Stow, 1908). Most of the time the lonely Moon man plays with his anti-gravity gas in London, but his mission anticipates that of more crude cinematic alien invaders of the 1950s.

Interplanetary exploits with plenty of invisibility or death rays eventually became the staple of cheap film serials based on comic strips. The most successful was *Flash Gordon* (1936–40) and *Buck Rogers* (1939).

Most notable, perhaps, of modern media science fiction was Orson Welles' Mercury Theater of the Air

broadcast of an updated version of H.G. Wells' *War of the Worlds* on the evening of 30 October 1938. Many Americans were willing to believe that the Martians had actually landed, and the programme's impact is chronicled in the TV movie *The Night That Panicked America* (J. Sargent, 1975) and made fun of in *Spaced Invaders* (Patrick Read Johnson, 1990). Those who tend to dismiss the sociological element in ufology should bear this media-inspired panic of 1938 in mind. Nine years before Arnold's sighting, there clearly was a readiness to believe in invading aliens.

After World War II, *The Purple Monster Strikes* (Spencer Gordon Bennet and Fred Brannon, 1945), a 15-part serial, had a Martian who takes over a scientist's body in an attempt to invade Earth. Once the 'flying saucer' craze broke in 1947, low-budget film-makers quickly jumped on the bandwagon. For example, another serial, *Bruce Gentry – Daredevil of the Skies* (Spencer Gordon Bennet and Thomas Carr, 1948), had the Panama Canal attacked by flying discs. Taking its cue from the headlines, *The Flying Saucer* (Mikel Conrad, 1950) showed the Russians stealing a saucer from a scientist in Alaska.

These initial stories of flying saucer inventors and Communist spies gave way to aliens from outer space gleefully stealing Earth women and radically altering (if not totally destroying) the American way of life. The aliens are usually emotionless, rational and scientifically advanced. Certainly they are often meant to represent thinly disguised, godless, scientific, Communist infiltrators, but they can equally represent other more fundamental social and psychological concerns.

Most of the 1950s films worry about or act out a possible World War III. The best example of this is *The Day the Earth Stood Still* (1951). The fears about nuclear power and East-West relations mirror the concerns that became expressed increasingly by contactees and ufologists in subsequent years. The depiction of the flying saucer, and Gort the robot, are probably the best examples of how people at that time imagined the technology of UFO beings.

Humanity is also shown as heartless and cruel in *The Man from Planet X* (Edgar G. Ulmer, 1951): an alien visits us to obtain help for his dying planet, but all we do in return is to blast his ship with bazookas. The same fate nearly occurs to the aliens who fall to Earth in *It Came from Outer Space* (Jack Arnold, 1953), but one man does have faith in them and helps them to repair their meteor-like craft.

What could stop all these destructive menaces who sought to rape and pillage our fair planet? The answer

A scene from *The Day the Earth Stood Still.*
20th Century Fox (courtesy Kobal)

usually came in the form of religion. George Pal's *War of the Worlds* (1953) has the beleaguered survivors of the invasion congregating in a church, where their prayers are miraculously answered by a fall of rain which kills off the Martians. As the voice-over boldly states, the God-given bacterium on Earth kills them but protects us. Furthermore, aliens like the humanoid Klaatu in *The Day the Earth Stood Still* are often equated with Christ-like saviours (Klaatu uses the alias Dr Carpenter), who are killed and resurrected.

Such films as *Invaders from Mars* (William I. Cameron Menzies, 1953); *Earth Versus the Flying Saucers* (Fred F. Sears, 1956); *Invasion of the Body Snatchers* (Don Siegel, 1956); *Plan 9 From Outer Space* (Edward D. Wood, 1956); *Invasion of the Saucermen* (Edward L. Cahn, 1957); and *Teenagers from Outer Space* (Tom Graeff, 1959) all showed 'them' in possession of our minds, bodies and property. In *This Island Earth* (Joseph Newman, 1956) the Metalunians even kidnap some of our scientists to help

them fight the Zahgons. The battle is unsuccessful, but we are shown beautifully coloured flying saucers and grotesque, lumbering monsters.

The image of a flying saucer is also depicted colourfully in *The Forbidden Planet* (Fred M. Wilcox, 1956). This time the craft is operated by us in the future, and its mission to look after the spaceways leads to a battle with the monsters from a crazy scientist's Id. *I Married a Monster from Outer Space* (Gene Fowler Jnr, 1958) shows us male aliens who kidnap men and take on their form so that they can breed easily with Earth women without detection. Beyond the poor special effects and silly story, it articulates amply fears of Communist invasion, as well as fears about the opposite sex.

The 1960s saw a change in viewpoint. Rather than 'them' out there, or beings able to take over our minds or bodies, *we* could be aliens. In *Quartermass and the Pit* (Roy Ward Baker, 1967), an ancient Martian spaceship is found during the excavation of a new subway tunnel in London. The ship comes to life and it is discovered that the Martians are insect-like, and that when they came here they accelerated our evolution so that we could become their slaves. Martians look like the Devil because they are an intimate part of our racial memory, and some of us are genetically aliens. The ultimate in humankind evolving into something else is demonstrated in Stanley Kubrick's *2001: A Space Odyssey* (1968). The same idea is parodied in *The Final Programme* (Robert Fuest, 1973), where Jerry Cornelius (Jon Finch) becomes a monster rather than a messiah.

¤ COME INSIDE

Rather than the fear of technology and Communism, we now have the fear of our own bodies revolting against us. Such a transition can be seen by comparing *The Thing From Another World* (Christian Nyby and Howard Hawks, 1951) and John Carpenter's 1982 remake. The former concentrates on male bonding. Their military discipline, allied with suitable leadership (which isn't blinkered by impersonal science and the rule book), enables the men to defeat the beast. In contrast, Carpenter's *The Thing* is far more cunning and insidious. Nobody is quite sure if the other person is part of the Thing or not, and there is no group consensus or leadership that can get them out of trouble. Instead of bacteria coming to our aid, as in *War of the Worlds*, an alien infection is our downfall and no religion on Earth is likely to help us.

The theme of giving birth to something devilish and

monstrous was to become a predominant theme of sci-fi and horror films. Mia Farrow gives birth to the Antichrist in *Rosemary's Baby* (Roman Polanski, 1968). In its wake, we have a woman giving birth to an extra-terrestrial child in the TV movie *The Stranger Within* (Lee Phillips, 1974), and the birth of a Christ-like baby as the result of rape by computer in *Demon Seed* (Donald Cammell, 1977).

This takes us to the influential themes of motherhood and birth in *Alien* (Ridley Scott, 1979). When the crew of the spaceship are woken from suspended animation, they are reborn only to face death at the claws of the alien. The male body, the final frontier, is ultimately invaded, violated and killed. As individuals or as a group, the men cannot fight the alien, and it is the woman (Ripley, played by Sigourney Weaver) who is able to outsmart and evade the creature. The sequel *Alien* movie (James Cameron, 1986) shows that Ripley has to fight both patriarchy and the alien matriarchy. She is inevitably a complete outsider in *Alien 3* (David Fincher, 1992), where she is as much a disruption to society as is the alien.

Less well known than the *Alien* films is Larry Cohen's *God Told Me To* (1976). The main protagonist, Peter Nicholas (Terry Lo Bianco), discovers that he is the product of alien intercourse, which occurred when his mother was abducted by a UFO. Rather than come to terms with his alien origins, he voluntarily enters an insane asylum.

Things have become so bad on planet Earth that we are now the corrupting influence on aliens, rather than vice versa. In *The Man Who Fell To Earth* (Nicholas Roeg, 1976), the Man is ruined by the US government and betrayed by science.

With Watergate, Vietnam and the undermining of social and moral values, it is no wonder that the films of the 1970s should reflect such changes in attitudes and beliefs. There is no longer anything to protect, and what was alien and 'out there' is likely to be inside us, waiting for the chance to get out.

¤ SALVATION

Just when everything seemed condemned to uncertainty and fear, the sci-fi boom of the late 1970s turned the tide. Salvation from the stars came in the form of Steven Spielberg's *Close Encounters of the Third Kind* (1977). This plays knowingly with governmental scientific-military cover-ups maintained and perpetuated through the TV mass media, and with our cinematic knowledge that UFOs are flown by hostile extra-terrestrials. The appear-

An alien from Metaluna threatens the lives of Earthmen played by Rex Reason and Jeff Morrow in *This Island Earth*.
Universal Pictures (courtesy Kobal)

ance of the UFOs disrupts family life and Middle American normality, but it puts Roy Neary (Richard Dreyfuss) in touch with life and the Universe in a manner similar to a religious conversion. The climax of *Close Encounters*, where humanity is united with the aliens, can be regarded as an early sign of *glasnost* between East and West, or as a metaphor for the cessation of hostilities between the US and Vietnam.

Likewise, Spielberg's *E.T. The Extraterrestrial* (1982) has religious overtones. E.T. is discovered hiding in a shed; he has the miracle of life literally at his fingertips and he suffers death and resurrection. E.T. is at one with nature and his death is 'caused' by the scientists, who seek to investigate and exploit rather than understand and love. Against the grain of prevailing attitudes, Spielberg shows that the monstrous in appearance can be loving and worthy.

After this sci-fi boom of the late 1970s, films about aliens turned away from the heavens and looked at our own culture and gender clashes. Such films were usually comedies about the alien not knowing how to act properly in our society, and they gave us a chance to see ourselves (and our ridiculous behaviour) from the viewpoint of an outsider – an alien. Examples are *My Stepmother is an Alien* (1987), *Alien Nation* (1988) and *Earth Girls Are Easy* (1989). Before them, Joe Dante's *Explorers* (1985) eloquently and humorously showed the influence of our post-modernist pop culture on alien teenagers.

¤ ABDUCTION

But the mood changed. *Communion* (Philippe Mora, 1989) kicked all the laughter into touch. Based on Whitley Strieber's bestselling book about his reported real-life encounters with aliens (see Chapter 7), it plays with images of fear and fantasy, to the point where even Strieber admits, 'I kinda went crazy'. He is abducted by blue, monk-like aliens and thin-faced, insect-like beings with large eyes. Inside their spaceship, he is raped in a small, reeking room by something that looks like a shower attachment. In another abduction scene, an alien reveals that it is wearing a mask – they are literally a mystery within a mystery that always eludes him. On the written page, Strieber's story is barely credible; transferred to the screen it is just silly and pointless. (John Sayles' *Passion Fish* (1993) has an actress recount how she endlessly rehearsed the line 'I didn't ask for the anal probe' for a film suspiciously like *Communion*.)

The main influence of *Communion* was to bring fictional reconstructions of 'real' UFO encounters to our screens. In its wake, a TV mini-series, *Intruders* (Da Curtis, 1991), based on Budd Hopkins' abduction research (see Chapter 11), was made by NBC. By the mid-1990s, dramatic reconstructions became the basis of British paranormal programmes (*Strange But True?* on ITV and *Out of the Blue* on the BBC). However, the TV movie *The UFO Incident* (Richard A. Colla, 1975), which dramatized Betty and Barney Hill's influential 1961 abduction story (see Chapters 7 and 11), gets the credit for beating them all to this concept.

Fire In The Sky (Robert Lieberman, 1993) gives us the best attempt at a big screen docu-drama. The centrepiece occurs when we see (in flashbacks) Travis Walton inside the flying saucer (see Chapter 11). In a surreal nightmare, Travis is 'reborn' inside a cocoon, and after trying to escape he is stripped naked and bound to an examination table. After being drilled in the head by a robot device, he finds himself back on Earth. At its weakest, the film is evasive about the 'reality' of the events it depicts, but it works magnificently when it concentrates on its powerful images of abduction, imprisonment, torture-examination, birth, death, horror, nightmare, mental breakdown and communal-personal fears and doubts.

Abductee, played by Christopher Walken, with 'gray', in a scene from *Communion*. New Line (*courtesy Kobal*)

In the same year, there was Abel Ferrara's remake of *Invasion of the Body Snatchers*, which had also been remade by Philip Kaufman in 1978. The first can be read as a metaphor for society/Communism turning us into robots, and the second shows that there is no escape from this fate. Ferrara's version equates the aliens with virulent disease (AIDS, ecological pollution), which infiltrates the very structures of society (the military and the family). In the same vein, *The Puppet Masters* (Stuart Orme, 1995) literally shows that the flying saucers are a Trojan horse for invading aliens who want our bodies.

¤ HUMANITY FIGHTS BACK

Independence Day (Robert Emmerich, 1996) confidently offers us an adrenaline rush of entertaining UFO and alien imagery. Without negotiation, the aliens simply and systematically destroy the cities of Earth. Even worse, they have the gall to destroy and subvert all that is American. To underline the point, they are even rude to the US president! He proves he is not a wimp by deciding to 'nuke the bastards' (the doubts caused by the Vietnam war seem to have been exorcised at last). The whole narrative plays with our knowledge of tabloid ufology and science fiction movies of this ilk. *Independence Day* shows us three dead aliens, artfully suspended in large floor-to-ceiling tubes, that had survived the Roswell crash (see Chapter 9) by a few weeks. Their usual appearance is really a biomechanical shell which hides an alien akin to more recent UFO lore. There is even an autopsy scene, which playfully scares us in the manner of a similar scene in *Alien* and simultaneously refers to Santilli's 'factual' alien autopsy film (see Chapter 9).

¤ MEANWHILE, ON THE SMALL SCREEN...

Fictional flying saucers and aliens on TV have mainly ended up in comedy sitcoms or paranoid sci-fi dramas. In the first group, we have been treated to *My Favorite Martian*, *Mork and Mindy* and *The Third Rock From The Sun*, while in the latter we have had *The Invaders*, *UFO*, *V*, *War of the Worlds*, *Dark Skies* and, of course, *The X-Files*. The phenomenal success of this particular show in the 1990s is due to the fact that it deals stylishly and seriously with the weirdest stories from the tabloids. Conspiracy is piled on conspiracy, so that no one really knows anything except that 'the truth is out there' – somewhere. This

Extra-terrestrials are destructive and utterly unsympathetic to humanity, as indicated in this scene from *Independence Day*.
20th Century Fox (courtesy Kobal)

appeals to curious, intelligent, affluent X-Generation viewers who had long been misunderstood or neglected by the broadcasting networks. Certainly it has popularized, on a weekly basis, such arcane aspects of ufology as brain implants, missing time, abductions, retrievals, hybrid alien-human babies, Area 51 and the shady machinations of government-military departments.

Many specific films and programmes can be seen as being directly responsible for stories provided by real-life abductees, and in turn their stories become the basis for further films and programmes. The images of UFOs and aliens in the past 50 years have been so prevalent that the boundary between fact and fiction is totally blurred. These films and TV shows are popular because there is a fundamental belief that we are on the verge of encountering extra-terrestrial life; on a deeper and longer-term level, they act as a metaphor for personal, social, psychological or physical alienation. Equally, they can be a symbol of optimism and beauty, and a means of escaping our mundane troubles.

The success of *The X-Files* and *Independence Day* makes it likely that our TV networks and cinemas will be swamped with even more alien invaders and allied sci-fi themes as the millennium approaches and the second half of ufology's first century opens.

4

Seeking Patterns

FLAPS, WAVES AND WINDOWS

I T WAS 4AM, that wee hour of the morning when the world is dark and quiet. Police constables Clifford Waycott and Roger Willey would have been quite happy if it had stayed that way for the rest of that October night in 1967, as they coasted along in their patrol car on the road between Okehampton and Holsworthy, Devon, England. But the velvet darkness of the Dartmoor night surrounding them was suddenly punctuated by a strange glow up ahead of the patrolling policemen's vehicle. 'The light wasn't piercing but it was very bright,' Waycott was to say later. 'It was star-spangled – just like looking through wet glass – and although we reached 90 miles an hour it accelerated away from us.'

The glow was created by a group of lights clustered into a cross shape. It sailed silently at tree-top height, keeping just ahead of the police car, as if playing a game. The constables radioed their headquarters to tell of their action in chasing the UFO. The car squealed around bends and swooped up and down dale in a vain effort to catch up with the light form. They just couldn't get closer than about 400yd (370m). Knowing that they would never live it down if they crashed their patrol car while pursuing a UFO, Waycott and Willey finally abandoned the chase. To insure against ridicule, they pulled up behind a Land Rover parked at the roadside. Inside was farmer Christopher Gardner, who was taking a nap after a long drive. The police officers woke the man, and he was able to witness the brilliant flying cross formation in the distance. Before it disappeared, a second cross-shaped light form joined it, and they both flew off.

This is one of the better-known sightings to come from the 1950 wave. The object was photographed by Paul Trent at McMinnville, Oregon, USA, on 11 May. *Fortean Picture Library*

The incident received big press coverage, and the papers took the men's accounts seriously. Journalists were learning to do so, because UFOs were being sighted everywhere in Britain that year by the sort of witnesses not usually associated with uncontrollable imaginations – policemen, airline pilots, high-ranking military officers, suburban housewives and so on. In the days following the Devon incident, reports of glowing, flying crosses, not to mention other strange aeroforms, came in from locations around the country hundreds of miles apart.

Britain was in the midst of a UFO 'flap'. No one was to know at the time that it was just part of a massive worldwide wave of UFO activity.

✳ FLAPPING AROUND

It is a characteristic of the human mind to seek patterns and connections in the complexity of the world around it, whether in the scatter of stars across the night sky, astrological correspondences, population distribution, consumer demand or the myriad other aspects of the physical and sociological environment. It has been the same in ufology: people soon tried to find recurring signs of order and connections in the growing data supplied by the UFO reports which were accumulating in the files of military agencies, individual investigators and the expanding band of civilian UFO organizations in various countries. In addition, researchers pored over archival sources and newspaper reports for accounts of strange phenomena, and the works of earlier authors were studied for any data they might yield. It became obvious to ufologists that there were variations in the occurrence of UFO reports: they could cluster in both time and space.

Ufologists initially borrowed the Air Force term 'flap' – meaning a panic or ungovernable crisis – for specific periods of time during which an increase of reported UFO sightings occurred. In later years, most ufologists adopted the term 'wave' to describe such outbreaks revealed in chronological analysis of report data, especially when a wide geographical area rather than a localized district (a 'window' – see page 53) was involved.

Kenneth Arnold's 1947 sighting of nine glittering objects (see Chapter 1) occurred in the midst of what with hindsight ufologists saw was a UFO wave. After Arnold's sighting was publicized, the news media became keenly alert to reports from the public of flying saucers. In turn, the public itself had become excited about the media tales of things seen in the sky, and either because of these facts, or because there was a genuine wave of aerial phenomena (or perhaps because of a combination of both situations), the numbers of claimed sightings of flying saucers soared. A woman even saw discs 'like silver plates' flying over the Cascades only three days after Arnold's sighting. By 16 July, the peak of that perceived wave, the US Air Force itself had received over 850 reports of UFOs, and a 1988 survey by ufologist Loren Gross revealed a further 142 accounts in California newspapers alone. Numbers of claimed sightings began to dwindle in the following weeks.

We have also described the outbreak of mystery airship sightings in America between 1896 and 1897 (see Chapter 1). That this has come to be seen by ufologists as a flap pre-dating the contemporary ufological era is due in no small part to preliminary research conducted by Charles Fort. Born in Albany, New York, in 1874, Fort devoted much of his adult life to the tireless trawling of book and newspaper libraries, seeking evidence of anomalies ignored by mainstream science. He compiled a voluminous record of unusual events and incidents, and published four books: *The Book of the Damned* (1919), *New Lands* (1923), *Lo!* (1931) and *Wild Talents* (1932).

Fort packaged his raw data in an offbeat, humorous commentary, aimed mainly at the pomposity of a dismissive science. In *New Lands*, he picked up on the widespread news reports of strange airships, lights and balloons seen in American skies in the latter 1890s. He divined that there was hoaxing and joking in the mix of the reports, but sensed that there was also a real, underlying phenomenon. 'The indications are that voyagers from some other world are nearby,' he wrote, always ready with a provocative hypothesis (he refused to settle on a single, cast-iron 'explanation' for anything, preferring a more inclusive and organic approach to the mysteries of the Universe).

In the process of assembling his uniquely compendious record of unusual events, Fort began to spy possible connections that virtually no one before him had had the range of data or wit to perceive. He would note, for instance, how on a given day curious events such as falls of frogs from the sky or unexplained booming noises could erupt at various widely separated points around the world. Some of his observations were particularly sharp: in *New Lands* he noted that on the night of 9 February 1913, coincident with a lapse of activity in the 1912–13 British airship wave, there were either 'groups of meteors, in one straight line' or 'a procession of unknown objects, carrying lights' that flew through Canadian skies. He also linked strange aerial lights with earthquakes, pre-dating modern geological ideas of 'earthquake lights' and 'earth lights' (see Chapter 10), and made still-challenging connections between earthquakes and meteoric rock falls. Fort further commented on the recurrence of such phenomena over decades and centuries in specific regions that in the age of ufology would become known as 'windows'. It is no wonder that some of today's researchers have dubbed him 'the first ufologist'.

A number of modern ufologists took on research into UFO waves, but folkorist and ufologist Thomas E. Bullard nowadays takes a somewhat jaundiced view of the subject, and observes that what we might call 'wave literature' was more prevalent in the earlier decades of ufology than currently. He suggests that this is because the idea of waves, initially so full of promise as a royal road of UFO research, has subsequently proven to be more complex and difficult to define, and a sense of frustration with the approach has set in.

The French-born pioneer UFO researcher Jacques Vallée, together with his wife Janine, published an important study of UFO wave phenomena in their 1966 book *Challenge to Science*. The following year, Ted Bloecher produced a study of the 1947 wave, and in the 1960s and 1970s John Keel made studies of various waves and flaps and instituted the concept of 'windows'). Numerous other ufological researchers have produced studies of both historical and contemporary waves in the US, Scandinavia, Britain, Belgium and elsewhere on through to the 1990s.

Ufologists realized early on that Fort's example had to be followed – namely, that if patterns were being sought, the database had to be adequate for the job. A number of UFO databases have been compiled, but probably the major one is UFOCAT, initiated by David Saunders in 1967 and based on 3000 reports submitted by Jacques Vallée to the Condon Committee (see Chapter 7). In 1975, UFOCAT was donated to the Center for UFO Studies (CUFOS) in Evanston, Illinois, the organization set up by J. Allen Hynek. By 1980, it contained well over 100,000 entries of various kinds. After lying fallow for the following decade, the catalogue was resumed on mainframe computer by Donald Johnson.

Despite the work that had gone into it, and its general usefulness, UFOCAT was criticized by Allan Hendry, who for a period was a funded, full-time investigator with CUFOS and one of America's most incisive and balanced ufologists until his retirement from the scene in the early 1980s. He felt that the quality of data contained in the catalogue varied greatly. Some of the sources of the entries were 'less than inspiring as arbiters of complete and accurate information', and the parameters of information contained within each entry were not uniform, so they were difficult to use for statistical purposes. Among other factors, such as an unconscious bias by the catalogue's coders towards 'more interesting' cases and the inclusion of more IFOs (Identified Flying Objects such as planes, astronomical bodies and meteors) than were noted in the entries, he also pointed out that the number of American cases in UFOCAT was disproportionately large compared to those from the rest of the world – a function of the ease of data-gathering in North America rather than a reflection of actual global incidence of UFO activity. 'As a bibliography of raw UFO reports, UFOCAT is without peer,' Hendry concluded, but warned that it could be treated only as a reference guide to the original sources for the details. 'Otherwise, the distinction between poorly investigated reports and exhaustively studied sightings is completely lost.'

This underlines one of the chief problems faced in ufology: all that researchers really have to go on are UFO *reports*, not UFOs themselves. Photographs have been shown to be next to useless, as so many fakes have been uncovered, and the ease of creating sophisticated photo-

A SELECT CHRONOLOGY OF MAJOR UFO WAVES

1896–7	US, Canada
1909	Great Britain, Russia
1912–13	Great Britain, New Zealand, Russia
1932–7	Scandinavia
1946	Scandinavia, Greece
1947	US
1949	Soviet Union, South-west US
1950	North Africa, Spain, US
1952	Western Europe, US, Canada
1954	France, Western and Eastern Europe, North Africa, South America, Australia
1955	US
1957	Brazil, US
1958	Japan
1959	New Guinea
1960	Tasmania, New Zealand
1962	Argentina, Brazil
1964	South America, US
1965	Australia, Central Africa, Chile, US
1966	Australia, US, Great Britain, South Africa Soviet Union
1967	US, Great Britain, Soviet Union
1968	Spain, Western and Eastern Europe, South America
1972	Central and Southern Africa
1973	US, Western Europe
1975	South Africa, Australia
1977	Soviet Union, Great Britain, Chile
1978	Italy, New Zealand, Australia, South America
1978	Italy, Kuwait, New Zealand
1981–3	Norway, South America
1982	South America
1987–8	Great Britain
1989–91	Belgium
1991–?	Mexico

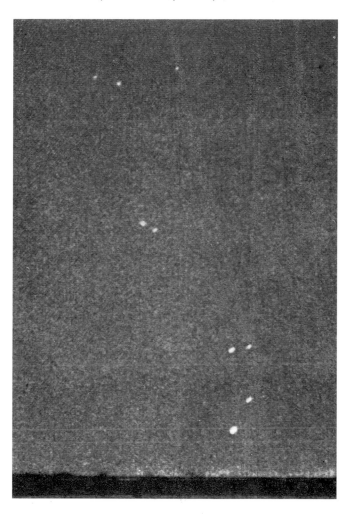

A daytime 'lights in the sky' sighting from the 1952 wave. This is a frame from about 30 feet of film taken on 2 July at 11.10 am by Navy Warrant Officer Delbert C. Newhouse in Utah, USA. Newhouse, a veteran Navy photographer, was accompanied by his wife and two children while driving on an open highway north of Tremonton. As the objects flew westwards, one broke away and reversed its course.
National Archives (Modern Military Branch)

graphic hoaxes has only become greater over the years. Even authentic pictures of genuine unusual phenomena tend to yield very little information, and the need for more thoughtful photographic techniques, together with instrumental data, has become a pressing matter within the field.

Despite the difficulties of assessing data, ufological research has nevertheless managed to identify a considerable number of apparent UFO waves over the decades, as a glance at the panel reveals. The earliest identified waves related to mystery 'airships', 'balloons' or 'ghost planes', with the exception of the 'foo fighters' of World War II. The first wave after that war seems to have been the rash of primarily Scandinavian 'ghost rockets' (see Chapter 1). Kenneth Arnold's sighting came, we have noted, in a wave of sightings affecting large areas of the western US.

The 1950s brought their own waves, and what is often but erroneously called the 'French wave' of 1954 was subjected to study by French ufologist Aimé Michel and, later, by the Vallées, who uncovered twice the number of cases reported in the French press compared to those used by Michel. From the French perspective, this wave started in the east of the country in mid-August and continued to the end of November. Four reports on 11 August were followed by a case at Precy-sur-Thil, in which a shiny object moving in a jerky fashion and leaving a trail was observed. A few days later, at Dole, a 'cloud-cigar' was seen, moving slowly across the sky and illuminating the whole town. On 20 August, reports of UFO landings began (the validity of these has been much contested by some researchers). On 23 August, a landing was reported on the shore of Lake Geneva near Thonon, and an aerial 'cigar' was observed at Vernon for three-quarters of an hour by policemen, a businessman and an Army rocket enginer, all from separate locations. The flood-tide of reports then broke: the Vallées collected

One of the claimed Spanish sightings of the 1954 wave. This picture was taken by Juan Coll and Jose Antonio Baena near Malaga, Spain, on 2 November. *Fortean Picture Library*

nearly 1000 unexplained sightings covering the following three months.

'It was the number of reports, the quality of the descriptions, and the reliability of the observers that made the 1954 wave the subject of so much controversy and a standard for the various theories of the UFO phenomenon,' the Vallées observed in '1966. But they noted something else. The records of the US Air Force showed that Germany was the first Western European country where numbers of reported sightings rose sharply. And studying a wide range of records for September 1954, they found that reported UFO events for that month 'covered all of Western Europe, from Scandinavia to Portugal, and extended into Africa'. On 5 September, for instance, discs were seen flying over Graz, Austria, in the morning, and by the afternoon a disc-shaped object the size of a plane was observed over Tangiers for ten minutes. On 17 September, thousands of witnesses in Rome, Italy, saw an object looking like a half-cigar at an altitude of under 1 mile (1.6km) above the city. Witnesses included military pilots and high-ranking army officers. The object was tracked by radar as it sped at up to 175mph (280km/h) per hour, only to stop dead in its tracks. It would drop in altitude, then turn, and rise again. It performed for over an hour, before moving away to the north-west. Reports of curious lights, objects and 'luminous plates' leaving trails behind them came from airline pilots over the Atlantic, from the Azores, the Ivory Coast of Africa, Scotland, and even as far afield as Dhubri, India.

In France, the wave had peaked by 12 Ocotber, but its apparent centre of activity moved eastwards to Italy and Yugoslavia. By the end of October, additional reports had come in from Angola, Algeria, Morocco and Madagascar, as well as from Eastern European countries. By November, the wave had petered out in France, but reports increased in South America, Africa, Australia and Spain. It was almost a global wave, although, according to the Vallées, North America did not show any marked increase in reports.

Two French investigators, Gerard Barthel and Jacques Brucker, dismissed the 1954 'French wave' as an artefact of media distortion and a mass fear reaction: '*la grande peur Martienne*'. But the Vallées, demonstrating the extent of the wave, stated firmly that 'the idea that the events of 1954 essentially centred on France, are confined to the facts related in Michel's book, and should be interpreted within the framework of a mere sociological phenomenon affecting one small country with very dense population, is simply incorrect'.

¤ TIDAL WAVE

UFO wave activity started the 1960s modestly enough, with flurries over South American countries and Australasia, but from about 1964 to 1968 a huge wave of reported UFO activity rolled virtually around the globe: it was 'a wave of waves', a UFO tidal wave.

'If the classic wave is an epidemic,' Thomas E. Bullard has written (in Clark, 1996 – see Bibliography), 'some periods qualify as pandemics because wave-level activity continues unabated for several years on an international scale... UFOs cavorted through the skies during 1964–8 with a complexity of activity defying description. Localized waves rippled here and there around the country [the US] and about the world continuously...'.

The first swells of the tidal wave spread out from South America throughout 1964, with heavy reported UFO activity there. The southwestern US started to pick up on reported sightings in the early summer, and by late summer the whole country was experiencing sightings. In 1965, Britain started to be affected, with the small Wiltshire town of Warminster beginning to emerge as a 'hotspot'. (Much of the initial interest surrounding this famed sightings locale was instigated by the energetic involvement of local reporter and author Arthur Shuttlewood, and much of what was seen could be dismissed as misperceived observations of military activity. Even a carefully faked photograph was produced. Nevertheless, there were also repeated reports of what stolid local ufologists felt was a real phenomenon, a cavorting orange-gold lightball they nicknamed the 'Amber Gambler'.) In the same year, while parts of South America continued to produce many UFO reports and Mexico experienced a wave, reports began arriving also from Australia and central Africa. In the US, the front of a UFO wave appeared to advance from New Mexico north to the Dakotas overnight, with dramatic sightings of multi-coloured lights, 'Saturn-like' and 'egg-shaped' objects, together with military and weather-bureau radar tracking of unknown objects.

In 1966, Britain continued to be active, and increased sightings reports came in all year from Australia, especially from Victoria in April. Particularly intense activity was reported within the US in Michigan, Wisconsin, Minnesota, Arkansas, Utah, the Ohio Valley and the

This cylindrical or 'cigar-shaped' object was photographed in Wichita, Kansas, on 27 June during the 1967 UFO wave. This is one of 6 pictures of the object taken by Jefferson Villar. *Fortean Picture Library*

Wanaque Reservoir, New Jersey (but see page 53). Some of the US sightings involved dramatic highlights, such as car chases and reported landings.

In 1967, the wave crested: North American activity continued, it picked up in Britain, and during the latter half of the year there were extensive sightings in Russia. One of the present authors, Paul Devereux, saw two remarkable phenomena himself during the British activity of 1967. One (see Chapter 1) was of a round, black object, the other a glowing orange rectangle of light above open fields near Bromley in Kent. Numerous other witnesses in various locations saw the same glorious-looking object, which came to a halt several hundred feet in the air, changed its perfect rectangular outlines into other forms, and finally collapsed into a rose-tinted, amorphous cloud that grew duller and duller and finally dispersed in the atmosphere. The whole year was a period of time that can now be recalled like some visionary novel: airline pilots flying into Shannon airport, Ireland, complained of being 'buzzed' by green fireballs; mysterious lights in the sky affected police telecommunications in the English Midlands; and there were many sightings of mysterious cross formations of lights, as described on page 45. In 1968, the tidal wave rolled back into South 'torpedo-shaped' and glowing 'egg-shaped' objects. In some cases, vehicles' lights and motors failed and an object would touch down on the road ahead.

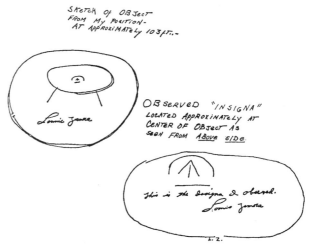

Zamora's sketch of the Socorro object.

People in a Madrid street gape skywards at a UFO photographed with a high-powered telephoto lens that appeared over the Spanish capital on 4 September 1978. Spanish Air Force jets failed to reach the object, which disappeared at 90,000 feet.

The still-enigmatic Socorro case of 24 April 1964 is another example, shortly after the commencement of the 1960s UFO tidal wave, in which a police officer in New Mexico named Lonnie Zamora claimed to have seen a roaring cone of blue flame, which landed in the desert. Tracing its position, Zamora saw a metallic-looking object with small beings near it. It took off again, leaving physical damage at the site and indentations in the ground. Zamora claimed the object had an arrow-like insignia on it (curiously like a surveyor's benchmark).

Valensole, in June 1965, is another, well-investigated, case in which a farmer apparently encountered an egg-shaped object and small beings in a French lavender field.

America, with eddies and ripples circulating in both Eastern and Western Europe, especially Spain.

After the 1960s crescendo, UFO activity reverted to mainly shorter-term waves in many places around the world, including South Africa. Major multi-state waves were to occur in the US only twice more during ufology's first half-century, in 1973 and 1974.

Some of the most celebrated UFO encounter reports occurred during waves, a factor easily overlooked when concentrating on case histories to the exclusion of the more general context of UFO activity. The Levelland, Texas, case is an example. In the space of a few hours around midnight on 2 November 1957, at the peak of a UFO wave, police patrols received multiple reports from drivers around the town concerning close encounters with

One of the marks (protected by stones) left by the object Zamora claimed to see land in the desert. *Fortean Picture Library*

Despite later investigations by ufologists, this sighting remains unexplained, although it was discovered that the area had been selected as a possible installation site for missiles and the French sixth fleet was in the area at the time of the incident, when helicopters, for example, would still have been unfamiliar sights to inhabitants of the district. The UFO tidal wave was touching the shores of Europe (the British Isles) at this time, although France has not generally been implicated specifically in this by ufologists.

In October 1973, amid a wave affecting both the US and Western Europe, Army reserve Captain Lawrence J. Coyne and crew were flying in a helicopter which had a close encounter with a gray tubular object, sporting red and white lights and emitting a green fan of light, near Mansfield, Ohio. The UFO came to a halt near the helicopter, then took off at speed, causing curious behavioural effects, with the Army machine in its wake. The encounter was seen by ground witnesses as well.

On 21 October 1978, during an Australasian wave, young Frederick Valentich disappeared while piloting a light aircraft over Bass Strait, Australia. Shortly before communication from him ceased, over his radio he reported encountering a long, shiny object with a green light. And so on.

¤ OTHER WAVE MECHANICS

Apart from logging their frequency and scope, ufologists have attempted to understand other aspects of UFO wave mechanics. They have noted that waves of UFO reports can start suddenly with a deluge across the affected area, or gradually build in frequency until the level of incidence is such that a wave is in place. Waves can likewise end either suddenly or gradually. At one point, it was thought that the appearance of waves might correlate with factors such as the nearness of Mars during its cycles relative to the Earth: the 1950 and 1952 waves, for example, coincided with oppositions of Mars, and allowed prediction of the wave in 1954. Alas, a reliable sequence of such correlations could not be maintained.

In 1980, the longer (roughly 11-year) cycle of sunspots, another correlative favourite, also began to be checked: Swedish researcher Ragnar Foshufvud took UFO data that had been 'screened' and selected by J. Allen Hynek, and ranged these against sunspot cycle data. He found that UFO sightings increased towards the onset of the two sunspot maxima which occurred in the timespan of his sample (late 1940s–1970), and decreased afterwards. Forshufvud was actually seeking correlations between

This was one of six photographs taken by Roy Manifold at Crayfish Bay, Bass Strait, Melbourne, Victoria, Australia, on 21 October 1978, shortly before the mysterious disappearance of Frederick Valentich. Manifold was intent on photographing the sunset, and did not see the dark, 'soft' object pictured here. *Fortean Picture Library*

UFO incidence and geomagnetic factors, and as sunspot activity disturbs the Earth's magnetic field, this was one obvious aspect to test. French researcher Claude Poher had already found correlations between increased reported UFO activity and rises in geomagnetic activity levels, and other researchers, such as Michael Persinger of Laurentian University, Ontario, went on to conduct numerous sophisticated mathematical analyses of correlative factors with large samples of UFO reports, including solar-geomagnetic ones. In 1981, for example, Persinger found that UFO activity appeared to increase one to three years after a decrease in geomagnetic (or solar) activity. This careful way of wording findings indicated apparent trends that were not greatly at variance with the pattern revealed by Forshufvud's simpler graph.

One particularly bizarre correlation was made by John Keel. He had noticed that in the 'flap' areas he investigated there were also often reports of sudden poltergeist outbreaks concurrent with the reported UFO activity. Going back over the work of paranormal researchers, he found a similar pattern in historical data, and produced a

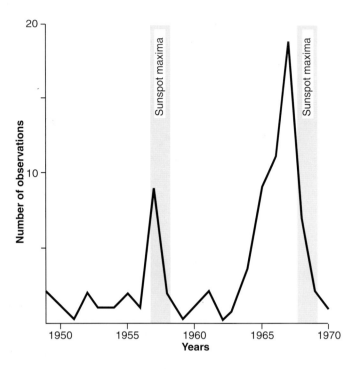

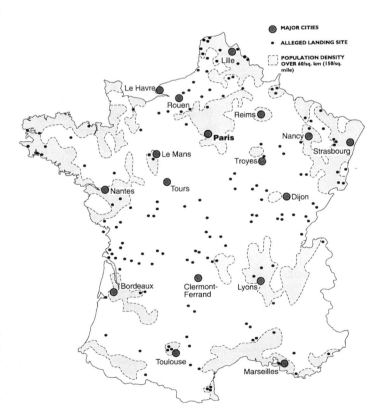

Swedish researcher R. Forshufvud compared 20 years of UFO reports with sunspot activity. It can be seen that peaks in both sets of data closely correlate.

graph covering the years 1900–13. UFO flaps, Keel concluded, were either immediately preceded or followed by poltergeist outbreaks, or they were accompanied by them. This may seem a ridiculous correlation at first sight, but if we forget ideas about poltergeists being spirit entities, and think of them rather as perhaps forms of energetic and highly localized natural phenomena based upon electromagnetic effects, such patterns might be telling us something about the nature of the UFO phenomenon. In Chapter 10 we will return to the 'poltergeist connection', without paranormal connotations.

It was thought that the behaviour of waves themselves showed progressive features: in 1956, Aimé Michel thought that he could discern a general global drift eastwards in UFO wave activity. Calculations indicated a 30-degree eastwards advance around the globe for each successive 61-month wave. Making certain allowances and distinctions, and working to data at hand, Bullard (writing in Clark, 1996 – see Bibliography) noted that 'waves have adhered to this predicted pattern into the 1980s'.

There has also been a keenness on the part of ufologists to identify patterns of UFO behaviour within waves. For instance, it was thought for a time that UFOs would come closer to witnesses, or exhibit increased strangeness (landings, entities, and so on) from one wave to another

– but such patterns did not hold up to serious analysis. The Vallées, however, made an interesting observation in the French data of the 1954 wave. They found that of the 200 reported UFO landings (involving some 624 witnesses in all), most of them occurred in rural areas. Not a single report came from the six *départements* surrounding Paris, containing nearly one-third of the French population. This is unexpected, as UFO sighting reports can come only from persons who think they have seen a UFO and report it: consequently, one normally expects a positive population bias to be present in any geographical distribution of reports. The French 1954 data would therefore suggest, at least superficially, that something other than 'mass hysteria' or a similiar hypothesized sociological phenomenon was at the heart of the 1954 French UFO reports, even allowing for a mix of probable hoaxing and political elements.

Other such 'internal' UFO wave patterns included Aimé Michel's perception that UFOs sighted in the French part of the 1954 wave followed a straight-line course or 'orthoteny' – but this turned out to be based on faulty

Most sightings of the 1954 UFO wave in France occurred outside the areas with greatest population density. *After Jacques and Janine Vallée* mathematics. Another French researcher, Ferdinand Lagarde, found a correlation between reported low-level and landed UFOs and geological faulting.

Another key analysis of characteristic behaviour patterns on the part of reported UFOs came from J. Allen Hynek himself. On poring over the data with which he had such intimacy, he arrived at the now well-known basic categories of sightings:

¤ **Distant UFOs** Phenomena seen at a distance – 'nocturnal lights', 'daylight discs', and 'radar-visual', where radar echoes seem to have been confirmed by visual observation at the same time. (Hynek acknowledged that nocturnal lights and daylight discs need not be mutually exclusive.)

¤ **Close Encounters of the First Kind (CE-I)** The 'simple' close encounter of witness with UFO, where the phenomenon does not interact with its environment.

¤ **Close Encounters of the Second Kind (CE-II)** The close observation of a UFO in which the object interacts with its environment in some way, such as leaving marks on the ground or damaging foliage.

¤ **Close Encounters of the Third Kind (CE-III)** The now famous classification, in which close observation of a UFO includes the perception of 'occupants' or 'entities' in or around the phenomenon. This is not necessarily the same as 'contactee' reports, where someone claims to be in telepathic or other contact with 'space beings'.

To these categories, some subsequent ufologists have added 'Close Encounters of the Fourth Kind (CE-IV)', in which psychic or extremely high-strangeness, subjective events are claimed, such as physical abduction, time lapses (amnesia), the appearance in a witness of unusual mental or physical abilities after close encounter, and suchlike.

¤ WAVING OUT OF WINDOWS

What the UFO wave is to time, the UFO 'window' is to space. A total global wave is exceedingly rare, if it has ever existed at all. The geographical areas covered by UFO waves, especially large-scale ones, can only ever be judged approximately. Unlike the political boundaries of countries and states, they do not have clearly marked extents.

'Our first consideration in a "flap" study should be geographical,' stated John Keel, the veteran American

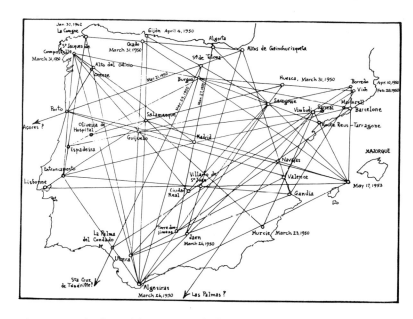

It became popular for a while to see straight-line patterns, 'orthotenics', in geographical distributions of UFO report data. This example shows the supposed orthotenic network in Spain and Portugal, as plotted by A. Ribera.

ufologist who coined the term 'window' for a flap area, in 1969. In studying reported UFO activity in the US, he came to the conclusion that sightings in a given area during a specific period of time were confined to regions having a radius of about 200 miles (320km). This was his original conception of windows, and he felt that each state in the nation probably had from two to ten of them. Then, as he explained in his *UFOs: Operation Trojan Horse* of 1970, Keel suspected that these window regions were themselves part of larger circles of activity. He came to this idea because of his observations surrounding a brilliant meteor seen by many people arcing over Canada and the north-eastern US on 25 April 1966. Keel discovered that exactly at this time there was a huge earthquake in Tashkent in the then Soviet Union. Reports emerged of extraordinary light phenomena accompanying this cataclysm: it was dark early morning when the quake struck, and people saw room interiors and streets bathed in brilliant white light; afterwards, there were glowing spheres floating through the air 'like lighted balloons'. 'Tashkent is at exactly the same latitude and longitude as the north-eastern US, precisely on the opposite side of the earth,' Keel observed. 'Our "meteor" and the Tashkent earthquake occurred simultaneously... '.

It is doubtful if any mainstream geologist or seismologist would give any credence to Keel's idea, but Keel was in no doubt that on the smaller scale many windows centred on areas of geomagnetic deviation and faulting and, like Charles Fort before him, he sensed a connection between bizarre 'meteors' or light phenomena and tectonic disturbance.

Subsequent to these pioneering observations by Keel, the window idea has settled deeply into ufological thinking. While few ufologists would now attempt to define windows rigidly as areas 400 miles (640km) across, there has been the recognition that relatively small and fairly specific areas seem to have harboured unusual light phenomena for very long periods of time. The incidence level in these places, always above the average baseline in surrounding regions, can itself fluctuate. American examples of such specific windows include the Yakima Indian Reservation in Washington State, where there was an outbreak of light phenomena in the 1970s that was witnessed, photographed and triangulated by fire wardens and other observers, or the wave of lights and seemingly metallic daylight objects in the remote Uintah Basin of Utah in the same decade. But the prime American example is the region around Marfa in the Big Bend area of Texas, where light phenomena have been reported for a century or more. In Britain, the Pennine Hills, among various other locations, have hosted unusual lights for generations, and these still flare out in special displays in specific valleys up to the present time. A particularly interesting example of these highly localized windows is the Hessdalen valley in Norway, where, again, unusual lights have been seen for decades, and which had an exceptional outbreak in the early 1980s (see Chapter 10). This was studied in the field by a team equipped with a range of instrumentation, who succeeded in obtaining many photographs of the lights, some of which were very large, and these were witnessed navigating their way along rocky moun-

An investigator sets up camera equipment in bitterly cold conditions during the outbreak of UFOs or light phenomena in the Norwegian UFO 'window' of Hessdalen, in the 1950s. *Project Hessdalen*

This sign at the viewing spot for the 'Marfa Lights' on Highway 90 between Alpine and Marfa, Texas, tells the story of this UFO 'window'. *Paul Devereux*

tain ridges for over an hour at a time. Recurring UFOs seen in windows like these are sometimes subtly downgraded to 'spooklights', and ufologists who believe that UFOs are extra-terrestrial craft consider them to be something other than UFOs. Paul Devereux has termed them 'earth lights', and their study is the only one within ufology at the end of the first 50 years where scientific data are begining to accumulate and evidence is expanding beyond the anecdotal to include instrumental readings and ongoing, funded fieldwork which involves mainstream scientific observers. This aspect of ufology is considered in greater detail in Chapter 10, but it can be noted here that some ufologists feel it is likely that such lights and apparent metallic objects are in fact exotic, little-known geophysical phenomena rather than ET craft.

Again, Keel was prescient. His study of waves and windows convinced him that the UFOs were not alien spaceships but something else, something which belonged to this planet, although equally unknown. By 1969, he was pointing out that most of the sightings in the so-called airship waves around the turn of the century were of manoeuvring lights, just as are the majority of modern reports. It is all too easy for witnesses unconsciously to 'fill in' what their expectations dictate. 'We have done ourselves an injustice by concentrating on the reports of "hard" objects (seemingly mechanical objects) which represent a minority of all reports,' Keel declared. 'It is erroneous to assume that all "soft" objects (lights, and transparent or translucent objects which change in size, shape and colour while remaining in view) are merely visible portions of "flying saucers". The "soft" objects are the real phenomenon.'

¤ CLEANING WINDOWS

Trying to clarify the objective nature of waves and windows is not easy. We are dealing with waves of *reports*, not directly with phenomena, and there are great difficulties in separating a genuine increase of UFO incidence from an artefact of reporting. As a simple example, at the time of the 1957 wave the Russians had launched the first space satellites, the Sputniks. 'All eyes turned towards the sky,' remarked the Vallées. 'Suddenly "flying saucers" shared the headlines with the satellites.' Simplistic explanations might thus ascribe the 1957 wave to misidentification of new, unfamiliar man-made lights in the sky – the satellites. But the Vallées pointed out that 'the brief flare-up of interest on the part of newspapers made the wave appear to have a peak of short duration... In reality, the wave had been going on for a long time'. Undoubtedly, the novelty of artificial satellites, not to mention underlying tensions in the American public at such an unexpected Russian advance in space technology (thus implying military superiority), must have contributed to erroneous UFO reports. Yet how is that separated out from the brute fact that more people's attention would be directed to the sky, and so if there were genuine UFOs, reports relating to them would be bound to increase at such a time? The same conundrum applies to the recent Mexican wave (see panel, p.56).

Another example of this kind of problem also showed up in the 1950s. It was noted that more UFOs were reported in warm-weather periods, but this was because during that decade air conditioning was rare and people spent more time out of doors! Clearly, caution is called for: all possible mechanisms that could increase the numbers of reports have to be sought out and weighed by the thoughtful ufologist before it can be proclaimed that there was an actual increase in unusual aerial phenomena.

Then there is the role of the news media. This is always a fraught matter, as we have already remarked more than once. If a local newspaper decides to repress reports of sightings, then no wave will be apparent. John Keel pointed this out in 1969:

The sightings around the Wanaque Reservoir in New Jersey received considerable publicity early in 1966, but during my repeated trips to the area I found witnesses who had been seeing UFOs almost continuously for two years before one of the objects blatantly appeared directly over the reservoir and created a 'flap'. That 'flap' still continues sporadically but the police and the local officials are weary of the crowds and the publicity and keep the new sightings to themselves. They haven't been 'censored' or 'hushed up'. They are merely trying to keep interest in the phenomenon at a minimum to make things easier for themselves...

I have found many other sections of the country which have seemingly been inundated by UFOs for months – even years – and the local press has not carried a line about them.

Paul Devereux found a similar situation during research in Wales in 1987. A woman who had come to live in the remote Elan Valley had noted strange lights flashing off the top of surrounding mountain ridges. She called together a meeting at the town hall in the tiny town of Llanidloes at one end of the valley, suspecting that the lights might be something sinister to do with occasional experiments conducted by British Aerospace in a forest in the valley. Local BBC reporter Phil Rickman covered the meeting, but discovered that shepherds and other long-time residents of the region were well acquainted with the lights. 'I've seen them since I've been a child,' one told Rickman. The lights had been there long before British Aerospace had been doing its thing in the forest. (The company said it used the site as it was well removed from electromagnetic interference.) Devereux found younger country folk in the valley whose parents and grandparents had seen the lights and who forbade them to talk to outsiders about them, for fear of being laughed at as superstitious country bumpkins. In fact, the only ones prepared to speak were those whose parents were deceased. Local beliefs about the lights ranged from fairies to electrical effects arising from metal ores in the mountains.

Conversely, if a newspaper or TV station decides to fill in odd gaps in its page space or broadcasting time with examples of the sporadic UFO reports that are commonly made and are usually ignored by the press, then it can appear falsely as if there is the beginning of a wave. This may encourage many people to look for and expect to see something unusual, so misperceived mundane objects such as a cloudy Moon, shooting stars, Venus, balloons, aircraft, meteorological effects and the like increase their share of the reports. Such a rising media tide would attract the hoaxers, liars and attention-seekers who are always with us, and so the mirage of a wave is created. Likewise, if there is a particularly active ufologist living in a specific area, the enthusiasm of such a person in chasing up all reports and rumours in the district and feeding these to local newspapers can by itself make an area which normally has no excessive incidence of reported aerial phenomena look like a UFO hotspot.

Then there is the even more tricky situation where the

A UFO wave erupted in Mexico in 1991, and brought a new dynamic into the phenomenon – the wide availability of amateur video cameras in the affected population. The wave was precipitated by a total solar eclipse that occurred on 11 July. This rare and spectacular event naturally captured the public imagination, and it was filmed by the country's leading TV stations. The public, too, took many photographs and much video footage of the eclipse, which was directly visible from Mexico City and the whole of the Valley of Mexico.

The eclipse triggered UFO interest because, generally, it attracted mass attention to the skies, and, specifically, many people noted on their photographs and video sequences of the event a diffuse point of light in the sky, which became brighter as the sky darkened during the progress of the eclipse. Here was a sensation – a clearly filmed daytime UFO over Mexico City, one of the most populous places on Earth! Mexican TV producer Jaime Maussan, who had shown interest in UFOs in a few earlier programmes, broadcast some clips from the many amateur videos of the eclipse, showing the 'extra-terrestrial ship'. He organized UFO watchers, 'Los Vigilantes', among the TV population. People enthusiastically scanned the skies, camcorders in hand; they were to send in their video footage to Maussan. (In an interview in August 1996, Maussan told Paul Devereux that he had by then received some 6000 video sequences of strange aerial objects.) Within months of the eclipse, UFO excitement within Mexico had reached high-tension levels.

'The UFO atmosphere in Mexico was ripe,' reported skeptical UFO researcher Hector Escobar Sotomayor. 'In a few months there were reports of landings in many parts of the country such as Tula,

Jaime Maussan (left) with Paul Devereux. *Paul Devereux*

Hidalgo, Poza Rica and Veracruz. There was a wave in Atlixco, Puebla, in which hundreds of people spent all night waiting to see the UFO (always at the same hour). The UFO was a bright yellow light with two smaller lights at its sides, one green, the other red. A similarity to the lights of an aeroplane or just a coincidence?'

There was a cascade of books, magazines, videos, TV shows and lectures on UFOs. Moreover, after teasing the public for some time, in 1993 Maussan revealed UFO contactee Carlos Diaz, a professional photographer from Tepotzlan, Morelos, who brought ecological messages from the extra-terrestrials and who had photographs showing a yellow flying saucer rising up behind rooftops and trees.

What did the video clips sent to Maussan show? The TV producer felt that they recorded genuine anomalous objects. Devereux looked at about a dozen sequences selected for him by Maussan, in addition to others shown to him by members of Los Vigilantes. He felt that most looked easily identifiable as kites, balloons and, in several cases, distant car headlights descending steep roads on hills lost in the darkness (much of the valley floor in the area of Mexico City is a glittering sea of city lights, and surrounding hills are totally invisible at night – especially on video). Devereux saw no more than a couple of sequences in the sample he was shown which may possibly have featured something of real interest.

The UFO during the eclipse that had triggered the sequence of events generating the UFO wave did not fare well on analysis, either. Calculations showed conclusively that the spot of light captured on video was Venus. As the sun darkened, Venus naturally emerged into a measure of visibility, strengthening in brightness as the eclipse became total. It was claimed that the object viewed in enlargement appears to be rotating, but this is an effect produced by mechanisms within the video system, which become noticeable upon amplification. Another factor which turned this UFO into an IFO was the fact that video sequences taken from Mexico City showed the object in just the same way as did sequences taken from Puebla and other locations 60 miles (100km) or more away. No local object hovering above Mexico City could have shown up similarly in such distant views.

In addition to Venus, some of the still photographs taken of the eclipse showed a spot of light which proved on analysis to be flares generated within the lens systems of some of the cheaper cameras by the points of sunlight around the eclipsed sun.

It is clear to any dispassionate observer that there never was a real increase of UFO activity in Mexico. The wave was a sociological phenomenon generated by factors that must be obvious from this account. While there is no reason to believe that Jaime Maussan is anything other than the sincere, warm individual he presents himself as, he is open to the criticism of being too uncritical of the material he has received and of his own role in generating the Mexican 'UFOria'.

Nevertheless, despite all these problems thousands of people have been scanning the skies above Mexico, so if there are unusual phenomena crossing the heavens then the likelihood of them being spotted, and possibly even filmed, has increased. This still would not denote a wave of UFO activity, but it could possibly mean that amid the loud sociological noise of this Mexican UFO wave there may be a few faint signals concerning genuine anomalous phenomena. The fact that strange lights are routinely claimed to have been seen by rural Hispanics and Indians in Mexico, who do not possess the citified concept of 'UFOs', further supports this idea.

news media might be responding to a genuine increase in sightings reports, but by publishing them it creates a kind of 'feedback loop' in that the published reports spark off the sorts of effects indicated above.

Social conditions have also to be taken into consideration. The media can act as a lubricant of the collective social mind, and can to some degree stoke psychological phenomena such as 'Great Fears' and mass hysteria. A crowd of people can sometimes act like a single organism, and there is little doubt that the modern media machine can make whole populations behave in the manner we once associated only with physical crowds. It can focus and enlarge what is felt in a society when there are fears of impending war, foreign dominance, economic upheaval or uncertainty, or social unrest and tension of any kind. In such mass states, a society tends to project its fears onto some tangible thing such as an ethnic minority, or a political figure or faction, or into some unifying image of the 'other' such as damned foreigners or... strange craft in the skies. By the same token, at times when life seems too hard, uncertain or spiritually barren, fears can be transmuted into hopes of salvation. So miracles are sought – remarkable healings and visions at some shrine, perhaps, or a religious cult, or... strange craft in the sky bringing wise and benign beings who will help that society out of its troubles.

As well as the news media, there is also the role of the mass dream machines of TV and the cinema, which were discussed in Chapter 3. Some UFO skeptics such as Martin Gardner predicted that there would be a UFO wave after the opening of Spielberg's *Close Encounters of the Third Kind*, but although this movie undoubtedly caused a massive revival of interest in the subject of UFOs, no major waves occurred where they might have been most expected – in North America and Western Europe. So cause and effect in mass psychology cannot easily be identified, and the actual existence and nature of mass states of mind is not as thoroughly proven and explored as is sometimes supposed.

In the end, whether or not a wave is a true wave can only come down to a matter of judgement and careful research. Some waves are probably no more than mirages, but it would seem that there is also some real evidence of fluctuating levels of reported UFO activity, whatever that may be – whether anomalous aerial phenomena, or some poorly understood mechanism affecting the flow of information in complex societies. It might also yet prove to be the case that some of the correlative factors, such as geomagnetism, that ufologists have started to study may hold genuine secrets that could help to unravel the UFO mystery.

The Far Side

ANCIENT ASTRONAUTS, LINES AND CIRCLES

ACCORDING TO SOME neo-Nazi beliefs, Hitler escaped at the end of World War II through a hole at the South Pole into a world inside the Earth. Other rumours say that he sent elite troops on an expedition aimed at locating the polar entrances to the underworld before the war even began.

Such stories are based on the eccentric but abiding belief in there being a 'hollow Earth' containing the civilization of an advanced race. An early proponent of this notion was the American John Cleves Symmes, at the beginning of the nineteenth century. He vainly petitioned Congress to grant funding for an expedition to the poles, and claimed that there were five concentric spheres within the Earth which could sustain life. The obsession was picked up by Cyrus Reed Teed (called 'Koresh' by his followers), who developed a cult in America. This was introduced to Germany by World War I pilot Peter Bender, where it eventually came to Hitler's attention.

In the 1940s, the idea that flying saucers were based within a hollow Earth was promoted by Ray Palmer, editor of *Amazing Stories* and *Fate* magazines. Elements of this obsession have surfaced periodically on the fringes of modern ufology ever since, especially in South America. The general scenario is that flying saucers enter our world from and disappear back through holes at the poles. In this scenario, the ufonauts are

not extra-terrestrials but intra-terrestrials – representatives of the peoples from within the Earth, who are survivors of lost Atlantis or Lemuria. This represents the meeting of ufology with occultism. British ufological writer Brinsley le Poer Trench (who became Lord Clancarty) even deluded himself into thinking he had discovered a space-satellite photograph of a polar hole. In reality, the picture was comprised of a montage of satellite images which built up the picture of the polar region over a period of time. The evolving polar night occupied a rotating part of each photograph, creating the impression of a dark circle or 'hole' at the centre of the montage.

¤ ANCIENT ASTRONAUTS

Other Earth-related ideas have run curiously influential strands through ufology's history, affecting large numbers of people. Perhaps the best known is the 'ancient astronaut' school of thought. Calling on biblical writings and the ancient texts of India and elsewhere, and pointing to remarkable or unexplained features in archaeological artefacts and sites, these proponents argue that Earth was visited in remote antiquity by extra-terrestrials, or that there was some great, technically advanced former civilization on Earth that has since disappeared – or a hybrid of both ideas. Some claim that the ancient extra-terrestrials interbred with humans; others are more cautious and merely ascribe achievements such as the building of great megalithic structures in South America, the Great Pyramid and the megaliths of Europe to the technological guidance of the ancient space visitors. Otherworldly cultural heroes

Stonehenge, England. *Paul Devereux*

such as the Mayan Kukulcan ('Feathered Serpent', the Aztec Quetzalcoatl), who brought and taught the skills of civilization, are interpreted as extra-terrestrials enlightening a benighted humanity. Yet most cultures have such legends, and they can equally be seen as a mythological anthropomorphization of the rise of knowledge within a society, and also perhaps of contact with more advanced neighbours or foreign influences. The variations on the thesis therefore pay scant regard to human skill and genius, and so diminish our human heritage.

Crop circle at Lockeridge, Wiltshire, made and photographed by Robert Irving.

Various ufological writers have championed the ancient astronaut theme. In addition to Trench, mentioned above, there was – among numerous others – George Hunt Williamson (who accompanied contactee George Adamski on his desert encounter with a spaceship), W.R. Drake, T.C. Lethbridge and Desmond Leslie. Leslie co-wrote *Flying Saucers Have Landed* with Adamski in 1953, and was therefore particularly influential. In that book, he chases after all kinds of evidence for ancient astronauts. He delves into the ancient Vedic literature of India, and discusses the references to *vimanas* or 'air-boats', used by the elite and the military in that remote society, and the apparent references to fierce weaponry. Whether these are literal descriptions of flying craft, mythological imagery, or symbolic accounts of social class or mental states and apocalyptic visions, is not clear at this distance in time and culture, but Leslie opted for their being Atlantean technology. The flying saucer is 'only an interplanetary, more advanced, model of the ancient *vimana*', he suggested.

After his sorties into Sanskrit, Leslie sought similar evidence in the Celtic myths, analysing in 1950s' terms what he perceived as the super-weaponry of culture heroes such as Chuchulain of Ireland and Siegfried of Germany. It was obvious, Leslie maintained, that Chuchulain had use of heavy tanks and missiles, powered in some unknown way.

Influenced by the claims and interests of the turn-of-century Theosophists, Leslie toyed with that old occult chestnut of sound: how the great blocks of stone for ancient monuments might have been levitated and moved by sonic engineering. Even if true, it is unclear what this has to do with the thesis of ancient spacemen – other than the implication that such skills could only have come from some source other than the stream of humanity we know and are part of. He pondered on anti-gravity devices energized by personal, human vibration – a secret of the ages.

By the confused end of Leslie's ramblings it is unclear what he is suggesting, but the general thrust seems to be that space people – the 'Lords of Venus' or whatever – came to

A depiction of the prehistoric engraving on the rocks at Val Camonica, Italy. Von Daniken considers the headgear on the figure to represent antennae, but archaeologists would say the figure is wearing a deer-antler head-dress, mark of the shaman or religious functionary.

A depiction of a prehistoric rock carving in the Coso Range, California. Left by Numic Indians, the figure relates to the vision quest, accomplished with the aid of the hallucinogenic plant, Jimson Weed. The figure is not holding space-age weapons, but a 'medicine' bundle, and the designs on the body relate to 'entoptic patterns' seen under hallucinogenic trance. The Chumash Indians, also in California, produced similar imagery for similar reasons. They are not 'technical' or related to spaceman imagery, as von Daniken would have his audience believe.
David S. Whitley

Earth before the Flood and founded a hybrid race of terrestrials and extraterrestrials, forming what we now refer to as the civilization of Atlantis and raising terrestrial, animal-man to new intellectual and spiritual heights. What we discern in our own prehistory are the technological remnants of that remotely ancient, advanced civilization.

It is against this sort of background that the 1960s wave of ancient astronaut speculation needs to be viewed. Without doubt, the most famous (or infamous) writer of this persuasion is Erich von Daniken, whose 1968 *Chariots of the Gods?* was a worldwide bestseller. The Swiss ex-hotelier essentially took a random selection of unconnected archaeological mysteries to fuel his speculations; a few examples of this technique must suffice here.

Von Daniken suggests that the headgear worn by a figure carved in prehistory on the rocks of Val Camonica, Italy, is 'very much like some kind of aerial'. He wonders aloud if this means that it is the representation of a cosmonaut. In fact, the figure is obviously wearing deer antlers, the standard 'crown' of that universal tribal religious figure, the shaman. Similarly, von Daniken considers the radiating lines around the heads of other figures in prehistoric rock art as being possible antennae, whereas such depictions are known to symbolize cross-culturally the 'solarization' – that is, the enlightenment of high states of consciousness – of shamans and other tribal religious characters (Halifax, 1982 – see Bibliography). The halo in medieval European art is probably a descendant of this depiction. Von Daniken looks at rock paintings left in rock shelters by the Chumash Indians of California, and similar prehistoric rock art, and argues that rather than being depictions of gods, they look 'more technical than divine'. In fact, it is well known that such rock art was produced under the influence of the hallucinogenic Jimson Weed, and consists of figures containing abstract

Prehistoric rock painting of a masked figure with deer-antler headgear at Tassili, in the Sahara Desert. This ritual figure is holding – and his costume is bristling with – mushrooms, probably of the hallucinogenic psilocybe variety. But to von Daniken, they have to be antennae. *Drawing by Paul Devereux*

imagery known as 'entoptic patterns' – effects produced in the visual cortex during trance states. The ethnology, neurophysiology and archaeology of this is now becoming well researched (Lewis-Williams and Dowson, 1989; Whitley, 1994 – see Bibliography).

Von Daniken turns his attention to imagery on Australian Aboriginal ceremonial boards and paintings, considering their dots and coiled, linear circles to be stylized depictions of planetary systems, unaware of the anthropological reality that such markings actually represent genealogies and other tribal and individual information. To him, it seems, all Aboriginal rock art is peopled with images of the ancient cosmonauts. In the Algerian Sahara, he argues that forms sprouting from the outlines of a masked figure in the rock art of Tassili are 'antenna-like excrescences'. Yet they look much more like mushrooms than antennae, and it has been suggested that that

is exactly what they are. (The use of hallucinogenic mushrooms and other plants was widespread in antiquity – indeed, archaeologists are themselves only just coming to terms with what an important factor this was in ancient religious life.) Another Tassili figure was nicknamed 'the Martian' by archaeologists, and of course von Daniken took that literally.

In his bull-in-a-china-shop rampage through the artefacts

Another Tassili rock figure, nicknamed 'the Martian' by archaeologists.

of the ancient world, von Daniken sees Egyptian effigies of the human soul – *ka* – as models of aircraft, Native American ritual costumes as copies of spacesuits, ornate headgear in any culture as space helmets, a ceramic Aztec incense burner as 'a bad copy of a jet engine', and so forth. He completely eclipses the inner, spiritual, ritual and intellectual life of prehistoric humanity by his attempts to project his crude, twentieth-century mechanistic interpretations onto the material remains of the past.

Sometimes, in his quest for evidence of spacemen in the past, von Daniken does alight on truly intriguing objects, such as the 'Bagdhad Battery', a ceramic vase with copper inserts that can, indeed, work as a simple battery. There is no reason to suppose that such knowledge was not available at times in the past, and there is nothing about such objects to suggest other than the technological capabilities of the day.

Two of the worst of Daniken's misinterpretations, and yet probably among his better-known pieces of 'evidence', relate to a carved Mayan slab and the lines on the desert near Nazca, Peru. The slab is a tomb lid beneath a pyramid in the ancient Mayan city of Palenque, and on it is carved the image of a human figure surrounded by complex designs, all depicted in the characteristic flowing Mayan style. This assemblage of imagery looks to von Daniken like a helmeted spaceman piloting a rocket ship from a reclining seat, in the manner of our own astronauts. To archaeologists, it is the image of the Mayan shaman-king, Pakal, shown between the worlds of the living and dead, falling into the Otherworld atop the deified plate of sacrifice. His 'helmet' is a smoking axe, a standard Mayan symbol of great spiritual power. Moreover, the slab is meant to be viewed vertically, at 90 degrees to the way von Daniken always shows it.

A depiction of the cover of the Mayan king Pakal's sarcophagus at Palenque. This is the way round that von Daniken always shows it, to fit in with his 'astronaut' notion, but in fact it should be viewed with what is here the lefthand side as the top.

¤ LINES

The linear markings on the desert tablelands, the so-called 'pampas', of the Nazca area are truly mysterious. They are straight, ranging in width from narrow pathways to large, geometrically rectangular areas. They were made around 2000 years ago by the removal of the desert pavement, revealing the lighter subsoil. It hardly ever rains on the pampas, and the wind long ago removed anything that could blow away. Consequently, markings made on the desert pavement remain visible for centuries and even millennia – a fact clearly known to the makers of the Nazca lines. To von Daniken, the lines look like 'an immense airfield with radiating and converging landing strips'. He pushes his thought to the next step. 'Was it once a space centre for the "gods"?' he asks.

The answer is flatly and simply, 'no'. It is now known that the Nazca lines are only one example of dozens of straight track and road features laid down throughout the prehistoric Americas (Trombold, 1991 – see Bibliography): versions of straight lines like the Nazca examples occur from as far north as Ohio in the US, through the California sierras and the south-west, throughout Mexico and Central America, and down the Andean region of South America; there are even newly discovered examples in the Amazon basin. Everywhere, these features have been associated with tribes who practised shamanism (ecstatic, trance-centred divination and healing), usually using hallucinogenic plants (Dobkin de Rios, 1977; Schultes and Hofmann, 1979/1992; Schultes and Raffauf, 1992; Devereux, 1992 – see Bibliography). They represent a kind of spirit geography, a mapping of the out-of-body, soul flight experience of the entranced

One small section of the mystery lines on the Nazca pampa.
Tony Morrison/South American Pictures

shaman. Subsequently, in some societies they became roads of the dead, spirit ways and expressions of political power by priestly elites (Aveni *et al*, 1990; Trombold, 1991; Devereux, 1993 – see Bibliography).

So, the lines mark out a landscape of the ancient mind and soul, and have nothing to do with von Daniken's spaceships. Quite apart from the archaeology and ethnology now available to offer explanations of the lines (even though they remain strange to our ways of thinking), the physical facts could not support the Swiss fantasist's notions. The marks made on the 'runways' by any craft would still be perfectly visible. None are. The exhaust of rockets, jets or other propulsion units would have left their effects behind. They didn't.

But if not ancient spaceships, von Daniken's dubious notions have themselves left their mark. 'Certain entertaining space-phantasies, which have found wide acceptance, have attracted numerous visitors, who have left footprints and cart-tracks which threaten to obliterate the drawings completely,' Maria Reiche reported in 1976. She is the German scholar who has dedicated much of her life to studying and protecting the Nazca lines. Fantasies are not always harmless.

Von Daniken has chosen to overlook the inner, religious nature of human experience at the expense of crude notions of ancient spacecraft and spacemen, and those, moreover, in the image of the technology of our own times. Nevertheless, one could perhaps find some forgiveness for von Daniken if his naivety had been confined to the 1960s. Anyone can be over-enthusiastic and ill-informed (and, to be fair, understanding of some of the features he spotlighted has only been forthcoming in recent years). And if he struck lucky with a successful, financially rewarding book, then no one could really blame him.

Alas, such presumed innocence cannot be maintained indefinitely: as recently as September 1996, at the close of ufology's half-century, von Daniken appeared in a new, hour-long documentary programme on network American television, churning out his old stories. He either has not bothered to research what he is talking about, or chooses to ignore it – so another generation risks being seduced into false ideas about the marvels of the human past (that is why we have taken time out here to describe this problem in more depth than we might otherwise wish to do). And even before this, von Daniken had been regaling his huge German-speaking audiences for some years with the new round of his tales, and added erroneous, New Age ideas about 'ley lines' to his mix of misinformation. This brings us to another type of line that has become attached to ufology's flank.

The origins of ideas about 'leys' or 'ley lines' go back to the 1920s, when Englishman Alfred Watkins wrote about straight, cross-country alignments of ancient sites that he felt he could see and track in the landscape and trace on maps. He felt he was rediscovering the traces of traders' tracks laid down in prehistory by line-of-sight surveying methods, which accounted for their straightness. Watkins surmised that markers on these alignments – standing stones, sighting mounds and suchlike – had come to take on religious significance, and some had been Christianized, thus explaining why he often found old churches on his alignments. For several years, Watkins used the Anglo-Saxon word 'leys' (meaning cleared strips of ground) as a name for his alignments, but he eventually opted for the more straightforward terms 'old straight tracks' and 'archaic tracks'.

Watkins' books and lectures caught the public's interest, and a club was formed for 'ley hunters' called the 'Straight Track Club'. Watkins died in 1935, and the following year the occultist Dion Fortune wrote a novel, *The Goat-foot God*, in which she talked about alignments of sites in terms of

A typical ley in Saintbury, southern England, marked out on an air photo. The alignment runs through a medieval crossroads and cross, along the course of an old road, through an ancient church, and on through prehistoric mounds and ritual centres for nearly three miles. *Paul Devereux*

'lines of force'. In 1939, Arthur Lawton, a member of the still extant Straight Track Club, linked dowsing ('water witching') work in France and Germany with the idea of leys, and pronounced that ancient sites were laid out to a pattern of subtle but dowsable cosmic energy. After World War II, the club was disbanded and just a handful of individuals kept the ley idea alive. One of these was Egerton Sykes, who was a believer in Hans Hörbiger's theory of 'cosmic ice', which had become such an influential one within the Nazi elite in Germany and had eclipsed even notions of a hollow Earth there. (This theory maintained, among more bizarre ideas, that comets were made of ice. This has subsequently been found by modern space research to be true – dramatically so with the announcement by the Pentagon in December 1996 that cometary ice has been discovered at the Moon's south pole.)

The great revival of the subject came in 1961 through the person of Tony Wedd. Wedd was an ex-RAF pilot, a free-thinker, a critic of modern materialism, and a man with both technical and artistic leanings. He had read Watkins' main work on leys, *The Old Straight Track* (1925), and his own field investigations led him to think that

It was suggested that when viewed from the air, Stonehenge had the shape of a flying saucer. *Paul Devereux*

clumps of trees were also key ley markers. Wedd was also a flying saucer enthusiast, and became convinced that telepathic contact with what he called Space People was a real possibility. In 1960, a psychic called Mary Long was visiting Wedd's home in Kent and found herself drawn to a source of 'magnetic force' near the house. Visiting the spot, Wedd found a large, old sycamore tree. Claiming that she was receiving information from 'Attalita', a Space Being, the psychic said that the spot was a permanent magnetic node 'at the crossover of two important lines of force'. She, Wedd and others felt that 12 lines of force radiated out from the point, and tree clumps and other 'ley markers' were found to fall on those lines. Wedd checked local UFO reports, and found that some sightings were reported over certain of the tree clumps on his lines. 'I began to suppose from that date,' Wedd later wrote, 'that saucers' crews knew about leys.'

Wedd was impressed by two UFO books containing ideas that he pressed into service in supporting his vision of leys being lines of terrestrial force navigated by UFOs. One was Aimé Michel's *Flying Saucers and the Straight Line Mystery* (1958), in which it was claimed that during the French part of the 1954 wave or 'flap', UFOs sightings fell into straight lines or 'orthotenies' in any 24-hour period (see Chapter 4). The other book was *My Trip to*

Leys and orthotenies were the bricks of Tony Wedd's conceptual edifice, and the mortar was the 'magnetic current' of Buck Nelson and the 'force' of Wedd's sensitive, Mary Long, who may well have been influenced by her reading of Dion Fortune's 1936 novel *The Goat-foot God*, for Fortune was a famous occultist. Fortune herself may have got her idea of endowing leys with 'force' from the classic work on Celtic fairy lore *The Fairy Faith in Celtic Countries* by W.Y. Evans Wentz, which had originally been published in 1911. Wentz includes the following footnote in the book: 'An Irish mystic, and seer of great power... regards "fairy paths" or "fairy passes" as actual magnetic arteries, so to speak, through which circulates the earth's magnetism.'

Desmond Leslie had already introduced the idea of 'magnetic paths' into the flying saucer literature in 1953, ahead of Buck Nelson. 'Some of the vimanas travelled in great waves, approaching and receding from the earth,' wrote Leslie. 'This may or may not have been due to their following certain definite magnetic paths now known to surround and interpenetrate the planet. These magnetic forces were known to the Atlanteans....' Wedd must have read the Leslie-Adamski book (see Chapter 2), and perhaps unconsciously absorbed these observations, in addition to recognizing the claims made by Nelson (who in turn may also have picked up on Leslie's ideas).

It is all a corridor of mirrors. At the end of it, all that can be said is that to date modern science has not found an organized grid of magnetic pathways crisscrossing the planet – although of course telluric forces do exist in the Earth's crust.

Mars, the Moon and Venus (1956), written by American flying saucer contactee, Buck Nelson. The author claimed that the spaceships travelled along magnetic currents, each of which was named and numbered. 'The Space People tell me that the places where magnetic currents cross is comparable to a crossroads sign,' Nelson wrote. Wedd associated these claimed currents with Michel's orthotenies, which gave him licence to state that 'the spaceships do appear to travel along certain well-defined routes'. He also assumed that the famous 'falling leaf' motion in flying saucer flight behaviour, often remarked on in earlier reports, related to the craft changing directions at a 'crossroads' of magnetic currents. Wedd's argument was completed in these words:

> *Since flying saucers have been visiting the Earth throughout recorded history, such crossroads signs would have to be prehistoric. With the publication in 1925 of Watkins' book on* The Old Straight Track *people have in fact become aware that there are landmarks across the country, lying along quite straight alignments.*

Wedd clearly had an old-fashioned pilot's view of the matter: after traversing unknown distances from their interstellar or interdimensional origins, the Space People required out-of-the-porthole visual landmarks like tree clumps, stone circles and earthworks to follow the magnetic currents that powered their craft!

Wedd started a new Ley Hunter's Club in 1962, as well as creating the Star Fellowship, which promoted information about UFOs and the Space People.

Leys, or 'ley lines' as they began to be called, along with occultism and ufology, became part of the heady brew of the psychedelic decade. UFOs were a particularly hot topic, as the 1960s saw the greatest worldwide UFO wave ever recorded (see Chapter 4). In his *The Flying Saucer Vision* of 1967, John Michell, an erudite man who was something of a maverick scholar, provided a bridge from the old occultism of Theosophy, visions of Atlantis, ancient astronauts, and early flying saucer and contactee material, to the new interest in UFOs and the new breed of ley hunters. He saw in the tales of the UFO contactees certain archetypal themes, and did not necessarily take them as being literal accounts of physically real events. Nevertheless, he supported the idea of ancient gods being the human memory of space visitors, and felt that if we could understand the effect that extra-terrestrial visitation had on ancient cultures, we would be better prepared to face such an encounter in modern times. In a number of his writings of the period, he remarked that when viewed from the air, Stonehenge looks like a flying saucer. So he encouraged specific associations with ancient monuments.

In his 1969 work *The View Over Atlantis*, an exceedingly influential book within the New Age movement,

Michell strengthened ideas about leys being lines of force. It must be noted, however, that Michell can use prose in a semi-poetic way, and it has been the hallmark of much of his writing to be scrupulously unclear about what exactly he does mean, and he uses this ambiguity as a kind of smokescreen to allow him the freedom to conduct various intellectual adventures without becoming pinned down as representing any specific position. But Americans, in particular, take their use of the language far more literally, so some of Michell's subtleties passed them by. By the mid-1970s, 'ley lines' were firmly established in American (and international) New Age literature as lines of dowsable energy.

Even though a core of research-based 'ley hunters' have long since moved on from such notions, and employ scholarly study involving archaeology, ethnology and other disciplines to understand such features as the Native American straight lines, straight 'death roads' in Europe, and concepts of shamanic paths in Siberia, the false New Age representation of leys as energy lines remains their most dominant public image. It is this idea of leys that Erich von Daniken has picked up on.

Two popular books by the New Zealand writer Bruce Cathie – *Harmonic 33* (1968) and *Harmonic 695* (1971) – provided a fusion of many 'far side' beliefs. Cathie maintained that the Earth was covered by an energy grid which was the power source of flying saucers, and that this grid was known by ancient civilizations. (Subsequently, a plethora of 'planetary grids' has been proposed, and the association of leys with UFOs, dwellings, murders, depressions, ecology and a thousand other supposed factors has been claimed.)

¤ CIRCLES

Straight lines and grids became subordinate to circles in another topic that emerged into increasing public awareness in the 1980s and 1990s: the matter of the mysterious 'crop circles' that initially appeared in southern England. Were these markings left by UFOs? Certainly, the phenomenon had an effect on ufology. So much so, in fact, that by the late 1980s Jenny Randles, one of Britain's leading UFO researchers, was bemoaning the way in which some ufologists and journals were rushing onto the crop circle bandwagon, and, in 1990, the journal of the British UFO Research Association (BUFORA), the *UFO Times*, screamed on its cover, 'CIRCLE MANIA'. In the US, the assumed association between crop circles and UFOs was even stronger than

in Britain, where other 'explanations' such as the mystery markings being messages from the Earth Mother, Gaia, were entertained. And not only ufology, but 'ley lines' and dowsing were soon caught up in the whirl of excitement. Within the course of a bare decade, virtually all the themes seen weaving their way through the 50-year evolution of ufology have been re-run in the crop circle saga. Even that perennial maverick, John Michell, popped up as the founding editor of a journal devoted to the topic, *The Cerealogist*. For a while, it was like old times.

For the final section of this chapter, we have asked Montague Keen to overview the rise and rise of the crop circle story (an earlier version of this account appeared in *The Anomalist*). Keen is a journalist specializing in international farming affairs, and has been an editor of agricultural journals for nearly 25 years. More recently, he spent three years as scientific adviser to the Centre for Crop Circle Studies. He has therefore been intimately involved with the evolution of the crop circle phenomenon.

¤ AROUND AND AROUND WE GO

By all the precedents, it should have been a seven-year wonder, but the crop circle phenomenon has shown no sign of abating. More specifically, the repeated assertion that hoaxing can explain all, so please let's get on with something more serious, has done little to dent the enthusiasm or diminish the conviction of those for whom these represent wondrous symbols from outer space, pregnant with meaning for mankind (although just *what* meaning remains obscure).

But to begin at the beginning – as Alice said. (That is already a problem: there is no agreement about where or when the story does begin.) For the first few years of observation, crop circles were exclusively comprised of more-or-less circular areas of cereal crops neatly flattened to the ground, with edges sharply delineated and plants swirled around either clockwise or anti-clockwise with a precision which clearly eliminated natural crop-lodging by wind and rain as the cause. Or rather, the start was not so much their appearance in the cornfields of southern England as the *observation* of their appearance, since one school of investigators – the meteorological school led by physicist Dr Terence Meaden – were emphatic that these circular 'cut-outs' had always been around but had simply remained unremarked, or at least unrecorded. According to the Meadenites, the markings could only be due to a hitherto unrecognized natural phenomenon they called a 'plasma vortex'. Others argued that the appearance of a steadily growing number of these artefacts over an ever-widening area of Britain could not possibly have gone unreported for centuries, and if they did indeed represent a novel phenomenon, they could hardly be the product of previously unrecognized meteorological forces.

From as early as 1983, this conviction grew steadily stronger, as the formations began to abandon their simple, single circular shape and embark on a voyage of elaboration that has yet to end. First, there were quintuplets: a large central circle surrounded by four equidistant satellites linked by a thin line. There followed ringed circles, multiple rings, then scattered grapeshot circles arbitrarily strewn over the field as though a departing spacecraft had jettisoned its motley load.

The pioneer investigators tried to go about studying this mystery in a quiet and thorough way – but as an example of how not to undertake scientific investigation it stands without rival, although it is easy to be critical after the event. Virtually no proper tests were set up to establish what could and what could not have been attributed to man. Assumptions made about the behaviour of crushed plants at different growth stages were frequently wide of the mark, and seriously misleading. Dr Meaden's theory, elaborated in a series of books, was that the circles were formed by a static, vertically descending vortex of ionized air, created when certain climatic and topographical features were present. The reluctance of the meteorological establishment to back this theory could be attributed to the novelty of the stationary vortex concept, but the real weakness was the dearth of supporting evidence linking the formation of these phenomena with clearly defined factors of humidity, wind, temperature, elevation, distance from escarpments and the like. To supply this data would not have been an easy task, since the precise time, let alone the date, on which formations were created was invariably unknown. The only reliable date was that of the observation, and even in relatively crowded Britain that might not be until weeks after the event.

Vigorously promoted by Dr Meaden and his supporters, the vortex theory began to falter as formations became increasingly elaborate and, worse still, began to show signs of an intelligence. As they became more geometrical, as circles developed non-circular adornments or their components exhibited complex mathematical relationships, so the postulate of a spinning vortex hovering stationary when all meteorological precedent required it to move fast, became less and less tenable. The fact that, in the face of overwhelming evidence to the contrary, it persisted for so long illustrates a common peril

A crop circle formation produced in 1996, near Avebury, Wiltshire, southern England. *Frederick C. Taylor/Fortean Picture Library*

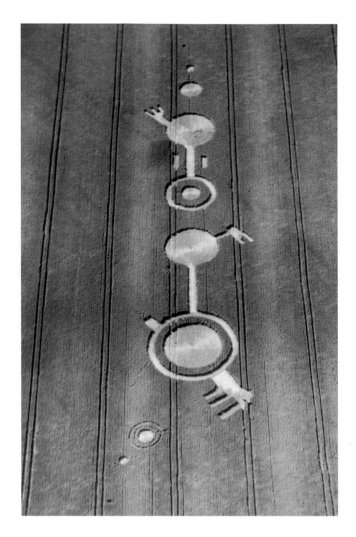

A pictogram-type crop circle formation, Alton Barnes, Wiltshire, 1990.
Frederick C. Taylor/Fortean Picture Library

in scientific inquiry to which American researchers were later to succumb: the retention and defence of a hypothesis well past its jettison date.

It is easy to express astonishment at the ease with which the pioneer investigators appeared to disregard William of Occam's advice to beware of the introduction of novel hypotheses when well-established and simpler explanations were at hand. Surely it was obvious that they were all hoaxes? It was not. Why should hoaxers want to make formations in fields so distant from public view that many were never even noticed until ready to be chewed up into the combine harvester? Who would want to venture out at dead of night, often in wet weather and at the risk of discovery, armed with heaven knows what tools? By the late 1980s there were hundreds of crop markings reported every year, and in a dozen countries

as well as Britain: and yet no one had been discovered in the act. What's more, it would surely be impossible to make formations of such precision in the dark. And what sort of hoax was it when no one ever came forward to mock the true believers?

Had the believers relied solely on this collection of presumptions, all of which were to be undermined decisively within the following two or three years, they would certainly have merited the derision which many of them were later to earn. But there were more substantial reasons, and most of them remain puzzles for which none of the hoaxers or their protagonists have satisfactorily accounted. These are discussed later.

By the high summer of 1991, this was how things stood: the circles had grown into pictograms, complete with oblongs, squares, tails, volutes, dumb-bells, link lines and multiple swirls. Several books, all lavishly illustrated, had been published, most of them concentrating on formations seen and recorded in Britain, but by then reports had come in from a score of countries, although not on anything like the same scale in number or complexity. Worldwide interest had been engendered. The British royal family was reputed to be so interested that they invited the veteran scientist Lord Zuckerman to make his own private assessment. This he did, sharing his qualified doubts of authenticity with readers of the *New York Review of Books*.

At least three bodies claiming to undertake research had been set up. These included Meaden's outfit, dedicated to a severely prosaic explanation aimed at conforming, no matter how uncomfortably squeezed, within the confines of orthodox physics; a more evangelical organization called Circles Phenomenon Research and run by Colin Andrews, an electrical engineer, who now commutes between Britain and the US mesmerizing audiences with his apocalyptic visions and aerial photographs; and the more recently formed Centre for Crop Circle Studies (CCCS), still struggling on, but dedicated to a more scientific examination of the evidence. Dozens of magazines and local newsletters furnished abundant evidence of acute public interest and bewilderment.

Evidence of authenticity more substantial than mere conjecture was beginning to emerge, much of it from the US. It was in two parts. The more complex came from the biophysics laboratory of an elderly scientist in Michigan, Dr W.C. Levengood. His analysis of plant samples sent from England in 1990 and 1991 was leading him to conclude that detectable, albeit minute, changes in the structure and appearance of parts of the sampled plants could have been attributable only to the rapid infu-

Dave Chorley (left) and Doug Bower, the original crop circle hoaxers, in Dave's Southampton studio. *Rob Irving*

sion of energy of a type inconsistent with the activity of hoaxers. More strikingly, another establishment in the US had used gamma spectroscopy to examine samples for radioactivity, and the results appeared to indicate that minute, barely detectable, emissions from no fewer than 13 different short-lived radioactive isotopes were discernible, all with half-lives significantly shorter than any occurring naturally in background radiation or derived from atomic fallout. It later transpired that the procedure was faulty and the conclusions incorrect, but at the time the results were rightly considered sufficiently startling to warrant full-scale testing during the following season, when a small international team collected dozens of samples for examination.

There was accumulating anecdotal evidence that something abnormal was occurring: strange luminosities in the sky, constant reports of defective electrical equipment in crop circles, the inexplicable gyrations of compasses, odd photographic anomalies, disturbing animal behaviour, unpleasant physical, and less frequently euphoric, effects experienced by visitors, and the absence of footprints or damage signs in the densely cropped approaches to forma-

tions distant from the tramlines left by the repeated passage of spray-delivering tractors.

Taken together, all this was sufficient to overwhelm the protestations of two elderly hoaxers, universally known as 'Doug and Dave'. Their claims to have originated and perpetrated the entire phenomenon were lavished over the front pages of the tabloid press early in September 1991. The two men gave a lacklustre performance of their technique before the world's press, and produced some evidence to support their claims. They appeared surprised and hurt to find that, instead of admiration for pulling off the hoax of the century, they were accused of being government disinformation stooges and pretentious liars. While the rest of the world breathed a sigh of disappointment and turned over to the other side, the crop circle devotees, having muffed their chances of ever conducting an objective assessment of these claims, made ever more determined efforts to discover a litmus test which, once and for all, would distinguish between a

The tools used by one of the contestants in the 1992 crop circle-making competition. Rob Irving

man-made and a genuine formation.

One consequence was a crop circle-making competition held in July the following year. Prodded by Lord Zuckerman's proposal that the competence of hoaxers should be tested, a committee under the impartial aegis of Dr Rupert Sheldrake, plant physiologist and world-notorious popularizer of the morphic resonance theory, was formed to devise a test. The aim was to incorporate in a specially designed pictogram as many of the features the experts considered difficult if not impossible to counterfeit as could reasonably be undertaken at night by competitive teams operating in realistic conditions. It was promptly denounced by half the circle enthusiasts as little more than an invitation to potential hoaxers to hone their skills and practise yet more illicit invasions of farmers' property. Its defenders argued that it was the sort of basic scientific work which ought to have been done years ago, and was aimed solely at testing the validity of some of the circle investigators' assumptions. In the event, both sides proved correct. It undoubtedly gave a fillip to what was rapidly becoming a nocturnal art form, and it did show how skilfully several of the competing teams, many claiming to have had no previous experience, could produce impressive, even persuasive, pictograms.

Having been chiefly responsible for devising the prize pictogram and setting the rules, Montague Keen was unable to witness the outcome for himself, since he was in Albuquerque for a UFO convention where, to his surprise, he found interest in crop circles even more ardent than in Britain. But whereas in North America the phenomenon was assumed to be closely associated with UFO activity, this was rarely the case in Britain, where there was much debate about the phenomenon's curious preference for a relatively small area of mid-southern England. Was it the abundance of prehistoric ceremonial sites there, or simply a superfluity of hoaxers? Perhaps it was simply a by-product of malobservation (who, after all, is going to notice a crop circle in the endless, treeless vista of a Kansas landscape?).

The 1992 season marked the high-water mark of scientific investigation. Funded substantially by the Robert Bigelow Foundation of Las Vegas, investigators crawled over dozens of the 1992 formations, taking crop and soil samples. The main object was to check the previous year's evidence of bombardment by unnatural isotopes – no supporting evidence was found. Additionally, a mass of samples was sent to Levengood's laboratory. The results percolated through in the following months. The season produced a veritable cornucopia of formations, many of them bearing symbolic glyphs of alchemical and mythological significance, the implications of which were gravely dissected in various learned contributions to such magazines as *The Cerealogist* and *The Circular*, while the qualified supporters of the Meadenites sniped from the wings through the medium of their own journal, the *Crop Watcher*, and outright skeptics used their *Skeptic* magazine to alternate between excoriation and ridicule of the whole shebang.

Just before the last field of wheat was ready to harvest, and hard by the mysterious prehistoric mound known as Silbury Hill, there appeared the most spectacular formation of the season: a large ring with a central bow-tie feature, the circumference embellished with seven different symbols, most of which had featured in that season's crop of designs. It was dubbed the 'Dharmic Wheel' or the 'Shamanic Mandala'. This was hailed as a masterpiece. What was particularly significant was the manner in which the main ring had all but struck a water trough, the profound symbolism of which was exposed in more than one interpretative article by those who know about these things. Likewise, one of the symbols was a bull's heart, which every knowledgeable student of the Eight Paths Between the Worlds will recognize as a symbol of male fertility. Similarly, the crescent Moon adornment is obviously linked to the sacrifice of two freemartin bulls on the sixth day of the new Moon in November...

When Jim Schnabel's book *Round in Circles* appeared the following spring, casually claiming authorship of this supreme example of intelligent communication from beyond, there was fury. Schnabel, a young American PhD student, had interrupted his research at Oxford to study and then involve himself actively in the crop circle business. He had all but won the circle-making competition, and was the only sole operator to compete. His book was regarded as scurrilous, if highly amusing. Not everyone was prepared to believe that he was responsible. Some samples from the formation were sent to Levengood: they appeared to pass his test of genuineness.

¤ RE-INVENTING THE WHEEL

Schnabel was invited to demonstrate his expertise on Montague Keen's farm in East Anglia before an audience. He did so on 3 July 1993, toiling away for more than five hours on the hottest day of the year armed with metal rods, cord and a plastic roller. He made a jokey version of the 'Dharmic Wheel'. The water trough, he explained, had surprised him. In the darkness he hadn't noticed it, and it slightly messed up his design. The bull's heart? Well, that was to have been a Mandelbrot set (in honour of the much marvelled at and beautifully fashioned pictogram, based on iterated chaos, which had appeared the previous year and was spotted, suspiciously enough, near Cambridge, England). But by that time he was getting tired, and had accidentally produced a bull's heart. Viewers of the jokey version the following year were equally divided between those satisfied that he must have perpetrated the original, and those who considered him an industrious fraud. Indifferent to skepticism, Schnabel offered a conclusive piece of evidence. He had posted a letter to himself some days before making the 'Dharmic Wheel', he said, and inside had included a rough sketch of his intentions. On the front was the stamped date, two or three days before the formation had been made. For further proof, he had sketched a miniature of the design on the envelope and put his postage stamp over it, so that the datemark would be embossed over it.

Television cameras were present as the crucial envelope was opened, but it was pointed out that this was far from definitive proof, since experiments showed it possible for a stamp to be lightly affixed down one end, receive the date evidence from the post office, and to have the post-hoc design inscribed underneath before sealing the stamp down completely! The opening ceremony was accordingly abandoned; the letter remains as a testimony to the hazards of attempting to devise a surefire proof. Schnabel retired to his native land, marvelling at the resolute manner in which believers maintain their beliefs whatever the evidence.

Interest in this formation had been greatly heightened by a more absurd drama some months earlier – the Schnabel tape hoax. It arose from the widespread belief, fomented by a controversy arising from the Doug and Dave claims, that a government conspiracy was at work to rubbish the phenomenon in order to allay public anxiety. It was clearly linked with the US government's efforts to keep the UFO information under wraps and continue its dissembling over the Roswell crash (see Chapter 9). More sinister still, the CIA was in it, too, linking hands with Opus Dei, the mysterious arm of the Roman Catholic Church: all of them determined to pour sufficient scorn on the whole UFO-linked phenomenon to stem the gadarene rush over the cliffs of occult paganism.

A finger had been pointed at Schnabel. A dubious character named Henry Azadehdel, or Armen Victorian, was encouraged to trap Schnabel into admitting that he was part of an international conspiracy. Tapes of various recorded telephone conversations appeared to show how, cautiously and reluctantly, Schnabel was coaxed into an astounding admission, while Victorian, eager to join the conspiracy and posing as a Nigerian with a Hungarian accent, proffered his services as a spy, and was eventually given details of how to apply. Only when the tapes had been given wide circulation, and credence, did it became known that Schnabel had been alerted to Victorian's game by a fellow circle-faker, Robert Irving, and that the whole operation was a backfiring confidence trick.

But to return to the events of 1993. While Schnabel was licking his wounds and drawing his royalties, the season saw a further attempt by the CCCS to find the elusive litmus test. As the organization's research panel convenor – a title which concealed the fact that there really was no panel to convene – Montague Keen had concluded that further tests on samples of crops were unlikely to prove fruitful. He was beginning to harbour doubts about the reliability of Levengood's procedures and conclusions (for reasons given in some detail in the lengthy report published that spring on the outcome of the previous season's research activities). As a result, it was concluded that a series of acoustic, electromagnetic and other electrical sensory devices should be installed at a key point in order to catch a formation in progress and obtain some permanent record of the energies involved in the process. Elaborate monitoring equipment was specially designed and centred on Alton Barnes in Wiltshire, at a large arable farm where some 20 formations had appeared the previous season and which appeared to be the regular epicentre of crop circles.

Alas, what was recorded was ambiguous. Perhaps the hoaxers had got wind of the monitoring and had steered clear? Others believed the mystic circle-makers had no intention of having their mechanisms exposed and origins revealed by mere science. There were formations a-plenty, but not where they were needed. Some odd blips on the computer record were tenuously linked to the formation of a somewhat sinister creation of a treble-six design, the Number of the Beast, relatively nearby, which was either attributed to identified pranksters or regarded as a biblical symbol of diabolical interference. Evidence that something electromagnetic was involved, and might leave a residue, was abundant if human testimony was to be credited; but instrumentation failed to bolster it.

While this monitoring was in progress, further blows to the credibility of the phenomenon were beginning to accumulate. Doug Bower, the leading original hoaxer, resurfaced. In two crowded public meetings he demonstrated just how he and Dave Chorley had done it, and they supported their claims with a wealth of photographs and diagrams, many of previously unrecorded events. Doug's demonstrations of how apparently impossible effects were produced quite simply, were impressive, at least to those not in the irretrievable clutches of true belief.

Worse was to come. Another renegade, no less than a documentary film producer who had long been regarded as among the faithful, was surreptitiously photographing the elderly pair engaged in their impish nocturnal deeds. One of these was claimed to be the fabrication of a particularly impressive pictogram which Montague Keen was among the first to examine, and which was subsequently found to have been made with the connivance of the farmer. The film was shown to a crowded audience in London in December 1993. Most found it convincing. Others accepted that it was good evidence that hoaxing was rife, but not that the entire phenomenon was phoney.

Every year since 1991, the last formation of the season had turned out to be the most spectacular and controversial, and 1993 was no exception. Long after most of the winter wheat had vanished from the fields of southern England, there appeared in a late-sown wheat crop in a field overlooking a major road in Northamptonshire, 100 miles (160km) from the main circle region, what was agreed by general consent to be the most elegant and intricate pattern of all. This was the 'Bythorn Wonder'. It had geometric shapes which embodied the Golden Ratio and comprised a series of rings, between the outer two of which were petal-shaped features. A Star of David, in the form of inverted triangles, was neatly embodied in the design. It bore the hallmarks of a circle-obsessed

youngster whose compulsive urge to practise what was now a recognized agrarian art form could neither be suppressed nor written off as a hoax, since he made private confessions to a few crop circle cognoscenti. (Public admission ran the risk of inviting prosecution for criminal trespass: hence the reluctance of claimants to be specific about their misdeeds.)

Once again the crop circle world was divided, and a bitter row ensued. The following winter, Keen conducted an inquiry at which the young claimant, having obtained assurances against prosecution, explained how he had made the circular parts on one night, then decided to elaborate the next night by adding the double triangle. There was strong evidence against him, including local witnesses who claimed that the complete pictogram was visible after the first night. The clinching evidence came in a close examination of blown-up photographs said to have been taken at the halfway stage. If there was a detectable difference, the claimant would have made his case. There was. This made no difference to many of the true believers. In the last resort they could argue – and did, with indefensible logic – that hoaxers might well be acting as unwitting instruments of the 'intelligence' ultimately responsible. Investigators were urged to stop wasting time and money on trying to detect and argue about hoaxers and hoaxing, as it diverted attention from contemplating and seeking to fathom the true message.

Absurd though this may sound, it must be judged against the fact that nearly all the so-called hoaxers, Doug and Dave apart, seem to believe there is a genuine phenomenon. Some are inclined to share the 'lost paradise' view of Dr Meaden: that only the simple, pure original circles are genuine and the rest reflect man's corruption.

¤ CIRCULAR SCIENCE

But we have lost track of Dr Levengood and the mounting volume of his reports on samples from North America and England. They had served to sustain the belief, growing into a conviction as the reports mounted in number and apparent conclusiveness, that an objective way had been found to distinguish man-made from genuine formations. There were problems, however. It is the fate of the pioneer, slogging away in his remote laboratory, to meet indifference from the outside world. Levengood tried to inject some science into this morass of unsupported assertion and unsustainable belief systems. He made false starts, changed his approaches, tested new assumptions, and came up with closely argued evidence that measurable, statistically significant alterations in microscopic tissue were present in the genuine and not in the man-made samples of crops from formations.

Yet it is also the fate of many a scientist whose preliminary evidence appears encouraging, to promote tentative hypothesis to plausible theory, and thence elevate it a short distance to persuasive proof, a process aided by unconscious selection of supportive evidence or favourable interpretation of subjective evaluations. It is unkindly dubbed 'pathological science', and it is the commonest disease around. That Dr Levengood, as honest and industrious a man as ever dedicated himself to an unrewarding task, may have fallen victim to this malaise demands evidence which would take us beyond the legitimate boundaries of this review, but there are pointers, and they point to the heart of the controversy.

If Levengood is correct in having authenticated a considerable number of complex formations from which samples were taken in England, notably in 1992, and which were later claimed as hoaxes, although with insufficient evidence, then he would have to accept that intelligently directed energies of unknown origin, location and mechanism are responsible. That is what the faithful believe, but most certainly not what Dr Levengood does, since he has long declared his conviction that his discoveries can be reconciled within known physical laws, and he has postulated the phenomenon of deterministic chaos to account for it. But there is no evidence that chaos in whatever shape, either in the laboratory or in nature, can produce or has produced geometric patterns which vary from location to location, have lots of alchemical and mythological symbols linked to them, possess a striking symmetrical beauty, change from year to year, and follow no known or predictable rules of climate or topography. These reservations, and the rejection of Occam's cautionary razor, inevitably make one look with added caution on Levengood's methodology. His claim looks inconsistent with physical laws. More than that: it presupposes the existence of an unknown, directing intelligence operating an equally unknown energy with remarkable but erratic behaviour patterns. Such disturbing implications impose on the experimenters a duty to meet standards of proof, and adhere to protocols, of draconian severity, well beyond those normally required where no rules are broken or novel postulates advanced.

Levengood's findings were explained in an impressive contribution to a peer-reviewed journal. His paper on 'Anatomical Anomalies on Crop Formation Plants' appeared in *Physiologia Plantarum* 92: 356–363 in 1994. It was the first time that a serious contribution on the subject had ever made it into a refereed journal and it was regarded as a breakthrough, certainly by those who neither read it nor perceived its weaknesses. This journal, the exclusive domain of plant physiologists, makes no provision for correspondence or contradiction, otherwise it might have been able to inform its readers of Keen's failure to find a single piece of supporting evidence in the several footnoted citations.

¤ THE HOLE STORY

One of the key features of Levengood's evidence turns on measurements in the diameters of minute pit holes in cell walls. The results appear to support the claim that they are significantly larger, than those from controls. There had been questions raised by others about the precise manner in which Levengood obtained a random sample of pits for his analyses, questions which Levengood brushed aside. But more serious was the fact that the statistical evidence was based on measurements of diameters of pits averaging only $2\mu m$. Their validity depended on whether it was possible to calculate diameters to a precision of $\pm 0.3\mu m$ or less, using an ocular micrometer of 450x magnification. (A 450x magnification is equivalent to measuring differences in tick marks over a distance of 0.9mm with the naked eye.) Sensory limitations preclude this. The wavelength of light is about $0.5\mu m$, so it is doubtful whether optical magnification could satisfactorily differentiate diameters to the level of accuracy required for the sort of statistical calculations made by Levengood. There is a strong subjective element here, which must cast serious doubt on the reliability of the measurements made and conclusions drawn.

This was by no means the only technical reservation made about Levengood's work. There were, and remain, inherent difficulties in obtaining reliable controls against which suspected changes can be judged. In order to use artificially flattened plants as controls against which differences in sampled crops are measured, it is necessary not only to have a standard artificial flattening procedure, using the same implements at the same velocities and weights to flatten the crop, but to perform this operation at the same time as the sampled formation is made — otherwise the crop may be at a different growth stage and exhibit all manner of chemical and physiological differences. But this is impossible: nobody knows where or when crop formations occur, only when they are noticed. Such an objection may appear pedantic, but this is an area where we can afford to allow no rough edges.

While this dispute was brewing on the scientific side, there was mounting evidence that hoaxing, as an alternative explanation, was a misnomer. Whatever mischievous motives may have prompted Doug and Dave, and those who copied and improved on their techniques, by the summer of 1993 and beyond many so-called hoaxers had been identified or had confessed and most had mixed motives, rarely of a purely mischievous character. Some wanted to respond to the mystical intelligence in its own graphic language; others were simply unable to resist the thrill and challenge of a nocturnal adventure; still others entered into an informal competitive league to make the most impressively artistic creations. The steady elaboration of designs, and the skill and precision with which many had been created, were either hailed as further demonstration of the human night landscape artists' prowess, or proclaimed to signify the increasing desperation of the communicating intelligence to convey its message, whether of hope or impending disaster, ecological or spiritual, to dim-witted humankind. Those who sought the best of both incompatible worlds found comfort in the view that the hoaxers were the unconscious tools of the 'real' circle-makers. Thus the interminable argument about genuineness or fraudulence was irrelevant – they were all genuine.

In the late summer of 1993, an American circle sleuth, Peter Sorensen, took samples from a couple of neighbouring formations which he and an English colleague, Busty Taylor, had spotted in Wiltshire. By that time the wheat crop had already been harvested and the straw baled and removed, but some of the crushed samples were to prove of singular interest and ensure that the fires of controversy were not to die down. On some parts of the formations there was a brown smear, apparent also on some chalk clods: but these were seen only inside parts of the two formations, not outside. Samples were sent to Levengood. Some months later Levengood and a physicist colleague, John Burke, circulated a draft report. It was sensational. Even Levengood and Burke described the results as an important breakthrough. After months of work, the brown smear had been identified: it was magnetically susceptible. Spectroscopic analysis revealed it to be coated with a glaze composed only of iron and oxygen. Had it come from the soil, there would have been traces of silicon and calcium, at the very least. Tests proved there to be dramatic differences between formation samples and controls on the basis of two measuring criteria: the rate of growth of seeds and the electrical conductivity of the bract tissue surrounding the seed heads. It was not, therefore, a hoaxed formation. The authors concluded that minute particles of iron contained in the late-summer Perseid meteor shower had been drawn down from stratospheric heights by a plasma vortex. On entering the Earth's atmosphere, the heat had generated microwaves of sufficient intensity to moltenize the iron particles, some of which were found to be embedded in the stalks running from the base upwards.

As rumours of this revolutionary discovery filtered through the following spring, a leading circle-maker and *bête noire* of the circle investigators, one Robert Irving claimed that all Levengood and Burke had actually found was the residue of finely ground iron filings taken from a standard chemistry laboratory bottle which had been posted to him (labels preserved with evidence of delivery date) by Schnabel some weeks earlier from the chemistry department of one of the Oxford University colleges, and some of the contents of which had been arbitrarily sprinkled over parts of two formations which he and others had made before being rained off. By the time the rains had ceased, the crop had been harvested and the land compressed by combine harvesters, reception wagons and baling machines. The squashed remnants were well and truly impacted into the stubbles from which Sorensen had garnered his samples. Sorensen later let Irving have some.

Irving then issued a challenge to Levengood and Burke. He undertook to provide control samples of chalk and wheat from the original site, together with samples of the contaminated crop from the samples left with him by Sorenson, accompanied by some of the original batch of ordinary iron filings: let them be submitted to independent examination, along with Levengood's lot. Alternatively, just dampen a piece of chalk or wheat, sprinkle iron filings on it, wet it again, leave outside to mellow, and then see whether any difference can be detected compared with Levengood's samples.

But answer came there none. The dispute bubbled over into the columns of the prestigious *Journal of Scientific Exploration*, to which Levengood and Burke contributed a learned paper heavily adorned with supporting references of layman-wilting complexity. A series of doubts Keen had the temerity to express were crushed from a huge height by a defence which made it clear that Levengood and Burke had done their scientific stuff, and that ill-informed sharpshooters would be better employed on matters of which they had a glimmering of understanding.

Nevertheless, there are other odd things about the whole of the so-called 'H-Glaze report'. Despite Levengood's apparent belief that similar evidence would be found in subsequent years at around the same date, none was reported in 1994 or either of the following two seasons. The Perseid shower hypothesis appears not to have received any support from those who study the antics of passing comet trails or the eccentric behaviour of plasma vortices. One could look in vain for signs that any form of deterministic chaos could fashion itself into the elaborate idiosyncratic and unique assemblages of patterns which were now regularly decorating odd patches of the English countryside, and occasionally beyond. But without such independent evidence the explanation advanced by the two scientists would appear extremely shaky. There being no other feasible alternative explanation, it followed that the ostensible proof must fall under heavy suspicion. By the end of 1996, Irving was still awaiting his open invitation to demonstrate how to produce the very phenomenon which Levengood and Burke had subjected to electron microscopic analysis and pronounced genuine.

By the same date, the original proponents of a naturalistic explanation, led by Terence Meaden, had entered a Trappist retreat. Belatedly accepting that a plasma vortex was not consistent with anything more than a circle or two, all the pictograms were ruthlessly cast into the void whence rejected data may ne'er return. What emerged, purified and fresh, was the original theory of a straightforward plasma vortex creating uncomplicated and non-geometrical, circular patterns, but still providing us with no way of distinguishing its product from the revellers' handiwork, and hence valueless as raw material for a database, itself the raw material for all feasible theories.

✄ CROP CIRCLE SMEAR

Faced with ever more complex, beautiful and hence puzzling formations, the CCCS searched with growing desperation for someone to guide them to the pinnacle of Mount Litmus Test. He duly appeared, bearing a testable hypothesis. This was Jim Lyons, an engineer with a special interest in nature's subtle energies. Lyons believed that the process of circle formation was essentially geophysical, and therefore closely related to natural processes occurring in the Earth's biosphere. He hypothesized that strong vertical electrostatic fields might interact with low-impedence points on the Earth – the crossover of energy lines on the Earth's 'energy grid'. Such fields would be expected to have a strong influence on atmospheric nitrogen and oxygen. Normally, these remain separate, but under ambient transient electrical fields they could combine to form nitrogenous gases. It is known that lightning strikes form oxides of nitrogen in the soil, so the theory had some semblance of scientific respectability. Since the results would be clearly present in the vicinity of the crop and the soil, Lyons argued, they should leave tell-tale effects capable of subsequent analysis, in particular soil tests for nitrates.

Accordingly, with the help of sympathetic members of the Agricultural Development and Advisory Service (ADAS), tests were carried out in 1995 on a fairly wide range of formations. The aim was to measure nitrate-N levels inside and outside formations. The results were published the following year. Alas, the variations recorded in soil nitrate levels were mostly within the variability that might be expected within a field, and although there were interesting anomalies there was no consistent trend. The results overall were negative. To dampen ardour further, one of Britain's leading soil scientists has pointed out that even positive results, in the form of consistently and significantly higher nitrate levels inside formations, might simply be due to the inability of crushed crops to absorb nitrogen, which is then left to augment the soil readings.

So, what are we left with? Many, but still essentially anecdotal, reports of strange luminosities, and odd electrical and magnetic anomalies; disturbing accounts of strangely knitted barley tops over a wide area of a Sussex formation; photographs showing inexplicable shadows and blotches where none ought to be...

Could we all have been witnessing a variant of the infamous Philip experiment? Some 23 years ago, members of the Toronto Society for Psychical Research formed a group which sat regularly in a seance room where they deliberately created a totally imaginary character called Philip. The aim was to see whether, and how far, Philip could reproduce the communication skills and physical accomplishments of an apparent spirit contact, and to create an objective thought form. It succeeded alarmingly. Philip had been given a fictitious historic identity, complete with wife, home, mistress and seventeenth-century English Civil War role. He answered questions by the traditional table-tapping method. Gradually, Philip assumed a personality of his own, normally giving answers which were in accord with the group's expectations, although on one startling occasion insisting – correctly, as it later transpired – that Prince Rupert was not Elizabeth of Bohemia's brother-in-law, as a participating professor had believed. Apart from strange raps, bangs and scratches, the seance-room table was swirled around and half-lifted – all in broad daylight and under the suspicious gaze of observers.

Could the circle phenomenon also be a physical projection of a universal subconscious, generated by the sort of energy which produces poltergeist eruptions in the presence of psychologically stressed persons? Is this an artefact of the mind, projecting images through inexplicable psychic energies? Or can a combination of malobservation, exaggeration, spoof and mankind's instinctive lust for the mysterious account for all the anomalies?

6

The UFO Prophets

FLYING SAUCERS FROM HEAVEN AND HELL

N O ONE, LEAST of all ufologists, can really be certain what a UFO is. So various are the reported phenomena and so multifarious the claims as to the behaviour of UFOs, that the best an objective observer can say is that unexplained UFO reports are probably generated by a variety of phenomena. Some may be the product of rare natural events; some may be hallucinations (of which in turn there are many kinds); some may indeed be extraterrestrial craft – although we think the likelihood of that is extremely slim. Even if they are ETs, the aliens with whom people have claimed to converse have made a boggling series of claims about their origins. They have maintained that they come from nearby planets – Venus being a favourite – and from distant galaxies and star clusters (such as Draco or the Pleiades), and from places known on no map of the sky – Zircon, Clarion, Meton, Martarus, even 'the galaxy of Guentatori-Elfi'. Even the most convinced believer in the ETH ought to wonder whether the aliens are all lying, or if Earth unwittingly has some rare quality that only intergalactic travellers can appreciate.

Aliens, as reported by those who have seen them, are also extraordinarily disparate in their appearance. Even in 1996, despite increasing claims that the aliens are 'all' small gray creatures with large heads, huge eyes and no sex organs (the 'grays'), there were reports from Varginha, Minas Gerais, Brazil, that spoke of a creature that 'looks like a man but it's not. It has gray/brown skin, big red eyes, big feet and three little horns on its head'. Sisters Liliane de Fatima Silva (16) and Valquiria Aparecida Silva (14), and a friend, Katia de Andrade Xavier (22), were surprised by this alleged 'extraterrestrial' when they were walking home on 20 January 1996.

In South America alone, one study of 65 cases from 1947 to 1965 featured entities described as giants, 'normal'-sized, under 3ft (1m) tall, 'hairy bellicose dwarves', hairy giants, greenish creatures, small men with long hair and tall bald men, tall men with one eye – and creatures 32in (80cm) high with one eye. There were also three-eyed creatures and one with 'various extra eyes up and down the body'. There are encounter cases from elsewhere of creaking, talking or flying robots, silver-tongued 'angelic' beings, headless horrors with wings and reptilian monsters. Some wear

A 'Pleiadean' spacecraft over Switzerland, photographed by Eduard 'Billy' Meier in the late 1970s. It has been suggested Meier achieved his effects by suspending models from helium balloons with fishing line.
Fortean Picture Library

clothes (often described as 'suits', usually tight-fitting, but with little else in common) and helmets of diverse configurations, and carry what seems to be breathing apparatus. Some do not.

Nearly all ufologists agree that UFOs come from the sky, from some Great Elsewhere. Some say they come from 'other dimensions' – although it is not always clear whether these are to be understood as the physical or mathematical dimensions of 'hyperspace' or as the otherworldly 'etheric' or 'astral' dimensions inhabited by elementals, ghosts, spirits, sprites and goblins. The UFOs themselves may be round, crescent-shaped, tubular, triangular or even amorphous, capable of changing shape at will but for no discernible reason. Once again we are faced with both vagueness and variety.

Not surprisingly, it has proven possible to project almost any belief onto this inherently nebulous mass of information. The psychologist Carl Jung was not surprised at this: 'Should something extraordinary occur in the outside world, be it a human personality, a thing, or an idea, the unconscious content [of the mind] can fasten itself upon it, thereby investing the projection carrier with numinous and mythical powers,' he wrote in *Flying Saucers: A Modern Myth of Things Seen in the Sky* (1959).

The 'projection carrier' that Jung had in mind was the UFO phenomenon, which, he went on, 'has a highly suggestive effect and grows into a saviour myth whose basic features have been repeated many times.' Jung saw the circular shape of the UFO as an archetypal symbol of healing wholeness 'to compensate the split-mindedness

of our age', while the 'present world situation' – by which he meant the threats of nuclear annihilation and the rivalry between American and Soviet forms of imperialism – 'is calculated as never before to arouse expectations of a redeeming, supernatural event.' The prospect of a metaphysical or miraculous, overtly divine intervention was unacceptable to a scientistic, post-Christian, ostensibly rational age, so:

> *It is characteristic of our time that, in contrast to its previous expressions, the archetype should now take the form of an object, a technological construction, in order to avoid the odiousness of a mythological personification. Anything that looks technological goes down without difficulty with modern man. ...Consequently the UFOs can easily be regarded and believed in as a physicist's miracle.*

Carl G. Jung, probably the most distinguished thinker to have pondered the meaning of the UFO phenomenon at length. Jung recognized that all ufology had a religious theme at its heart. *Fortean Picture Library*

Nevertheless, only seven years after the first 'flying saucers' flitted across the Cascade Mountains, and five years before Jung published his book on UFOs, the first UFO messiah had had his first call from on high.

UFO photographed by Paul Villa near Albuquerque, New Mexico, in June 1963. Analysis has shown the picture was faked, but Villa maintained UFOs were 'a small part of God's huge armies that will soon invade planet Earth and redeem humanity from their present immoral fallen condition, while aliens living among us are helping to prepare for the great day when we shall meet our maker'. *Fortean Picture Library*

¤ JESUS ON VENUS

In March 1954, a taxi-driver, George King, was alone in his flat in Maida Vale, London, washing dishes when he heard a voice in his ear make the astonishing proclamation: 'Prepare yourself! You are to become the voice of Interplanetary Parliament.'

Most half-sane people might immediately have sought medical advice, but King seems to have taken this startling news in his stride, apart from dropping a plate in surprise. Eight days later, according to his own account, 'an Indian swami of world renown' (but whom King does not name) teleported himself to King's flat and instructed him further in his mission, particularly in how to achieve telepathic contact with a 'Cosmic Master' from Venus called Aetherius. In August 1956, in response to growing interest in his subsequent accounts of contacts with this being, King set up the Aetherius Society and proceeded to pass on to his followers information that he received telepathically, having been 'relayed over millions of miles of etheric space'. Some of these channellings came from the Cosmic Master Jesus (also alive and well on Venus), and others named Mars Sector 6 and Jupiter 92.

More, or worse, was to come. King claimed to have made out-of-the-body journeys to Mars and Venus, and told his (surprisingly) still growing band of adherents that Mercury was the only uninhabitable planet in the solar system. On his very first such trip, he managed to survive an encounter on Mars with a hostile dwarf armed with a ray-gun, and was then recruited by the Martians to combat a sentient asteroid 'the size of the British Isles' that was attacking their space fleet. When the Martians' best military efforts failed, King himself – who else – led a final 'death or glory' assault that defeated the object 'with a weapon of love'. This spectacular battle conveniently took place well away from all other human witnesses, some 40 million miles from Earth.

Over the years, King developed a combined cosmology and theology that drew heavily on Hinduism and kundalini yoga, European occultism (notably the writings of Madam Blavatsky), Christian millenarian beliefs and a blithe disregard of modern astronomical knowledge of the solar system. According to King, humanity's original, spiritual and material home was the planet 'Maldek', which orbited the Sun between Mars and Jupiter. The Maldekians attained a high level of technological civilization, but blew their planet apart in a spectacularly efficient thermonuclear explosion. We know the remains today as the asteroid belt. However, 'according to the perfect Law of Karma', the 'lifestreams' of the Maldekians had to be born again within the solar system. Earth (or 'Terra'; King regards Terra as both planet and sentient goddess) was the only suitable site: the other planets' cultures were too advanced to accommodate the long, slow process of reincarnations required to bring the Maldekian souls to the same refined level as theirs.

The first Terran civilization to re-establish contact with other planets developed in Lemuria, a continent in the Pacific ocean, but in time lust for power corrupted a faction and Lemuria went the way of Maldek – shattered by an atomic blast. The next centre of Terran civilization evolved on Atlantis, a continent in the Atlantic ocean. History repeated itself, and 'down fell the civilization of Atlantis into charred radioactive ruins'. A few of the Atlantean spiritual elite were saved by Martian spaceships before the cataclysm.

Today, King observes, an Earthly civilization has yet again discovered the power of nuclear forces and is poised on the brink of self-destruction. 'These are the last days of the old order,' writes King, at his most apocalyptic, in *The Nine Freedoms* (1963). But this time, by Karmic decree, the planet will not be destroyed, even if humanity incinerates itself. Instead, humanity will be reborn on a 'young, primitive world... in the solar system orbiting behind the Sun following exactly the same trajectory as Earth and... thereby not visible.'

¤ EYE IN THE SKY

Thus, despite all evidence of human fecklessness, spiritual darkness and incorrigible bad habits, the Space Intelligences or Great Ones of the solar system are watching over the Earth, hoping to avert a fourth disaster. And for 'several periods each year' (the precise dates are always revealed beforehand to King) the Third Satellite, a 'colossal Spacecraft' controlled by Mars Sector 6, orbits 1550 miles (2480km) above the Earth, during which time 'all truly selfless Spiritual activities performed on behalf of mankind are potentized exactly 3000 times because of the highly concentrated and carefully balanced energies radiated from Satellite No 3.' This is achieved by focusing the Sun's rays through large pyramid-shaped crystals and beaming the 'energies' to Earth via an ovoid crystal 30ft (10m) high that floats 'immobile in the Operations Room apparently defying the known laws of gravity'. So selfish and spiritually backward are most Earthlings (Aetherius Society members are apparently an exception) that most of this energy bounces off them, unabsorbed. George King has published graphs to prove it.

The existence of this amazing vehicle has long gone undetected, for it 'is totally invisible to physical human eyes and it cannot be detected by radar'. Of course, this coyness has nothing to do with secrecy, let alone hopelessly unprovable claims; the faith of King's disciples is bolstered by a careful explanation: 'So minutely exact are the energy radiations from Satellite No 3 that their delicate balance and predetermined results would be upset by normal light reflection and certainly by radar pulse reaction.'

While it is perfectly plain that King's cosmology is a mish-mash of pseudo-science, mythology and elements taken from earlier self-appointed seers and would-be messiahs, his basic message is closely allied to that promulgated by many other contactees of the 1950s. It is also a perfect expression of Jung's dictum that: 'Anything that looks technological goes down without difficulty with modern man' – King cannot resist justifying his religion through technical marvels, the modern equivalent of biblical miracles.

King is a creature of the post-war era of flying saucers and men from Mars, but is unusual in having maintained a following for over 40 years. During that time the claims of other contactees have generally been mocked and debunked by mainstream ufologists. Those who now energetically promote a belief in alien abductions have been particularly careful to distance themselves from the contactee 'movement'. At the same time, the Aetherius Society has continued to grow, and its spokesmen are treated by the media as representatives of those who 'believe in' UFOs. King himself – today resident in Santa Barbara, California – has accrued an extraordinary collation of titles of obscure provenance, starting with an academically worthless 'Doctorate of Divinity' acquired from a spurious and now outlawed British 'university', and culminating in his current appellations of 'His Eminence, Prince George de Santorini, Count de Florina'.

One has the impression that mainstream ufology does not quite know what to think about King and his Aetherius Society, and never has known. Ufologists tend either to ignore them in public or dismiss them in private as unscientific cranks. This is both to miss the lesson that King holds for ufology (not least if one looks at it from Jung's perspective) and to presume that there is a rather greater degree of scientific expertise and attitude within ufology than is demonstrably the case.

¤ LADY WITH A PAST

The Aetherius Society is by no means the only long-lived UFO cult to see salvation in the saucers. One of the most bizarre, with an internal mythic history and ritual so elaborate as to beggar the epithet *kitsch*, has been Unarius (Universal Articulate Interdimensional Understanding of Science), also founded in the mid-1950s, by Californians Ruth and Ernest Norman. Unlike those of the 'secular' saucer contactees, but like King's and other overtly religious UFO movements, Unarius' claims depend not on face-to-face encounters but on information received through telepathic or 'channelled' messages from the extra-terrestrials, first received by Ernest and, after his death, by Ruth. The central tenet of the Unarian faith is that spaceships of the Intergalactic Federation, with the 'Space Brothers' aboard, will land on Earth – at a specially constructed landing strip in the mountains near San Diego – in 2001CE. They will begin a new age of peace, plenty, free energy and philosophical enlightenment, brought about by the reconstruction of long-lost Lemurian and Atlantean technology. Ruth Norman, who died in 1993, will return with them to unify and lead the nations of the Earth.

Belief in reincarnation is also crucial within the Unarian mythology. Ruth Norman believed not only that she was once the Pharaoh's daughter who discovered Moses among the bulrushes – she and her husband were also reincarnations, respectively, of Mary Magdalene and Jesus of Nazareth. Their followers ritually admitted their guilt in persecuting Jesus (a sin they had committed in former incarnations). 'Readings' of Unarians' past lives have produced long, complex narratives in which the 'students' have often known one another in previous historical eras or on other planets. They have on occa-

sion actively opposed the Unarian scheme of things: present students, in one previous group incarnation, tortured Ruth Norman (then incarnated as the spiritual leader of the Pleiades) for no less than ten centuries.

Like George King, Ruth Norman adopted a number of grandiose titles during her lifetime; unlike his, hers were cosmic rather than temporal and secular. She was generally known to her students as Uriel ('Universal Radiant Infinite Eternal Light'), and, variously, also as The Universal Seeress, Spirit of Beauty, Healing Archangel, the Goddess of Love, and Queen of the Archangels. Norman never failed to dress the part as she saw it, decking herself out in shiny or diaphanous high-collared gowns and capes, with glittering tiaras, fur stoles and sceptres as additional impedimenta. For personal transport she had the Space Cadillac or Cosmic Car, which sported a lit-up flying saucer on its roof. The vehicle awaits her on her return in 2001.

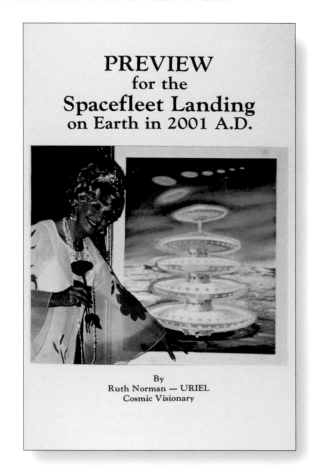

The late Ruth Norman, the Barbara Cartland of ufology, who like Eduard 'Billy' Meier maintained she had a special relationship with Pleiadeans, if in a former life. Norman's followers look forward to a mass landing of Space Brothers in 2001. *Fortean Picture Library*

While Norman's less impressed neighbours in El Cajon, California, derided her as 'Spaceship Ruthie', her teachings undoubtedly provided – and still provide – some badly needed sense of meaning and coherence to her followers. Her promise of a new Golden Age, and her claims of martyrdom, actual death and vow to return, contain distinct echoes of Christianity and other hero-myths.

Ufology was as bemused by Ruth Norman as it was by George King, tending to ignore them both except as curiosities and subjects for deadpan encyclopedia entries. The nature of King's and Norman's claims may have contributed to this: they were intrinsically insusceptible to what would pass in either the courtroom or the laboratory as proof or disproof. Everything resides in the good faith and integrity of the recipients of the channelled messages on which both founded their cult followings. While astronomers might point out the good reasons why no known form of life exists on other planets within the solar system, King and Norman would insist that the beings they contacted existed on a 'higher etheric level' than ours, thus shifting the ground of argument from beneath scientists' feet and into the mystic realm.

By 1975, hardly anyone in the Western world could be excused for being ill-informed about space. Six years earlier, the first attempt to put men on the Moon had succeeded brilliantly, while a host of unmanned craft had been launched to explore remote space, sending back extraordinary pictures of the solar system along with a mass of information about its strikingly inhospitable planetary environments. All the planets were shown to be clearly desolate of, and incapable of sustaining, any advanced form of life recognizable by Earthly standards. Questions remained as to whether microbes may have developed on Mars, which had at some point been scoured with water.

¤ BORN AGAIN (AND AGAIN)

Just after 2pm on Tuesday 28 January 1975, a one-armed farmer and odd-job man named Eduard 'Billy' Meier was walking near his home at Hinwel, in the canton of Zurich in Switzerland, when he saw a silvery, disc-shaped craft swoop down out of the sky with a strange throbbing sound and land about 100yd (90m) away from him. Intrigued, he began to run towards it, but some invisible force halted him after about 50yd (45m). A figure then emerged from the disc, which was about 25ft (8m) in diameter, and approached him. When it and its vehicle departed 1 hour 45 minutes later, Billy Meier knew he

had met a cosmonaut from the Pleiades star cluster (of which seven are visible to the naked eye on Earth), 430 light years away from the Sun in the constellation of Taurus.

In all, between January 1975 and August 1991 Meier met five Pleiadians – Semjase (a female of some pulchritude), Ptaah, Quetzal, Plaja and Asket – in over 700 encounters. He took over 1000 photographs of their five different types of flying disc, collected extra-terrestrial artefacts from them, and wrote over 3000 pages of notes on their conversations and general wisdom. According to Meier, the Pleiadians look like terrestrial Scandinavians, although their lifespan stretches to the equivalent of 1000 of our years. They came from a planet named Erra 'in the system of Taygeta' in the Pleiades. Before that, they lived on a planet in the constellation of Lyra, from which they had emigrated millions of years previously. They had reached Earth thousands of years ago, during a continuous programme of space exploration, in ships capable of travelling faster than light through 'hyperspace'. Meier himself has travelled through time with them, and has photographed cavemen, dinosaurs and even the eye of God to prove it.

Their general message for mankind was that we should concentrate on the arts of peace and cultivating the life of the spirit – they could not interfere in Earth's affairs, although they diagnosed terrestrial civilization as 'an insane society rushing headlong to... destruction'. The Pleiadians communicated with Meier both through telepathy and by speaking his own dialect.

While assiduously recording all this data, Meier seems not to have pondered some basic facts about the Pleiades star cluster. By astronomical standards, the Pleiades is young: a mere 150 million years old. Its 500-odd stars are virtually all 'B' type – ferociously hot, very large blue stars that burn themselves out very rapidly. The majority have, in fact, already consumed most of the hydrogen in their cores. In contrast, our Sun, a relatively cool, slow-burning 'G2' yellow dwarf, is some 4.49 billion years old, and it took a further 2.5 billion years or so before conditions on Earth were able to support even the most primitive forms of life. Should any planet have formed in the Pleiades, the chances of it being habitable are about zero.

The best that can be said for the Lyran emigrants is that they chose a remarkably inhospitable place to claim to have settled. This is all the more surprising in the light of their statement that they are '3000 years ahead of us' in terms of civilization and intelligence – although the excruciating triviality of their 'philosophical' utterances may lure one into thinking otherwise.

But it was less Meier's lack of astronomical exactitude than his admittedly elegant photographs that attracted the attention of ufologists. Meier's chief champions in the US have been Wendelle Stevens and Jim Dilettoso, who first presented the pictures in a lavishly produced coffee-table book in 1979. They maintain that they have subjected the photographs to exhaustive computer analysis and confirmed the 'unearthly' nature of 'Pleiadean' metal samples through laboratory tests. In the early 1980s, Ground Saucer Watch, an Arizona-based, increasingly skeptical UFO research group, did its own digital interrogation of Meier's pictures and pronounced them a 'grandiose' hoax. At about the same time, ufologist Kal Korff systematically took Meier's claims, and those of his American supporters, to the cleaners in a short but devastating book. Not least among Korff's achievements was to show that the 'computer enhancements' published by Wendelle Stevens were absolutely fraudulent.

Far from retiring abashed, Meier merely multiplied his claims, which in turn have generated a minor industry in the shape of at least eight lavish picture books and hagiographies. Meier has also produced what he calls the *Talmud Immanuel*, the 'last true testament of Jesus Christ'. Meier was led to its translator by the Pleiadeans. Unfortunately, but perhaps predictably, the original scrolls have since been lost. By his followers, who maintain him in some comfort on a 50-acre compound, Meier has been acclaimed as the one true prophet for the New Age. And he now proclaims himself to be the reincarnation of Jesus of Nazareth – who can add to his list of miracles the ability to be reborn in two bodies at once, if both Ernest Norman (died 1971) and Meier (born 1937) are to be believed, and to live on Venus at the same time (according to George King).

In 1991, Korff went to Switzerland and infiltrated Meier's 'Semjase Silver Star Centre' under an assumed

Eduard 'Billy' Meier in the 1970s with a portrait of 'Semjase', his favourite Pleiadean. A photo taken of the lissome blonde cosmonaut was later revealed to have been of a Scandinavian model in a magazine advertisement. *Fortean Picture Library*

name, and at the same time garnered a mass of early Meier pictures and documents from the family of a disillusioned early admirer. He digitally enhanced the pictures anew, using the commercial Adobe Photoshop program – so that their fakery can easily be verified by anyone else. In a new book published in 1995, he tore Meier's photos to pieces (the 'eye of God' turned out to be the Ring Nebula), shredded the claims that Meier's 'alien' metal samples are genuine, dismantled what he called the 'assorted claptrap' that has come out of the mouth of Jim Dilettoso, and dismembered the evasions and double talk of Wendelle Stevens.

None of this has endeared Korff to the Meier disciples. His reputation had preceded him to Switzerland. In his false persona, he asked some of Meier's disciples what they would do if Kal Korff came to visit. 'We would not let him in, or we would never let him leave,' came the somewhat chilling reply. No less creepy was the reaction to Korff's book by another Meier follower, who wondered (in an Internet posting) if Korff – whom he denounced variously as a 'liar', a 'skunk' and a 'scumbag' – had been financed by 'the Anti-Defamation League... that is known in the US as the "Jewish GESTAPO", whose members long to exterminate UFO groups and others by means of underhanded murder and other methods?'

Somehow, this kind of thing tends to confirm the suspicion that Kal Korff has been right to doubt Meier's integrity all along. Meier's mistake, of course, was to try to provide 'proof' of his contacts with his 'Pleiadeans' – an error that channellers such as George King, Ruth Norman and numerous others in psychic contact with off-world, space-age 'divinities' have wisely avoided. Meier is thus unusual as a flying saucer prophet in having attracted sustained attention from ufologists, and in being roundly rejected by all but a few – who, coincidentally, make money by publishing credulous books about him.

¤ SPEAK OF THE DEVIL

In direct opposition to those who maintain that ufonauts are here to guide humanity to greater things are those convinced that UFOs and aliens are full of evil intent, if not indeed agents of Satan himself. For reasons that are not immediately clear, ufologists – some of them highly influential within their chosen field – have endorsed such ideas with a good deal more ease and alacrity than they have accorded the salvationist scenario. Possibly this is because, almost without exception, the salvationist con-

tactees – from Adamski to Meier – had been saturated with occult lore long before they had, or said they had, physical or psychic contact with extra-terrestrials, around whom they wove a new, quasi-scientific quilt of their pre-existing beliefs.

In contrast, the demonological tendency in ufology has arisen either from contemplating the UFO 'data' (which in some cases included commentators' own UFO experiences), or from fundamentalist Christianity. The former group are not that far divorced from ufologists who embrace the darker conspiracy theories. The testimony of salvationist contactees like Adamski shaded very rapidly into the testifying of the UFO cult leaders; in a parallel movement, the dark musings of Jacques Vallée about a shadowy group that directs the UFO phenomenon as a means of social control, and appears able to manipulate spacetime in the process, is only slightly removed from the supernaturalist rantings of Gordon Creighton about demons and *djinns* or the tricksterish 'ultraterrestrials' discerned by John Keel within the phenomenon (of which more below). In the late 1980s, the theme of the demonic nature of UFOs and aliens would find its way back into conspiracy theories that began (also in the 1950s) as political, not supernatural or religious, perceptions of ufology. Thus a circle was completed, as materialist speculations on UFOs joined hands with metaphysical ones. It suggested to some that all ufology should be examined from a religious perspective, and to others that ufological history had ended, and a monstrous pluralism of yet more undisciplined conjecture was about to loose itself on the world.

The demonologists of ufology are distinguished by a still more tenuous connection with any 'evidence' for their suppositions than the salvationists could offer. Gordon Creighton, for decades a force within the UK's once-respected *Flying Saucer Review* (*FSR*) and now its editor, has long warned that journal's readers of the hellish nature of ufonauts. As early as 1967, Creighton was suggesting that some, if not all, aliens 'correspond very closely indeed to the traditional concepts held, in all parts of our world, of "demons", "goblins", "trolls", and so on.' This was long before Jacques Vallée intimated that elves, pixies and UFO occupants were aspects of the same phenomenon. Two years later, *FSR* assistant editor Dan Lloyd announced openly that UFOs were a Satanic device and delusion, intended to focus the mind of man on purely material matters and cripple human spiritual evolution.

By the mid-1970s Creighton, who is reportedly a Buddhist, was in full apocalyptic flow: 'Demons... are

The Four Horsemen of the Apocalypse – Death, Famine, Plague and War – descend upon a hapless humanity at the Battle of Armageddon. Visions of universal chaos, debauchery and destruction, orchestrated by ufonauts in the service of Satan, fill the minds of a surprising number of ufologists. *Fortean Picture Library*

already here in immense strength,' he assured readers, and were selecting a chosen few for their genetic superiority (a quality he had the rare good taste to leave undefined). And 'before the close of the century, cataclysmic and apocalyptic events will rend the planet... and as the signs of moral and spiritual decay multiply, who can doubt that certain of the "UFO entities" have a hand in... the stirring of the nauseating brew?'

No one could, if Creighton were correct in his assertion that in the interim governments and nations were telepathically controlled by the evil entities. In the 1990s, *FSR* was regularly publishing articles affirming that, for instance, UFOs represented 'a hellish plot aimed at complete enslavement of humanity'. In March 1997, *The Times* of London quoted Creighton as saying unequivocally: 'I do

believe the great bulk of these phenomena are what is called Satanic.' Creighton represents a tropical case of the ufologist at odds with his material, for *FSR* also published many, often admirably detailed, case histories – none of which seemed to offer much to substantiate the exotic conclusions that its editor drew from them. As Jerome Clark remarked of *FSR*'s editor, such 'peculiar beliefs... represent a flight from reason by virtually any definition'.

¤ UNEVEN KEEL

Creighton's imaginings can at least be placed in the context of milleniarist fantasy. In predicting the advent of the Four Horsemen, he is explicitly rewriting prophesies of Apocalypse, Armageddon and the End Times in ufological language. At least we know there will be a horrible crisis and then all our troubles will be over. Rather more depressing, even depressive, is John Keel's vision of the demons in flying saucers. Jerome Clark quotes what he calls 'a particularly ripe paragraph' from a Keel article in *Strange* magazine:

> *While we grovel on our way to the twenty-first century, someone or something is watching with amusement.... We are biochemical robots helplessly controlled by forces that can scramble our brains, destroy our memories and use us in any way they see fit. They have been doing it to us forever.*

For Keel, as for Creighton, ufonauts were not extra-terrestrials, but demons in modern disguise. They took on shapes and sizes of all kinds, however, not just those of 'aliens': they may be monsters, angels, fairies, even poltergeists. In *UFOs: Operation Trojan Horse*, widely regarded as his *magnum opus*, Keel wrote:

> *The Devil's emissaries of yesteryear have been replaced by the mysterious 'men in black.' The quasi-angels of biblical times have become magnificent spacemen. The demons, devils and false angels were recognized as liars and plunderers by early man. These same impostors now appear as long-haired Venusians.*

These grotesquely manipulative entities Keel dubbed 'ultraterrestrials'. They may manifest themselves in the material world, but truly inhabit another 'dimension' of existence: Keel calls it the 'superspectrum', but it is to all intents and purposes the same as the 'etheric world' beloved of spiritualists. Their intention – or their achievement – has been to enslave humanity, for they control religion, politics and individuals. There may be more than one faction among the ultraterrestrials, and humans have been used as helpless pawns in their battles.

In Keel's pessimistic, even masochistic metaphysics, humanity is powerless and eternally doomed to be the plaything of the god-like ultraterrestrials. In this he echoes a subtext of the religions derived from the *Tanach* (the Hebrew Bible), which presents God as all-powerful, omniscient and yet frequently inexplicably cruel, a creator of evil as well as good, and possessed of moral standards that only intermittently connect with human ideas of justice, compassion and reason. Keel shows no sign of being aware of this troubled tradition but, as a diabetic, he is himself a victim of an incurable condition, which if not regularly palliated (or, in religious language, propitiated) can – for purely biochemical reasons – produce bouts of irrationality. It is rarely helpful to raise such personal matters in discussing anyone's ideas, but in this instance might we, perhaps, discern the roots of Keel's singularly depressive vision of a world at the mercy of uncontrol-

lable, evil, unjust and inescapable forces from elsewhere?

It is easier to follow the reasoning – if that is the word for it – behind the insistence among fundamentalist Christians that UFOs and aliens are 'limbs of Satan'. The train of thought runs thus: first, UFOs and aliens are deemed to be real, and their claims to be extra-terrestrial are taken at face value – as claims. However, in fundamentalist belief there can be no life on other planets, as the Bible says nothing about such a thing. According to the fundamentalists, the aliens (and, incidentally, anyone else who claims there even just *may* be life elsewhere in the Universe) therefore deny the Bible, and therefore deny God. Fundamentalists have also taken to heart the notions that the aliens are scientifically, morally and perhaps physically more evolved than humans, and that they are here to accelerate our own evolution. The very concept of evolution is, of course, anathema to fundamentalists, to whom the account of the Creation in Genesis is absolute and literal truth. Whichever way they look at the UFO phenomenon, it is clearly designed to bamboozle people into rejecting the Bible and the biblical account of creation. Not only that, but people will think salvation is to be had from the Sky People or Space Brothers, not from Jesus of Nazareth. And *who else* but Satan and his demons would create such a cunning scheme?

There are several logical flaws in this argument, not least its first assumption. As theologian Professor Ted Peters says, 'It is logically possible for things to exist that are not mentioned in the Bible. Toyotas and Swiss watches and Big Mac hamburgers exist indisputably, but they are not mentioned in the Bible.' One could argue (and many Christians have) that evolution, the book of Genesis, and a caring God are all compatible. Indeed, as Peters has pointed out, Judaism, Christianity and Islam are not at root opposed to the idea of extra-terrestrial intelligence. Nonetheless, there is a grain of truth even in the fundamentalists' obsessional perspective on ufology: that is their perception that much of its mythology is essentially salvific, inspired by the hope that the ufonauts will bring us peace, understanding and plenty.

And here lies the real importance of the UFO cults. They are no more irrational than any other religion, if rashly prone to garble the vocabulary of modern science and put it through an occult mangle to serve their various cosmologies. But they do demonstrate the ready *capacity* of ufological beliefs to act as fertile soil for religious beliefs. Whether this is a parasitical growth upon the back of ufology, an aberration within it, or a clue to the true nature of its seemingly unsystematic assortment of ideas, is a question we will leave dangling for the time being.

7

Ufological Wars

FLYING SAUCERS OF THE MIND

I N THE NAIVE days of early ufology, the witness report of a UFO tended to be equated unthinkingly with the UFO itself, but ufologists came to realize that they actually deal only with the reports from people about their experiences. This is true even in those rare cases where other forms of evidence such as vegetation damage are found. All of ufology is based primarily on witness statements, with, occasionally, some circumstantial evidence. This realization assumed primary significance for some investigators, and ultimately led to a strong movement within modern ufology that is usually referred to as the 'new ufology' or the 'psychosocial school'.

The psychosocial ufologists usually do not take a witness's account at face value without considering the cultural context in which it is made – that is, the current ideas, attitudes, beliefs, myths, values, influences and tensions existing within the society in which the witness lives – and the psychological state of the person concerned. This can cover a wide range of factors. Is the person fantasy-prone: does she or he daydream a lot? Is the individual creative in an artistic sense? Was the witness subject to trauma (such as child abuse) in the past, resulting in an acquired ability to dissociate (enter vivid other mental realities to escape stress within the waking state)? Are there personal crises being struggled with by the witness that could be affecting his or her psychological state?

A particularly crucial consideration is what the circumstances were in which the person had the experience. It is a fact that over three-quarters of all 'alien abductions' are reported by people who are in their homes, often their bedrooms, or engaged in driving at night, and psychosocial researchers argue that people who have genuine high-strangeness experiences are in one or other form of an altered state of consciousness, in which dream or hallucinatory material invades the waking state. An individual can experience such altered states by slipping unawares into marginal sleep states, by 'road hypnosis', by seeing something strange and alarming (even if it is a misperceived mundane object), by exposure to electromagnetic fields (perhaps associated with an anomalous 'earth light' – see Chapter 10), by shock, and by other external stimuli. For witnesses who happen to be undergoing considerable psychological crisis at the time of the UFO experience, or who are particularly susceptible to dissociated states for whatever reason, the external trigger can be surprisingly slight.

Consideration of the psychological state of a witness can also include less dramatic perceptual errors, such as 'confabulation', in which a person embroiders non-existent details onto some unusual or misperceived sight. This can range from mild examples experienced by most people, such as when a piece of paper blowing in the wind is momentarily seen out of the corner of the eye as a bird or butterfly, to more complex cases. An example of one of these occurred when what was undoubtedly a brilliant meteor flashed across British skies many years ago, and a number of people reported seeing 'portholes' and other non-existent details on the dramatic object. Confabulation is coloured by individual and cultural expectations.

The psychosocial adherents, the new ufologists, point out that such operations of consciousness do not constitute deliberate fraud or hoaxing, but rather an involuntary process invisible to the witness. The experience is, to the person concerned, real and can be dreamed about as if having been an actual, 'event level' incident. It can be recovered (and expanded and strengthened) by regression hypnosis. Indeed, it can even be *created* during hypnosis if leading questions and projected assumptions are made by the hypnotist.

It is difficult to place an exact date on the appearance of the psychosocial strand of ufology. It was certainly foreshadowed by C.G. Jung's 1959 book, *Flying Saucers — A Modern Myth of Things Seen in the Sky*, in which the great psychologist deals primarily with the UFO phenomenon as a visionary rumour, which is itself real whatever UFOs themselves may or may not be. He urged that the 'psychological aspect of the phenomenon' should be investigated, and recounted dreams of patients in which archetypal motifs he saw as underlying the UFO phenomenon presented themselves. He identified similar motifs in the accounts of some of the flying saucer contactees. Jung also toyed with ideas of psychic projection onto perceptions of the physical environment. But whatever the actual nature of UFOs, there was, he insisted, a 'psychic relatedness' to the whole affair.

It was the publication of Jacques Vallée's *Passport to Magonia* a decade later, however, that most ufological historians think kickstarted the present element of psychosocial ufology. In this important book, subtitled 'From Folklore to Flying Saucers', Vallée argued that the basic motifs in modern UFO accounts parallel those to be found in ancient folklore. Like John Keel at about the same time (see Chapter 6), Vallée pointed out that the fairies and elementals, devils and visionary personages of former times and traditions bear striking likenesses in terms of role, behaviour and sometimes appearance to today's UFO entities. 'When the underlying archetypes are extracted from these rumours, the saucer myth is seen to coincide to a remarkable degree with the fairy-faith of Celtic countries...' he wrote. Although Vallée's development of this fundamental observation in the book is somewhat vague and ambiguous, it resonated with a lot of ufologists who were becoming dissatisfied with a literalistic extra-terrestrial approach.

Whatever its exact starting point was, the psychosocial position grew in the 1970s, and had become a distinct element within ufology by, 1980. It developed, really, in parallel with the topic of UFO abductions, for while psychosocial explanations can often be applied to even relatively simple events such as the sighting of a light in the sky, it becomes more relevant the higher *(cont. p.90)*

This woodblock print from an old English chapbook 'freeze-frames' many themes in fairy folklore, including the Green Man in the tree, the magic mushroom ('toadstool') and the hollow hill or fairy mound, with its door. Entrance into the fairy mound by humans was to invite enchantment, missing time from the human world, and confrontation with Otherworld beings. Was the fairy mound a forerunner to the flying saucer? Do both images relate to the same archetype?

From 1947 to the mid-1960s, the resources, energy and dedication that the USAF put into UFO investigations varied enormously, from all-out efforts by a large team to gather and analyse the best available data, to desk-bound information gathering and lackadaisical assessments of sighting reports. In addition, the investigators had to contend with some highly vocal ufologists who insisted that the USAF 'knew' that flying saucers were from outer space, but was determined to hide the truth. This view had hardly been corroded by the USAF's policy of classifying the work of its various UFO studies, up to and including its last, codenamed Project Blue Book.

Dr Edward Condon meets a being from Venus – otherwise known as Constance Viola Weber Menger, wife of contactee Howard Menger. Condon, noted for his impatience with 'crackpots', seems to be enjoying his close encounter.
Fortean Picture Library

Blue Book's chief scientific consultant, astronomer J. Allen Hynek, believed that the phenomenon might yet yield 'scientific paydirt' if it were to be examined comprehensively. But, Hynek felt, not one unexplained case had been mined exhaustively for its possible scientific profit. At the same time, the USAF had a massive public relations problem. Constantly announcing that UFOs were of no significance brought the equally constant refrain: why then is the Air Force bothering with them?

The problem was solved by a scientific advisory committee, whose secret report was issued in March 1966. Its key recommendation was that the USAF should contract with a number of universities to investigate 'perhaps 100 sightings a year' in depth, as 'such a programme might bring to light new facts of scientific value'. Only the University of Colorado agreed to take on the work, with Dr Edward U. Condon as project director.

Condon had a well-developed sense of the ridiculous. As the project evolved, he was particularly entertained by stories of contactees such as George Adamski (see Chapter 2) and his imitators. Condon's irreverence extended to practical jokes. One prank led to a reception committee representing the governor of Utah, complete with brass band, waiting several hours at the Bonneville Salt Flats racetrack for a telepathically predicted UFO landing. While amusing himself in this fashion, Condon regularly gave speeches that made it plain that he thought there was 'nothing to' UFOs. His staff became increasingly uneasy, and the UFO organizations who were passing him data finally withdrew their support from the project when it appeared that its objectivity was compromised.

The notion that Condon deliberately set out to produce a 'negative' report has haunted the Colorado project ever since. Much of the ufological outrage at its final report is inspired by the notion that what is not explicable in the case studies must be extra-terrestrial. It was at least a tactical error by Condon not to anticipate the believers' reaction and address the issue of the ETH in much greater depth and detail. But he did say this:

> When confronted with a proposition of such great import [as the reality of alien visitors to Earth], responsible scientists adopt a cautiously critical attitude toward whatever evidence is adduced to support it. Persons without scientific training, often confuse this with basic opposition to the idea, with a biased desire or hope, or even of willingness to distort the evidence in order to conclude that [the actuality of UFOs being visitors from outer space] is not true.
>
> The scientists' caution in such a situation does not represent opposition to the idea. It represents a determination not to accept the proposition as true in the absence of evidence that clearly, unambiguously and with certainty establishes its truth or falsity. [emphases added]

Thus it was not surprising to scientists, if disappointing to ufologists, that Condon, working largely with the 'anecdotal gossip which was the bulk of the raw material' of his subject, cautiously concluded:

> ...the emphasis of this study has been on attempting to learn from UFO reports anything that could be considered as adding to scientific knowledge. Our general conclusion is that nothing has come from the study of UFOs in the past 21 years that has added to scientific knowledge. Careful consideration of the record as it is available to us leads us to conclude that further extensive study of UFOs probably cannot be justified in the expectation that science will be advanced thereby.

But he also declared that if scientists thought the report's findings were wrong, and had ideas for more accurate studies, 'such ideas should be supported...

each individual case ought to be carefully considered on its own merits.' The philosophical and logical crux of the matter, however, was that his team was obliged to adopt a reversal of the principle implicit in every other attempt to enlarge knowledge in the history of the scientific disciplines. Its task had been to investigate:

> ...curious entities distinguished by lack of knowledge of what they are, rather than in terms of what they are known to be. [emphases added]

The distinction is crucial: every scientific advance, however revolutionary, is made by standing on the shoulders of knowledge acquired over generations. Newton had Galileo's calculations, an incontrovertible fact – things fall to Earth – and centuries of mathematical subtlety to help him conceive and express his laws of gravity and motion. Einstein's insights into gravity would in turn have been impossible without the genius of Newton and his nineteenth-century successors. When ufologists claim to be scientific, they are deluding themselves. There is scarcely anything to match the objective solidity and consistency of real scientific findings (let alone the quality of reasoning that deals with them) in ufology's mountains of reports and reams of speculation.

The *Final Report of the Scientific Study of Unidentified Objects* was published in January 1969. Its effect on ufology was dramatic. UFO organizations and publications suffered a huge loss of support. And on 17 December 1969, Secretary of the Air Force Robert C. Seamans Jr announced the closure of Project Blue Book.

The reaction of ufologists to the demise of Blue Book was almost one of relief. NICAP said, as if Condon had never issued his report, that the Air Force decision opened the way for 'a fresh look at the UFO problem'. Indeed it did. The ETH took a massive battering from Condon, and the 1970s saw a free-for-all among ufologists vying for the most intriguing alternative way to account for the UFO phenomenon. This was the background against which the 'psychosocial' school of ufologists emerged.

(*cont. from p.87*) the factor of strangeness that is contained in a UFO encounter report.

It is quite widely perceived that psychosocial ufology has its greatest base in Europe, especially France and Britain, while the 'nuts-and-bolts' extra-terrestrial approach is the foundation for most ufology within the US. Although this is a stereotypical view – some of the best psychosocial work is done by Americans, and there are plenty of extra-terrestrial believers in Europe – there is some truth in it. This ufological transatlantic 'war' is actually a conflict between fundamental attitudes towards the UFO problem: does it have a physical basis, or is it, to put it crudely, 'all in the mind'?

To the red-blooded, all-American ufologist of an extra-terrestrial bent, psychosocial ideas are the fruits of abstract and even effete European intellectualizing. But the following case – a rare two-witness abduction that was remembered without hypnotic assistance – which occurred in the US and was unravelled by a North American investigator, eloquently attests to the strength of the psychosocial position. The case, which we believe has never reached the ufological literature, is merely summarized here, the full account being given in his book *Fire in the Brain* by neuropsychological researcher Ronald K. Siegel, a distinguished professor at UCLA (see Bibliography).

¤ A FUNNY THING HAPPENED ON THE WAY TO CALIFORNIA

Mr Jack Wilson was a white-haired man in his fifties. When he met up with Siegel he was wearing a baseball cap, a checked lumber jacket and khaki trousers. Wilson had deliberately sought out Siegel because he had heard the researcher talking about UFOs on a radio programme.

'Day before yesterday I was on a UFO for seven hours,' Wilson announced when pleasantries were over. Siegel gulped, and arranged for the man to tell his story in a relaxed atmosphere.

Wilson had been returning to California from Florida by car. After an all-night drive, he reached the Arizona state line. Stopping just long enough to refuel his car and buy extra bottles of water, he continued on, driving across a lonely, high-desert landscape ringed with distant mountains. After a time, he heard a strange sound coming from the rear of the car, so he stopped and got out to inspect the vehicle. As he walked along the shoulder of the road, Wilson felt dizzy and faint, and was aware of a blinding light in the sky. He suddenly saw a humanoid figure, no more than 4ft (1.2m) in height. It wore a gray, seamless suit and was surrounded by what appeared to be a force field, rendering its outlines indistinct. The entity had a glow of light around its head. Alarmed, Wilson backed his way into the car, with the small being apparently following him at a distance. Suddenly, he became paralyzed, and his body began to feel very light. He started to float, and was drawn upwards towards the bright light. As he approached, he saw it was a craft – a 'goddamm gen-u-ine UFO'.

The next thing Wilson knew, he was inside the craft, floating down a long corridor which had bright metal panels on its walls. There were intricate geometric designs carved on the panels. He then found himself in a room that looked like an operating theatre. Several gray-suited figures gathered around him, and then he saw stars, as if he had been hit on the head. 'That's when... they drained me,' Wilson muttered with emotion. He explained that by this he meant that the aliens had taken 'my fuckin' memories!'. There was a TV-like screen in the room, and he saw vivid images and sequences from his past flash on it as the beings drained his brain. The last picture showed him sitting in the car. He merged with the image and found himself awake and physically present in his vehicle. There were seven hours of missing time.

Siegel's first reaction was that the man had experienced a complex and vivid dream. A bad dream, a nightmare, but a dream nonetheless. But then Wilson released his bombshell. 'Friend, it was no dream,' he said firmly. 'My son, Peter, was with me. They drained him, too.' Siegel reeled somewhat from this, for he felt sure the man was telling the truth as he knew it.

The next morning, he took the detailed medical and personal histories of the man and his 24-year-old son. They seemed to contain nothing unusual. Wilson agreed to undergo a full physical examination, which included blood and urine tests to see, among other things, if there were traces of any anaesthetic that might have been used on him inside the UFO (there were no such indications). Siegel explained that he would need to check the car and speak with Peter, and Wilson agreed to this. So while Wilson went for his examination, Siegel had the car checked by mechanics to see if there had been any unusual electrical or other faults, as these are sometimes reported as resulting from UFO close encounters. There was nothing amiss. Nor did the vehicle show any signs of exterior damage. The professor rummaged around in the car, and found a map in the glove compartment, which he took.

Siegel interviewed Wilson again in depth, studying his facial expressions closely (certain directional shifts of the eyes, for instance, can indicate when a person is speaking fantasy or recalling memories directly). The fellow was able to decribe the exact route the two men had taken in their car (and this had also been marked in felt-tipped pen on the map Siegel had found), and precisely where and when they had stopped. Wilson claimed not to believe in the paranormal, that he had never read a book on UFOs and had not seen any of the popular films on the subject, such as *Close Encounters of the Third Kind*. Siegel conducted a series of psychological tests on the man, who also underwent a battery of personality and intelligence tests. In addition, he was asked to draw the small gray humanoid and the UFO's interior. Everything indicated that Wilson was not engaged in fanciful elaborations, and was not the type to get lost in daydreams. Siegel also managed to interview Peter without Wilson being present. The investigator made various other enquiries, and was eventually ready to confront Wilson with his findings.

Siegel showed the claimed abductee the results of the medical examinations. He had a clean bill of health, although there was a history of orthostatic hypotension – that is, a tendency to become faint and dizzy when standing up suddenly after being seated for long periods – and slight photophobia, or sensitivity to bright light. Pleased with his medical results, Wilson was not in the mood to be told he had had a dream, and Siegel carefully explained that he had come to the conclusion that the 'abduction' had resulted from a mix of objective events and mental states. Although Wilson and his son had shared the driving, neither had slept very well, as they journeyed non-stop for 30 hours. When Wilson pulled up the car he had been at the wheel for a solid 11 hours. As the car rolled to a halt at the side of the road, it was facing west. Siegel had confirmed from the weather bureau that sunrise at that location had occurred two hours earlier, and there was a slight mist. When Wilson stepped out of the car he experienced a sudden dizziness. As he looked to the rear of the vehicle to check for the cause of the mechanical noise, he was blinded by the glare of the sun shining at a low angle through the mist. He turned away involuntarily, and so was now facing west, towards the 'antisolar position', the point in space directly opposite the sun. This was where he saw the little gray man. The antisolar point was directly ahead of Wilson, on the ground at the head of his own shadow. What Wilson saw was a 'glory', also known as a 'Heiligenschein', or 'holy light'. It is an optical effect that appears as a glow of light around the upper part of a person's shadow when it is projected onto a surface containing droplets of moisture, such as grass laden with dew, a cloud or a mist. The small points of moisture act like tiny lenses or prisms that refract the sun's rays. Peter had jumped out of the car when his father had appeared to faint, and as he grabbed the older man from behind he too saw the gray figure, with its glow and blurred edges. Back in the car, the two men discussed the figure, Peter recalled. The young man had speculated on it being some kind of radioactive creature, or a ghost – or, indeed, a creature from outer space. Both men drifted into sleep as they talked (Peter recalled this, but Jack Wilson had obviously forgotten).

Extremely tired people often get particularly vivid flashes of imagery in the transitional phase between waking and sleep known as the 'hypnogogic' state. Elements of memory are combined into snatches of fantastic and unfamiliar scenes, and sometimes odd sounds are fleetingly heard. It is the 'germinal stuff of dreams' states Siegel, a scientist well known for his important work on altered states of consciousness induced by hallucinogenic drugs and other means. Some characteristic hypnogogic (and trance) imagery is in the form of abstract, geometrical patterns called 'entoptics', and are common to all human beings, as they are produced by poorly understood processes in the visual cortex. Flashes of light are also frequently seen and these, along with the geometric forms, can quickly transform by association in the mind's eye into the passing image of a flame or a bright reflection, or some object or scene from memory. Such involuntary interpretations imposed on the abstract imagery by the dissolving rational, conscious mind at the onset of sleep (or trance states) are known as 'construals'. As the person drifts through the hypnogogic state closer towards sleep itself, the brain's alpha rhythms of wakefulness change into the slower theta frequencies. This causes the onset of a sense of paralysis (in certain stages of sleep, only the eye and respiratory muscles remain unparalysed) and a general loss of conscious control. This deep hypnogogic condition is very similar to the highly suggestible hypnotized state.

Siegel suggested that while Wilson and his son were drowsily muttering about strange beings and UFOs, Wilson drifted deep into the hypnogogic state on his way to sleep and experienced what is known as the 'Isakower effect' – one of the universal entoptic forms appearing as an illuminated circle or similar roundish, symmetrical shape that grows bigger, and so appears to be approaching. As this grew larger, Wilson felt as if he were floating along a tunnel towards the light (a common description in many out-of-body and near-death experiences), and the mental geometric imagery mixed with the construal scene. His fading consciousness linked the

ABDUCTION AS VIRTUAL REALITY

When it was re-examined in 1980, the Maureen Puddy abduction case in Australia in 1972 gave ufologists pause for thought about the actual nature of such reported experiences. Early in 1972, Puddy reported seeing a disc-like object in the sky. In July, she claimed that the object had reappeared by hovering over her car and halting it. Some months after this, she described being taken aboard the UFO, where she saw an entity and considerable detail. These events seemed to cause her genuine emotional upset, yet the 'abduction' happened in the presence of two UFO investigators! When Puddy claimed she had been aboard the UFO, her physical body was still in the car with the two other people, but she had lapsed into unconsciousness. On a later occasion, she claimed the entity had appeared to her once more, when she was driving her car.

It can hardly not be mentioned that Maureen Puddy was under personal stress over this period of time, with two young children and an invalid husband (who died about six months after the supposed abduction).

Isakower light to the glare he had seen outside the car, and turned it into the construal image of a UFO. He dreamed of gray beings, and experienced flashbacks of the Florida trip and other memory pictures. Peter also fell asleep and dreamed of floating inside a hallway and the gray figure, and saw flashback images. When they awoke, they traded accounts of their dreams as they drove along, smoothing out their disjointed nature. (Although Siegel doesn't mention it, it may also have been the case that both men experienced fragmentary lucid dreaming states, a condition of consciousness which causes mental imagery to take on such vividness as to appear – literally – virtually real, while the dreamer's mind has the sense of being awake. This extraordinary and paradoxical altered mind state has been confirmed instrumentally and is currently subject to international research – see Epilogue.) 'By the time they arrived in LA,' Siegel says, 'the fleeting images of the dream had coalesced into a solid abduction story.'

Siegel laid out before the unhappy Wilson dozens of drawings made by hypnotized subjects who had been told simply to imagine a UFO abduction. These showed long corridors, little gray men, geometric patterns and medical examinations that matched Wilson's own pictures perfectly. Siegel decided not to tell the man that his son felt he had become over-enthused by the idea that he had been abducted. The young man was not so sure it had happened, although he speculated that perhaps their astral bodies had been taken up by a spacecraft. Also, he couldn't explain the gray figure he and his father had seen.

'What caused the mechanical noise?' Wilson asked with a forced smile, as the two men parted.

'How should I know?' retorted Siegel. He was merely a brain scientist, after all, not a mechanic.

¤ SLUGGING IT OUT

The 'war' between ufological ideologies has been openly acknowledged in some UFO journals. For example, the *International UFO Reporter*, organ of the Center for UFO Studies (CUFOS) set up in Illinois by J. Allen Hynek, ran an issue in March 1989 with the cover headline 'UFO Wars: Europe vs America'. One article in this was by Italian ufologists Edoardo Russo and Gian Paolo Grassino. They felt that American ufology had 'gone back to square one... we Europeans stand bewildered and astonished as American ufology seems to be re-entering the 1950s'. They saw some modifications to this: the earlier contactee syndrome had now become the abductee complex, so that now 'you don't even need a trigger sighting... you need nothing more than a vague fear for suspecting a suppressed alien abduction memory!', and the Freedom of Information Act had rocketed conspiracy theory from earlier suspicion of military cover-ups to assumptions of wholesale governmental chicanery and the setting up of mysterious secret bodies such as MJ-12. The Italians noted the nostalgia evident in the reopening of 40-year-old cases such as the Roswell incident (see Chapter 9). They pointed out that European ufologists no longer considered Identified Flying Objects (IFOs) as 'false UFOs', as was the case in America, for they believed that misperceived mundane objects could trigger UFO reports just as remarkable as

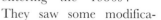

any that might be produced by genuine unknown phenomena, if such existed.

'UFO sightings are just the proverbial tip of the iceberg both for American abduction researchers and for the European sociopsychological "new ufologists"', the Italians wrote as part of their conclusions. 'But those are very different icebergs: the first is a massive genetic-testing campaign by alien intruders, the second is just one facet of a multifaceted "modern folklore" phenomenon.'

Editor Jerome Clark responded, admitting that American ufologists were all too guilty of not hearing other views aimed at solving the UFO riddle. But he maintained stoutly that American ufology was more pragmatic than the 'new ufology', paying more attention to actual evidence than over-arching theories. He accused the new ufology of taking a 'skewed view', dealing with extreme cases and the wild claims of dubious individuals in order to make their points about the psychological and cultural origins of the UFO phenomenon. He claimed that as ufology became more sophisticated in the 1970s and into the 1980s, authentic evidence of the physical nature of some reported UFOs began to accumulate: radar-visual sightings, vegetation damage and so on. He also placed value on the wealth of secondhand evidence being gathered from the great retrospective inquiry into the Roswell UFO crash that several American ufologists had earnestly embarked upon.

Clark felt the Italians were making a fundamental error, 'in common with all European new ufologists', in equating contactees with abductees. These were not the same types of people, he maintained, and the contactee movement was really a subset of 'occult visionary religion' and was 'viewed disdainfully by nearly all American ufologists'. (In the skeptical British journal *UFO Brigantia*, Hilary Evans, a leading British proponent of the new ufology, was later to challenge this supposed distinction: 'abduction stories used to be told shortly after there had been a long and highly visible epidemic of contactee stories in the United States... This situation is so blatant that even the "abductions-are-real" proponents cannot sidestep it; nevertheless their position generally is that the contactee manifestation and the abduction manifestation are two entirely separate things... This is a shoddy evasion... if the contactee phenomenon is now dismissed as devoid of physical subtance, we must surely wonder whether the same may be true of the abduction phenomenon'.) 'My point is simply that, from the point of view of us pragmatic Americans who are paying close attention to the evidence... the ETH [extra-terrestrial hypothesis] seems at the moment the approach that begs fewest

questions,' was Clark's carefully worded conclusion.

On the other side of the Atlantic, the British journal *Magonia*, a balanced and scholarly champion of psycho-social ufology, similarly became embroiled in the 'war'. Its pages were (and still are) often filled with the jousting and fencing of international contributors over the pros and cons of the new ufology. The clash of ideologies reached a peak in issues spanning the late 1980s and early 1990s. In reviewing the differences (*Magonia* No 34), American folklorist and ufologist Thomas E. Bullard admitted that Americans had 'turned a deaf ear to social and psychological explanations for UFO phenomena'. Even though there were American ufologists seeking alternatives to the ETH, that nevertheless remained the dominant explanation in America. But he still felt that psychosocial explanations fell far short, and argued that while it undoubtedly contained many inconsistencies, the ETH answered the basic UFO problem 'without need for intellectual gymnastics'. As a folklorist, he felt that while there were many similarities between modern UFO accounts and traditional fairy lore, there were also significant differences.

Dealing with the psychological argument accounting for alien abductions, Bullard skimmed over their dreamlike aspects and cited such factors as multiple witnesses, cases where recall is without need of hypnosis, and coherent narratives as making the case for abductions being actual events. (With our presentation of the Jack Wilson case above, we can now see that none of these assertions is necessarily true.) He cited Mark Rodeghier of CUFOS in stating that European ufology worked 'from the top down', starting with highly abstract theories and making the actual evidence support them, while American ufology operated 'from the bottom up, wallowing in facts'.

Bullard was rounded on by opponents in the following issue of the journal, *Magonia* No 35. Two of the most powerful contributions to the debate were, ironically, by American ufologists. Denis Stillings referred to Bullard's article as 'a Cock and Bullard story'. He pointed out that even a cursory review of abductees' reports shows that they have a dream-like experience, but this is 'always glossed over or reinterpreted' by the literalists who believe in actual, physical abductions. He also cast scorn on the claim that American ufology uses a 'bottom up' approach based on case evidence alone, remarking that the dominant ETH was as much a 'top down' theory as anything the new ufologists could come up with.

In the same issue, Martin Kottmeyer, one of the most powerful proponents of the psychosocial approach, provided details showing that the dramatic, unfolding sequence of the basic abduction account followed an 'intuitive ordering principle' that could be traced even in old *Buck Rogers* cartoons. He rammed home what he saw as the science fiction influence on the whole ETH approach to UFOs and abductions by giving a wide range of examples of motifs and themes from pre-ufological films and stories. In particular, he instanced the most famous science fiction story of all time, H.G. Wells' *War of the Worlds*, in which the Martians were described as being possessed of 'vast, cool and unsympathetic' intellects, just as abductees claim is shown in the attitudes of the aliens who kidnap them. Even more remarkably, Wells' aliens had intense dark eyes, lipless mouths and grayish-coloured skin, and appeared to be without

gender. This matches perfectly most of the 'grays' described by abductees.

Kottmeyer then dwelt on a claim in Bullard's article that in the 'interrupted journey' of Betty and Barney Hill, the first abduction report to appear in the mainstream American ufological literature (although it wasn't the first reported abduction), the two witnesses 'had no cultural sources from which to derive the experience they reported'. To Bullard, and other abduction literalists, this suggests that the Hills experienced an 'event level' (physically real) encounter with aliens rather than some psychological phenomenon.

The Hill case took place in 1961. The couple were motoring home through New Hampshire after a long journey. Late in the evening near Lancaster, west of the White Mountains, they noticed a bright light in the sky. Barney checked the object with his binoculars and thought it was a plane. The light seemed to get closer and to circle them. Betty looked at it through the binoculars and told Barney that she could see a large craft with rows of windows. The silent light dropped to tree-top height and the Hills stopped their car. Barney got out and walked towards the large, pancake-shaped, glowing object. Through the binoculars, he could see that it had occupants. He suddenly felt he was in danger of capture and ran back to the car in a panic, and they drove off. The onward journey to the Hills' home in Portsmouth, New Hampshire, seemed to have taken two hours longer than it should.

Betty reported the experience to Pease AFB (who confirmed that radar had picked up an airborne 'unknown' in the area at that time) and to a UFO group, and avidly immersed herself in the UFO literature. Barely a week after the experience, Betty wrote to the popular UFO writer of the time, Donald Keyhoe, telling him about their adventure and stating that they were considering seeking a 'competent psychiatrist' to regress Barney hypnotically in order to find out the cause of his sudden panic. In the following weeks, she began to suffer a series of nightmares in which humanoids appeared on a road and in which she and Barney were led aboard an alien craft, where they were examined. Barney showed medical symptoms of stress – presumably a consequence of the encounter, or of the harsh commuting schedule he had to maintain.

In 1963, both the Hills started a series of hypnotic sessions with a respected professional therapist, Dr Benjamin Simon. They both told basically the same story (although there were differences of detail) of a UFO abduction and medical-style examination by alien entities with slit-like mouths, who communicated by telepathy.

Artist's impression of the Betty and Barney Hill UFO encounter in New Hampshire, 1961. *Mary Evans Picture Library*

Betty initially said the aliens had 'Jimmy Durante'-type noses, and Barney mentioned their large, 'wraparound' eyes. The couple were shown a star map, and were returned mysteriously to their car. The accounts pretty well matched Betty's dreams, which she had described to Barney in the years prior to the hypnosis sessions. Simon concluded that the pair had indeed encountered an unidentified object of some kind, but had had an imaginary experience. He stressed that hypnosis can reveal only what the subject believes to have happened, which may not necessarily equate with a physical reality. The Hills' case received considerable public exposure as a result of John Fuller's 1966 book *The Interrupted Journey*, and 'engraved itself on the unconscious of a generation', as Martin Kottmeyer has put it.

To the psychosocial researcher, the Hills encountered something they could not explain (a secret military aircraft, perhaps, or an unusual geophysical phenomenon such as an 'earth light' – see Chapter 10), but the abduction itself was of a complex psychological nature. There are grounds for thinking that Barney was echoing Betty's descriptions of her dreams, and her story contains many inconsistencies. Psychosocial ufologists also note that Betty went on to report many other UFO sightings and encounters in the years that followed. What Kottmeyer emphasizes is that Betty had read Keyhoe's book *The Flying Saucer Conspiracy* just before she started having her nightmares, and that it cites nearly a dozen occupant cases, at least two of which echo specific aspects of the Hills' reported experience. He goes on to note that two movies, *Invaders From Mars* (1953) and *Killers From Space* (1954), had medical motifs that might have triggered a dream image of the 'examination'. In particular, *Invaders From Mars* has a woman abducted by aliens who perform an examination on her, which matches aspects of Betty's reported experience. Betty even originally described the noses of the aliens in a way that recalled the appearance of the noses of the movie Martians! (Betty dropped this detail, it seems, due to the reaction it caused – the 'Jimmy Durante' analogy made the whole case seem ridiculous.) Kottmeyer was thus able to argue that there was nothing in the Hills' experience that had not already figured in images provided by elements of the popular culture.

The jousting in *Magonia* continued. In issue No 37, Bullard responded to his detractors. He admitted that they had seriously damaged parts of his case, but persisted in his perception that abduction accounts were remarkably consistent with one another, and in this respect did not follow the laws of folklore, indicating that

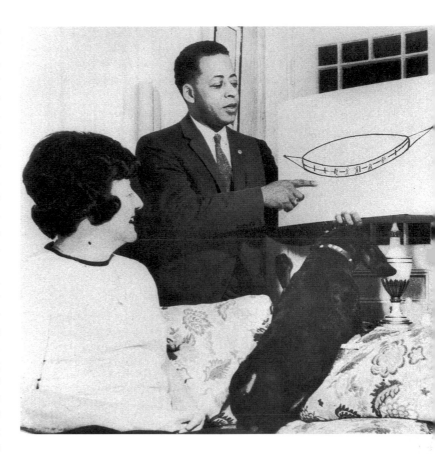

Betty and Barney Hill looking at a sketch of the UFO they claimed they saw. *Fortean Picture Library*

they were more likely to relate to actual events. In the following issue, *Magonia* columnist Peter Rogerson pointed out that while the general framework of the abduction scenario was fairly standard, there were variations in individual accounts. In *Magonia* No 42, Hilary Evans questioned whether there were the rules in folklore that Bullard claimed, and argued that in any case the psychosocial view of abductions was that they were more complex than simple folklore, but nevertheless stood as modern-day social narratives that could be paralleled with certain aspects of folklore.

The point seems not to have been made during the *Magonia* debate that the consistency in abduction accounts that Bullard complained of can come about in a culture where ideas and images are rapidly broadcast, augmented and homogenized by the mass media; the dynamics of folklore narrative in such a high-speed technoculture have yet to be assessed and understood properly. The old models will no longer apply – at least in a complete way. It can be seen in the Jack Wilson case above that even where the witness claims not to read UFO literature or watch science fiction movies, the now classic 'abduction scenario' can readily colour an hallucinatory-dream experience. We underestimate too easily what a phenomenal barrage of fleeting imagery and ideas we are subjected to almost constantly on TV shows and commercials, on videos, in film trailers (even when we have gone to a cinema to see something entirely different), in newspapers and magazines (whether actually read or not, they can enter our subconscious minds subliminally while we are standing at supermarket checkouts or passing a newstand), and on posters and book jackets. This is not to mention whole TV shows, movies and literature dedicated specifically to UFO themes.

The simple fact is that there cannot now – or for a considerable time hitherto – be anyone in a modern society who does not have the basic abduction scenario imprinted in the back of their minds, whether they consciously think about it or not. We have all seen the face of the 'gray' staring at us; we have all had the close encounter which originated in the ufological literature and then invaded our sensibilities through the mass media. As far as the psychosocial ufologists are concerned, and, indeed, as common sense dictates, there can no longer be such a thing as an abduction experience uninfluenced by the current culture. And this fact probably goes back, as we have seen, even to that 'first' abduction involving Betty and Barney Hill.

The presses rolled, and in *Magonia* No 44 Bullard came back and doggedly held onto his view that the abduction phenomenon was based on individual experience rather than psychosocial forces. But this cut no ice with the new ufologists. In the same issue, American journalist and ufologist Dennis Stacy observed that even Bullard's own studies had revealed 'a decidedly non-physical attribute to the average abduction to which he gave the name "doorway amnesia"...'. This refers to the

¤ ABDUCTION AS SOAP OPERA ¤

The influence of the cultural environment on the abduction phenomenon is well illustrated by a 1988 case investigated by British ufologist Andy Roberts and colleagues. Alerted to the report of an alien abduction by leading UFO researcher Jenny Randles, Roberts and friends visited the claimed abductee at her home in northern England. The woman was in her forties, and was clearly distraught by her experience. She said she had been taken from her bedroom by two strange entities with 'leathery skin' who 'floated' her to a nearby field, where she was taken inside a large spaceship that was illuminated 'like a fairground'. She was subjected to an intrusive examination, and showed the investigators faint marks on her arm where she said a tube had been inserted. She mentioned noticing a smell like that of cinnamon while events were taking place on the spaceship. She eventually found herself back in her room, and the next day suffered physical symptoms she ascribed to the abduction.

The investigating ufologists interviewed the woman just two days after the claimed abduction, and they felt her emotional distress was genuine. However, Randles felt caution was called for, as the reported events occurred on the same night as the TV broadcast of the final episode of the American soap opera *The Colbys* (a spin-off from *Dynasty*), in which Fallon, a character in the series, was depicted as being abducted by a UFO. The investigators raised this with the woman, who openly admitted that she had seen the programme, but strongly denied it had influenced her experience. Nevertheless, Roberts and colleagues noted that the detailed description of the woman's UFO closely matched that in the TV show, and that the smell of cinnamon and the leathery skin of the aliens were components of the soap opera drama as well. The investigators felt that 'the chances of someone genuinely being abducted on the same night as the *Dynasty* [i.e. *The Colbys*] abduction and having an almost identical experience are pretty slim'.

If this case had not been checked so speedily, the '*Colbys* factor' could easily have been overlooked in a later investigation. The cultural influence is subtle but all-pervading. And the effect of the media can be of a 'feedback loop' kind: in this case, the scriptwriters of *The Colbys* had themselves picked up the leathery skin and cinnamon from the UFO literature. Round and round it goes.

curious fact that abductees fail to recall exactly how they actually enter a 'craft' or how they physically leave it. As Stacy implies, this type of scene-shifting is a classic feature of dream or hallucinatory experience.

This airing of the arguments in the UFO literature in recent years has at least confirmed one matter beyond argument – namely, that the psychosocial approach has American champions every bit as trenchant and erudite as their European colleagues. The only cultural difference that can be seen to exist is simply that on the European side of the Atlantic alternative views to the ETH are given greater coverage in the UFO literature and have a more attentive audience than on the American side.

¤ QUESTIONS AND ANSWERS

In 1991, the psychosocial school got a backhanded boost from a surprising quarter – Whitley Strieber. The irony of the situation could not have been greater. Strieber's book *Communion*, describing his mysterious encounter and apparent abduction, sold millions of copies, and its cover depiction of the classic 'gray' glowered from bookstore counters and posters to such an extent that it saturated the cultural environment. More than any other single source, *Communion* concretized the image of the alien, and the book, along with the *Communion Newsletter* and abductee support groups, more than any other influence helped to establish the abduction scenario as a significant social phenomenon, especially in the US. And yet Strieber was always careful not to state that he had had a literal abduction, or that his abductors were necessarily extra-terrestrial. In the April issue of the *Communion Newsletter*, it became clear that he had had enough. He found ufologists to be 'probably the cruellest, nastiest and craziest people' he had ever encountered. He was also fed up with media pressure and cynicism. He had come to the conclusion that many abduction reports were the 'artefacts of hypnosis and cultural conditioning'. Whatever lay behind the 'visitor experience' was intense and demanded explanation, but he was now satisfied that it was 'a human thing' that had existed within the psyche for a long time. We and our world are far more strange than we have ever dreamed, he suggested. Strieber had inadvertantly described the very case the new ufology had been brought into existence to present.

While neither side of the debate can claim the knockout punch, the arrival of the new ufology has clearly given the standard extra-terrestrial explanation a severe mauling – and continues to do so as the second half of ufology's first century begins. But it is far from plain sailing.

The supporters of the ETH make what seems to be a valid criticism, for instance, about the inability of the psychosocial ufologists to offer a clear-cut alternative explanation for the UFO phenomenon as a whole, as they claim their approach essentially does. The new ufologists are seen as being evasive, putting forth one explanation, then another – this piece of sociology, or perhaps that piece of psychology. It looks patchwork, and is unsatisfying to those who seek a simple answer.

The new ufologists counter by pointing out that the ETH is not the solid, one-shot answer to the problem that its supporters claim it to be, either. For instance, how can there be so many different types of alien craft visiting our planet? Whatever happened to the airships of the nineteenth century, or the ghost planes of the early twentieth century? They also make the telling point that the 'flying saucers' that became all the rage in the early era of ufology were based on a journalistic misinterpretation, not on Kenneth Arnold's actual description of what he saw (see Chapter 1). It is not only the alarming variety of craft: the occupants, too, seem to be composed of more species than are contained in the average zoo. It is only with the recent advent of the questionable abduction phenomenon that the UFO occupants have settled into small, spindly 'grays' occasionally accompanied by taller beings. Where have the tall, fair-haired Venusians gone? The robots? The elf-like creatures? And why do aliens who have such advanced technology that they can cross interstellar space, out-perform even the most advanced human aircraft, render their vehicles and themselves invisible, and spirit human victims through walls and across cities and fields, allow themselves to crash just like any old Earthly aircraft? And if they did do so, where are the dead occupants and wreckage – the nuts and bolts? If there is a government cover-up, if the Americans have possession of alien

Where have all the Venusians gone? This is a sketch by Alice Wells of the space being who supposedly met George Adamski in the California desert near Blythe in 1952. Wells was said to have been a distant witness to the event, viewing it through binoculars. *Flying Saucers Have Landed: Desmond Leslie and George Adamski, 1953* technology, and, perhaps, are in contact with the extra-terrestrials, how come we never see it? Why the traceable sequence of aircraft technology? Why the Apollo mission? Why the space shuttle series? If the aliens have been landing on Earth for decades or even centuries, why have such advanced beings spent so long picking up bits of rock or vegetation – are they slow learners? Why do they ask abductees repetitive, stupid questions ('What is a vegetable?'; 'What is yellow?') – do they not compare and collate the information they have gathered from their victims over all these years? The list of ludicrous inconsistencies is almost endless.

The ETH believers come back with answers such as: the extra-terrestrials are so alien we cannot fathom their behaviour; the early contactees were (we now see) devious people and so we need not bother about the imaginary occupants they described; we know crashed saucers have been swept up and kept secret by the government, so there is no need to address the deeper questions. The hypothesis becomes self-serving, and the believers in extra-terrestrial explanations show thay can fudge just as well as the new ufologists.

There is no one version of the ETH that answers all the facts of the UFO problem, any more than there is one, tidy psychosocial solution. And that, the new ufologists argue, is the point. There are too many facets for there to be one answer – or even one phenomenon. There is hoax, misperception, error, mirage, confabulation, cultural influence and filtering, expectation, hallucination and media mayhem. Different combinations of cultural, psychological, physiological and possibly geophysical explanations are required from one case to another. Furthermore, the new ufologists insist that there is no single, monolithic psychosocial school of thought. The movement is comprised of different people with differing opinions and areas of expertise struggling with one of the great riddles of our times.

But credible ufologists favouring an extra-terrestrial explanation have a further, valid criticism. They see new ufologists as being too keen to embrace an 'all in the mind' approach, ruling out any form of anomalous physical event in any sighting. There is occasionally persuasive evidence of physical effects – burnt grass, singed vegetation and even burn marks on witnesses, not to mention a few good photographs – that tend to be studiously ignored in too many psychosocial models. This bias was highlighted in 1982, when considerable resistance was shown to the proposal that exotic geophysical phenomena, 'earth lights' (see Chapter 10), were involved in some UFO sightings. From the perspectives of the new

psychosocial ufological zealots of the time, it was a cardinal sin to suggest that there was an actual, physical, unknown factor at the heart of certain UFO reports.

In subsequent years, however, there has been sufficient accommodation of this idea to allow at least some new ufologists now to accept it. While cultural and psychological explanations are seen as the way to tackle most UFO sightings and, certainly, abductions, they realize that there is also the possibility that there are unexplained geophysical phenomena that can shine out in all colours at night like good UFOs should, that can appear metallic in daylight as plasmas can, and that are able to leave physical marks where they touch down, as well as possibly affecting the brain function of close encounter witnesses, giving a further spin to the psychological aspects. This added extra dimension to the psychosocial approach is exemplified in the papers and books of scientists such as Michael Persinger, and books such as Paul Devereux's *Earth Lights Revelation* (which includes material provided by Paul McCartney, David Clarke and Andy Roberts), or *Phantoms of the Sky* by David Clarke and Andy Roberts – see Bibliography. It allows the psychosocial model to tackle virtually all aspects of the UFO enigma.

¤ THE SHOW GOES ON

Nevertheless, the main strands of research within current new ufology remain the many and varied cultural and psychological aspects. In the cultural bag, the influence of science fiction is a recurring topic. It was noted in Chapter 1 that science fiction was in at the birth of ufology in the person of pulp-king Ray Palmer. Hilary Evans remarks in *UFO Brigantia* No 51:

> Anyone who studies the American SF pulps ... of the 1920s/1930s will quickly discover that there is virtually not a single theme of current ufology which was not anticipated there – domed discs overflying Earth; visits by aliens, some concerned with our welfare, others with less benevolent intentions; humans drawn up into spacecraft by beams of light; abductions and physical examinations by aliens (women laid on their backs on tables in spacecraft while aliens surround with probing devices, etc). Even the 'Bermuda Triangle' was anticipated many years before the name was coined.

He also points out that *Amazing Stories* and other magazines of the late 1930s era made space travel an imminent possibility – so much so that the famous 1938 radio broadcast by Orson Welles of H.G. Wells' *War of the Worlds* caused people in America to run into the streets in terrified expectation of an alien invasion (see Chapter 3). Evans argues that there was a predisposition to fabricate an extra-terrestrial scenario in a large section of the American population, and the idea had been seeded before World War II had even begun.

French 'new wave' ufologist Bertrand Méheust has similarly pointed out that early science fiction stories match later accounts by UFO witnesses, contactees and abductees remarkably well, and has identified a French story of the 1920s that parallels a Brazilian abduction of the 1970s! Méheust has also found startling parallels between accounts of abductees and the themes of primitive legends: tales of dreams, visions, abductions by the spirits and initiation rituals.

The underlying patterns of folklore, archetypal imagery, the dynamics of narrative and other associated arcane subject matter are all grist to the mills of those psychosocial ufologists trying to get a grip on the true context of the UFO phenomenon. The work goes on.

The other prime area of ongoing concern for the new ufologists naturally revolves around the psychological factors affecting UFO witnesses and abductees. Attempts have been made to identify a special psychological 'type' prone to seeing UFOs or experiencing abductions. Some psychological studies indicate that they tend to be above average in creative and imaginative capacity, but there have been no clear identifications of characteristic mental abnormalities. There is some evidence that abductees as a section of the population may show a higher than average incidence of having suffered child abuse, may operate in 'boundary deficit' conditions in which areas of mental experience slip and slide between reality/fantasy, inner/outer and other mental categories clearly distinguished by most people, and may exhibit fantasy proneness. Some psychosocial investigators have even claimed to note indications of Munchausen syndrome (mood disorders, voluntary production of psychological symptoms, manipulative characteristics) in some abductees. Naturally, all such findings are extremely controversial, and certainly no such research has yet proved conclusive. But the investigations continue.

Despite this, however, the psychosocial ufologists have far from fully addressed the literature that exists on altered mental states. Highly qualified psychological

Large-headed, big-eyed aliens with minimal noses and slit mouths abduct human beings and conduct medical examinations on them. Such is the basic plot of most of today's abduction accounts, yet here the theme is pictured on the cover of a 1935 edition of *Astounding Stories*. It illustrated a fictional story entitled 'The Invaders'.
Mary Evans Picture Library

experts remain aghast that the abduction phenomenon, in particular, could have taken such a grip on so many people. Robert Baker, professor emeritus of psychology at the University of Kentucky, Lexington, for instance, is quite categoric. All of the reported symptoms of an alien abduction, he states, are 'very well known by trained and experienced clinicians... For students of sleep disorders, hypnosis and suggestion, iatrogenesis, memory aberrations, and hallucinatory phenomena, there is nothing whatsoever puzzling or unexplained'.

(The term 'iatrogenesis' means the creation and shaping of a disorder by the therapist – in the case of abductions, this usually means the hypnotist, who is all too often merely an amateur. Iatrogenesis is a well-known problem in psychology, and psychosocial ufologists are confident that it is prevalent in the abduction phenomenon, even though abduction protagonists howl indignantly that this is not true. Baker points out that even trained therapists have been known to compound clinical error with adherence to trendy ideas – this has occurred with so-called Multiple Personality Disorder, for example – and he notes sadly that this has happened to a few professional therapists who have allowed themselves to become seduced by the abduction scene.)

But there is a further body of extremely important and relevant literature and expertise that has barely been touched by anyone within the field of ufology, psychosocial or otherwise, and that is the two decades or more of research into the effects of psychoactive drugs: LSD, DMT, ketamine and other hallucinogenic substances. This is partly because such literature tends to be kept off centre stage due to political and legal pressures, but the material that is present in this body of research speaks directly to deep factors within the human psyche that could have a great bearing on the nature of the 'alien' encountered within the abduction experience, and on how the mind can model perceptions of reality. Its study acts as a strong corrective to those who persist in dismissing ideas of altered mind states as explanations for events so 'real' as abductions or close encounters. This failure is due to our culture's woefully inadequate knowledge of consciousness outside of a very narrow range that society deems 'normal'. Even some psychosocial researchers who understand this intellectually are still too experientially ignorant of the power of the other mental realities such extended states of consciousness can produce. To mature fully, the new ufology will need to look to this research, written and practical, as well as to ethnopsychology, which records the knowledge of older tribal societies where altered states are regularly induced and intimately mapped. Only then will it be possible to understand better the vivid mental states people in our modern societies may enter unawares.

As the psychosocial show rolls on, then, it is important to realize that the new ufologists are not 'debunkers'. They accept that there is a UFO phenomenon, and that there is a real alien abduction experience. The debate is over the nature of such things.

¤ OH BABY!

Much attention has centred in recent years on the nature of the now-classic alien, the large headed, big-eyed 'gray'.

It is obviously a key concern of the psychosocial ufologists to understand where this image comes from, if there are no actual extra-terrestrials involved in the abduction experience. In attempting to answer this conundrum, the new ufology fashioned one of its first Big Theories – and one of the few, interestingly, in which hallucinogen research is referred to.

It was noticed early on that the 'gray' bore a marked resemblance to the human foetus. American researcher Alvin Lawson suggested that was exactly what it was the image of, and proposed the 'Birth Trauma Hypothesis'. His claim was that during their harrowing experience, abductees were reliving their own birth. This was not as unlikely as it first sounds, because extensive therapeutic use of LSD by psychiatrist Stanislav Grof had already revealed that patients were quite capable of remembering, or mentally reconstructing, their own birth trauma. Grof observed that his subjects 'assume postures and move in complex sequences that bear a striking similarity to those of a child during the various stages of delivery'. He noted recurring imagery in subjects' hallucinations, such as moving down tunnels, or feeling inexplicable bodily pressures and constraints, that suggested stages of the birth process, such as progress down the birth canal. In addition, some subjects told Grof that they quite explicitly relived their own births. (The psychiatrist R.D. Laing told Paul Devereux in 1967 that he had managed to recover his own pre-birth memories by means of a carefully administered programme of LSD sessions.) Grof also noted – as have other researchers – that many people in the profoundly altered states induced by the action of certain psychoactive drugs report inner experiences centring on contact with beings from other worlds or dimensions. (Grof went on to develop a powerful therapeutic model of altered states of consciousness based on the stages of what he terms the 'perinatal' process.) Lawson was additionally informed by other therapists that terminal patients on certain drug regimes 'commonly have spontaneous abduction fantasies'.

Lawson realized that recurring imagery in the alien abduction experience could be interpreted as symbolic in birth trauma terms. Abductees often reported being taken aboard a craft by means of a tube of light, a 'tractor beam', and of moving through doorways and passages on board the craft. They would find themselves in womb-like rooms and would undergo painful medical examinations,

An artist's impression of a 'gray' or alien based on witness descriptions. This is the current 'standard form' of how an extra-terrestrial is supposed to look. *Debbie Lee/Fortean Picture Library*

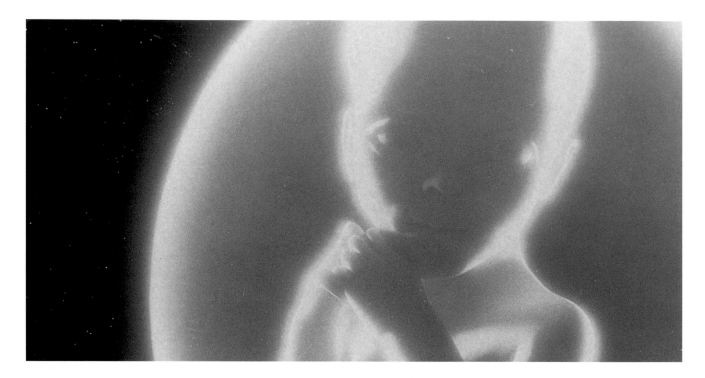

The 'cosmic foetus' in Stanley Kubrick's trailblazing 1968 film, *2001: A Space Odyssey. MGM (courtesy Kobal)*

often with emphasis on the navel and urogenital areas, and experience unpleasant odours and tastes and suffer breathing difficulties, as well as feeling subject to physical pressure. In 1982, Lawson summed it up like this:

> UFO 'abductees' unconsciously use major components of the birth process as a matrix for a fantasized abduction experience.... the foetus, taken from warmth and comfort and subjected to prolonged distress in the birth 'tunnel', emerges into a strange world with bright lights, unconfined spaces, 'entities', an 'examination', and various sensory stimuli. Similarly, 'abductees' are levitated through a tunnel of light into a UFO's vast, brilliant interior where alien creatures examine and probe their bodies, often painfully.

According to Lawson, the universal experience of birth accounted for the similarity of descriptions in abduction reports – the factor that so baffled Bullard. Lawson identified the craft itself, the flying saucer, as an image of the placenta, which is a circular, inverted bowl-shaped organ connected to the embryo by the umbilical cord. He was able to show that this placenta/umbilical archetype appeared in both Eastern and Western religious imagery as celestial placenta-shapes with descending tubes. Hildegard of Bingen's twelfth-century image of an airborne form with a descending tube connecting with a mother's navel, for instance, was supposed to show how the soul enters the human foetus. The Immaculate Conception is often shown as a celestial tube, a beam of light, reaching down to the Virgin Mary, and in at least one Renaissance painting of this, there is actually a saucer-like image shown in the sky. Lawson also felt that memory of forceps delivery was indicated in some abduction reports where abductees described being picked up by clamps instead of a tractor beam, or of having clamp-like objects attached to them while undergoing the examination on board.

Dennis Stacy has more recently put forward a variant foetus hypothesis. He suggests that for abduction, read abortion: the abduction experience is really a memory of abortion. He considers that parallels between abductions and abortions on both a physical and emotional level 'are simply too numerous and tempting to overlook'. It is undoubtedly true that a major theme within the abduction scenario is the idea that the aliens are cross-fertilizing with humans, producing hybrid human-alien offspring that are being incubated and raised off-Earth. Many female abductees consider they were impregnated by the aliens and their unborn child later taken from their wombs. There are numerous abduction accounts, both female and male, of what are effectively rapes or forcible seductions. A variant in male cases is that semen samples are taken. Stacy comments that in abortion we lose our own DNA – it is our own future selves that are flushed or vacuumed away. To Stacy, the grays are 'psychic projections, an imaginal caricature of a foetus'. The alien is the avenging spectre of the unborn dead, an ageless, sexless hybrid creature, gazing accusingly at us with its dark, penetrating eyes from across the void.

¤ WHAT BIG EYES YOU HAVE...

And it is those great dark, glistening eyes that are the most powerful feature of the gray. Abductees are terrified by the intense alien gaze, which commands, penetrates, and is often the outward sign of telepathic contact.

Like most of the key images and themes in the abduction scenario, the precedent for the large-eyed alien is again to be found in the prototypical Betty and Barney Hill case. Barney described (and drew) the alien entities as having long, 'wraparound' eyes. He first revealed this during a hypnosis session dated 22 February 1964. Martin Kottmeyer has discovered that only 12 days before that session, a science fiction film called *The Bellero Shield* was broadcast on the TV series *The Outer Limits*. Wraparound eyes are an extreme rarity in earlier science fiction films, Kottmeyer notes, and the only example he knows of is in... *The Ballero Shield*. 'If the identification is admitted, the commonness of wraparound eyes in the abduction literature falls to cultural forces,' Kottmeyer comments tellingly (*Magonia* No 35).

But the eye is so fundamental to human psychology that the dominance of such a feature in the image of the alien probably hints at deeper sources than mere cultural precedent. The eye is the window on the soul, and the soul is the unfathomable alien we harbour within ourselves. The eye has been the image of God, another unknowable alien being, from remote antiquity – we can think of ancient Egypt's Eye of Horus, for example. The 'divine eye' is a universal motif in mythology.

Above all else, the eye is the most powerful channel of human communication. A glance can signal authority, anger or love. Eye-to-eye contact is considered the most direct and unhindered form of communication. And it goes deep. When a mother talks to her baby, it watches her eyes, not her lips. And a mask showing just two eyes and the basic form of a nose can cause an infant to smile – it is the eyes causing the reaction.

Princeton psychologist Julian Jaynes refers to what he calls the 'eye index'. On the normal human face, the globe of the eye is about 10 per cent of the height of the head. But in the statues and idols of antiquity, from Mexico to the Euphrates, there are 'eye gods' and 'eye goddesses', many looking incredibly like the 'ET' of modern invention, in which the eye index is 18 per cent or more: 'huge globular eyes hypnotically staring out of the unrecorded past of 5000 years ago with defiant authority'.

Jaynes has a controversial theory claiming that up until a few thousand years ago, the human mind was bicameral: that is, the left and right halves of the brain operated in more separate ways than the integrated manner we experience today. In the bicameral age of consciousness, he proposes, people heard 'voices' that originated in the right brain. This was how that hemisphere communicated with the left brain. As with unmedicated schizophrenics today, these voices could carry great authority, and seem to come from points in the environment. To the ancients, they were the voices of the gods. Jaynes has proposed that bicameral societies had highly organized systems of auditory hallucination, of which the eye idols were an integral part (In earlier societies still, the skulls of the ancestors played the same role.) They were the points in space where inner voices were culturally recognized to be located. Their giant eyes, sometimes fitted with glistening, hypnotic gems, commanded and held the people rapt, as their half-open mouths uttered their orders or oracular pronouncements. The idols were the concretization of the hallucinating mind.

Has the gray become the large-eyed idol of our times? If so, we need to ask what it is that gazes at us so intensely out of the depths of the psyche. Is the alien a foetal image of ourselves? Or is the abduction experience a psychodrama performed by the increasingly estranged soul of modern humanity? If so, what is it trying to tell us?

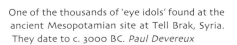

One of the thousands of 'eye idols' found at the ancient Mesopotamian site at Tell Brak, Syria. They date to c. 3000 BC. *Paul Devereux*

Out of the Shadows

CONSPIRACY AND PARANOIA IN UFOLOGY

IN THE SUMMER of 1996, a message from an individual known only as 'Branton' was posted on the Skywatch International List on the Internet. Part of it read:

I've had 'altered state' contacts with the humans who live within the underground system, those who I refer to as the 'Melchizedeks'. These are members of a metaphysical lodge with connections to the deep initiatory levels of Mormonism, Masonry, the Mt Shasta/Agharti network, Mayans, Sirius, Arcturus, Saturn, etc. They had formerly maintained cautious territorial treaties with the branch of grays/reptiloids that are native to the underground levels, and the reptiloids took advantage of this agreement in order to infiltrate their society.

Between 1979 when the Dulce and Groom wars broke out leading to the takeover of 'our' joint operational bases and 1989 when the reptiloids/grays took control of the Alternative-3 bases on Luna and Mars, several of the Melchizedek bases were also attacked as the reptiloids/grays turned on these native subterran residents.

During the two-year period when the executive branch of our government broke relations with the Grays following the Dulce-Groom wars, the intelligence community split into two factions: the American-Navy backed COM-12 agency which no longer desires interaction with the Grays, but seeks to maintain contact with the Pleiadeans instead and is fighting to preserve Constitutional government; and the Bavarian-CIA backed AQUARIUS agency which seeks to maintain contact with the Grays, etc in that they are depending on their mind control technology, abductions and implants to impose a joint human-alien fascist 'New World Order' dictatorship.

Between the Archuleta Mesa of New Mexico (the main headquarters of the malevolent reptiloid forces) and Death Valley in California (below which lies the main headquarters for the benevolent humanoid forces) there are several bases where things are 'out of control'. These consist of huge cavern systems linked together via artificial tunnels... with main 'bases' below Deep Springs, CA; Mercury, NV; Dougway SW of and Granite Mt SE of Salt Lake City; Page, AZ; Creede and also the Denver International Airport in Colorado, etc.

Many of the uninitiated reading the post must have wondered what this bizarre and (quite literally) labyrinthine saga was all about, where it came from, and what possible evidence there could be to support it. Surprisingly, it is regarded by a substantial body of UFO devotees as not entirely low-rent science fiction, and is even underwritten by a few ufologists who retain the respect of their peers. This epic myth is the latest, and still evolving, version of a series of only slightly less extraordinary claims that began to circulate in the early 1980s. It represents the latest of a welter of beliefs, which are as old as ufology itself, in a concerted, ubiquitous and sinister cover-up of the truth about flying saucers. It alleges not only a fundamental challenge to Western ideas of liberties and constitutional government, but a threat to all humanity. 'Branton' continued:

> *The benevolent humanoid Federation forces involved are from the Andromeda and Pleiades constellations, and also Tau Ceti, Vega Lyra, Procyon, Wolf 424, Alpha Centauri, etc. The malevolent reptiloid Empire forces are from Draconis and Orion, and also Epsilon Bootes, Zeta Reticuli II, Capella, Polaris, etc.*
>
> *Both sides have more or less been at a state of war or truce for centuries. However in recent years the 'war' has been escalating, and has raged more or less through Arcturus, Bernards Star, Altair Aquilla, Aldebaran, and especially Sirius-B where Pleiadean humanoids, Draconian reptiloids and joint 'collaboration' forces are currently at war. The epicentre of this war is now gravitating to the*

An alien spacecraft, known to aficionados of UFO lore as the 'sports model' form Area 51 S-4, peeps out of a hangar at the US Air Force base at Aviano, Italy. This is black-and-white proof that the US government is in league with aliens. Or is it? The picture is a digital combination of real and artificial images that demonstrates how easy computer technology has made the work of jokers and hoaxers. *Rob Irving*

> *Sol system where the Draco-Orion forces are using Nemesis (a 'Dark Star' beyond our system in the direction of Orion yet closer than Alpha Centauri, a protostar which was not quite large enough to ignite into a star and instead became a nearly invisible frozen planet about the size of Jupiter). Nemesis has been sending planetoids to earth's vicinity*

which are actually hollowed carriers which have served as staging bases for the Grays' abduction, implantation, mind control programming, mutilation, and infiltration agendas in collaboration with a network of secret Bavarian-based societies. These planetoids have been here since at least 1953 when two of them took up geosynchronous orbits around earth simultaneously, which led to the CIA's contacts with the Grays and the subsequent landing at Muroc-Edwards AFB in 1954 and the resulting GREADA54 treaty.

To see how this myth arose, we have to go back to the beginnings of the conspiracy/cover-up allegations in ufology. But we may note before we begin that there are at least three other conspiratorial scenarios on the loose in American ufology, and they are promoted by people whom no other American prominent in the field seems to regard as unusually eccentric. This should be an insight into the condition of the subject in the US. As we shall also see, things are rather different in Europe.

¤ SAUCERS FULL OF SECRETS

The grandfather of conspiracy theories in ufology was Donald Keyhoe (see Chapter 2). On 10 May 1949, over lunch in New York, the editor of *True* magazine, Ken W. Purdy, suggested to Keyhoe that the USAF was trying to manipulate public opinion about flying saucers. First, there had been massive secrecy about the Air Force's investigation of the phenomenon. This was known to the public – including Keyhoe – as 'Project Saucer'. Its classified name was Project Sign, until late February 1949, when it changed to Project Grudge in the wake of Sign's unacceptable suggestion that flying saucers were from outer space. With the new regime

Donald Keyhoe's third book, published in 1955, which elaborated in characteristic, breathless first-person narrative on his entirely imaginary version of struggles within the USAF between a mythical 'silence group' anxious to maintain a cover-up, and the 'censor-fighters' intent on bringing the truth about UFOs to the public.
Fortean Picture Library

came a more open attitude to public relations.

At the end of April that year, Grudge issued a long report on its findings which, while admitting not all sightings had been 'solved', generally came down on the side of misperceptions of stars, planets, balloons and aircraft as the explanation for what people saw as 'flying saucers'. A few days later the first of two articles by Sidney Shallett on UFOs appeared in the *Saturday Evening Post*. Shallett had had Grudge's co-operation in preparing the pieces. The first concluded: '...if there is a scrap of bona fide evidence to support the notion that our inventive geniuses or any potential enemy, on this or any other planet, is spewing saucers over America, the Air Force has been unable to locate it.' In his second article, Shallett described how he had persuaded a pilot to chase a weather balloon. The pilot reported that (to his own surprise) the balloon appeared to behave just like a flying saucer. Shallett used his finding to confirm the Air Force interpretation of a 'classic' case – the pursuit by Lieutenant George Gorman of a particularly elusive UFO at night over Fargo, North Dakota, on 1 October 1948, which was eventually identified as a lighted weather balloon.

To Purdy and Keyhoe, the USAF's new openness and the Shallett articles reeked of what today would be called 'disinformation'. In historian Curtis Peebles' words, they assumed from the start that 'any statement or explanation by the Air Force was deception and trickery. Every comment, every action, every rumour was fitted into this pre-existing belief.' To this presumption, Purdy added the suggestion that the saucers were 'interplanetary'. Then it dawned on Keyhoe: *this* explained the secrecy, and the gradual release of information. Keyhoe's own article (and his ensuing books) were, he was soon convinced, part of this strategy. The public would be *slowly* acclimatized to the saucers and their extra-terrestrial nature, so that when the official revelation came there would be no mass panic – as there had been, for example, in 1938 when many believed that the docu-drama radio presentation of H.G. Wells' *War of the Worlds* was announcing a real invasion from space (see Chapter 3). Such a disclosure, Keyhoe was the first of many to say, might be imminent. These simple ideas were to fuel Keyhoe for the rest of his ufological life, and they are still common currency in ufology today.

True published Keyhoe's article just after Christmas 1949. By June 1950 Keyhoe had elaborated it and had it published as a book, *The Flying Saucers Are Real*. The immediate appeal to Americans of Keyhoe's thesis may have its roots in many complex social and psychological factors: we would note particularly the generalized fear of invasion and surprise nuclear attack by Soviet Russia; the outbreak of war in Korea on 25 June 1950; and (on the same day) the first of many allegations that the US government was riddled with communists, made by the junior Senator from Wisconsin, Joseph R. McCarthy. The staying power and development of cover-up and conspiracy theories in ufology do, however, owe something to the USAF.

The USAF harboured the world's first ufologists, and by the time it closed Blue Book in 1969 (see Chapter 7) it had spent more time, money and resources on investigating saucer sightings than any other body in the world. But it did most of its work well away from the public gaze, issuing debunking reports that were sometimes taciturn to the point of arrogance. Inevitably – and especially in the climate fostered by Keyhoe, whose books sold in hundreds of thousands – this fostered the belief that the USAF had something to hide. Ironically, in 1953 the CIA-sponsored Robertson panel had recommended in a report – itself needlessly kept secret – that:

> ...the national security agencies take immediate steps to strip the Unidentified Flying Objects of the special status they have been given and the aura of mystery they have unfortunately acquired....
>
> We suggest that these aims may be achieved by an integrated programme designed to reassure the public of the total lack of evidence of inimical forces behind the phenomena, to train personnel to recognize and reject false indications quickly and effectively, and to strengthen regular channels for the evaluation of and prompt reaction to true indications of hostile measures.

Little was done to implement the advice, so that – and even more ironically – it was to be none other than Edward Condon (himself alleged to be part of the cover-up) who put the case against official secrecy most trenchantly. And he wrote as a skeptic:

> It would have been wise at that time [1953, after the Robertson panel report] to have declassified all, or nearly all of the previous reports of investigations of flying saucer incidents such as those making up the bulk of the Project Grudge and Project Blue Book reports 1–12. ...Had responsible press, magazine writers, and scientists been called in and given the full story, or had a major presentation of the situation been arranged at a large scientific convention... they would have seen for themselves how small was the sum of evidence and in particular how

> totally lacking in positive support was the ETH idea. ...
>
> But secrecy was maintained. This opened the way for intensification of the 'aura of mystery' which was already impairing public confidence in the Department of Defense. Official secretiveness also fostered systematic sensationalized exploitation of the idea that a government conspiracy existed to conceal the truth.

This last was a pointed dig at Keyhoe, who had invented a whole raft of factions at work within the USAF's UFO projects, including a shadowy 'Silence Group' who were, of course, intent on suppressing the 'facts'.

¤ THE PLOT THICKENS

There were more elaborate notions than Keyhoe's doing the rounds. Leon Davidson, at one time a scientist at the government's Los Alamos laboratories, was convinced that UFOs were secret military machines; part of the cover-up involved distracting the public by creating outrageously incredible contactee claims. Davidson believed George Adamski had been duped by the CIA and, as if to back him up, Howard Menger once claimed that *his* contactee stories and films were all set up by the CIA (see Chapter 2). Adamski himself first claimed that his stories had been 'cleared' by the Air Force and the FBI and then, when they read him the riot act over that

Picture by contactee Howard Menger purporting to show a Venusian man with his craft (strikingly like that photographed by George Adamski years earlier) in the background, and a flying disc landing near a Moonbase. Menger told different stories at different times about his pictures: they were either the real thing, or were supplied to him by the CIA to spread 'disinformation' about UFOs and alien visitors to Earth. *Fortean Picture Library*

fiction, maintained they had tried to silence him.

Meanwhile, there were stories told by just plain folks about the sinister Men In Black (MIB). They would usually crop up (often in threes) on the doorsteps of people who had seen a UFO but not yet reported it to anyone, and tell them, with greater or lesser threats of violence, to keep quiet about their experience. How the MIB knew about the experience was never revealed. They gave every appearance of being government agents, but fixed in a 1940s or 1950s time-warp in dress and language. Even their cars were out of date, and usually vastly more expensive than G-men get issued. The MIB behaved so weirdly that it is difficult to resist the conclusion that they were apparitions of some kind, but ufologists have taken them to be either exactly what they said they were, or agents not of government but of the aliens themselves. Reports of MIB still surface occasionally, and there is currently available on the Internet a set of instructions for defending oneself against the MIB when they come to call. This sub-plot of the conspiracy legend is still alive and well.

Nonetheless, the obsession with cover-up and conspiracy faded from ufology for a while after Condon published his Report. Then, in 1974, the scope of the US Freedom of Information Act (FOIA) was extended to allow members of the public to obtain copies of government documents on all conceivable subjects. Ufologists fell on this new facility like tramps on a kipper, and have since extracted tens of thousands of pages of UFO-related documents from the archives of the USAF, the CIA, the FBI and other agencies and arms. Just as Donald Keyhoe's conspiratorial imaginings need to be seen in the light of the Cold War, ufologists' reactions to this flood of information in the 1970s become clearer in the light of contemporary events.

Between 1974 and 1975, President Richard Nixon resigned just in time to avoid impeachment over the Watergate scandal; the wars in South-east Asia ended in a Communist victory, and with it the last vestiges of the illusion that over 50,000 young Americans had died in a worthy cause; and a Senate investigation of the CIA revealed that for years the agency had indulged in a panoply of illegal activities that ranged from domestic surveillance to experiments in mind control. It became received opinion that government in the US was corrupt – a suspicion proclaimed until then only by incorrigible cynics and opponents of the Vietnam war. This was a sea-change in public perception, and ufologists were as susceptible to it as anyone else.

Discovering that, despite official denials, the USAF had been collecting UFO reports long after Blue Book closed, that the FBI had done the same since the 1940s, that the CIA had hundreds of pages of UFO documents and that yet more lodged in other agencies' archives, all prompted ufologists to cry 'cover-up!' with some considerable energy. This was merely the latest in a line of government deceits if, in ufologists' eyes, possibly the worst of the lot. The recent cases newly revealed under the FOIA were, on close inspection, susceptible to rational explanations, but most ufologists chose to regard them as mysterious. And, as before, the presumption was that if these accounts could be released, some larger and more sinister business lay unrevealed at some higher level of secrecy. Events were to solidify this belief.

¤ THE INVISIBLE PROOF

The most notorious UFO document to surface from FOIA requests was released in 1982 by the National Security Agency (NSA), whose task is to monitor electronic communications worldwide for their defence significance. A decade and a half later, one or two ufologists still like to wave this heavily censored paper about in public at every opportunity to 'prove' that there is a cover-up in operation. It is a top-secret affidavit that came to public view after a lawsuit brought by Citizens Against UFO Secrecy (CAUS) against the CIA under the FOIA revealed that there were UFO-related papers in the hands of the NSA. (That sentence contains six acronyms, which may be a record even in a UFO book.) The NSA refused to release them on security grounds. On appeal, the NSA allowed the judge to see this affidavit, but not the documents themselves – and he upheld the NSA's case. CAUS lost a further appeal, and the Supreme Court declined to review the case.

The affidavit was 582 lines long; on its first release, 412 of them had been censored. Eleven pages had been blacked out entirely. What was all the black ink hiding? The NSA produced a public affidavit as well as a secret one. Its description of the documents, and its reasons for not releasing them, boiled down to this:

The COMINT [communications intelligence] reports being withheld... are all based on intercepted foreign communications. The disclosure of these records would identify the communications that had been successfully intercepted and processed for intelligence purposes. No meaningful portion of any of the records could be segregated and released without identifying the communications underlying the communications intelligence report. ...Disclosing them would permit foreign intelligence officials to draw inferences [and] to take countermeasures... to defeat the capabilities of NSA's intelligence gathering techniques.

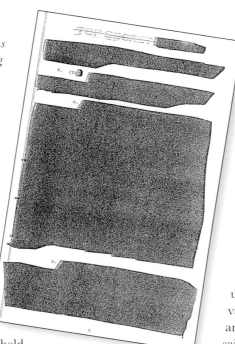

Top-secret document from the US National Security Agency, released to ufologists in the early 1980s. Under the black ink, said conspiracy theorists, lay startling facts about UFOs. Time was to prove them wrong again. *US National Archives*

True believers in the UFO cover-up such as Stanton Friedman and Timothy Good rarely, if ever, bothered to mention the NSA's straightforward explanation for its actions. Even among moderately skeptical ufologists, there was a nagging belief that the documents must hold some major secret about UFOs. Jenny Randles reasoned that the secret affidavit was censored 'not for reasons of NSA procedure but precisely because of the UFO content'. Unreconstructed ETHers believed the NSA would not release the documents because they prove there has been contact with aliens. Stanton Friedman refused to accept that the UFO material could not be segregated from the sources of the intelligence and echoed Jenny Randles' belief that the information NSA was hiding must therefore be about UFOs.

In a previous book, Peter Brookesmith offered a simple analogy to show the falsity of this leap of logic. Suppose the material was all about railroad locomotives. The CIA admits to an enquiring trainspotter that it has 57 documents mentioning steam trains but, backed by a federal judge and the Supreme Court, denies access to the papers. What possible security interest could be compromised by releasing files on a few obsolete locomotives? And the trainspotter insists that all he wants is the data on the trains. But even admitting it knows that a narrow-gauge 2–4–2 is rusting in a shed in the Pandemonian mountains could blow several CIA covers. It reveals that the CIA can see inside train sheds in Pandemonia. From that snippet of information foreign counterintelligence agents might be able, eventually, to deduce that the Pandemonian minister of transport, ostensibly a revolutionary zealot, is a CIA agent; or that its sister agency the NSA has satellites with X-ray vision; or someone has hacked into the ministry of transport's encrypted UHF communications system – the only place that antique train has received a mention in 30 years. Much investment by the CIA goes straight down

the tubes, and all without uttering a peep about how they obtained the information. Translate all this into ufological terms, and the NSA's mysterious stubbornness becomes entirely comprehensible.

Unlike other believers in a cover-up, ufologist Tom Deuley actually saw the relevant files when he was an NSA employee, and recommended continued denial. He has said they contained nothing of scientific interest, no indication of follow-up activities, and no evidence of NSA interest in UFOs as such. None of these arguments changed the minds of those who were already convinced that the NSA has more to hide than its own tradecraft.

Events were to bear out the accuracy of the analogy, and of Deuley's account. In January 1997, the veteran, much-abused UFO skeptic Philip J. Klass announced that he had succeeded in obtaining new releases of the secret NSA affidavit and copies of the documents originally requested by CAUS. Parts were still censored, but with good reason – for the documents were intercepts of messages from Soviet radar sites from 1958 to 1979. Their identities, and other clues to the NSA's eavesdropping capabilities, were blacked out. The biggest irony was that the much-vaunted UFOs mentioned in these reports were, in the NSA analysts' opinion, usually balloons – which the Soviets used to 'fly' by the height-finding radars to check their (and their operators') performance. Thus a typical report reads:

███████UNIDENTIFIED FLYING OBJECTS (UFO): (A) 0028–0325, FOUR UFO (PROBABLY BALLOONS) MOVED SLOWLY FROM SE OF ████ TOWARD SW AND PASSED ████. (B) 0325–0515, ONE UFO (PROBABLY A BALLOON) MOVED SLOWLY FROM ████ TOWARD WEST, PASSED ████ AND FADED ████. (C) 0325–0515, ONE UFO (PROBABLY A BALLOON) MOVED SLOWLY FROM NORTH OF ████ TOWARD WEST AND FADED ████. (D) 1355–1630, 19 UFO (PROBABLY

BALLOONS) MOVED FROM ███ AND ███ TOWARD WEST AND FADED ███ AND ███, ALT 69,000–79,000 FT. ███

The NSA was so fed up with being pestered by ufologists that after 1979 it stopped using the term 'UFO' to describe what were, in fact, unidentified flying objects, even if not flying saucers manned by aliens. Thus the day-to-day work of the agency could continue without irrelevant distraction. Nonetheless, some intriguing visual sightings crop up in the NSA papers. For example:

███ SIGHT THREE UNIDENTIFIED FLYING OBJECTS ███ AT 1915 ███, THREE LUMINOUS OBJECTS WERE SEEN IN THE WESTERN PART OF ███. THE FIRST OBJECT WAS SHAPED LIKE A HORSESHOE AND WAS WHITE IN COLOR. THE OTHER TWO WERE ROUND AND YELLOW IN COLOR. ███

Which just goes to prove that the Soviet military were as capable as anyone else of producing reports of lights in the sky that were as useless and uninformative as most of their kind.

¤ INTO THE DARKNESS

If so-called 'mainstream' ufologists can misread the attitude of security agencies so radically, it should amaze no one to learn that conspiracy theories in 'fringe' ufology inhabit a realm beyond the surreal. Somewhat more disturbing is the way it is becoming increasingly difficult to tell, in the 1990s, where mainstream ufology ends and the fringe begins. The major UFO organizations around the world rarely mention the startling assertions of 'Branton' and his cohorts (of whom more shortly), and, one presumes, their members remain more interested in UFO experiences and alleged hardware – accounts of sightings, abductions, crashed saucers – than in his kind of paranoia. But step outside the few thousand people and the relatively disciplined thinking that the established organizations represent, into the world of flying saucer magazines and the Internet, and it becomes apparent that vast numbers of people seem to be eager to lap up this kind of thing.

Known politely as the Darkside Hypothesis, the saga of warring tribes of aliens, underground alien bases throughout the US (some say the connecting tunnels stretch into South America and even beneath the Atlantic

to Europe), grisly experiments on humans and so on has its immediate roots in an apparent abduction reported by Ms Myra Hansen and investigated by Dr Leo Sprinkle in 1980. One of the unusual features of the victim's narrative that emerged under hypnosis was a journey by 'spacecraft' to a point in the New Mexico landscape. Here, she was taken into an underground base, where she managed to escape briefly from her captors. She found herself in a room full of what appeared to be water tanks, and was horrified to find they were vats in which were floating human body parts, including an arm with a hand attached to it. Witnessing the hypnotic session was Paul Bennewitz, a representative of APRO, who was also an electronics expert.

Bennewitz became convinced that the aliens had implanted some kind of communication device in Myra Hansen's head, which they were using to control her actions. He decided to intercept the aliens' signals to their victims, and then to try to jam them. From his home in Albuquerque, New Mexico, near Kirtland Air Force Base, Bennewitz seems to have picked up low-frequency radio signals. He believed they were 'alien' transmissions, but they appear to have been part of a secret military experiment. Thus, when Bennewitz presented his findings to the US Air Force Office of Special Investigations (AFOSI) at Kirtland, the Air Force decided to play along with him in the hope of discrediting his story and keeping the lid on their secret projects. Whether the stories Bennewitz began to tell came entirely from his imagination, or were partly fed to him by AFOSI, is not clear. It is certainly true that he suffered a mental collapse as the result of what he believed he had discovered through taking photographs and 'decoding' the 'alien' signals he monitored.

Bennewitz announced his findings in what he called *The Beta Report*. Here, edited for spelling and punctuation, are some of its main claims:

¤ *Constant reception of video from alien ship and underground base view-screen; typical alien, humanoid and at times apparent* homo sapiens.

¤ *Subsequent aerial and ground photographs revealed landing pylons, ships on the ground – entrances, beam weapons and apparent launch port – along with aliens on the ground in electrostatically supported vehicles; charging beam weapons, also apparently electrostatic.*

¤ *The computer communications and constant interaction with the alien in this manner without direct encounter has given a reasonably clear picture of the alien psychology, their logic and logic methods and their prime intent [which was to construct a race of humanoid hybrids – part human, part alien].*

¤   *The total alien basing area apparently contains several cultures (all under the designation 'Unity'), and is approximately 1¾ miles (3km) wide by 5 miles (8km) long and located in the middle of nowhere on the Jicarilla Indian reservation west of Dulce, New Mexico. Based on the number of ships presently in this area, the total alien population is estimated to be at least 2000 and most likely more.* [The heart of this base, Bennewitz alleged elsewhere, was over 3000ft (900m) below the surface of Archeluta Mesa near Dulce.]

¤   *Cattle mutilations – it appears that the humanoids are fed by a formula made from human or cattle material or both and they are made from the use of the female encounter victim's ovum. The resultant embryos are referred to by the alien as an 'organ'. Time of gestation appears to approximate one year.*

¤   *The aliens are picking up and 'cutting' (as the aliens call it) many people every night. Each implanted individual is apparently ready for the pull of their 'switch'. Whether all implants are totally effective I cannot predict, but conservatively I would estimate at least 300,000 people have been implanted in the US and at least two million worldwide.*

In the mid-1980s relatively few people knew about Bennewitz's startling assertions. But some time around 1987 his story reached John Lear, who among other things was an airline pilot with 14,000 hours logged in the air (some of them for the CIA), the holder of an impressive string of airspeed records, and a recently converted UFO buff of a distinctive order.

Lear met Bennewitz in August 1987, absorbed what he had to say, and applied it to a highly selective version of UFO history, including what was then the hottest news in ufology. That was the release by Timothy Good in the UK, and by Jaime Shandera, William Moore and Stanton Friedman in the US, of the Majestic-12 papers, which purported to be top-secret US government documents concerning the recovery of a crashed UFO and alien bodies from near Roswell, New Mexico, in the summer of 1947 (see Chapter 9). And then, on 29 December 1987, Lear posted a 4000-word document on the Internet – bypassing the critical scrutiny of more experienced ufologists but reaching a vast audience.

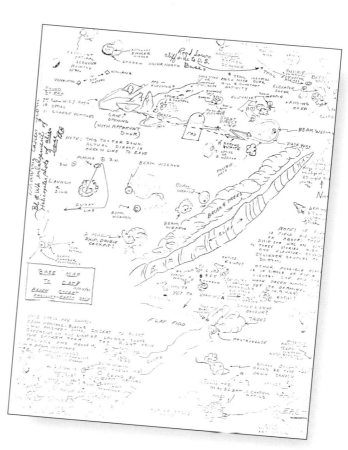

A drawing by Paul Bennewitz of alien bases, beam weapons and other exotica that he said he had discovered in New Mexico, and the official minute of his meeting with US Air Force officials to tell of his findings. *US National Archives; CUFOS*

¤ A FAUSTIAN PACT

The 'Lear Document' was an elaboration of the Bennewitz story, mingled with yet more rumour and hearsay and outright fantasy. The heart of the matter was this:

> During the period of 1969–1971, MJ-12 representing the US government made a deal with these creatures.... The 'deal' was that in exchange for 'technology' they would provide to us, we agreed to 'ignore' the abductions that were going on and suppress information on the cattle mutilations. The EBEs [Extra-terrestrial Biological Entities] assured MJ-12 that the abductions (usually lasting about 2 hours) were merely the ongoing monitoring of developing civilizations.

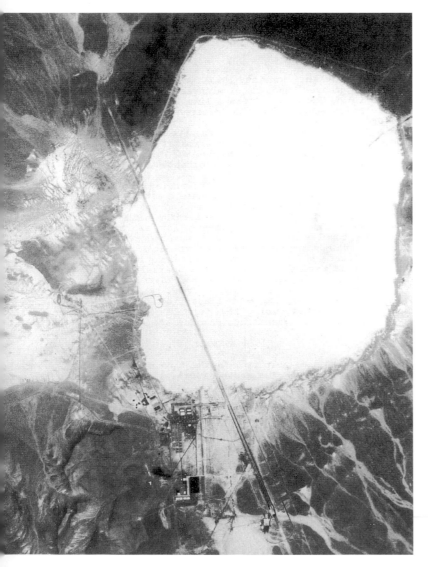

> In fact, the purposes for the abductions turned out to be:
> (1) The insertion of a 3mm spherical device through the nasal cavity of the abductee into the brain. The device is used for the biological monitoring, tracking, and control of the abductee.
> (2) Implementation of Posthypnotic Suggestion to carry out a specific activity during a specific time period, the actuation of which will occur within the next 2 to 5 years.
> (3) Termination of some people so that they could function as living sources for biological material and substances.
> (4) Termination of individuals who represent a threat to the continuation of their activity.
> (5) Effect genetic engineering experiments.
> (6) Impregnation of human females and early termination of pregnancies to secure the crossbreed infant.

Lear also claimed that 66 US Special Forces troopers were killed in a 1979 'altercation' at the Dulce laboratory, trying to free 'a number of our people trapped in the facility, who had become aware of what was really going on' and had apparently mutinied against their alien hosts. The best sources for his information that Lear could offer were a 'confidential informant' and Project Grudge/Blue Book *Report No 13*, an almost certainly non-existent (or at best faked) document that only two people in the world have ever claimed to have seen. One of them was Milton William Cooper who, when asked about *his* sources, tended to respond by accusing those who doubted his revelations of working for the CIA.

In Internet postings from early 1989, Cooper was to take over where Lear left off, and introduce new elements of his own into the farrago. In May 1989, Cooper published *The Secret Government*, which took the notion that 'MJ-12 has total control over everything' to its logical, if unlikely, conclusion: the group really ran the country, and in a fashion that made nonsense of everything that everyone took for granted about life, liberty and the pursuit of happiness. The core of his 'argument' is this:

> By secret Executive Memorandum, NSC 5410, Eisenhower... establish[ed] a permanent committee (not ad hoc) to be known as Majority Twelve (MJ12) to oversee and conduct all covert activities concerned with the alien question. ...Meetings are held by the 'Policy

Soviet satellite photograph of the Area 51/Groom Lake base. Some ufologists maintain, in the face of all evidence, that this is the entrance to a massive underground base beneath the desert floor.
Fortean Picture Library

Committee' when necessary on a Nuclear Submarine beneath the Polar Ice Cap. The secrecy is such that this was the only method which would ensure that the meetings would not be bugged...

Throughout our history the Aliens have manipulated and/or ruled the human race through various secret societies, religion, magic, witchcraft, and the occult.

The secret government, Cooper said, is in cahoots with the aliens and has a plan

to exploit the alien and conventional technology in order for a select few to leave the earth and establish colonies in outer space. I am not able to either confirm or deny the existence of 'Batch Consignments' of human slaves which would be used for manual labour in the effort as part of the plan. The Moon, codenamed 'Adam', would be the object of primary interest followed by the planet Mars, code named 'Eve'. As a delaying action, [the plan] included birth control, sterilization, and the introduction of deadly microbes to control or slow the growth of the Earth's population. AIDS is only ONE result of these plans.

There was much more, about the self-destruction of Earth 'by or shortly after the year 2000'; plant life flourishing on the 'dark side of the Moon'; an assertion that in the 1960s future US president George Bush established the international drugs trade as part of a scheme to encourage street violence, generate revulsion against guns and thereby disarm the American people; plus claims that one in every 40 people carries an alien implant, and that the US space programme is a gigantic hoax. Cooper maintains that when President Kennedy announced the plan to put a man on the Moon:

In fact a joint alien, United States, and Soviet Union base already existed on the Moon at the very moment Kennedy spoke the words. On 22 May 1962 a space probe landed on Mars and confirmed the existence of an environment which could support life. Not long afterward the construction of a colony on the planet Mars began in earnest. Today cities exist on Mars populated by specifically selected people from different cultures and occupations taken from all over the Earth. A public charade of antagonism between the Soviet Union and the United States has been maintained over all these years in order to fund projects in the name of National Defense when in fact we are the closest allies.

¤ FANTASY FEEDBACK LOOP

Naturally, someone had to be responsible for all this. Rather unimaginatively, Cooper chose the Jews to carry the can. In his book, he went so far as to reproduce the entire text of *The Protocols of the Elders of Zion*, a notorious document that pretends to reveal a hideous Jewish plot to dominate the world. It was exposed as a fake in the early 1920s, but was enormously popular in anti-Semitic circles in Russia and Germany before World War II. However, the accusation, mad as it is, is a good illustration of how ufology has essentially consisted of a limited number of ideas that rise and fall from fashion only to be resurrected in a fresh mutation after a few years. Cooper was only the latest in a line of unsavoury characters in ufology who have fastened on anti-Semitic mythology to 'explain' human inadequacy in the face of the aliens, or even in the face of life's irremediable difficulties.

George Hunt Williamson, a so-called 'psychic' channeller and long-time associate of George Adamski, wrote as early as 1953 of 'negative space intelligences' that were controlled by both evil aliens and the 'International Bankers' – like 'cosmopolitans', a code word among anti-Semites for the Jews. Said Williamson:

These secret world rulers will never allow official UFO announcements to be made to the public. If they did allow it, it would spoil their doom. If the technology of the space visitors is revealed it will immediately limit the need for... practically everything... that... keeps every family in America on a credit-buying spree....

Williamson also explained that the 'Silence Group' identified by Donald Keyhoe was an 'ancient, hideous conspiracy that is nothing but the spirit of the Antichrist'. This more or less completes the circle that links Williamson's batty splutterings with those of 'Branton', with whose epic, if derivative, ravings we opened this chapter. Apart from mistaking constellations of stars for star clusters – both have evil ufonauts coming to Earth from Orion, for example – and seeing a wicked Jew behind every one of the world's problems, the Darksiders produce nothing solid to back their ramblings. That, sadly, is to be expected. The grandest claims in ufology have never been backed by much solid evidence, yet have unfailingly drawn forth dedicated supporters from the rank and file, some of them highly educated.

But the consistency of the data is not really the issue here. What is revealed in the long link between George Hunt Williamson, George Adamski and the present-day

Darksiders is how much they have in common with the likes of George King, Ruth Norman, Gordon Creighton and Billy Meier (who has unashamedly anti-Semitic followers as well as his own apocalyptic vision) – see Chapter 7. Consciously or not, much of the structure of the conspiracy buffs' thinking derives unmistakably from the Christian tradition and the New Testament's book of Revelations – which is obscure enough to support almost any destructive belief. For many, if not most, ufologists of the late 1990s, UFOs and ufonauts were either demonic or harbingers of fundamental, revelatory and creative change. In either case, it was clear to those who nursed such ideas that existing terrestrial power structures would have every reason to silence those who had recognized the imminent advent of such cataclysmic events.

Presumptions of cover-up and conspiracy were ubiquitous in ufology in the 1990s, and their uncritical dissemination gave some faint glow of respectability to the ravings of the Darkside. Worse, in a different way, was the way the paranoid habit of thought made many otherwise rational ufologists assume that anyone outside whatever passes for 'serious' (that is, belief-driven) ufology is engaged in something called 'disinformation' – a nebulous concept somewhat elusive of definition.

One of the authors of this book has been subject to this treatment already. In a series of Internet postings in January 1997, a dedicated ETHer who objected to various interpretations of ufological history in one of Peter Brookesmith's books more or less openly accused the writer of being a 'disinformer' in the pay of some unnamed intelligence agency. The only 'evidence' offered to back this sensitive individual's suspicions was the seemingly expensive quality of the paper on which the offending volume was printed. There was no point in denying the accusation – a spook would, wouldn't he? Driving the whole rather fatuous episode seemed to be disbelief that skepticism could be an honest trade; any challenge to the dominant myths of ufology could issue only from a sinister arm of government – who alone, apparently, can afford decent paper for a popular book.

¤ SIGNS IN THE HEAVENS

A still more ludicrous instance of ufological paranoia surrounded the comet Hale-Bopp, discovered on 23 July 1995 by American astronomers Alan Hale of New Mexico and Thomas Bopp of Arizona. Various startling claims were made about the object: for example, that it 'changed course' from time to time (apparently because astronomers refined their calculations for its orbit), that it would collide with the Earth (its nearest approach was reckoned to be about 120 million miles/194 million km), or that NASA was suppressing its most recent photographs of Hale-Bopp taken through the Hubble space telescope (in fact, the comet was so near the Sun that Hubble could have been damaged by focusing on it). There was a rumble of suspicion and speculation across the Internet – surely the most efficient rumour-mill in history – that a 'cover-up' was under way. For debunking such claims, Alan Hale

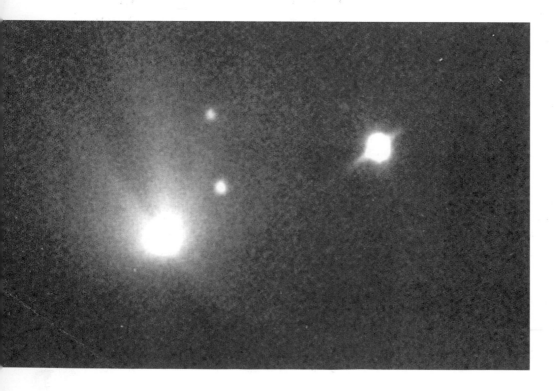

Comet Hale-Bopp (on the left) and an apparently Saturn-like 'mystery companion' digitally photographed through a telescope by amateur astronomer Chuck Shramer on 14 November 1996. In fact, the 'saturn-like object' is the star SAO 141894, which gained its odd appearance as the result of distortion in the optics of the telescope. There is no anomalous, planet-sized object near Comet Hale-Bopp. *Chuck Shramer*

was called an 'Earth traitor' by one Netsurfer. But what was being covered up?

Late in 1996, photographs of the comet appeared on the Web that purported to show an allegedly 'Earth-sized' object accompanying the comet (which itself is only 16 miles/25km in diameter). Some ufologists were reminded of the mythology of Branton, as well as earlier 'channelled' prophecies that a hollow sphere carrying 40 million reptilian aliens ('reptoids') from the constellation Draco was due to arrive in the solar system in 1996 or 1997. This had originally been predicted to turn up in 1986, but when it didn't materialize those in the know said, with straight faces, that the aliens had had to turn back for extra food supplies for the journey. None were better reminded than Dr Courtney Brown, a professor of political science, who maintained that a member of the Farsight Institute he owned in Atlanta, Georgia, had examined the object by 'scientific remote viewing' (a fancy name for clairvoyance) and found it to be a 'possibly sentient' space vehicle full of – sure enough – reptoids. Further, Brown placed on his Website a picture of the object and the comet that, he said, had been handed to him by a reputable astrophysicist, who would shortly be making a public announcement on the matter. No statement was forthcoming: it seems the distinguished scientist suddenly stopped returning phone calls. And, a day after the picture appeared on the Net, astronomer Oliver Hainaut of the University of Hawaii denounced it as a doctored version of a bona fide picture taken the previous September.

Meanwhile, the other 'mystery' objects in pictures of Hale-Bopp had been explained as artefacts of the digital cameras with which they had been taken. They were simply distorted images of known stars in the backdrop of the comet pictures. Confronted with the fraudulent nature of 'his' picture, Dr Brown told Michael Lindemann of CNI News:

> To tell the truth, we've been so thunderstruck. ...We're talking about [an astronomer that the 'remote viewer'] had taken courses with, a confidante and advisor – and you know, you don't get cheated by someone like that. We know for sure – we've caught people in the act – that our phone and fax are bugged. Someone is listening to our phones and found out who we were calling to get corroboration. ...Two days ago we were reminded, believe it or not, by one of our contacts, 'Get ready, you are in the middle of a disinformation campaign, a really big one.' And then we woke up this morning and heard this. Our contacts are really accurate.

So 'disinformation' – and all the shadowy controllers the word evokes – raised its ugly head again. But Dr Brown's crowning remark was surely this:

> Just because someone has created a fraudulent picture doesn't mean the actual thing doesn't exist. But this was done to discredit what we're doing, and it was done very cleverly, hooked in to a very impeccable source. ...And then what's going to happen is, the ETs are going to do something. See, this Hale-Bopp thing, it's not us. They were the ones who came, not us. ...This Hale-Bopp thing is here for a reason. And they're showing themselves for a reason. It's just a matter of time before something else happens. The remote viewing will be shown as correct.

The possibility that the mystery astronomer planted a fake picture on Dr Brown to test, perhaps even expose, his gullibility has never even been considered here. Instead, a conspiracy against 'the truth' is invoked, leaving intact Dr Brown's rooted belief in a vast spacecraft crammed with scaly aliens flying toward the millennium to save us or consume us.

¤ FOOLING SOME OF THE PEOPLE

'Disinformation' was once a useful term in ufology. It remains useful in counter-espionage, where the idea first arose. The strategy is simple enough: if your adversary suspects or knows that you have a particular plan in mind, you divert his attention from your real intentions by confirming his general impression but misleading him grossly as to details. A good example is the huge and entirely imaginary force that was stationed in eastern England before the D-Day invasion of France in World War II. It was replete with radio traffic, cardboard aircraft and pump-up rubber tanks, but commanded by an entirely real and suitably flamboyant US General, George Smith Patton III. This gigantic fiction persuaded the German Army to concentrate its forces well away from the beaches where the Allied landings in northern France would actually take place. The disinformation campaign worked because the Germans knew an invasion was inevitable: what they did not know were the all-important details of where and when, and they were cleverly misled on both points.

Ufologists, especially a vocal assortment of American ones, brandish the term 'disinformation' in the belief that 'the government' has deep secrets about UFOs and aliens from which it wants to distract the public's – and pesky

UFO researchers' – attention. That is the 'given' in the theorem that automatically brands a skeptic as a paid lackey of whomever is running the 'cover-up'. Paradoxically, almost anyone who comes out of the woodwork claiming to have a background in military intelligence and spouts the most outlandish nonsense about saucers and aliens, cattle mutilations and underground bases, is welcomed with open arms by this wing of ufology – although these whistleblowers might rationally be expected to be the very people best placed, and trained, to disseminate real disinformation. As things stand, everything that has so far come to light from documented, *bona fide* US government sources would suggest that the armed forces, CIA, NSA and related agencies have nothing of ufological interest to conceal and, insofar as they have concerned themselves with UFOs at all, have been as perplexed as anyone else by them. Archives in other countries reveal the same pattern.

However, the US and possibly other governments *may* have generated genuine disinformation on UFOs – but not to hide saucer wreckage, pickled aliens and nefarious dealings with extra-terrestrials. Rather, as William H. Spaulding suggested in his 'Federal Hypothesis' in the early 1980s, governments have occasionally let sightings of their own secret hardware, and of foreign hardware they would be embarrassed to admit had entered their airspace, take on the mantle of 'UFO' or 'flying saucer'.

The Soviet Union certainly seems to have been happy to encourage a UFO myth to grow up around the jellyfish-shaped trail of a rocket launched from the space centre at Plesetsk, Russia, in September 1977. It is also very possible that in early 1981, USAF security exploited some wild tales of UFOs being put about by US airmen based in Suffolk, England – some say in the hope of charming young ladies off their feet. Tracing the growth and spread of the stories, some of which may have been planted by US intelligence, would have provided extremely useful information about which airmen had loose tongues. As the USAF was then taking delivery of cruise missiles at several UK bases, this would have been more than an exercise in curiosity.

American ufologists have historically been highly resistant to such mundane explanations for their cherished mysteries, although Europeans seem to be more amenable to alternatives to the ETH and largely indifferent to claims of cover-up. The Spanish Air Force, for example, has opened all its UFO files to researchers, while the Belgian Air Force was anything but furtive in its handling of the famed 'triangles' that haunted the country in March 1990. From one point of view, these moves in themselves are a good indication that there are

no great government secrets lurking anywhere else. It does not make much sense for *one* government to hide evidence of any contact with ETs – especially not a crashed saucer. There is no reason to suppose the ETs would respect an Earthly nation's desire for secrecy. Therefore, the economical move would be to announce the ETs' presence as fast and as widely as possible, lest the ETs take sides with one's political adversaries.

Implicitly recognizing this, the thinking of the conspiracists leads inevitably to the allegation of an *international* conspiracy, for in their logic no news is bad news. Because no government will admit to ET contact, ruling elites *everywhere* must be in on the secret. As on no other issue, they are united in their determination to keep the truth about UFOs from the world's peoples. This itself is bereft of political sense, as such a situation would give any tinpot ruler the power to blackmail the rest of the world's leaders. But to the believers, the very absence of evidence thus becomes Exhibit A in the case for a cover-up, and the idea of a cover-up has naturally evolved into imaginings of a monstrous tentacular conspiracy of the powerful. The trouble with paranoia, as Jerome Clark has remarked, is that it explains *everything*.

¤ PLAGUES AND PARANOIA

These ufologists, and others more rational, seem to be unaware that in adopting this response to an intractable mystery they are following an age-old pattern. The social history of disease provides some remarkable parallels, and even more remarkably has recently become entangled in the UFO myth.

When the people of fourteenth-century Europe found themselves reeling before the onslaught of the Black Death (which they called the 'Great Dying'), their religion-drenched culture led them either to blame themselves and their sins for the catastrophe visited on them by a vengeful God, or to lash out at the Jews, strangers in their midst who in Christian thinking were also estranged from God. From there it was not difficult to believe Jewish people were devil-worshippers intent on destroying good Christians. Finicky questions as to how, exactly, anyone at all could possibly control and direct such an indiscriminate disease were brushed aside or ascribed to demonic, magical powers. (A favourite explanation was that Jews were poisoning the wells of Christians.) Countless innocents were murdered as a consequence of this kind of thinking, if 'thinking' it can be called, but it is alive and well in Darkside ufology.

One suspects sometimes that there is something in

European and American societies that fosters the invention of conspiracy theories and makes them attractive to otherwise rational people. When cholera raged throughout Europe in the nineteenth century, those at the bottom of the social heap inevitably suffered more from the effects of such crude defensive measures against the disease as quarantines and *cordons sanitaires* than did the rich. Resentment among the poor at rocketing food prices turned soon enough to a search for causes of the disease – for someone to blame. Rumours flourished that cholera was a sickness caused by a poison put about by the rich to rid themselves of a troublesome underclass. It has to be remembered that this was the era – the late 1840s and early 1850s – that saw half the nations in Europe seized by revolutionary fervour: 1848 saw uprisings and insurrections across the whole continent, as well as the first publication of Marx and Engels' *Communist Manifesto*. The conspiracy theories about cholera fastened onto a pre-existing social tension, just as those about ufology were to do over a century later.

The medical profession became the focus of the poor's discontent and fear of cholera. *Cordons sanitaires* and other measures designed to keep cholera out provoked riots in Russia and Hungary, where physicians, army officers, magistrates and nobles were killed. In Prussia, a rumour spread that physicians were being paid three silver thalers for every death from cholera among people under their care. Doctors were stoned in Paris, France. In India, cholera was said to be not a disease at all, but a campaign of poisoning rebellious subjects of British rule. In Britain itself, it was believed that doctors were using the disease as a cover to murder patients and sell their bodies for dissection in medical schools. As the epidemics retreated, so did the conspiracy theories, if not the state of mind that produced them.

The US and Europe in the 1980s and 1990s saw the rise of AIDS conspiracy theories. British doctor John Seale published an article in the *Journal* of the Royal Society of Medicine in 1985 which claimed that the US Army had concocted HIV out of genetic material from viruses causing bovine leukaemia, visna in sheep, lentiviruses from horses and goats, and human T-cell leukaemia/lymphocyte virus. The recipe had been cooked up at Fort Detrick, Maryland, in 1977. Lying behind Seale's thesis were two articles that appeared in the same year in *Literaturnaya Gazeta*, the journal of the Soviet Writer's Union, and told much the same story. According to Professor S. Drozdov of the Research Institute of Poliomyelitis and Encephalitis in Moscow, the CIA had let the virus loose by testing it on federal prisoners in the US and in the field in Africa.

By the late 1980s, the claim that AIDS was a product of biological warfare experiments in Africa had metamorphosed itself to haunt the imagination as home-grown folklore. By this time, the threat of the virus to heterosexuals was widely recognized, along with the disproportionate spread of AIDS among young black people – and among many African Americans the legend grew that AIDS was a genocidal attack on them. Stephen Thomas and Sandra Quinn, from the University of Maryland, polled black Americans in seven states between 1988 and 1990 on attitudes to the disease. Nearly 40 per cent of the black college students surveyed in Washington, DC, agreed with the statement: 'I believe there is some truth in reports that the AIDS virus was produced in a germ-warfare laboratory', while of a representative sample of black churchgoers, one in three agreed strongly with the statement: 'I believe AIDS is a form of genocide against the black race.'

In 1996, Dr Leonard G. Horowitz, a dental health expert and former faculty member of Tufts and Harvard Universities, published (at his own expense) a 592-page hardcover 'exposé' – *Emerging Viruses: AIDS & Ebola: Nature, Accident or Intentional?* – of the links between AIDS, the National Institutes of Health, US biological warfare research establishments and a list of several favourite targets of conspiracy addicts, such as the Rockefeller family, the CIA, the Council on Foreign Relations, the Alfred P. Sloan Foundation and the Nixon administrations of 1968–74. According to Dr Horowitz's book, AIDS researcher Dr Robert Gallo did not discover HIV in 1984, but had already invented it by 1971. The virus was deployed in Africa as a means of population control, and the whole plot was originally put together by Dr Henry Kissinger as early as 1969. Dr Horowitz also claims that 'the world's most feared and deadly viruses' – Marburg and Ebola – were likewise man-made, and 'share the dubious distinction of breaking out in or around areas of CIA/NATO operations' in Africa (where, incidentally, NATO does not operate), and were put to good use in diplomatic blackmail.

Circumstantial evidence and a powerful belief system can prove almost anything. Horowitz's 'critical examination' of 'the *New York Times* bestselling "non-fiction" book *The Hot Zone* by Richard Preston... reveals Preston's book is undoubtedly counterintelligence propaganda seemingly intended to prepare the world for future epidemics and additional virus outbreaks.' Horowitz says 'a final serendipitous discovery identified... Preston as the recipient of a $20,000 literary grant from the Sloan Foundation'. This fact, bar the actual sum involved, could be deduced by looking at the first few pages of the book.

¤ ALIENS AS DISEASE

Ebola and other haemorrhagic viruses have a later provenance according to Captain Joyce Riley, a former USAF flight nurse, but are nonetheless man-made. In a lecture in Houston, Texas, on 15 January 1996, she asked:

Have you been seeing anything in the newspaper about Dengue fever in South America, or about these 'strange' viral haemorrhagic diseases that are 'suddenly attacking us' from 'nowhere'? Guess what. They came out of the Gulf War! And, they are now calling it 'emerging viruses'. Haemorrhagic fever viruses are among the most dangerous biological agents known. The Ebola virus. You didn't hear about that before the Gulf War, did you?

Captain Riley blames haemorrhagic fevers and Gulf War Syndrome on an international cartel of drug companies who, she says, are deliberately wiping out the armed forces of the US and those of other members of the Desert Storm coalition. She does not explain why anyone should regard this as a good idea. As presented on one Website, her essay is laced with comments by Val Valerian (aka John Grace, an associate of William Cooper and John Lear), a sample of which illustrates how far-reaching, as well as far-fetched, current paranoia about the US government has become. Says Valerian/Grace:

The reason for the Gulf War, upon analysis, was three-fold. It was to infect the US military and subsequently the US and world population, and secondly to reacquire Kuwait oil fields, which are owned by a well-known family in London [This is code for HM Queen Elizabeth II, in conspiracy-speak], and thirdly to test weaponry on Iraq, to whom factions sold weapons to be used against our own troops. ...Do you understand, yet? Other reasons for securing the area involved control of vital earth grid points in Southern Iraq. Interestingly, there are also large underground facilities in the Middle East, some of them of rather ancient, and alien, origin, which still today contain high-tech equipment.

So here we have politics, the arms industry, the British monarchy, earth magic and mysticism, and aliens and UFOs all tangled together in one horrendous stew along with emergent viruses. As usual, no explanation is offered as to why whoever is supposedly behind this farrago of nonsense wants to infect 'the world population'. But the point of conspiracy theories is less to satisfy logic than to articulate and dramatize emotions – often ones, it would

appear, that the purveyors of these convoluted schemes are unaware of enduring.

None of these claims bears much relation to scientific facts or history. The earliest identified AIDS cases date back to 1959, when the concept of genetic coding was unknown. Reverse transcriptase was discovered in 1970, and retroviruses were discovered in people in 1978. But it was not until 1983 that the technique of polymerase chain reaction, which revolutionized research into and manipulation of DNA, was invented. Essentially, the cloning technology that the 'invention' of HIV requires did not exist in 1977, let alone in 1969. After the fall of the Berlin Wall in 1989, the Soviet Academy of Sciences apologized for suggesting AIDS was a deliberate invention, a move it admitted had been inspired by the KGB. The US State Department had already concluded as much, and believed the accusations were designed to discredit the US in developing countries. Of the haemorrhagic fevers, Ebola fever first emerged in Zaire in 1976, Lassa fever in Nigeria in 1969, and Marburg fever in Germany (although it originated in Uganda) in 1967 – all well before the biotechnology existed to engineer them into existence, and vastly in advance of Operation Desert Storm. Facts have never stood in the way of a good conspiracy theory, however.

Professors Dorothy Nelkin of New York University and Sander L. Gilman of Cornell University have pointed out that in this context, 'blaming' and conspiracy theories are 'a means to make mysterious and devastating diseases comprehensible and therefore possibly controllable'. (Dr Horowitz invokes the hope of redress by appealing to his readers to 'make a difference by contacting their congressional representatives' to demand appropriate investigations.) Even when plagues were deemed to be the work of a wrathful God, the ultimate cause was believed to be human wickedness which lay within human control. 'But diseases are never fully understood,' say Nelkin and Gilman and, despite our medical science, 'we still make moral judgments for misfortune. ... If responsibility can be fixed, perhaps something – discipline, prudence, isolation – can be done.' When confronted by incurable, invisible and potentially universal afflictions like AIDS:

These are situations where medical science has failed to serve as a source of definitive understanding and control, so people try to create their own order and to reduce their own sense of vulnerability. In effect, placing blame defines the normal, establishes the boundaries of healthy behaviour and appropriate social relationships, and distinguishes the observer from the cause of fear.

As the anti-Semitic outbreaks during the Great Dying illustrate, this does not mean that the perceptions of what is 'normal', 'healthy' or 'appropriate' are necessarily humane, urbane or morally defensible. Blame for disease is most often poured on those who are feared, powerful or, simply by being unconventional, a threat to social cohesion. Fear of intrusive, over-mighty and uncontrollable 'big government' and big business is clear enough in the outbursts of Dr Horowitz and Captain Riley, as it is in the rage of ufological conspiracists. It is hardly insignificant that Horowitz reserves his greatest venom for members of the Nixon administrations, whose betrayals of trust remain beyond all attempts at rehabilitation in the popular mind.

Sooner or later, conspiracy theorists from ufology, the 'patriot' movement and elsewhere were *bound* to conscript AIDS and emerging diseases to their cause. One can substitute the one word 'science' for 'medical science' in the passage quoted above and apply it to ufology without disturbing its truth. Scientists have largely ignored UFOs, especially since their skepticism was endorsed by the Condon Report, and so have goverments. In the eyes of believers, this has been a betrayal; and so scientists and governments are demonized, made part of the psychodrama in which 'the aliens', who seem so powerful, pose an uncontrollable and unfathomable threat to all that is ordered and peaceful – as if they were a kind of chronic, irremediable disease of the night skies. The aliens are also intrusive, according to the abduction scenario, coming upon you unawares, reading your mind and, like an incurable plague, able to defeat any protective measures you take against them.

The emergence of AIDS occurred at almost the same time as the popularity of abduction accounts and the birth, in the Bennewitz affair, of the latest rash of conspiracy theories in ufology.

Is this mere coincidence?

Sign for the one watering hole in the tiny town of Rachel, Nevada: 'Area 51' has become a tourist attraction as the UFO myth, once the concern of a few, has emerged into the public domain. *Fortean Picture Library*

Biting the Dust

CRASHED SAUCERS: UFOLOGY'S LAST STAND?

I
N 1947, THE reported finding of a crashed 'flying disc' in the desert near Roswell, New Mexico, was a two-day wonder. By 1997, that same supposed crash had spawned a major industry within and without ufology and had been the subject of argument for nearly two decades. Fifty years after the modern UFO was born, the abduction phenomenon and the Roswell incident (together with its various ramifications) were absorbing most of the energy of mainstream ufology, and therefore of the skeptics too.

In the years in which it has grown, the Roswell legend has both powered and been fuelled by the conspiracy beliefs that have been present in ufology since its inception. Without Roswell, and artefacts like the MJ-12 papers that are offered in its support, it seems unlikely that the more unhinged beliefs surveyed in Chapter 8 would have gained much currency. Without the revelations during the 1970s of irrefutably genuine conspiracies, machinations, intrigues and plain dishonesty in American government, intelligence and military circles, the claim that there had been a massive cover-up of alien contact would probably not have been seized upon as it was when the Roswell incident was revived in 1980.

As the 'evidence' that an alien spacecraft had crashed in 1947 has mounted in volume, if not validity, over the years since 1980, so has the boggle factor in the claims

Leased Wire

Associated Press

Roswell E

ROSWELL, NEW MEX

VOL 42 NUMBER ESTABLISHED 1888

Gen.RameyEmp

Lewis Pushes

Sheriff Wilcox Takes Leading Role in
Excitement Over Report 'Saucer' Found

Arrest 2,0
In Athens

of the conspiracy merchants. But in that time, ufology's general boggle threshold has been hiked, too. In both abduction and crashed-saucer lore, 'evidence' that mainstream ufologists would have rejected out of hand ten or 20 years previously has been accepted as fact. The same happened with stories that aliens were mutilating cattle – a legend that continued to grow despite being dismantled time and again by scrupulous investigators. As we have seen, at the apex of paranoia all three phenomena merged and connected in a cloud of factoids and fantasy. At a lower level, believers and researchers in the Roswell saga at least dressed up their arguments with a species of logic, but the reasoning was underwritten by a fundamentalist attachment to some variant of conspiracy theory, however mild. This led to logic being bent out of shape on many occasions to accommodate the train of assumptions brought to the subject: that there are extra-terrestrial saucers; that one, two, maybe even a dozen have crashed; and that the truth is being hidden from the people.

This chapter is devoted largely to observing this process at work. Without question, if just one of the crashed-saucer stories could be shown to be true, and the saucer shown to be extra-terrestrial, the ufologists' belief in the ETH would be vindicated. Equally plain is the

Two-day wonder: the original newspaper reports from the *Roswell Daily Record* of Tuesday 8 and Wednesday 9 July 1947. The full text of the report headlined 'Roswellians Have Differing Opinions On Flying Saucers' on 8 July is intriguing from today's perspective: not one of the citizens quoted thought flying saucers were from outer space. As late as 1950 Gallup reported that 92% of Americans thought UFOs were secret US aircraft, whereas only 5% thought they were extra-terrestrial and 3% thought they came from Russia. *Fortean Picture Library*

Reconstruction in the Roswell UFO Enigma Museum of the site where an alien spacecraft allegedly crashed somewhere in New Mexico in June or July 1947. In the 1990s, UFOs became big business in this quiet desert town. *Fortean Picture Library*

corollary: the more ufologists barricade themselves within the stockade of Roswell, the less credible will be their entire position when their little wooden fort is overrun.

¤ MAJIC IN THE MAILBOX

Some of the original Roswell newspaper accounts of the incident, which give all the necessary background, are reproduced in this chapter. At the time, the case seemed to be open one day and closed the next: end of story. For 30 or so years after Frank Scully's tales of downed saucers – his craft had soft landings – were published and debunked in the early 1950s, stories of crashed UFOs with dead or dying aliens scattered nearby surfaced from time to time and disappeared again.

The Roswell case lay virtually forgotten until nuclear physicist Stanton T. Friedman happened to be put in touch with the leading witness, Major Jesse Marcel, the intelligence officer at Roswell Army Air Field in 1947, who had a remarkable tale to tell. In a way, his story of the amazingly tough, lightweight, super-thin material found at the crash site rang true, just because he was making no unlikely claims about dead aliens. On the other hand, what Marcel said he found on Mac Brazel's ranch was hardly credible as the remains of a complete flying saucer. There was no sign of a power plant, crew,

control panels or anything else that could pass muster as an entire UFO.

Diligent research uncovered a secondhand story told of one Barney Barnett, a surveyor, who allegedly came upon the rest of the craft, and its crew, on the Plains of San Agustin, 200 miles (320km) north-west of Roswell. Barnett was joined by a group of archaeologists from the University of Pennsylvania shortly before a convoy of US Army vehicles roared up, shooed them away and cordoned off the area. This was the bare bones of the tale as recounted in Charles Berlitz and William L. Moore's *The Roswell Incident* (1980), for which Friedman had, without acknowledgement, done the bulk of the research.

In 1987, the Roswell story received a new boost with the release of the 'MJ-12' papers, which had actually first surfaced in 1984 and had been mentioned in hoaxed documents and ufological scuttlebut since 1980. On 11 December 1984, TV producer Jaime Shandera had received in the mail at his Burbank, California, home a double-wrapped, heavily sealed package containing un-developed 35mm film. Some time before this, Shandera had been approached by Roswell researcher William L. Moore, who believed he had made contact with a group of dissidents in USAF intelligence. This small circle – whom Moore later dubbed 'The Aviary' – allegedly wanted to make public the military's involvement with aliens and crashed saucers.

The film pictured two documents, one dated 18 November 1952, the other 24 September 1947. The first was a briefing document addressed to President-elect Dwight D. Eisenhower by Rear Admiral Roscoe H. Hillenkoetter. Each page was stamped TOP SECRET/MAJIC EYES ONLY. The second, an attach-ment to this, was perhaps more momentous. It purported to be a TOP SECRET memo – referred to as Special Classified Executive Order No 092447 in the briefing, but not so marked – signed by President Harry S Truman to Secretary of Defense James Forrestal. Interpreted in light of the briefing to Eisenhower, it authorized Forrestal, after due consultation with nuclear scientist Dr Vannevar Bush, to establish a board of suit-ably qualified persons to be answerable directly and only to the President, and to be known as 'Majestic 12'. Their job, the presidential briefing made clear, was to investi-gate a crashed saucer that had been recovered near Roswell, New Mexico, in July 1947.

The briefing for Eisenhower described the members and progress of the MJ-12 group since 1947. The MJ-12 panel consisted of 12 eminent scientists, engineers, mili-tary men and intelligence experts – some of whom, such

Harassed Rancher who Located 'Saucer' Sorry He Told About It

W. W. Brazel, 48, Lincoln county rancher living 30 miles south east of Corona, today told his story of finding what the army at first described as a flying disk, but the publicity which attended his find caused him to add that if he ever found anything else short of a bomb he sure wasn't going to say anything about it.

Brazel was brought here late yesterday by W. E. Whitmore, of radio station KGFL, had his picture taken and gave an interview to the Record and Jason Kellahin, sent here from the Albuquerque bureau of the Associated Press to cover the story. The picture he posed for was sent out over AP telephoto wire sending machine specially set up in the Record office by R. D. Adair, AP wire chief sent here from Albuquerque for the sole purpose of getting out his picture and that of sheriff George Wilcox, to whom Brazel originally gave the information of his find.

Brazel related that on June 14 he and an 8-year old son, Vernon were about 7 or 8 miles from the ranch house of the J. B. Foster ranch, which he operates, when they came upon a large area of bright wreckage made up on rubber strips, tinfoil, a rather tough paper and sticks.

At the time Brazel was in a hurry to get his round made and he did not pay much attention to it. But he did remark about what he had seen and on July 4 he, his wife, Vernon and a daughter Betty, age 14, went back to the spot and gathered up quite a bit of the debris.

The next day he first heard about the flying disks, and he wondered if what he had found might be the remnants of one of these.

Monday he came to town to sell some wool and while here he went to see sheriff George Wilcox and "whispered kinda confidential like" that he might have found a flying disk.

Wilcox got in touch with the Roswell Army Air Field and Maj. Jesse A. Marcel and a man in plain clothes accompanied him home, where they picked up the rest of the pieces of the "disk" and went to his home to try to reconstruct it.

According to Brazel they simply could not reconstruct it at all. They tried to make a kite out of it, but could not do that and could not find any way to put it back together so that it would fit.

Then Major Marcel brought it to Roswell and that was the last he heard of it until the story broke that he had found a flying disk.

Brazel said that he did not see it fall from the sky and did not see it before it was torn up, so he did not know the size or shape it might have been, but he thought it might have been about as large as a table top. The balloon which held it up, if that was how it worked, must have been about 12 feet long, he felt, measuring the distance by the size of the room in which he sat. The rubber was smoky gray in color and scattered over an area about 200 yards in diameter.

When the debris was gathered up the tinfoil, paper, tape, and sticks made a bundle about three feet long and 7 or 8 inches thick, while the rubber made a bundle about 18 or 20 inches long and about 8 inches thick. In all, he estimated, the entire lot would have weighed maybe five pounds.

There was no sign of any metal in the area which might have been used for an engine and no sign of any propellers of any kind, although at least one paper fin had been glued onto some of the tinfoil.

There were no words to be found anywhere on the instrument, although there were letters on some of the parts. Considerable scotch tape and some tape with flowers printed upon it had been used in the construction.

No strings or wire were to be found but there were some eyelets in the paper to indicate that some sort of attachment may have been used.

Brazel said that he had previously found two weather observation balloons on the ranch, but that what he found this time did not in any way resemble either of these.

"I am sure what I found was not any weather observation balloon," he said. "But if I find anything else, besides a bomb they are going to have a hard time getting me to say anything about it."

---

as Hillenkoetter, combined more than one of these roles. It even included Harvard astronomer Dr Donald Menzel, who in his public utterances was a ferocious opponent of any suggestion that UFOs were remotely real.

To scholars of UFO-related conspiracies, Hillenkoetter's involvement was hardly less fascinating. The Admiral had been the first Director of the CIA, which was also established in September 1947. He retired from the US Navy in June 1957, and soon afterwards joined the Board of Governors of Donald Keyhoe's NICAP, possibly the most influential UFO organization of the 1950s and 1960s. Conspiracy theorists have always maintained that Hillenkoetter was a fifth columnist of the first water; William Spaulding, for example, had made much of the heavy presence of ex-CIA members in NICAP's higher echelons. No ufologist has drawn the equally plausible alternative conspiratorial conclusion: that their presence turned NICAP into a disinformation funnel.

Shandera, Moore and Friedman made the MJ-12 papers public on 29 May 1987. They said they had spent the intervening two-and-a-half years trying to verify the documents, and released them only because British ufologist Timothy Good had announced that he, too, had

Rancher W. W. 'Mac' Brazel's account of how he found mysterious wreckage on his property on 14 June 1947. This key date is altered to early July in reconstructions of the Roswell incident, although Brazel had no reason to alter the truth. If the debris was indeed of a huge train of balloons belonging to the top-secret Project Mogul, as the USAF now suggests, it is not surprising he did not recognize it.
Fortean Picture Library

copies, and was about to publish them. The American researchers also told how cryptic postcards had suggested they look in a certain file in the National Archives: and there, in July 1985, Shandera claimed he found a memo to General Nathan Twining – head of Air Material Command, in which Project Blue Book was located, and an MJ-12 member, according to the 'briefing'. The note referred to a briefing by the MJ-12 panel during a National Security Council (NSC) meeting with President Eisenhower on 16 July 1954 and so appeared to corroborate the existence of MJ-12 and validate the papers sent to Shandera.

Moore, Shandera and Friedman soon claimed to have contacted a 'highly placed military intelligence operative' who could authenticate the story. But the 'highly placed' source turned out to be a lowly USAF sergeant – Richard

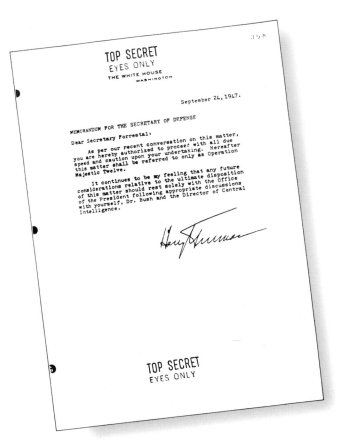

The notorious 'Majestic 12' documents that, if genuine, would prove that an alien craft did indeed crash in New Mexico in 1947. Although they have not conclusively been proved fraudulent, evidence and arguments against their authenticity far outweigh the case for their being genuine.

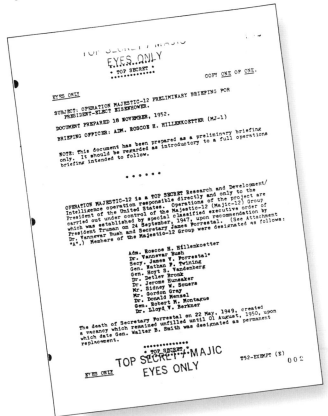

L. Doty, an Air Force Office of Special Investigations (AFOSI) agent who had been involved in the Bennewitz affair and had, allegedly, been instrumental in feeding Bennewitz much of the material that went into his accounts of strange goings-on in underground alien bases in New Mexico (see Chapter 8). In 1980, while at Kirtland AFB, New Mexico, Doty had been connected to an anonymous letter, full of fictions but based on an official UFO sighting report, and he had already passed a doctored (and fake, the USAF says) AFOSI document to Moore that referred to 'MJ Twelve'. Also, in April 1983 Doty had shown mute researcher and TV director Linda M. Howe a 'presidential briefing' (which president was not stated) on 'unidentified flying vehicles' that described at length 'extra-terrestrial biological entities' retrieved from crashed UFOs.

In the course of that meeting with Howe, Doty also mentioned MJ-12. 'MJ', according to him, stood for 'Majority'. The Twelve were a policy-making body in charge of contacts with extra-terrestrials and directing the cover-up. Doty then gave Howe the runaround for months on end, while promising her official footage of alien contacts and even a face-to-face interview with a live alien. In July 1986, Doty was removed from AFOSI for faking reports of contacts with Communist agents while stationed in West Germany. In October 1988, he left the Air Force; MJ-12, however, was now inextricably part of the Roswell saga.

¤ THE CRASH OF YOUR CHOICE

In 1991, Kevin D. Randle and Donald R. Schmitt published the results of their lengthy research into the events of June – or July – 1947, *UFO Crash at Roswell*. Randle and Schmitt dismissed the story that Barney Barnett had found a crashed saucer on the Plains of San Agustin. The Roswell UFO had crashed only a few miles from where it had shed debris onto the Brazel ranch, and was spotted from the air. Before the military could reach it overland, Barnett and the archaeology students stumbled upon it. There were only three decaying bodies. The awkward detail that Barnett's wife's diary put him near Pie Town, over 300 miles (480km) to the west, they ascribed to Barnett's submission to patriotic duty: even to his wife he was covering his tracks. They accepted Marcel's version of events. One of the 'star' witnesses in the book was former Brigadier General Arthur E. Exon USAF, who had heard of the research into the remains of the UFO and its alien crew while serving at Wright

Field as a Lieutenant Colonel in July 1947, and speculated at length about how this would have been organized and who would have been involved.

The next year, Stanton Friedman and his new co-author Don Berliner published *Crash at Corona*, which reasserted the authenticity of the MJ-12 papers and restated the argument that a UFO had fallen on the Plains of San Agustin on 2 July. The invention of the transistor, it was hinted, might have been one fruit of studying the wreckage. The authors produced a star witness who, with his family, had actually seen the downed saucer, the alien bodies, and the arrival of both the archaeologists and the military. Gerald Anderson, who was aged five when the crash occurred, particularly recalled a flame-haired officer and a black sergeant among the military, and put together an identikit picture of the leader of the archaeological team that matched the features of New Mexico historian Dr Winfred Buskirk. Anderson's powers of recall were acknowledged to be phenomenal.

In a further twist, Friedman and Berliner concluded that *two* saucers had crashed – after colliding in the sky. Altogether, eight alien bodies were recovered; one or two may have been alive. And Glenn Dennis, a mortician and Roswell's part-time ambulance driver, told how the airbase had requested child-sized, hermetically sealed caskets, how he had seen some of the saucer wreckage in the back of an Army ambulance, and had later been told much about the alien bodies by a nurse from the base hospital.

Randle and Schmitt returned to the fray in 1994 with *The Truth About the UFO Crash at Roswell*. By then, the writers were well known to be on less than cordial terms with Friedman and Berliner. Meanwhile, Karl T. Pflock had produced a revisionist history, *Roswell in Perspective*, which suggested that a then top-secret Mogul balloon array had landed on Brazel's field. *The Truth...* gave their 'rivals' short shrift. Randle and Schmitt now informed their readers that the UFO (just one) had crashed some 35 miles (55km) north of Roswell on 5 July. They now dismissed the Barnett story, which they had previously endorsed in part, as hearsay (it had always been that), and listed the forgeries, lies and evasions that Gerald Anderson's testimony had turned out to be. These included a fake diary, a doctored phone bill and shifts in his story that moved the site of his encounter with the UFO and the recovery team to at least three different locations. The identikit picture Anderson produced of Dr Buskirk was the result of having been taught by Buskirk at high school, ten years after the Roswell incident. Anderson at first denied having been to the school in

question, but he mysteriously appears in class photographs at the time Buskirk taught there.

However, Randle and Schmitt had found a new archaeological team, this one led by Dr Currey Holden. They wrote that 'there is no reason not to believe he had been there' at the crash site, although Holden's diaries powerfully suggested he had been in Texas the whole time, doing anything – such as attending a wedding – but archaeological work. A 'star witness' in *The Truth...* was one Jim Ragsdale, who with his girlfriend 'Trudy Truelove' had actually seen the UFO crash on the night of 2 July. Like Gerald Anderson, he soon began to alter and embellish his story, and by the end of 1995 Randle had repudiated him. He had also fallen out with his co-author Don Schmitt, who had misrepresented his qualifications and the nature of his employment. Another 'star' was Frank Kaufmann, who appeared in the book under different names. In his first incarnation he is presented as having been flown specially from Roswell AAF to White Sands Proving Grounds, to spend 24 hours gazing at a radar tracking a mysterious UFO – the one that crashed. So concerned not to miss anything was he, that an elaborate system of mirrors was set up to relay the radar image to the bathroom. Randle now says this was his own misinterpretation of Kauffman's account, but he has not explained why White Sands was so short of radar operators that Kaufmann – and Kaufmann alone – had to be flown there for an eye burning 24 hour shift.

The summer of 1995 saw the appearance of the first apparently solid evidence that aliens had been recovered from a crashed UFO in 1947 – about half-an-hour of shots from the autopsy of one of the ET corpses. According to Ray Santilli, the British entrepreneur who acquired the film, the man (known only as 'JB') who shot it was a military cameraman who had been flown especially from Washington, DC, to the crash site, where he had filmed wreckage and dead and dying aliens and later, in Dallas, the autopsy.

As we write, two more pieces of Roswellian evidence have emerged into the public eye. One is a video interview with 'JB', released by Santilli to Japanese television early in 1996. The other is a further MJ-12 document, a *Special Operations Manual (SOM)*, which details how alien crashed-saucer sites and wreckage should be managed. This, too, turned up unannounced in the mail, this time delivered to California UFO researcher Tim Cooper in 1992, and was made public by Stanton Friedman late in 1996. The MJ-12 *SOM* is dated April 1954 and, amid much bureaucratic language, requires that most of such

Brigadier General Roger M. Ramey, commander of US 8th Air Force, with wreckage from the Brazel ranch. Ramey has long been held responsible for initiating the immediate 'cover-up' of the Roswell incident. *Fortean Picture Library*

wreckage should be delivered to the facility at 'Area 51 S–4'. Area 51, part of the enormous military reservation around Nellis AFB in Nevada, had since the late 1980s been the focus of enormous ufological attention. Here, it was said, captured alien craft were 'reverse-engineered' to extract the secrets of their amazingly advanced technologies. Stealth technology, which made such aircraft as the USAF's F-117A fighter and B-2 bomber virtually invisible to radar, was alleged to have been developed from captured UFOs.

¤ MEMORIES ARE MADE OF… THAT

The Roswell evidence appears to be coherent and compelling – but only at a distance. Close inspection of its most important components has revealed flaw after flaw in the material, but the largest cracks are in the logic employed by proponents of a genuinely extraordinary event in summer 1947 in New Mexico.

All the Roswell researchers have made Major Jesse Marcel the cornerstone of their case. Marcel told ufologists that he had flown in bombers on combat missions during World War II as a waist gunner, a bombardier and a pilot. He had shot down five enemy aircraft, was awarded five Air Medals in consequence, and was shot down once himself. He said he had a bachelor's degree in physics from George Washington University, Washington, DC. His certainty about the high strangeness of the Roswell debris was based on his being 'acquainted with virtually every type of weather-observation or radar tracking device being used by either the civilians or the military'. Shortly after playing his part in the affair at Roswell, he was promoted Lieutenant Colonel, and in August 1949 was so highly regarded in intelligence circles that he 'wrote the very report President Truman read on the air declaring that Russia had exploded an atomic device'.

In December 1995, Robert Todd rather spoiled Marcel's pitch by publishing the results of an elementary piece of detective work that no other Roswell researcher had thought to undertake: he had examined Marcel's official service record. None of Marcel's claims stood up under scrutiny. His combat flying was limited to a passenger's job, as an observer for intelligence; and as such, for flying the required number of missions, he was awarded two Air Medals. He had no aircrew training or experience. Five kills as a gunner would have made him an official 'ace'. He was nothing of the sort: even his rating with small arms was dismal. He had no degree; he had no knowledge of radar tracking devices or weather balloons. As Todd pointed out, 'radar targets were a highly specialized piece of equipment unknown to most people except the relative handful... who used them'. Marcel's promotion to Lieutenant Colonel was in the reserve: it was never his active-service rank. There is absolutely no evidence that he was shot down in combat (like many other fantasists, he claimed to be the sole survivor of the incident), and none that he was even remotely involved in Truman's announcement of Soviet

A string of radar reflectors and other gear on a Mogul balloon array. The project launched aerial trains of all kinds of configurations, some stretching 600ft (183m) when in flight, and kept aloft by many balloons. These experiments were intended to discover the optimum design for a system that would drift at constant altitude in the upper atmosphere and detect Soviet nuclear tests. *Fortean Picture Library*

nuclear capability – which, as it happens, was not made on the radio.

Marcel's familiarity with meteorological equipment has always been taken for granted by ufologists, but researcher Jan Aldrich supported Todd's position in a Net posting in November 1996, based on his own long experience:

> *[Often] we find this idea put forth: the military people should have recognized a meteorological balloon. In my experience, 16 years as an Army meteorologist technician, this is not the case. The Field Artillery is the main consumer of the meteorological information. Yet we almost always caused a sensation when we moved into an area, everyone wanted to come over and see how weather data was gathered. I constantly had to explain how and why we operated. On my first tour in Korea, we took a lot of grief from the XO [Executive Officer] of the Air Defense. He was absolutely certain that the Rawin [RAdar/WINd] set we were operating interfered with his radar. A Rawin Set looks like a radar, but ours was a radio tracking device. Even when we showed him the [technical] manuals he was not convinced.*

Major Jesse Marcel, base intelligence officer at Roswell Army Air Field in 1947, with some of the wreckage found at Mac Brazel's ranch. Marcel insisted the material resisted attack by fire, knife and sledgehammer, but experts agree the fabric and spars in the picture are from a standard-issue weather balloon. This detail was not the least of Marcel's exaggerations. *Fortean Picture Library*

'Clearly Marcel had a problem with the truth,' Todd remarked with masterful self-control. This catalogue of Marcel's lies and grossly misleading statements amounts to rather more than a vice common among veterans, which is to elevate one or two wartime incidents to heroic proportions. It is different in kind, because it is consistent and comprehensive in its distortions and untruths. It is a very long way from the tendency of many other combat veterans – to say little or nothing at all about their experiences, except among their peers.

Marcel's reliability is crucial to the extra-terrestrialists' case. Yet he aggrandized most aspects of his life, not just his war record, to the point of losing touch with reality. If he acted true to that form and exaggerated about the Roswell wreckage, what substance is left to the notion that something extraordinary fell to Earth in New Mexico in 1947?

Another key Roswell 'witness' is former mortician Glenn Dennis. He was 22 years old when 'Nurse X' told him about the alien bodies that had been brought into the Roswell AAF hospital. Some time around 4 July he had driven an airman, injured in a motorcycle accident, to the base. In a couple of old Army field ambulances outside the base hospital, he caught sight of some strange wreckage with marks that reminded him of Egyptian hieroglyphics. Stepping inside the hospital, he was confronted by a red-headed captain and black sergeant whom he'd never seen before – the same pair, one infers, that the discredited Gerald Anderson had encountered at 'his' (constantly shifting) crash site. The soldiers warned Dennis to say nothing about a crash or, threatened the captain, 'Somebody will be picking your bones out of the desert.' The sergeant responded: 'Sir, he would make better dog food.' At this point, Dennis's friend Nurse X – whom he later named as Naomi Maria Selff – came on the scene and saw Dennis hustled out of the hospital.

The next day, Lieutenant Selff made an appointment for lunch with Dennis. Over the meal, she described the dead aliens that she had seen. Two were hideously mangled, and stank with 'the most horrible, most gruesome smell'. A third, less mutilated, lay nearby. Two doctors, not from Roswell, asked her to take notes as they examined the remains. The creatures were small, with disproportionately large heads, 'very, very large' eyes 'set so far back you couldn't tell what they looked like'. There were four fingers on each hand and two canals in each ear. Their bones were 'flexible'.

Lieutenant Selff made drawings and notes for Dennis, which he kept at the funeral home where he worked. Unfortunately, he left them behind when he left there in 1962, and they were thrown away. In the days after they met, Dennis tried to contact Lieutenant Selff, but was told she had been transferred elsewhere. A few months later, a letter he sent her was returned marked 'Deceased'. Dennis discussed none of this with anyone except his father. Later, he was told she had died in an air crash.

Randle and Schmitt claimed that they had tried to track down both 'Nurse X' and the five nurses who appeared in the base's 1947 yearbook. Schmitt told journalist Paul McCarthy that:

since 1989 he and Randle... had scoured the planet up, down, and sideways for those nurses... to no avail. The suggestion: the government had wilfully purged the nurses from the record, and, possibly, the Earth, in its effort to hide the alien crash at Roswell. After all, the assumption went, dead women tell no tales.

McCarthy was given a name for Dennis's nurse by Randle, and then checked Randle's and Schmitt's research. He found that Randle had delegated the quest to Schmitt, who delegated it to two assistants, neither of whom had taken the elementary step of contacting the National Personnel Records Center in St Louis, Missouri. McCarthy did approach St Louis, and found 'in three days flat' what Randle and Schmitt had allegedly spent five years trying to unearth: the histories of the five nurses in the RAAF 1947 year book. Only one – Lieutenant Colonel Rosemary J. Brown – was still alive, and she told McCarthy that she had 'no sense of anything weird happening at all' in the summer of 1947. Of Dennis's 'Nurse X' there was no sign in the records, and Lieutenant Colonel Brown remembered nothing of her, although she did remember the other four 'year book' nurses.

There are other dubious elements in Dennis's account. It is unlikely that in 1947 the military would have threatened him, or any of the other self-proclaimed witnesses to events surrounding the alleged saucer crash. It is much more probable that they would have politely but firmly appealed to the witnesses' patriotism in requesting silence. It stretches belief that none of these peripheral 'witnesses' spoke to each other about what had happened, even if they never revealed anything to anyone else. It is quite implausible that in 1947 a black soldier would have spoken to any white man, about another, in the language Dennis reports. If anything, Dennis's black sergeant talks in the language of the Vietnam era, not the late 1940s. It is incredible that Dennis would have left potentially priceless documentation of an alien visitation at his workplace, and for so long that it was taken 'to the town dump'.

Perhaps the best – certainly the kindest – interpretation of how Dennis arrived at his account was offered him by researcher Karl Pflock, who released a letter he had written to Dennis on 6 January 1997. Some excerpts are given below.

[Glenn:...] I think you need to know my current views on the Roswell case in general and your story in particular. The

first is easy: based on my research and that of others, I'm as certain as it's possible to be without absolute proof that no flying saucer or saucers crashed in the general vicinity of Roswell or on the Plains of San Agustin in 1947. ...

The other part – your story – is, well, another story. ... Newspaper accounts and other material turned up by a military historian reveal that, during the summer of 1947, there was a [tuberculosis] epidemic among the dependent children living in base housing on Roswell Army Air Field. Apparently, Army authorities feared a panic among the civilian population and so kept the lid on the situation until months later. It seems likely to me the calls you got had to do with contingency plans should any of the kids on the base die. As you have related, your caller told you both times the army needed the information for future reference.

The bodies. I think they were from some sort of accident, probably a plane crash, which involved an intense fire, and which the army was concerned to keep quiet – or at least completely under military control until an investigation could be completed. Without revealing their connection to Roswell, UFOs, etc, a colleague of mine showed your sketches to an MD who is an expert in aircraft-crash trauma. The expert's first words were, 'What crash are these from?' He said they had all the earmarks of bodies subject to crash trauma and intense fire.

Records turned up by the military historian mentioned above and others show a fully loaded B-29 crashed on take-off from what was by then Walker Air Force Base in, if I recall correctly, 1949. I believe the plane clipped a water tower or some other structure and crashed inside the base perimeter. All 13 (?) aboard were killed and very badly burned. The Air Force goes bananas when such things happen, and rightly so. They clamp down a tight lid of secrecy and conduct a very careful investigation. ...

The nurse. ...There is no record (military or civilian) of and no one interviewed remembers anyone named anything like Naomi Selff or of a crash in which several nurses were killed. There is no record or reliable recollection of any abrupt transfer of any member of the base-hospital nursing staff or of any mysterious activity at the hospital – including an order for regular staff not to report for duty – in early July '47; this includes the recollections of the man who commanded the hospital at the time.

The simple truth is, no matter how efficient and far-reaching a group of cover-up conspirators might be, there is absolutely no way they could possibly have eliminated all record and recollection of 'Naomi'. ...So what do I think is the truth? When you were approached by Stan Friedman in 1989 in his usual fashion, with leading questions and set-up lines ('I'm investigating the 1947

crash of a flying saucer and the discovery of the bodies of its crew, and I've been told you were involved', etc) and his advance 'packet of information' about himself and what supposedly happened near Roswell (which we know from your interview with Friedman you read before the interview), I believe you got to thinking: 'Hmm. You know, there was that time I got into trouble at the base hospital, that time my friend who was a nurse there got so shook up... I wonder if it had anything to do with that?' Then you quite honestly told this to Friedman and, realizing you had nothing to back up the story, you decided to mention both 'the pediatrician' and [go into detail about] the nurse, giving a false name for the latter... because you and she had been a bit more than friends and you were married at the time. Why? Because if she were still alive, you wanted to protect her from scandal.

Since then, naturally, you spent a fair amount of time trying to recall more details and fill in the blanks. Through the fog of many years, unrelated events became part of the story and you recalled or thought you recalled many more 'interesting' details and made 'adjustments'

The model of a dead alien featured in the movie *Roswell*, and now on display at the International UFO Museum and Research Centre in Roswell. The museum is owned by former mortician Glenn Dennis, who says he was told about alien bodies retrieved from a crashed saucer by a nurse at Roswell Field. *Fortean Picture Library*

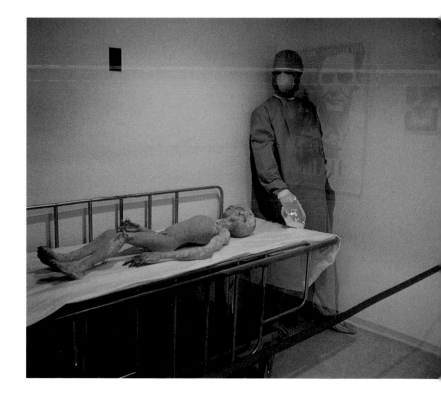

'to your story (like seeing the newspaper headline about the crashed saucer just hours after meeting with the nurse). As people began to question your story, you quite naturally tried to come up with people who could provide supporting testimony and, both consciously and unconsciously, embellished your story.

Glenn, I think you got into this whole business quite honestly, sincerely trying to help Friedman and others with their investigations. At some point, you probably began to realize what you recalled probably had nothing to do with a flying saucer crash, but you thought you were in too deep to say so. So you've just stuck with your story, always being careful to say you really have no idea what it was you got mixed up in, in 1947. What started out as an honest attempt to recall events you thought might be connected with a crashed flying saucer story got out of hand, grew into a tall tale, and became part of the Roswell myth, which now is more 'real' to thousands than the facts of the case.

'Glenn Dennis, ...by the way, is not the least bit upset with me. Ponder that for a while,' reported Pflock, a few weeks after communicating these thoughts to the now-retired mortician. Other Roswell 'witnesses' have very likely been through a similar process, and retrospectively reconstructed their memories with the utmost sincerity – and credibility – to those who believe there is something significant to remember in the first place.

¤ DEATH OF THE DOCUMENTS

The original MJ-12 papers have been savaged so many times by skeptics and ufologists alike (including Roswell specialist Kevin Randle) since their release that it would be tedious to rehearse here all the technical reasons why they fail to make the grade as bona fide government documents. But there is a scientific and forensic principle that bears repeating, which those claiming authenticity for the MJ-12 papers have never satisfied. It has been expressed most pithily by student of ufology Edward G. Stewart, directly to Stanton Friedman – who, outside the lunatic fringe, is now the only ufologist of any influence who retains any faith in MJ-12. Stewart turned a blistering sarcasm on Friedman's claim that he had established that astronomer Donald Menzel – an arch-skeptic toward UFOs in public life – was indeed a member of MJ-12 and that his findings about Menzel supported the reality of MJ-12. Referring to a comment from Jerome Clark, Stewart said the whole issue was a 'wild goose', and continued:

Notwithstanding were nuclear physicist Stanton T. Friedman's heroic and unprecedented personal efforts digging through the bowels of many, many, many archives... and uncovering, to an unsuspecting ufological community, that super-skeptic-astronomer, Director of the Harvard College Observatory and alleged MJ-12 staffer, Dr Donald H. Menzel, knew Japanese; knew a fellow Massachusettsian and a Harvard Alumni, Senator John F. Kennedy, by his first name 'Jack'; worked during WWII in the Navy as a cryptologist; continued to carry his association in that field as a consultant into what became the NSA; survived a loyalty hearing during the McCarthy era after fellow Massachusettsian, WWII buddy and alleged MJ-12 staffer, Dr Vannevar Bush, vouched for him; and after 'Jack' became President of the United States, hinted to 'Jack' that he wouldn't mind an appointment, as well as later tried to stick it to alleged MJ-12 staffer and non-Massachussettian, Dr Detlev W. Bronk, in the political 'buddy-buddy', Presidential appointments game. ...

All true, but none of the above has any direct linkage to establishing that the MJ-12 documents are real.

First, data by its nature is perceived by us interpretatively and interpretations are subject to error. So, how do we know what we know? We know what we know by multiple, independent, link-by-link, verified chains of evidence. That chain has to be unbroken from the premise all the way through the evidence that purports to substantiate the premise. All the links have to tie together from one end of the chain to the other end. One link is broken or missing and the premise is not validated.

As an example, suppose Mrs Menzel said that her husband used to utter in his sleep 'MJ-12, MJ-12', over and over again, but she didn't know what it meant? Or a note in Menzel's handwriting scribbled to himself that said 'must tell Jack about Bush/MJ-12' and found in his papers? Those would be direct links once authenticated through independent research to support that part of the chain that Menzel may have had something to do with MJ-12, but nothing such as that was found. ...

Also, since no agency has stepped forward and claimed the MJ-12 documents as their own, ownership has not been established. Ownership has also not been established at the front end. The source of the documents is anonymous. There is no genesis to the MJ-12 documents. The links are busted at both ends of the chain.

...After visiting fifteen archives, Stanton T. Friedman has not uncovered anything that establishes the genesis of the MJ-12 documents. And neither have the efforts of all other researchers that have attempted to find direct linkage to the claim that the MJ-12 documents are real.

...As you are so fond of saying: 'Absence of evidence is not evidence of absence'. Since the genesis/provenance of the MJ-12 documents has never been established, anyone with ample time to research an MJ-12 type scenario could have found out about the details and constructed a scenario around them. Not one detail provides a direct link to the authenticity of the MJ-12 documents or to the genesis of MJ-12. MJ-12 was floating around as rumour in the UFO grapevine for many years before Shandera received the rolls of anonymous film in his mailbox. Whoever felt motivated to, could have constructed MJ-12, whether it was an 'insider' or 'outsider', and had years to prepare and work bugs out of a working script.

Friedman was unable to refute these points, and ran into still more trouble over the purported MJ-12 *Special Operations Manual*, for research on which he was apparently seeking funds. As noted, the *SOM* made mention of the ufologically notorious Area 51. Peter Brookesmith was already aware from his reading in aerospace history that the Groom Lake Base in Area 51 had been developed no earlier than April 1955; before that it had been part of a USAF gunnery range. He also knew from prior acquaintance with both British and American military manuals that every new edition, and every change in a new version, is marked as such with soldier-proof clarity. The *SOM* was dated 1954, and it bore no sign of being a later revision. He soon discovered from aerospace archaeologist Peter W. Merlin that:

> *In declassified documents from the Atomic Energy Commision, the site is listed only as Watertown during the 1950s. Documents, beginning in 1960, refer to it as Area 51. It appears as Area 51 on official AEC, DoE, EPA, and USGS documents until at least 1977. The Nevada Test Site employee newsletter refers to the Area 51 sports teams and lists Area 51 phone numbers.*
>
> *The earliest official documentation I have yet found that uses the term 'Area 51' is dated June 1960. It is part of a set of fallout air sample data from the nuclear test programme. Specifically, it is a log sheet of measurements beginning on 1 June and ending on 1 July. Earlier log sheets, from July 1957 to December 1959 use the term 'Watertown.' On the June 1960 sheet, 'Watertown' is crossed out and replaced by 'Area 51.' It may be that when the June 1960 log sheet was begun (on 1 June) that it was still Watertown. Maybe the name changed during the month of June 1960. This would account for the change on the log sheet.*

Panoramic view of the Groom Lake Base in Area 51, Nevada. This site was first developed in 1955, for test flights of the U2 reconnaissance aircraft, and the surrounding area was first designated '51' in 1960. *Fortean Picture Library*

Ed Stewart performed a similar exercise and came up with matching, and more detailed, results. Stanton Friedman reacted to these rather conclusive discoveries with a mystifying objection:

> *Until we have access to the classified files, we cannot know the history of Area 51. Why is that so hard to understand? We are not talking about storage of apples and oranges, but of crashed saucer wreckage and alien bodies. The government has not admitted having either. Unclassified literature doesn't tell us about compartmented information. Proclamations are not the same as evidence.*

In the circumstances, the point seemed to his critics to be somewhat redundant. Ed Stewart responded patiently, and with steely exactitude:

> *What is clear from... the evidence presented is that there are clear unclassified open references to that area of Nevada that later became known as 'Area 51' that offer compelling evidence that the area in question was open territory, habitated by civilians and that there were no 'secret' facilities there prior to the U-2 programme which started in 1955. That makes your SOM bogus. Clear and simple. It is not an open question.*

A particularly piquant irony of Friedman's defence of the possible reality of the *SOM* was the reference to Area 51 'S–4'. The only person who had ever referred to an alleged S–4 compartment of Area 51 was Robert Lazar, who claimed to have worked there, investigating alien spacecraft. Friedman had been in the vanguard of those who had demolished Lazar's credibility and claims in excruciating detail. As Ed Stewart was to say, the MJ-12 affair was, by 1997, 'a sagging mystery'.

¤ THE CORPSE OF ROSWELL

The same difficulties faced those who promoted the authenticity of the 'alien autopsy' footage acquired, and energetically sold, by Ray Santilli. The initial skeptical attack – which was by no means mounted solely by 'traditional' UFO debunkers – on the sequence concentrated on dateable details such as the telephone that is visible in the autopsy room. It was eventually established that the phone was not an anachronism, but few remarked on the extreme unlikelihood that such a potentially dangerous microbe-gathering device would be in such a location in the first place.

British ufologists James Easton and Rob Irving independently addressed the problem of the alleged cameraman's journey from Washington, DC, to the crash site in New Mexico to make a record of the momentous events occurring there. 'Cameraman Jack', as he has become known, said in a statement:

I remember very clearly receiving the call to go to White Sands. ...I was ordered to a crash site just south-west of Socorro. It was urgent and my brief was to film everything in sight, not to leave the debris until it had been removed and I was to have access to all areas of the site.

He was told he was to film the wreckage of a Russian spy plane. In fact, he had no call to go anywhere near White Sands, but 'south-west of Socorro', New Mexico, which is never a short journey. This raises the question of why equally qualified people, with suitable security clearances, already in New Mexico at facilities at White Sands or Los Alamos or Albuquerque, were not given the job. But 'Jack' says:

I flew out from Andrews with 16 other officers and personnel, mostly medical. We arrived at Wright Patterson [then called Wright Field, in fact] and collected more men and equipment. From there we flew to Roswell on a C-54.

When we got to Roswell we were transported by road to the site. When we arrived the site had already been cordoned off.

This is not surprising. James Easton has noted all the likely stages of arranging such a journey:

- The crash has to be confirmed.
- The 'top brass' have to be notified.
- The cameraman and the SAC team have to be contacted.
- They have to collect all their equipment.
- They have to get to 'Andrews'.
- They fly from Andrews to Wright Field.
- They collect more men and equipment.
- They all fly on to Roswell.
- They have to unload all their equipment at Roswell.
- They have to reload all their equipment onto vehicles.
- They travel by road from Roswell to the crash site.

Andrews is about 400 miles (640km) from Wright Field as the crow flies, and from there it is about 1200 miles (1900km) to Roswell. The Douglas C-54 Skymaster had a maximum cruising speed of around 240mph (380km/h). Disregarding slower speeds for take-off, climb to cruising height, approach and landing, and assuming the plane was mechanically perfect, the team would have been in the air for at least 6 hours 40 minutes. The truck journey was at least another 180 miles (290km) to reach the main highway due south of Socorro. For the most part, even today, the road is a narrow, winding, two-lane blacktop that runs through two long mountainous stretches. To average 30mph (48km/h) on such a road in a US Army truck of the era would have been scorching the earth, and 20mph (32km/h) is probably nearer the mark. Then there was an unspecified distance on dirt roads or across country to the crash site itself – but already another ten hours or so have gone by.

So, it *is* surprising that when the cameraman arrived at the site, the craft, which 'it was plain to see... was no Russian spy plane', had 'heat still radiating from the ground around it' and 'nothing had been done as everyone was just waiting for orders'. Even more amazingly, it was decided to wait until the heat of the wreckage subsided before moving in 'as fire was a significant risk'. Even after so many hours? But then this was no ordinary craft. The inactivity was 'made all the worse by the screams of the freak creatures that were lying by the vehicle'.

They must have been screaming for about a day. But then they were aliens, not like us. Even granting the tiniest possibility that the film itself is genuine, on grounds of logic and logistics – and probably physics and biology too – the cameraman's story is clearly hokum. Yet only two of the world's thousands of ufologists have ever bothered to raise these fundamental questions about it.

Nevertheless, the film – or a video copy – exists. Mysterious to all was the cameraman's reported claim that the Pentagon somehow overlooked this historic record, which having been 'specially processed' at the time was never collected for viewing by the authorities. According to 'Jack':

The first two autopsies took place in July 1947. After filming I had several hundred reels. I separated problem reels which required special attention in processing. These I would do later. The first batch was sent through to Washington, and I processed the remainder a few days later. Once the remaining reels had been processed, I contacted Washington to arrange collection of the final batch. Incredibly, they never came to collect or arrange transportation for them. I called many times and then just gave up. The footage has remained with me ever since.

The rather thin excuse was offered that confusion arose in the change-over within the Air Force from being part of the US Army to becoming an independent service. Somehow, in the inevitable muddle, film of virtually the whole of an alien autopsy was strangely overlooked by *every one* of the military brass, scientists and politicians who would have been aware of it. Comment is superfluous.

Efforts to have the film stock dated ran into even worse difficulties. Santilli initially said that the film had been authenticated as genuine 1947 stock, but this was later revealed to be untrue. A few frames then supplied for testing turned out not to be from the autopsy sequence at all. At one point, Bob Shell, one of those who had offered to get the film tested, blamed Kodak for racking up their demands and strongly hinted that a conspiracy was afoot:

Kodak spokespersons have told others that they would test the film if brought to them, but when I have tried to do this they have backed out or changed the rules. Initially they said they only needed a tiny bit from one frame. When I informed them that I had film and would supply a frame, suddenly they needed a 20 inch strip. When it looked like I had gotten Volker [Spielberg, the keeper of the original stock] convinced to provide this, they suddenly wanted a 16 foot strip. It is my belief that Kodak has never been dealing with us in good faith on this issue.

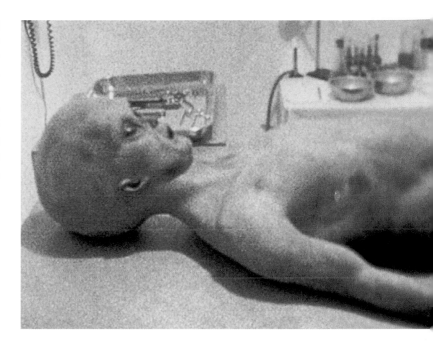

Shots from the 'alien autopsy' movie first aired in 1995. Dozens of theories have been offered to explain what the film 'really' is – but few, if any, ufologists have much faith in its being of a genuine alien.
Rob Irving

During September 1995, Tony Amato of Kodak was asked if he could clarify what had been specified for testing the film. He replied. 'We don't have a requirement. All we need is a few inches of film. ...It was Mr Shell that... suggested [he] provide an entire roll, therefore the roll would be authenticated.' As things stood at the beginning of 1997, no one outside Santilli's immediate circle had seen any of the original film or could even be sure that it existed. And were the film to be conclusively dated to 1947, there would still be no proof that the images on it were that old.

There were plenty of internal clues that the film was about as genuine as a Cornish £3 note. Model-makers from the special-effects industry testified that, to judge from the lie of its muscles, the 'alien' cadaver bore every sign of having been modelled from a standing figure, not one lying on its back (as the 'corpse' is in the film). It was striking that no sequence showed a scalpel digging into the skin of the alien, an act that tends to bloat a latex-covered model and reveal its artificiality. Apart from the initial incisions, the procedure seems to bear no relation to a standard autopsy. The pathologists work from no X-rays, and at remarkable speed. There seems to be only one cameraman, whose equipment is hand-held (and frequently out of focus), and no surgical artist – a strange arrangement for so important an event. And when it comes to the guts of the creature, they resemble nothing human, which raises interesting questions of evolution: at the least, it is a striking coincidence that the alien should so closely resemble an Earthly primate in exterior details, yet have such weird innards. Even the brain, when it flops out of the skull (whose trepanning is obscured from the camera), looks more like a liver than gray matter and, surprisingly, is apparently not attached to the skull, the spinal cord or the eyes.

The pathologists' cover-all suits are no less intriguing. A sharp eye can discern the top of the headgear moving up and down in time with the wearers' lungs. This clearly shows that, wherever the air was coming from, the suits were unpressurized. In that case, they were useless. What is known as a Biohazard Level 4 suit is kept under positive pressure, with air constantly blasting out of it to prevent microbes being wafted in. No breathing apparatus or airline is actually visible. About the only statement worth quoting from the interview with the alleged cameraman, shown on Japanese TV in January 1997, addresses this question rather clumsily: 'The protective suits made my job very difficult,' complains 'Jack'. 'Also the air feeds into the feet on those things and the surgeons were always getting in the way, but I expected that.' The idea that such a suit would have an airline dragging across the floor *to the feet* conjures up scenes of such slapstick humour that one is amazed that the 'pathologists' – who dart about quite a lot in the course of the film – remained standing quite as long as they did.

There are various other scenes allegedly shot in connection with the Roswell crash. Another section of the footage, unreleased to the public but viewed by us, shows what is supposed to be another autopsy performed in a tent, lit by storm lanterns. This too flies in the face of the most elementary anti-microbial precautions. The innards of the alien in this scene look like nothing so much as ectoplasm, or a catastrophic attempt at a cake mix. A pale, elastic substance is drawn at length from the 'body' (which is actually invisible) and dumped to one side. A third autopsy scene does apparently exist, which we have not seen. This is said to show an unscarred female alien having what has been called 'a gynaecological procedure' performed on it before being opened up – a pointless examination at best for a physician to conduct on a cadaver he was about to dissect. The suggestion that this was part of a dress rehearsal for the released version of the hoax seems plausible.

There are also shots of 'debris' from the crash that are notable only for the alien script seen on them. This looks like extracts from a cod version of the Greek alphabet, and nothing like the patterns or 'hieroglyphics' other eyewitnesses recalled. But then the Roswell footage shows a six-fingered alien, and those who said they saw the bodies all agreed the aliens had four fingers. Cameraman Jack, like most other supporters of an extra-terrestrial explanation for the wreckage Mac Brazel found, introduces a whole new set of dates for various events in the saga, entirely unrelated to Brazel's own account. In such ways – along with unlikely stories of tiring journeys across America – do hoaxers leave clues, laugh and cock a snook at those they are hoodwinking.

¤ NOT VERY ADVANCED TECHNOLOGY

Even the best-laid plans of mice, men and aliens go awry, it seems. The Roswell case, flimsy as it seems to us, is but the most thoroughly documented of dozens of such stories: a leading book on the subject by Kevin Randle gives a by no means exhaustive 'database' of 85 examples of UFOs that have allegedly crashed, all over the world. It is time to set the Roswell case in this larger context.

A rooted article of faith in the ETH has it that any alien visitors to this planet 'must' be hundreds, thousands or even millions of years 'more advanced' than humanity. By and large, the contactee and abductionist movements, which have more in common than the abductionists like to admit, agree that the aliens are spiritually as well as technologically ahead of us. The large questions of what is meant by the words 'spiritually', 'ahead' and 'us' we explore in our different ways in the Epilogue. Here and now, we want to turn over the problems associated with ET technology, as understood by ufology.

First, one can't help but feel that there is a contradiction, or at the very least a paradox, in the concept of the crashed saucer. Ufologists invite us to contemplate extra-terrestrials who, on the one hand, have so transcended the universal laws of physics that, among other accomplishments, they can float themselves and their human captives through solid walls and windows and up through the air, defeat gravity and the laws of conservation of momentum and energy and the light-speed barrier, communicate telepathically and control the minds and memories of their victims, bend light beams, and even, some say, become invisible at will – and yet they rely on flying discs that crash with such disheartening frequency.

It seems to us that the paradox can be resolved – if one steps back from this close-up confusion of nuts, bolts

Colonel H.M. McCoy, chief of intelligence for the USAF's Air Material Command at Wright-Patterson AFB, gave a lengthy briefing to the Air Force Scientific Advisory Board on 17 March 1948 – less than nine months after it is claimed that the Air Force recovered a crashed saucer near Roswell. Minutes of the meeting, originally classified SECRET, show that it was not until late in Colonel McCoy's presentation that he got round to discussing UFOs: 'We have a new project – Project SIGN – which may surprise you as a development from the so-called mass hysteria of the past summer when we had all the unidentified flying objects or discs. This can't be laughed off. We have over 300 reports which haven't been publicized in the papers from very competent personnel.... I can't even tell you how much we would give to have one of those crash in an area so that we could recover whatever they are.'

Long-time UFO researcher Dr Bruce S. Maccabee questions the new evidence and offers two alternative explanations for McCoy's statements: (1) McCoy – the USAF's top technical intelligence official – was not aware of the debris recovered from the Brazel ranch, or (2) McCoy knew about the incident 'but he lied about it.'

Those who claim that debris from a flying saucer was recovered from the Brazel ranch also claim that the debris was sent to Wright-Patterson for analysis. If so, Colonel McCoy would have been responsible for directing the analysis. During McCoy's 17 March AFSAB briefing he reported: 'We only have one recent item of captured equipment, which is a Russian IL-7 aircraft which crash-landed in Korea a few months ago....We have gone over that with a fine-toothed comb....It is a type (of) aircraft very similar to our P-47....'

If McCoy 'lied' to the AFSAB then he also lied to Major General C.P. Cabell, the USAF's Director of Intelligence, in a TOP SECRET memorandum dated 11 October 1948. Colonel McCoy was informed that Major General Cabell had requested an 'exhaustive study of all information' available on UFOs to assess what they might be. In a letter dated 3 November 1948, Major General Cabell pressured AMC for a response. On 8 November 1948, Colonel McCoy responded, saying: '...the exact nature of these objects cannot be established until physical evidence, such as that which would result from a crash, has been obtained.'

Maccabee also suggested that the TOP SECRET *Estimate of the Situation* rejected by General Hoyt Vandenburg indicated that the USAF was in possession of saucer wreckage. But that paper was based solely on sighting reports. It made no mention of a crashed saucer having been recovered barely one year earlier at Roswell. This is confirmed by former Major Dewey Fournet, who was the Project Blue Book liaison officer in the Pentagon. In a letter dated 23 May 1992, to UFO researcher Jim Meliscuic, Fournet said he had 'inherited a copy when I became programme monitor.... It recapped all seemingly unexplainable UFO reports received by the Air Force to that time. It very explicitly mentioned that absolutely no artefacts had been recovered'.

On 8 November 1948, only a few weeks after the report was sent to the Pentagon, Colonel McCoy wrote a letter dealing with UFOs, and classified SECRET, to Vandenberg. McCoy's letter included the following:

In attempting to arrive at conclusions as to the nature of unidentified flying object incidents in the United States, this Command has made a study of approximately 180 such incidents.... The possibility that the reported objects are vehicles from another planet has not been ignored. However, tangible evidence to support conclusions about such a possibility are [sic] completely lacking. ...Although it is obvious that some types of flying objects have been sighted, the exact nature of those objects cannot be established until physical evidence, such as that which would result from a crash, has been obtained.

Condensed, with permission, from *Skeptics UFO Newsletter* No 39 (May 1996)

UFOs flew in New Mexico from the earliest days of the 'flying saucer' phenomenon. Perhaps they still do. This picture was taken in January 1996, and at the time the photographer noticed nothing unusual in the sky. The most likely explanation: the 'UFO' is a reflection or lens flare. *Fortean picture Library*

outlook would see UFO lore as a new manifestation of these ancient tales and the fully – indeed exclusively – human questions that are their underlying concern.

The poet T.S. Eliot once suggested that the function of the surface meaning of a poem is to occupy the reader's mind while the poem did its 'real work upon him'. If tales of downed UFOs are seen as new growth in the forest of myth and legend, the careful labelling of individual cases on a scale from 'hoax' to 'authentic' becomes irrelevant, except to the extent that it reveals the singular incapacity of our utilitarian and technophiliac culture for symbolic thought. Because we *are* human, the symbols and metaphors bubble up and arrange themselves into myths and legends and folklore, whether we like it or not. But in failing to recognize and savour this process, we – or the nuts-and-bolts school of ufology and its many faithful adherents – cut ourselves off from the roots of our own wisdom. To state this argument in the bluntest terms: the literal interpretation of the Roswell legend and its many offspring is implicitly a denial of the human spirit. In this, it is of a piece with a culture that treats the human body (especially its sexuality) as pure mechanism, speaks of 'lifestyles' rather than ways of life, and considers 'standards of living' to be solely a matter of material welfare.

What are crashed-saucer stories trying to tell us? On one level, the downed UFO is an exact parallel of the legend of the Holy Grail in Christianity: the ultimate proof of the existence of the aliens who *come down to Earth from the heavens*. These godlings transfix us with visionary beams of revelatory light; they perform miracles beyond the understanding of all our science. They come perhaps to save us, perhaps to torment us: like theologians perplexed by the inscrutable ways of God, ufologists (and, most especially, abductees) are divided on this issue. Like other Beings from the Otherworld, they are humanoid but not quite human, physically or emotionally. Most significantly, they seem to lack gender, as well as warmth. It is as if, being like gods and elves immortal, they have no need to reproduce. At the same time, they are not 'perfect', existing in self-sufficient bliss, like the gods or prophets of the Semitic tradition. According to the abduction scenario (see Chapter 11), aliens do reproduce, but they seem to require human assistance to do so; some abductees even hint that humans are in charge of these breeding operations. This fallibility reaches in two mythic directions: back to the *maimed* and *immortal* Fisher God-King of the Grail legends, which form the template for the legend of Jesus of Nazareth, himself wholly human and wholly divine; and into the symbolism of the crashed

and wiring to view the whole mechanism: or, in pastoral language, to look at the wood, not the trees.

In all the stories that human beings have told each other down the ages – including the story that is science – it is only creatures or Beings from otherworldly realms who have displayed the kinds of powers ascribed to the aliens in their magnificent flying machines: gods, semi-divine heroes, elves, demons, elementals and fairies. But most especially gods. It is typical of 'extra-terrestrialist' ufology to regard this fact down the tunnel of its own parochial technological vision, and to see archaic accounts of otherworldly entities as evidence that aliens have been visiting us for aeons. A more parsimonious saucer. The wrecked UFO is the 'tragic flaw' in the godlings' magical technological prowess, and it complements the parallel flaw in their biological and emotional make-up. A closer look at the salient details of the Grail legend tends to bolster the feeling that in the aliens and their oddly unreliable craft we are imaging ourselves.

As a young man, the keeper of the Grail, Anfortas, went out looking for knightly adventures rather than concentrate on the responsibilities of his spiritual inheritance. He met a heathen knight, identified easily enough as a symbol of Nature, jousted with him, and caught a poisoned spear through the testicles. The doctors did their best, but when Anfortas beheld the Grail, the pain of his wound increased: for by gazing on this spiritual Ultimate he had become immortal. Anfortas, like 'science', had neglected his true, moral and spiritual, duty to his fellow man, gained a privilege for which we all secretly hanker, and (like Faust) paid a terrible price. His fishing – for a single magic fish that will feed an entire company of guests – is limited by his pain, and what he actually catches can barely provision his own household. There are the correspondences with science's ideal of an 'answer to everything', and the eternal but unsatisfying, unnourishing truths that science harvests from the mutable waters of creation. And *there* are the parallels with the genderless, barren, coldly detached aliens, dependent on ordinary people whom they must parasitically drain for some vicarious experience of wholeness.

In *Creative Mythology*, Joseph Campbell makes a convincing case that the Grail – which is variously a 'wide and slightly deep' dish, a cup, even a stone, and in many traditions a spinning wheel, but always silver – is symbolically and inextricably related to the Moon. The Moon, like a UFO, is a silver disc. Grail symbolism reaches right back to Indo-European roots still visible in the Hindu epic of the *Panchatantra*. Campbell spells it out:

> *The image of the turning spoked wheel, which had... earlier... been symbolic of the world's glory, ...became a sign, on the one hand, of the wheeling round of sorrow, and, on the other, release in the sunlike doctrine of illumination. And in the classical world the turning spoked wheel appeared also at this time as an emblem... of life's defeat and pain... in the image of Ixion, bound by Zeus to a blazing wheel... to be sent whirling for all time through the air.*

And where did it come from? According to one chronicler of the Grail: 'A host of angels left it on the Earth, then flew off, high above the stars.'

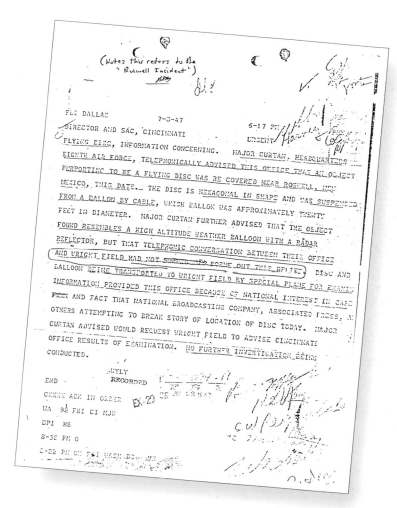

One of a tiny handful of official documents referring to the Roswell Incident that have been released by the US government. 'Believers' and skeptics alike have used it to argue the case for and against the crash of an alien craft near Roswell. The believers have yet to explain both why aliens would travel by balloon, and why the FBI conducted no further investigation. *US National Archives*

We have not found the Grail, nor can we display a crashed UFO for all to wonder at. Conspiracy and cover-up theories insist that there are Grail keepers – wounded and bemused scientists in Ohio or Nevada, pondering the wreckage of the magical, terrifying, addictive Other. But really, we are all Grail keepers, staring in pain and bewilderment at the debris of our spiritual life, which has been brought crashing to Earth, and we are as unable to mend it as we are to heal ourselves.

In such a way, we suggest, the legend of Roswell may be speaking to our condition, while the crippled, fallen aliens embody our secret knowledge of ourselves. And to look at the crashed-saucer stories in this way reveals something more: that beneath its faceted surfaces, the UFO myth – unlike ufology – is not compartmentalized into 'sightings', 'encounters', 'abductions' and 'crash/retrievals'. It is a seamless, web-like, articulate whole.

10

Planet Earth's UFOs

CHASING THE WILD LIGHTS

J OHN CLARE WAS walking briskly along between the villages of Ashton and Helpston in Cambridgeshire, England, when he saw a strange light gleaming out brightly in the night. Clare, who became famous as 'the Peasant Poet', described in his Journal of 1830 how the light came on steadily towards him. 'When it got near me... I thought it made a sudden stop as if to listen to me,' he wrote. It made a crackling noise and 'blazed out like a whisp of straw' surrounded by a luminous halo effect. The phenomenon had 'a mysterious terrific hue', Clare reported in his inimitable style. The light it cast lit up Clare and the surrounding bushes with a stark illumination which had a distorting effect that frightened the countryman. 'I held fast by the stilepost till it darted away when I took to my heels and got home as fast as I could,' Clare recorded.

Although Clare was the only one to have such an unnerving close encounter, many people in Helpston had been seeing lights at a distance. There was 'a great upstir' according to Clare. Up to 15 lights at a time were seen over Deadmoor and Eastwell Moor. They flew back and forth, both with and against the wind. With other villagers, Clare had earlier seen two lights that moved towards each other, then danced and gyrated around one another until 'they mingled into one'. The lights would rise up from the ground and settle down onto it – or 'land', as we might say nowadays. It was only when he personally saw the lights that Clare admitted to feeling robbed 'of the little philosophical reasoning which I had about them'.

Modern ufology is in a similar dilemma.

While 'mainstream' ufology has been concerning itself with confirming the existence of crashed flying saucers and other evidence for the ETH, and psychosocial ufologists have been seeking purely psychological and cultural explanations for the UFO phenomenon, a third line of research has slowly been uncoiling. Though accepting that most UFO reports relate to misidentifications of mundane objects, hoaxes and little-understood psychological states, this approach states that there is a real 'signal in the noise' – that there are UFOs, not from some other world but from this one, Planet Earth itself. These UFOs, it is claimed, are exotic but natural luminous phenomena produced by processes within the Earth – perhaps meteorological-atmospheric, or tectonic-geological, or perhaps a combination of such mechanisms. Its supporters maintain that it is not a reductionist approach, for they insist that they do not claim that 'real' UFOs are 'nothing but' balls of electricity: it is accepted that the unexplained lights they feel are at the heart of genuine UFO sightings are unknown, anomalous phenomena, which while they probably do have electromagnetic properties, also have other aspects to them that will take our understanding of physics across new thresholds.

Those who consider themselves to be 'real' ufologists — that is, those who have set their hearts and belief systems on UFOs being alien craft — naturally find this approach to the problem an anathema. In their own minds, they have already identified Unidentified Flying Objects as extra-terrestrial spaceships, so how can the study of balls of light have anything to do with the subject? The light hunters, however, remind their detractors that, in reality, UFOs remain unidentified.

Whether abhorred or ignored by ufologists of the extra-terrestrial persuasion, the hard fact remains that starting from humble beginnings, the study of anomalous light phenomena has developed into a dynamic research area of ufology (not that the light hunters like to think of themselves as ufologists at all). It is better funded than other areas within ufology, it can call on better resources, it has been able to attract mainstream, 'hard' scientists, and, above all, it is the only aspect of ufology at the end of the first 50 years that is beginning to move beyond mere anecdote.

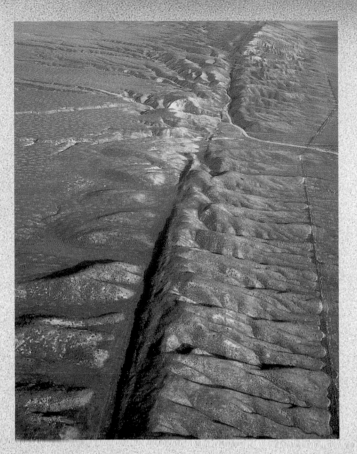

The San Andreas Fault, California. *R. E. Wallace/U.S.G.S*

⌑ GROWING TOWARDS THE LIGHT

Charles Fort was among the first to make the observation that strange 'meteors' appeared somewhat coincidentally with earthquakes and tremors. The 'first ufologist' had already made a connection between lights in the sky and tectonic activity (see Chapter 4).

It had to wait until the end of the 1960s for ufologists to take the next obvious step and link UFOs with geological fault lines, those areas of tectonic weakness in the Earth's crust. We have already noted (see Chapter 4) that veteran ufologist John Keel associated the appearance of unusual lights with areas of faulting and magnetic anomaly, as well as with the occurrence of earthquakes, but it was perhaps the French researcher Ferdinand Lagarde who focused in most tightly on the UFO-fault connection. In a 1968 article, he presented an initial survey of the French part of the 1954 UFO wave, in

which he found that 37 per cent of reported UFO sightings occurred on or in the immediate vicinity of faults, and that 80 per cent of the sighting localities were associated with faults. To counter the argument that 'anywhere' can be correlated with faulting, Lagarde compared *communes* with faults in the same areas: only 3.6 per cent of these fell on faults (or 10.8 per cent if margins of 1½ miles/2.5km were allowed for the faults). Later research showed a 40 per cent correlation between reported UFO incidence and fault lines.

Background: A light phenomenon photographed with a simple camera in 1973 by physicist David Kubrin at Pinnacles National Monument, California. The Pinnacles Fault is only a few miles from the San Andreas Fault. Kubrin and his first wife saw the light streak along at treetop height, creating shock waves in the air ahead of it. It then stopped without decelerating and began to spin and dissolve. As a physicist, Kubrin was amazed that the light had exhibited evidence of mass (shock waves) yet could seemingly stop without deceleration.

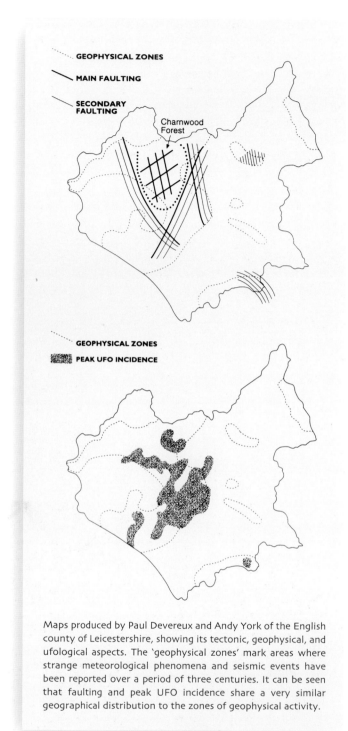

Maps produced by Paul Devereux and Andy York of the English county of Leicestershire, showing its tectonic, geophysical, and ufological aspects. The 'geophysical zones' mark areas where strange meteorological phenomena and seismic events have been reported over a period of three centuries. It can be seen that faulting and peak UFO incidence share a very similar geographical distribution to the zones of geophysical activity.

'UFO sightings occur by preference on geological faults,' Lagarde concluded. 'It seems as though faults, as such, are not merely the external aspect of an irregularity in the Earth's crust, but are also the scenes of delicate phenomena – piezo-electrical, or electrical, or magnetic, and at times perhaps of gravimetric variation or discontinuity.'

Although the lights–fault connection was a low-profile topic within ufology for several years, it gradually began to emerge from the shadows. In 1975, Paul Devereux and Andrew York published a two-part article called 'Portrait of a Fault Area' in a Fortean journal. In this, they surveyed their home county of Leicestershire in the English Midlands, mapping in great detail geographically and geologically the occurrences of a wide range of recorded strange phenomena and events over a number of centuries. Both meteorological anomalies ('strange lightning', 'balls of fire') and reported UFOs (lights in the sky, discs, spheres and cigar-shaped aerial objects) in the data were found to have had their greatest incidence over the tectonically active parts of the county. Although this was a relatively crude study, it did suggest that the influences causing the appearance of exceptional meteorological events appeared to be substantially shared by the phenomena termed 'UFOs'.

In 1977, Michael Persinger, a neuroscientist and geologist at Laurentian University in Sudbury, Ontario, together with Gyslaine Lafrenière, published *Space-Time Transients and Unusual Events*, in which they described a similar study of the entire area of the US. While this did not allow for the same kind of detail and individual accuracy obtained by the Devereux-York study, it used more sophisticated analytical methods. Their results indicated that reported UFO phenomena did tend to cluster in areas, supporting Keel's notion of 'windows' (see Chapter 4). They also found a correlation between the higher levels of reported UFO activity and the locations of earthquake epicentres. Persinger and Lafrenière concluded that 'the data consistently point towards seismic-related sources'. They argued that 'the existence of man upon a thin shell beneath which mammoth forces constantly operate, cannot be over-emphasized'.

Persinger and Lafrenière saw the interaction between stellar and planetary influences and the Earth's own processes as possibly providing the energy 'motor' that could generate light phenomena. While this interaction would affect the whole planet, Persinger and Lafrenière reasoned that it would result in outbreaks of lights and other unusual phenomena only in those locations where geological stresses were in a state of tension – primed to be triggered, so to speak. (Tectonic stress waxes and wanes in many places on the Earth's crust every day, producing numerous small, often imperceptible tremors which only occasionally escalate into major earthquakes.) These researchers visualized fields of forces operating evenly and quietly over very large geographical regions, which could become focused at any given time in a few small areas of particular geological resistance or instability such as fault lines, ore bodies or mineral deposits, stubborn rock outcrops, hills, mountains, volcanoes and so on. They likened this to the energies in the atmosphere being equally capable of producing a gentle breeze over a wide area or a localized ferocity like a tornado.

It had long been noted that unusual lights are often seen around physical projections within an active region. These include features such as mountain peaks and ridges, isolated buildings and church towers or spires, prominent rock outcrops, and transmission towers. Such features are charge collectors, so this obviously supported the assumption of there being an electromagnetic dimension to the lights.

Seeking a specific mechanism for the production of anomalous lights, Persinger and Lafrenière opted for a modification of the piezo-electrical effect, which is the term given to the production of electricity in crystals subjected to pressure. They felt that stress accumulating in a seismic area, perhaps over weeks or months, could produce an 'electric column' from a few feet to thousands of yards across. The high electric field in such a column could in certain circumstances ionize the air, creating glowing shapes. The column would move as the band of stress followed a fault or other line of weakness in the ground. Consequently, any glowing ionized shapes in the column would seem to be moving freely through the air.

This was the first outing of what has come to be known as the Tectonic Strain Theory, or TST.

In the decades following this work, Persinger, individually and with associates, has maintained a steady stream of research papers exploring the TST explanation in numerous locales within North America as well as in other countries, and he has also studied the possible clinical effects on the human mind and body of close proximity to anomalous light phenomena (see Chapter 11). The TST has also gradually been updated and refined. Now, for example, piezo-electricity has been joined by other possible mechanisms such as emissions of radon and other gases, and chemoluminescence. Another refinement has been associating the incidence of light phenomena not so much with numbers of quake epicentres, but with the intensity of such tectonic activity.

The idea of a 'strain field' crossing areas of increasing tectonic stress being the primary cause of light phenomena has stood up well to subsequent analyses, but it is now thought possible that there may also be more physical candidates, such as underground water moving through fault systems. It is also now recognized that even given the presence of a strain field, extra 'triggers' may be impli-cated in the occurrence of intense outbreaks of light phenomena. Such triggers could include lunar tides, the passage of air masses and geomagnetic storms – all of which have caused earthquakes. The passage of the Moon around our planet, for instance, causes a focal strain field to travel across the Earth's surface at around 625mph (1000km/h). Passing through a tectonically primed region, this could well set off a spate of luminosities.

In 1985, Persinger presented some evidence to support the observation that variations in the Earth's magnetic field would seem to be associated with the appearance of light phenomena, but only in regions where tectonic stress and strain were increasing. In 1990, he put forward further evidence to show that increased global seismicity could be linked successfully with worldwide UFO waves.

In the course of the 1980s, another important researcher into light phenomena made his appearance: John Derr, a leading US geologist who by then had already been pressing for a decade for scientific acceptance of earthquake lights. In 1986, he joined with Persinger to study a wave of lights that had been reported throughout the 1970s in the Yakima Indian Reservation, Washington State, and especially between 1973 and 1974. Fire wardens positioned in their lookout posts within the reservation saw red-orange and yellow-orange lightballs floating over various locations, such as Goat Rocks. These were quite large, although 'ping-pong balls' of light were also seen bounding along Toppenish Ridge

Fault-riddled Toppenish Ridge, Yakima Indian Reservation, Washington State, USA. This was one of the focal points for light phenomena during the outbreak in the 1970s. *Paul Devereux*

One of several photographs of the strange Yakima lights obtained by the then chief firewarden, W. J. Vogel. This was taken on 3 September 1971, with an 800mm lens using a 30 second exposure.
The Estate of W. J. Vogel

and Satus Peak within the reservation. In addition, columns and flares of lights were seen, as were white lights with smaller, multi-coloured lights apparently connected to them. Some lights were complex forms, and some displayed luminous protrusions or 'horns'. Over the years during which these remarkable sights were observed, there were also unusual meteorological effects, such as glowing clouds that fluctuated in brightness. The fire wardens organized themselves, and photographs were taken of the lights and triangulated observations using radios were made.

The Yakima analysis by Derr and Persinger showed that 78 per cent of the reported phenomena were lights seen in the night sky. They were seen most often in the vicinity of the ridges that cut across the reservation – each riddled with faulting – and with Satus Peak, the general area of a surface rupture and one of the stronger earthquakes in the region during the 13 years covered by the study. Successive reporting of lights occurred in the

A SOLUTION TO ARNOLD'S FLYING SAUCERS?

A particular significance of the Yakima lights is that the reservation is immediately adjacent to the Cascade Mountains, specifically the section where Kenneth Arnold saw his flying objects in 1947. In 1996, John Derr checked the seismic record of the area, and found that Arnold's sighting took place during a lull in seismic activity along the tectonic plate margin marked by the Cascades. Enormous strain had to be building in the region at the time of Arnold's encounter, because the next earthquake there, in 1949, was the biggest in the history of Washington State, with people being killed and injured. The Tectonic Strain Theory predicts that it is at the time of increasing strain when most light phenomena will occur.

The volatile nature of the Cascades was emphasized by the eruption of the Mount St Helen's volcano in May, 1980.

Mount St Helen's erupting. *US Geological Survey*

seven months preceding the biggest earthquake of the studied period, in June–July 1975. Regional seismic activity also increased during the times in 1972 and 1976 when most sightings were reported. The investigators took the opportunity to seek evidence for a stress field moving across the area. From June 1976 to March 1977, they noted 21 earthquake-light phenomena cycles, eight of which occurred in the time intervals between quakes located north and south of the sightings, and two more on the days when there were north–south shifts in epicentres. This strongly indicated a moving 'band' of stress within the local geology.

In addition to increasing the evidence for an association between outbreaks of lights and earthquake activity (for instance, Derr was able to make informal predictions to colleagues of an earthquake around Tennant Creek, Australia, in 1988 because of the earlier appearance of light phenomena in the district). Derr also made an important discovery regarding the role of liquids moving over or inserted into the Earth's crust near window areas. The liquids could be in the form of flooded rivers carrying much greater volumes of water than usual, the result of civil engineering enterprises such as the creation of new dams and reservoirs, or the high-pressure injection of water or waste liquids into the bedrock. The extra weight of water on the surface can add pressure to the underlying geology, as well as penetrate faults and fissures. Forced injection can cause cracks in rocks to increase and spread, thus shifting internal pressures, in addition to lubricating the surfaces of rocks meeting at a fault and thereby allowing them to slide more easily over each other.

The first case where this connection came to light was an outbreak of UFO sightings in the Uintah Basin in north-east Utah, around the towns of Vernal, Roosevelt and Duchesne, between 1966 and 1968. The main type of phenomenon observed was a large globe of light one witness described as having the golden-amber colour of the harvest Moon. It was rarely fully spherical, however, usually appearing as a sort of hemisphere with a flattened bottom. 'Rocket' and 'cigar' forms were also reported, along with infrequent sightings of metallic-looking discs. Many of the phenomena were observed by multiple witnesses, and some people reported hearing whistling and humming sounds on close encounter. Derr eventually discovered that the injection of waste liquids into the crust had been going on coincident with this wave. This had not been noticed for some time because the injection work had taken place across the nearby state line in Colorado.

In a 1990 paper, Derr and Persinger recorded that the forced injection of waste liquids into the bedrock at Derby, Colorado, triggered some 1500 small earthquakes, and a large increase of reported light phenomena within 60 miles (100km) of the injection site. They noted that some process within the Earth's crust, whether a strain field or whatever, diffused away from the site at a rate of 30–60 miles (50–100km) per month to distances as great as 190 miles (300km). Subsequently, Derr has made numerous other observations of a similar kind. For instance, an analysis of an 'epidemic' of light reports in southern Manitoba in 1975 showed a correlation with a strong earthquake in Minnesota near the source of the Red River (which flows into Manitoba). Derr and Persinger were able to show matching patterns between the numbers of reported light phenomena and the varying volume of the Red River.

¤ NATURE LENDS A HAND

But it wasn't just this kind of analytical research of earlier cases of light phenomena that moved the light-hunters' case along. Circumstances allowed two contemporary field studies of localized outbreaks of lights to be conducted. The first took place around Piedmont in south-west Missouri. The appearance of strange lights of various colours in the early months of 1973 coincided with TV and electrical interference in the area. Lights were seen not only in the sky, but also sitting in fields, hovering near transmitter towers, and even passing beneath the surface of a reservoir. Dr Harley D. Rutledge, a physics professor at Southeast Missouri State University, led field expeditions to the 'flap' area, and they took numerous photographs of light phenomena and made useful first-hand observations.

The second situation developed in the remote valley of Hessdalen, in a mineral-rich area famed for its mining of copper and other metals, about 70 miles (110km) south-east of Trondheim in Norway. For a few years after November 1981, Hessdalen hosted one of the most remarkable outbreaks of light phenomena ever reported. People living in the isolated farms that straggle through the valley saw lights spring into visibility near rooftops, or hover just above the ground. Mainly, however, lights were seen just below the summits and ridges of the surrounding mountains. The shapes of the light phenomena included spheres, 'bullet' forms with the pointed end downwards, and inverted 'Christmas tree' shapes. Colours were predominantly white and yellow-

An unexplained light within the valley of Hessdalen, Norway, photographed by Arne P. Thomassen in October 1982. In the original picture, a mountain ridge is visible near the top of the frame. *Project Hessdalen*

An inverted Christmas tree-shaped light in Hessdalen, photographed by Arne P. Thomassen on 25 September 1985. *Project Hessdalen*

white, although other colours were also reported, particularly small, flashing red lights on the top or bottom of larger white forms. Strong, localized white or blue flashes in the sky were also observed.

In March 1982, Norway's leading UFO group, UFO-Norge, became interested, as did the Norwegian defence department, who sent two Air Force officers to study the situation. (They discovered that people in Hessdalen had been seeing strange lights on and off since 1944.) By the summer of 1983, hundreds of reports of strange lights had been made by the inhabitants of Hessdalen. There were also complaints of curious underground sounds like rumbling trains. The situation had become so intense that Norwegian and Swedish UFO groups combined their resources to form Project Hessdalen. Field operations got under way on 21 January and ended on 26 February 1984. During this period, a continuous presence of monitors was maintained in the valley, along with a range of instrumentation including radar, a magnetometer, a spectrum-analyser, geiger counters and a variety of photographic equipment, including cameras with diffusion filters that could image the spectrum coming from a light source, allowing analysis to determine what elements were present. The project personnel had to work in difficult

In this near-panoramic view, Leif Havik photographed a bright light emerging from cloud and fog (*above*). The inset shows an enlargement of this light.

It moved left, in front of the mountain, and disappeared behind a hill (*above*). The photographs were taken on 12 February 1983. *Project Hessdalen*

Inside the trailer HQ used for the first field session of Project Hessdalen in 1984. *Project Hessdalen*

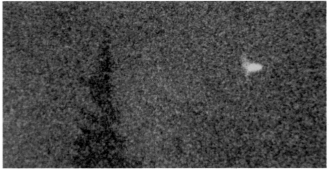

A shape-shifting light at Hessdalen photographed by Roar Wister on 18 February 1984. *Project Hessdalen*

conditions, with temperatures as low as −30°C. The headquarters of the effort was a trailer caravan high on a ridge, equipped with electrical power.

Project Hessdalen succeeded in taking many photographs of strange lights, and they also obtained a number of radar readings that were not 'radar angels'. In one baffling case, project personnel were watching a bright light cross the sky while the radar received an echo back from it only once every second sweep of the radar beam, yet it gave a steady appearance to the naked eye. A seismograph used for just a part of the field operation had its largest readings coinciding with peaks in sightings, but the cause of the earth tremors were not local to Hessdalen. The magnetometer showed changes in the Earth's field in apparent relationship with about 40 per cent of perceived lights. The geiger counters gave no unusual readings, although that could have been due to their distance from any lights.

Project Hessdalen conducted further fieldwork in the winters of 1985 and 1986, but it became apparent that the peak of the wave had passed between 1982 and 1984. J. Allen Hynek visited the site in 1985, and was impressed with what he learned about the phenomena there.

The Hessdalen phenomenon had massively raised the profile of the whole issue of mystery lightforms.

Left: Leading American ufologist, J. Allen Hyneck, at Hessdalen in January 1985. Hyneck was of the opinion that something very important for the future of ufology was happening at this Norwegian site. Unfortunately, he was approaching the end of his life at this point, but had he lived long enough to see the developments in the earth lights research, he may have been able to steer American ufology away from the 'all-or-nothing' extra-terrestrial obsession that has eclipsed it. *Project Hessdalen*

Leif Havik was one of the key figures in the original Project Hessdalen, and took some important photographs. Like several of the Project Hessdalen fieldworkers, he noticed a curious, undulating sensation in his chest when observing some of the lights, like a cork in a gentle ocean swell. Interestingly, the lights, too, seemed to undulate to a similar rhythm. *Paul Devereux*

¤ EARTH LIGHTS ARRIVE

In 1982, coincident with the onslaught of lights at Hessdalen, *Earth Lights*, the first book devoted solely to the phenomenon, was published by Paul Devereux. He made an attempt at summarizing and identifying clearly what until then had been a somewhat formless, unfocused area of enquiry. He provided the phenomena with the name 'earth lights' specifically to identify them as being something other than extra-terrestrial. The book reinforced the tectonic connection with the lights by presenting work the author had carried out with geochemist Paul McCartney, exploring detailed associations between light phenomena, epicentres and faulting in Britain. Even the great UK centre for UFO sightings, Warminster in Wiltshire, was shown to lie directly on an isolated fault line, and nearby Cley Hill, frequently the source of orange fireballs, was immediately adjacent to two faults.

The following year, Devereux, McCartney and chemist Don Robin brought earth lights to the attention

of a broader public through the pages of *New Scientist*, where they also discussed possible mechanisms within rock that could produce lights, such as piezo-electricity, triboluminescence (light produced by frictional forces), and thermoluminescence (the production of light by heating).

An important addition to the earth lights literature appeared in 1985 in the form of *Spooklights – A British Survey*, by David Clarke and Granville Oldroyd. Among numerous British earth lights haunts superbly documented by these authors was Burton Dassett, a now lonely church on top of an isolated group of hills set in the plain south of Warwick. It was the focus of an intense outbreak of light phenomena in 1922 and 1923. Reporters from the major local newspapers, as well as local people, saw many displays of mysterious lights, nicknamed 'the ghost'. The reporter from the *Birmingham Post*, together with other onlookers, saw a 'steady and vivid' light travelling a few feet above the ground. 'Its radiance was such that the sky was faintly illuminated for several miles,' he wrote.

Clarke and Oldroyd discovered that the church sits directly on the Burton Dassett fault, and that the mysterious light briefly reappeared on the night of 25 January 1924. That very night, there was a powerful earth tremor in Herefordshire, a county to the west. This obviously suggests a general tectonic connection of some kind with the Burton

In 1904 and 1905, concurrent with a great religious revival in Wales, bizarre lights began appearing along a coastal stretch of country between Barmouth and Harlech. The outbreak was heralded by an arch of aurora-like light stretching from the sea to the mountains. By January 1905, a large percentage of the local population had seen strange lights in the area.

Local journalist Beriah Evans kept publishing accounts of witnesses' sightings, including his own. 'Between us and the hills,' he reported on one occasion, 'there suddenly flashed forth an enormous luminous star with intensely brilliant white light, and emitting from its whole circumference dazzling sparklets like flashing rays from a diamond.... Another short half-mile, and a blood-red light, apparently within a foot of the ground, appeared to me in the centre of the village street just before us.'

All kinds of lights were seen. Sparkling diamond shapes attached themselves to the roof ridges of isolated chapel buildings, 'bottle-shaped' lights hung over hilltops, red lights popped out of the ground, rose into the air and fused together, and columns of light were seen to emerge from the ground – sometimes emitting smoke-like fumes – in which small balls of light could be seen. A set of such columns erupted in Dyffren, close to a 5000-year-old megalithic tomb, the Dyffren dolmen.

The story soon reached the ears of the national press, and correspondents were sent to the area. These hard-bitten reporters actually saw the incredible light phenomena, much to their surprise. The *Daily Mail* correspondent saw yellow balls of light of 'electric vividness' hovering 100ft (30m) above the Barmouth–Harlech road. They flickered 'like a defective arc-lamp', then went out. Travelling along the country road further to the south, the *Daily Mirror* journalist found himself engulfed in a 'soft, shimmering radiance'. Looking up, he saw 'a large body' overhead that had 'suddenly opened and emitted a flood of light from within itself'. Later on, the same reporter saw a light like 'an unusually brilliant carriage-lamp' barely 500yd (450m) away. He rush towards it, but as he got closer it changed its form into a brilliant blue bar of light about 4ft (1.2m) long. Observers on the other side of the light to the reporter *could not see the phenomenon at all*, even though there was nothing obscuring their view.

Local people tended to associate the lights with the religious Revival, and especially with local missionary Mary Jones, who frequently used the Egryn chapel for her meetings. Lights were often seen on and around this isolated building on the road between Barmouth and Harlech, and so the 1904–5 wave of lights is sometimes referred to as the 'Egryn lights'. But luminous phenomena were seen over a wide area of the district, and the correspondent from the *Guardian* felt even at the time that the lights would have appeared whether or not the Revival had been taking place.

The Dyffren dolmen.
Paul Devereux

Dassett light. The local *Leamington Chronicle* made just such an asssumption. 'Simultaneous with the appearance of the "ghost" of south Warwickshire comes the report of an earth tremor in the West of England,' it noted.

In 1989, Devereux's *Earth Lights Revelation* appeared, a sequel to his first book in which a much more comprehensive and updated scope of the subject was presented. The book also gave full information on a study by Devereux and McCartney of an 'earth lights zone' between Barmouth and Harlech in north-west Wales, which had been active in the early years of the century.

Because good, contemporary reports had been made of these Welsh lights, Devereux and McCartney found that by conducting thorough map and field research, the locations of quite a number could be mapped with great precision. These detailed positions were then matched with recent geological research in the region, and it was found that the lights followed the course of a major local feature, the deep-rooted Mochras Fault, like beads on a thread. Some of the lights had emerged from the ground directly on the Mochras Fault, and nearly all occurred within a 100yd (90m) or so of that or associated faulting. Indeed, the incidence level increased with proximity to the faulting. (To check if this was a random pattern or not, the investigators conducted a similar study of the St Bride's Bay area of south-west Wales, the focus of a UFO wave in 1977. The results were virtually identical to those obtained around Barmouth.)

The Barmouth–Harlech lights outbreak occurred in the midst of a period of unusual seismicity: between 1892 and 1906 there were several earthquakes in various parts of Wales. In October 1904, for example, immediately prior to the onset of the Barmouth wave, there was a quake at nearby Bedgellert.

On two occasions on 25 March 1905, balls of deep red light were seen to emerge from this field next to the chapel at Llanfair. In the second event, three lights rose up high into the air. The two outer ones divided, but the central one remained unchanged. They were observed by local people for 15 minutes. Recently, high-tech surveying has revealed that the Mochras Fault runs directly through this field. *Paul Devereux*

How the mapped lights from the 1904-1905 Barmouth-Harlech wave in Wales relate to the Mochras Fault.

¤ LIGHTS AND SITES ¤

A whole chapter of the history of earth lights could be written in which mysterious lights are associated with ancient sacred places. The holy Chinese mountains of Wu Tai shan and Omei shan, for example, apparently had large golden-orange lightballs that frequented their peaks at night. These were interpreted as 'Bodhisattva Lights'. A tower was specially erected at a summit temple on Wu Tai shan for viewing these holy lights.

Two pilgrimage shrines dedicated to the Goddess Bhagbatti on the sacred Purnagiri Mountain of northern India were likewise erected because of local light phenomena. The most sacred of the two shrines is situated on a fault and can be accessed only by a dangerous, narrow track. The lights are said to be votive lamps lit to the goddess by a holy man or sadhu. In his book *The Temple Tiger* (1934), Jim Cobbett describes his visit to the locale and his witnessing of three strange lights, each about 2ft (60cm) in diameter, in a gorge. One light merged slowly with another, then more lights appeared. They glowed in front of a sheer rock face.

The famous German Buddhist, Lama Anagarika Govinda, also saw lights in the mountains of India. While staying at Dilkusha, he spied fast-moving lights on distant slopes. The local Maharaja told him that the lights were often seen, and he had once witnessed them moving through his palace grounds towards a temple. That spot had always been considered a sanctified place, he said.

And it is not only in the mysterious East where such associations have been made. In 1919, a Mr T. Sington and colleague reported seeing white lights, 6ft (1.8m) in diameter, playing lazily over the prehistoric stone circle of Castlerigg, in the English Lake District. One globe of light broke away and approached Sington and his friend standing some distance away, but just as the men's nerves were about to crack, the sphere came to a halt and faded away. Sington later wondered if these were some unknown natural phenomena which occurred at that place from time to time over millennia. Had the megalith builders seen them, taken them to be spirits, and erected their stone circle there because of that?

There are numerous other eyewitness reports of lights being seen at prehistoric sacred sites.

Barmouth and Harlech are also adjacent to the Lleyn Peninsula, one of Britain's most active seismic areas, and epicentre in July 1984 of an earthquake registering 5.5 on the Richter scale. This event brought the lights back briefly to the Barmouth area: the evening before the quake, a resident saw a brilliant white light 'the size of a small car' float in from the sea and land just beyond the brow of a grassy dune on the beach. When he rushed over to examine the 'landing spot', there was nothing to be seen.

The 1980s saw the assembly of a wide range of research into the history of earth lights in early and non-Western cultures. It became abundantly clear that people had come up with explanations for the lights that suited their own cultures and times (see Chapter 1). What is particularly interesting is that throughout old Europe it was thought that veins of copper or other minerals are present where balls of light emerge from the ground. Although such beliefs were dismissed as mere superstition by the mining texts of the eighteenth century (the 'Age of Reason'), it is a fact that prospecting by means of studying light phenomena was conducted at Bere Alston, an important copper and arsenic mine in Devon, England, until the beginning of the twentieth century. This means that the skills involved in observing earth lights probably died out in the Western world only within the last couple of generations.

¤ IN THE LABORATORY

As well as field research, historical documentation, statistical analyses and theory-building, there have also been some laboratory experiments. In 1986, Brian Brady and Glen Rowell of the US Bureau of Mines fractured cores of granite, which has a high quartz content allowing piezo-electric effects, and basalt, containing no piezo-electric crystals. Their fracturing was performed in various gases (air, argon, helium), in a vacuum, and even underwater. Brady and Rowell used a spectroscope linked to image intensifiers to capture the spectra of any fleeting lights that might be produced as the cores broke up.

The results were most instructive. Both the granite and the basalt cores produced tiny lights – this challenged the theory that piezo-electricity could be the mechanism producing lights in the landscape. But the biggest surprise was that the spectra of the lights showed no trace of any elements from the rocks, only from the surrounding gas or liquid. Analysis of the spectra of rocks fractured in a vacuum showed only the gases in air (it is impossible to

Tiny flying lights shine out as a rock core explodes in the rock crusher during the 1986 experiments.
B. Brady and G. Rowell / U.S. Bureau of Mines

the original Project Hessdalen, has started a new Project Hessdalen. He launched it with a conference held in Hessdalen itself in 1994. Over 20 earth lights researchers, quantum and plasma physicists, and other interested scholars came from all over the world to share information and discuss ways forward. Working out of Ostfold College in Norway, Strand is overseeing the 'wiring up' of the entire Hessdalen valley with automatic monitoring equipment. It is a long and expensive operation (the project is continually in need of financial support), but when complete, the idea is to be able to monitor the valley remotely – it is even proposed that this can be done in real time by anyone sufficiently interested by logging onto the Hessdalen network using the World Wide Web. Although Hessdalen is not producing light phenomena at the rate it did in the early 1980s, there has been a slight increase in reported events. In any case, as

create a perfect vacuum on Earth). The experimenters concluded that 'an exolectron excitation of the ambient atmosphere is the mechanism responsible for the light emissions observed under rock fracture'. But although there were speculations about the radio fields produced by fracturing rock forming energy 'bottles' to hold the light emissions in spherical and other forms, there was (and still is) no satisfactory way of explaining how earth lights could travel freely in space and maintain specific, defined shapes.

There was another unexpected discovery resulting from the experiments. The energy produced by the cores fractured under water made the liquid glow and both atomic and molecular hydrogen was produced. It was realized by the experimenters that such 'molecular dissociation' might initiate chemical reactions 'of geological and biological interest'. John Derr interpreted this as meaning that this process had 'implications for biogenesis', or the origins of life.

Did earth lights trigger the creation of organic life in the primeval muds of our planet? Are they, in a sense, ancestor lights?

¤ OUTWARD BOUND

The earth lights research of the 1980s consolidated all that had gone before it, and reached out in many directions. There could no longer be any doubt that a whole new dimension to ufology had arrived.

The strength of earth lights research has continued to grow in the 1990s. Erling Strand, one of the directors of

Assembling the sophisticated equipment for the new Project Hessdalen.
Project Hessdalen

Strand points out, the frequency doesn't matter – the network of monitoring stations will be triggered *whenever* an earth light flies into its invisible, electronic web.

This new phase of Hessdalen research typifies a growing development in the 1990s: earth lights research is moving out into the field in a more resourced and co-ordinated way than at any time previously. Y-H Ohtsuki, a plasma physicist from Waseda University, Japan, is funded by both scientific and industrial sources to take his team of specialists and equipment to sites anywhere in the world where anomalous lights are being reported.

One such place is Marfa, in the Big Bend country of Texas, where lights have been reported for over a century. There is even a designated viewing spot on the

Japanese plasma scientist Yoshi-Hiko Ohtsuki explains to a specialized conference of fellow researchers held at Hessdalen in 1994, how he sets about field researching earth lights. *Paul Devereux*

Setting up one location of the earth lights observing station on the vast expanse of Mitchell Flat, Texas, in 1994. *Paul Devereux*

Alpine–Marfa road overlooking the deceptively undulating desert scrub of Mitchell Flat, and the little town of Marfa has an annual festival of the lights! Ohtsuki, who favours an atmospheric explanation for the lights, has made four expeditions to the area, and claims to have had one close encounter with a light which transformed from a glowing rod into a ball of light. His team has also monitored more distant lights.

While some hypothesizing about the nature of the lights and how they are produced is both inevitable and useful, Devereux, like Strand and Ohtsuki, thinks that the answers to the mysteries they present can ultimately be forthcoming only from careful, scientific observation of the phenomena in their natural habitat. So he, too, has moved the focus of his research into the field, chasing the wild lights. Working under the auspices of the International Consciousness Research Laboratories (ICRL), an interdisciplinary group of scientists and researchers conducting both pilot and extended studies of 'fringe' phenomena to see if they are worthy of further-reaching enquiry, he has been visiting areas of reported earth light activity. He has been accompanied by various colleagues and portable, lightweight recording and monitoring equipment in the hope of making the all-important visual-instrumental field study of a light phenomenon. Ironically, much of the work to date has resulted in some 'spooklight' locations being explained as cases of misperception of vehicle lights distorted by great distances or unusual viewing circumstances.

In 1994, Devereux visited Marfa for a ten-day field study along with his ICRL colleague Hal Puthoff, a physicist whose main research work is on the mysterious energy of the 'zero-point field' (an all-pervading electromagnetic field that exists in the vacuum – what is thought of as 'empty' space – even at the temperature of absolute zero).

Marfa proved to be a mixed case. By careful photographic mapping, it was possible to determine that the majority of 'Marfa lights' seen by most observers are vehicle lights tens of miles away across Mitchell Flat on

Physicist Hal Puthoff works with computerized equipment during a night observation session for earth lights in the desert near Marfa. *Paul Devereux*

'Light mapping' by means of long-exposure photography, as shown here, reveals that the lights most people at the viewing spot see, and think are the mysterious 'Marfa lights', are in reality vehicle headlights on a section of road about 30 miles away across Mitchell Flat. It is this misperception that keeps the story of 'Marfa lights' alive in the public mind. Nevertheless, there are also genuinely unexplained light phenomena in the Big Bend area of Texas. *Paul Devereux*

the Presidio–Marfa road or on tracks leading out to the isolated ranches in the vast landscape of the region. The lights are distorted by the great distances involved as well as by occasional mirage conditions that affect the district, and so often look strange and unfamiliar. It became

obvious that a great deal of misperception was keeping the legend of the Marfa Lights alive in the public mind. But discussion with Marfa researcher Judith Brueske and other investigators familiar with the area, such as Ed Hendricks, Bob Creasy and Dennis Stacy, as well as with reliable witnesses, made it equally obvious that on occasion there really did seem to be genuinely unexplained lights appearing in various parts of Big Bend country. In any case, lights had been reported from the region long before there were such things as vehicle headlights and motor roads. Some early travellers had thought they were Apache camp fires – until they started moving around.

The ICRL expedition spent long nights at isolated viewing locations on Mitchell Flat and elsewhere in the region. Nothing unusual broke the darkness of most nights. A blue-white light was glimpsed on one occasion by expedition member Charla Devereux moving near the dominant peak in the district, Chinati Mountain, but this could not be determined as anomalous or otherwise. However, acting on the tip of a local woman who had experienced a close encounter with a large ball of white light, the expedition journeyed 80 miles (130km) from Marfa to the Chisos Mountains on the Rio Grande. There they did see an earth light deep in an uninhabited valley. It appeared at the foot of a steep slope, about 1 mile (1.5km) from the monitoring station. It flared out brilliantly for about ten seconds, before flickering out.

In 1995, Devereux teamed up with Erling Strand and they visited the remote Kimberley region in Western Australia. They were responding to reports from a white bushworker who had seen balls of light at close quarters

¤ CHASING THE MARFA LIGHTS ¤

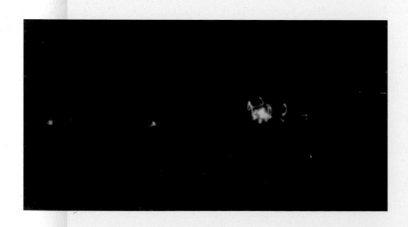

In March 1973, geologists Pat Kenney and Elwood Wright spent 20 minutes chasing lights through the scrub of Mitchell Flat, Marfa, in their jeep. The lights sped along about 4ft (1.2m) above the ground. A light would come to a halt, as if allowing the geologists to catch up with it, then shoot off again. 'It kind of looked like it was playing with us,' Kenney remarked later. The closest the two men could get to a light, which was the size of a basketball and had the colour and intensity of a normal household lightbulb, was about 200ft (60m). In the end, the lights simply vanished into thin air.

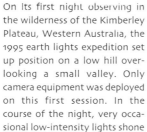

On its first night observing in the wilderness of the Kimberley Plateau, Western Australia, the 1995 earth lights expedition set up position on a low hill overlooking a small valley. Only camera equipment was deployed on this first session. In the course of the night, very occasional low-intensity lights shone out in the valley below. This location was far removed from any habitation or roads. The lights were blue-white, and some just blinked on and off, while a few moved a short distance before fading out. Because of their sporadic, fleeting nature, it was difficult to catch the lights on film, and it was thought that none had been captured. But analysis of the frame shown here, shows an apparent moving blue-white light (*extreme right*) below the skyline, and what may be stationary blue lights (*centre and bottom left*). The white light is shown in enlargement (*inset*). *Erling Strand/Project Hessdalen*

Paul Devereux waits for sundown alongside part of the camera array at the Australian earth lights expedition's final observation location. *Paul Devereux*

they were associated with unpleasant physical side-effects and 'poltergeist'-type events), the expedition members were disappointed, because their hope was naturally to be able to obtain close-up observations of the lights.

So, with their enthusiasm somewhat dampened, Devereux and Strand set up their monitoring station at various selected locations in the vast, largely uninhabited landscapes of the eastern Kimberley. Most nights were spent with no lights breaking them at all, except starlight and the momentary gleam of shooting stars. But on a few nights, distant moving lights, variously blue-white or soft, golden yellow in appearance, were seen. On one

on many occasions in a specific area when he worked in the Kimberley in the 1980s. Preliminary research conducted for the expedition by Australian ufologist Bill Chalker further showed that, indeed, a number of UFO reports had trickled out of this remote region over a 30-year period. Enquiries made in the field by Devereux and Strand among outstation managers and various Aboriginal informants revealed that while 'min-min' lights had been plentiful in the 1970s and the 1980s, their incidence was now much reduced. While the Aborigines were happy about this (they feared and disliked the lights, as

A mysterious light shines out on distant, uninhabited hills to the south of the expedition's observation point. The distance made it impossible for the investigators to confirm for sure whether or not it was an earth light, though its appearance did coincide with anomalous geomagnetic readings. Although this extended exposure photograph looks as if it was taken in daylight, it is in fact a nighttime shot with moonlight. See stars at top right of picture. *Erling Strand/Project Hessdalen*

These two sequential telephoto (200mm) shots show the same light moving to the left (eastward) relative to the foreground objects. *Paul Devereux*

occasion, a fan of brilliant light flashed silently from the surface of the desert. Then, in the final nights of the expedition's stay in the region, an important incident took place. Two bright yellow-white lights, appearing separately, shone out against the slopes of uninhabited hills about 7 miles (11km) from the field monitoring station. In the course of a few minutes they traversed a downward path and then disappeared. These hills had remained dark on previous nights, and the lights were the most distinct luminosities the expedition members had seen at any time in the Australian wilderness. Although quite possibly earth lights, by their very nature distant lights cannot be verified with complete certainty as anomalous phenomena. Frustration was cut short, however, by a shout from Strand. He had glanced at the printout from the magnetometer that was constantly measuring the Earth's magnetic field by means of a probe inserted in the ground a few hundred metres from the team's location. The chart recorder pen normally traced a gently undulating, narrow green line on the printout roll, but at the precise moment the lights had appeared the pen had started scrolling wildly from one side of the chart to the other, producing a huge trace. It was registering an unexplained and extremely anomalous change in the geomagnetic field some 800 times greater than normal. In varying degrees, the anomaly persisted for some hours, long after the lights had disappeared.

A reprise of this incident occurred on a further expedition in 1996, this time to the volcanic region around

The magnetometer probe is inserted into the ground 200 metres from the observation point. *Paul Devereux*

The great Mexican volcano, Popocatapetl. *Paul Devereux*

generated by El Popo each day. It was a promising environment for the appearance of earth light phenomena.

But the team had to undergo yet again the difficulties and frustrations inherent in chasing the wild lights. A nearby hurricane brought stormy weather that wiped out the possibility of observing visually or even instrumentally for many of the nights that the expedition was in Mexico. Some intermittent monitoring was nevertheless accomplished, although with no unusual results. Then, on the

The wild geomagnetic read-out that started when the lights appeared on the distant hills. The normal green trace is the thin penline at the bottom of the chart as shown here. *Paul Devereux*

Physicist David Fryberger (right) and Erling Strand study the magnetometer's bizarre readings near the base of Popcatapetl. *Paul Devereux*

Mount Popocatapetl in Mexico. On this occasion, which was being filmed for the *Equinox* TV documentary series on Britain's Channel 4, Strand and Devereux were joined by David Fryberger of the Stanford Linear Accelerator Center. The team were well aware of the sociological dimensions of the so-called Mexican UFO wave (see Chapter 4), but felt enough was being reported to indicate that there might be a genuine rise in actual light phenomena. Moreover, the expedition's enquiries among the rural population indicated that unusual lights (often interpreted as night-flying witches) were being seen fairly often in certain districts. In addition, Popocatapetl was in the midst of a phase of activity, issuing clouds of steam and thousands of tons of chemicals daily. Geologists monitoring the great volcano confirmed to the expedition members that there were many dozens of microquakes

final day, the weather cleared completely, and in the afternoon smoke, replacing the steam, erupted in vast plumes from the volcano's crater. Setting up camp near the foot of the almost 18,000ft (5550m) mountain, the expedition was able to deploy all its equipment. It was immediately noticeable that the magnetometer was recording extraordinary changes in the geomagnetic field, similar to the readings obtained in Australia although not so extreme. Night fell. The magnetometer readings continued their wild scrollings, but no unusual lights were to be seen. As this was the last night, the three investigators decided to pack up. While most of the equipment was being stowed, a faint area of soft, flashing light appeared high on the volcano's slopes. Again and again, the light flashed. In a frenzied rush, some cameras were unpacked and hurried shots taken – alas, none of them were suitable for reproduction.

With such field research on the increase, and instrumental readings linked to visual observations of unexplained lights beginning to be made, there is a general feeling that it is now only a matter of time before a major scientific encounter with an earth light is made. To the light hunters, that will be as important as the landing of a flying saucer on the White House lawn would be to an ET enthusiast.

¤ THE NATURE OF THE BEAST

Science now accepts that the Earth produces bizarre light phenomena in certain circumstances. Globes (and irregular shapes) of white, coloured and even black energy have been seen throughout the world springing into existence during storms, forming so-called 'ball lightning'. They have been witnessed exploding, and passing silently through solid walls and doors. They can be anything from the size of a pea to objects a yard or more in diameter. Nobody knows what this strange phenomenon is, although theories are legion. Even mundane lightning has its mysteries, such as 'superbolts' many miles long, which are relatively rare. And new mysteries appear as our observational capacities increase. In 1994, for example, shimmering fronds of red or blue light rising above thunderstorms for many miles were accidentally photographed by high-altitude aircraft. It is amazing that such gigantic phenomena have remained unknown until now. Nicknamed 'sprites', they mystify scientists. It is also now generally established within the scientific mainstream that

A nineteenth-century French depiction of ball lightning causing consternation during a storm.

This hemispherical earthquake light near Mount Kimyo, Matashiro region, Japan, was photographed at 3.25 am on 26 September 1966, with a fisheye lens by dentist T. Kuribayashi using a 36-second exposure. The light lasted for 96 seconds. *John Derr/U.S. Geological Survey*

there are such things as earthquake lights. Spheres, streamers, auroras, softly exploding hemispheres, flashes, rectangles and sparkles of light have all been described around the time of some earthquakes. These were reported anecdotally and documented for many years, but were ignored by most scientists until photographs of them were obtained during a swarm of Japanese earthquakes in 1967.

There is nothing clockwork about the appearance of such phenomena, however, for not all thunderstorms nor all earthquakes produce strange lights. The specific circumstances that make them appear are not understood.

Earth lights fit into this pageant of our planet's more mysterious light phenomena. To researchers like John Derr and Michael Persinger, earth lights are a form of earthquake light. To Ohtsuki, they are a plasma akin to ball lightning. Other researchers, such as Devereux, are less decided, feeling that while they are undoubtedly of the same family as earthquake lights and, possibly, ball lightning, they nevertheless have their own defining characteristics – the principal one being that they do not need an earthquake or a thunderstorm to accompany their appearance. Moreover, they can last for much longer than the reported lifetimes of ball lightning or earthquake lights: lights at Hessdalen, for instance, sometimes moved

back and forth along mountain ridges for over an hour.

No one knows what earth lights are actually comprised of. Some form of plasma (ionized gas) is assumed, but not a great deal is known about plasmas in any case, and some particularly baffling properties are seemingly possessed by the lights. According to recurring accounts, earth lights seem to be going 'on' and 'off' very rapidly, they can send their light in one direction only, and they can appear to have mass one moment yet seem weightless at another. The lights seem to hover on the very extremity of physical existence – here one moment, gone the next. Devereux has suggested that they may be macro-quantal events, displaying on our level of perception characteristics that owe something to the fluctuating probability field of the primal, subnuclear quantum sea out of which all energy and matter arise. Hal Puthoff has a suspicion that earth lights may be powered by zero-point energy. David Fryberger is developing a theory which has the lights resulting from a hitherto unknown particle he calls the 'vorton' – more exotic even than gluons, quarks and the other subatomic entities postulated by nuclear physics.

When they finally give up some of their secrets, earth lights could have a tremendous impact on quantum and plasma physics. And they may open doors to physics we do not yet know.

¤ INTO THE TWILIGHT ZONE

In fact, some light hunters think the earth lights may take us into areas where even non-scientists may at present fear to tread. While they clearly have electromagnetic dimensions, there are hints in the evidence that earth lights may have even more exotic properties. Specifically, the anecdotal record indicates that the lights can act as if they have a kind of rudimentary intelligence. Kenney and Wright, the geologists who chased lights around Mitchell Flat, Marfa, in 1973, told reporters that the lights 'had intelligence, definitely'. Dorothea Sturm, one of the fire wardens who saw light phenomena from her lookout station on the Yakima Indian reservation, was convinced that 'these things know when you're talking about them'. Intriguingly, even the field observers during Project Hessdalen felt that some of the lights were interacting with them. Precisely the same feeling was expressed by members of Harley Rutledge's field team who investigated an outbreak of light phenomena around Piedmont. Writer and ufological veteran John Keel saw purple balls of light hop out of the way of his flashlight beam when he was investigating strange lights in the Ohio Valley. He is utterly convinced that the lights had a crude form of reactive intelligence, however incredible it may sound to us. Biologist Frank Salisbury, who investigated the Uintah, Utah, UFO 'flap', found people who were convinced that the light forms they saw were interacting intelligently with them.

Such reports are extremely numerous across the world and through time. Could the lights be a form of geophysical consciousness? Do we share the planet with another, perhaps incredibly older, life form? Obviously, one has to be exceedingly careful not to overstate this matter – it is all too easy to confer intelligence on a distant light that may be moving in a random way. But many of the accounts are, in fact, far more specific than that.

It may yet turn out to be not such an impossible observation. As the millennium draws to its close, some leading brain scientists, such as Roger Penrose and Stuart Hameroff, are studying structures in the brain to see if they allow it to access the quantum field, for there is a

school of opinion that suggests consciousness may be an inherent property of the quantum state. If earth lights, too, emerge from this primordial level of existence, it may be that they do indeed possess some primary form of mind. And since the 1970s, Michael Persinger and Gyslaine Lafrenière have offered their concept of the 'geopsyche', a complex interaction between the electrical energies of the human brain and geophysical forces under special circumstances. Persinger reiterated this in 1990, when he pointed out that when we see a light phenomenon we may be looking in on just a tiny aspect of a vastly powerful and complex process which may indeed possess unusual emergent properties. This could result in 'unexpected interactions between the electromagnetic correlates of human cognitive processes and the UFO phenomenon itself'.

Another weird association with areas experiencing a wave of earth lights is poltergeist activity. A classic example of this afflicted the isolated hamlet of Linley, in the western English county of Shropshire. For several weeks in 1913, fiery balls of light were seen on the tower of the ancient church, and lightballs also flitted around the nearby cottages. Vaporous columns issued from the ground, and the residents heard curious explosions in the air. Metal door latches would fly open, chairs would hurtle across rooms, crockery would move of its own accord. When the lights were seen no more, these unusual side-effects also ceased.

These sorts of accounts could be repeated in dozens of other localities affected by earth light appearances. Even in the Yakima Indian Reservation, fire wardens remarked on odd sounds and the crunching of gravel around their lookout posts, as if it were being trod upon by ghostly feet.

The light hunters do not think such manifestations are paranormal in the commonly understood sense of that definition. Rather, they suspect that whatever the energetic environment is that gives rise to the lights can also produce side-effects such as these 'poltergeist'-type events. One candidate is change in the geomagnetic field, and in 1986 Livingston Gearhart and Michael Persinger conducted a statistical study comparing records of poltergeist activity and the index of geomagnetic activity for the same dates. This analysis 'clearly indicated that global geomagnetic activity (as an index) on the day or days after the onset of these episodes was significantly higher than the geomagnetic activity on the days before or afterwards'.

¤ BUT ARE THEY REALLY UFOS?

Ufologists of the extra-terrestrial persuasion have no time for earth lights, considering them to be something other than UFOs. The light hunters admit that small balls of light do not compare with structured craft, but point out that such reports have always been in the ufological record, where in the past they have been identified as 'drones' or 'probes' sent out from alien craft. So why dismiss them now if they suddenly take on importance as phenomena in their own right?

But, the extra-terrestrial school counter, what have lights to do with metallic discs seen in daylight? If earth lights are a form of plasma, then there is no problem with this, the light hunters state, because a plasma seen in daylight does happen to look shiny and metallic, and is likely to have a spherical, ovoid or discoid form.

Okay, the ET enthusiasts press, but what about the size usually ascribed to flying saucers or ET craft? Small balls of plasma, seen as lights or even as metallic forms can't account for those, surely? Yes they can, the light hunters retort. Some earth lights are reported as being huge – many yards across. A modest example of this was shown in Quebec, Canada, when 52 observations of light phenomena in the Saguenay region were studied by Quebec University. The lights were witnessed between 1 November 1988 and 21 January 1989 (the period around an earthquake on 23 November), in an area covered by a network of seismometers laid out by the university. Among a range of light phenomena, Professor Marcel Ouellet reported, fireballs 'a few metres in diameter often

popped out of the ground in a repetitive manner at distances up to only a few metres away from the observers'. Other balls of light, both stationary and moving, were seen several hundred metres up in the air. Some of these lasted for up to 12 minutes. The size, height and duration of some of these phenomena were clearly 'UFO standard'. The lights seen at Hessdalen were sometimes considerably larger than these Quebec phenomena, as can be deduced from some of the photographs reproduced in this chapter. So the size of earth lights is not a problem.

Yes, but, the ET ufologists persist, what about markings on the ground and damage to foliage associated with some reported UFO landings? These are quite consistent with localized damage caused by energetic lightballs, the light phenomena brigade maintain. Singed foliage, ground burns and grooves have been associated with ball lightning, for example.

But the exasperated extra-terrestrialists insist that there are specific reports of structured craft and entities in the ufological record. The light hunters admit this, but point out that they account for only a very small percentage of UFO reports. They maintain that the bulk of all *genuinely unexplained* sightings – those left when misperception and other psychosocial factors have been allowed for – can be accommodated by earth lights. This group forms only a tiny percentage of all UFO reports, and high strangeness cases in turn make up only a small fraction of *that*. These particularly exotic reports can be accounted for in a variety of ways: downright hoaxing, confabulation, psychosocial conditions affecting witnesses and, indeed, even mind-altering effects created by the energy fields associated with earth lights in the few instances where such an objective element is involved (see Chapter 11).

There is, of course, no reason why earth lights and alien craft should not coexist, but earth lights proponents consider that it is one hell of a coincidence that there should be a natural phenomenon that so matches the appearances of supposed ET craft. They feel that alien craft are not needed to explain what is required to be explained. They further argue that it would be a huge failure on everyone's part if a phenomenon that holds the potential to increase our knowledge of physics, that could provide a warning system for earthquakes, that might be responsible for the appearance of life on the Earth, and that might even offer us new insights into the nature and roots of consciousness, should fall victim to the preferred fantasies of ufologists on the one hand, and, because of that, the aversion or disregard of scientists on the other.

11

Beaming Us Up

TALES OF ALIEN ABDUCTIONS

STORIES THAT PEOPLE are being seized by aliens, hustled by virtually magical means into flying saucers and having horrible things done to them before being unceremoniously dumped back in their beds – or cars, or wherever they were snatched from – is now the biggest growth industry in ufology. Not even the energy that has gone into creating and questioning the Roswell and conspiracy and cover-up myths can match the number of calories, the gallons of sweat, ink and gasoline, the reams of paper and hours of online time that have been expended on the abduction scenario. Like the Roswell story, the matter of abductions is not an issue on which it is appropriate to take an agnostic stance. Either the evidence offered by those who promote the belief that these are real events, happening in real time and involving more-or-less flesh and blood extra-terrestrials, stands up to scrutiny, or it doesn't. That is the question we will address here.

Let it be said from the outset that the problems with abduction claims arise almost entirely from the approach of the investigators of the phenomenon, not from those who claim to have been abducted. Of course, we are not suggesting that there are not hoaxers and jokers among the claimants: some have admitted as much. One such 'witness', a Ms Donna Bassett, maintained that in 1962 she had sat with US President John F. Kennedy and Soviet leader Nikita Khruschev on board a flying saucer while they negotiated their way out of the Cuban missile crisis. The claim is incredible enough by itself, but it is even more incredible that one of the foremost abduction researchers and promoters, Professor John Mack of Harvard University, a psychiatrist and Pulitzer prizewinner, took Ms Bassett's story at face value. His most vocal associates in propagating the literal truth of abduction narratives have yet to be revealed holding quite such a gem of gullibility as that. But their evasions, omissions and intellectual idleness in many small matters amount to a credulity just as gross. And this is compounded with such a lack of scientific caution that it is hard not to conclude that they are deluding themselves. It is difficult, too, not to fear that their self-delusion may occasionally be far from helpful for their clientele.

These are uncompromising criticisms, but they are aimed squarely at those who have done so much to create the abduction scenario and make it a public event – not at those who have had a baffling or even terrifying private experience and have desperately wanted to come to terms with and make sense of it. What is the difference between the promoters of the abduction accounts and those who tell them? To answer that, we have first to see what constitutes the abduction experience. What follows is a skeleton: there is no longer a 'classic' abduction story, as different investigators have uncovered aspects of the experience that they present as being consistent among their own clientele – even if they do not appear in the accounts given by others' subjects. But these are the bare bones on which these variations have grown.

¤ THE ABDUCTION SCENARIO

First, in many cases, comes a UFO sighting, sometimes involving electromagnetic or other physical effects on the witness' home or vehicle. A key factor emerges after the experience is over and the UFO has departed: the events of what seem like a few minutes' duration turn out to have taken an hour or even several. In the following days or weeks, bizarre UFO-related dreams, memory flashes or even physical symptoms afflict the witnesses. In some cases, this is all that triggers the suspicion that an abduction has occurred; the memories and the sense of 'missing time' may be associated with a quite mundane event (such as a picnic, or seeing deer in a wood). Of their own accord, or encouraged by others, they may then undergo hypnosis to disinter the memory of what transpired in the 'missing time'. Roughly one-third of abductions, however, are recalled – sometimes in intricate detail – without the help of hypnosis. We have already discussed one such in Chapter 7.

Typical accounts describe being led into a disc-like craft by aliens of various shapes and sizes. Latter-day witnesses most often report small gray aliens, sometimes supported by taller humanoids on board the UFO. Recent accounts often tell of being floated through solid walls or windows and then up a beam of light to a UFO. It is rarely clear exactly how the craft is entered (a phenomenon known as 'doorway amnesia'). The interiors of alien craft are reportedly brightly but diffusely lit and clinically clean, often with white or metallic appurtenances. The reason for this sterility soon becomes clear, for the next stage in the abduction is a medical examination of some kind – usually a painful one.

Betty Hill and Betty Andreasson reported that they were examined with a machine from which needle-like wires protruded and that needles were inserted into their

The central scene from the 'abduction scenario': the medical examination. The painting is by David A. Howard, whose abduction experiences while in narcoleptic trance have developed over many years into a complex and detailed account of visits to a binary star system where his captors live. *Dr Sue Blackmore*

navels for a 'pregnancy test' (although both had had hysterectomies). Betty Hill had skin scrapings, samples of ear wax, hair and clippings from her fingernails taken. Charles Hickson said his body was 'scanned' by a floating instrument resembling a large eye. David Stephens had two blood samples taken, and was examined naked with 'a box-like device'. Whitley Strieber said 'an enormous and extremely ugly object', triangular in structure and with a tangle of wires at one end, was inserted into his rectum. These examinations may involve the removal or insertion of small 'implants' in the abductee's body. These are believed to be tracking devices of some kind. Others report being forced to have sex with aliens, and women have claimed to have found themselves pregnant as a result. Some victims also say they feel as if their minds are being scanned during the examination phase. Communication with the aliens is generally telepathic.

After this, typical witnesses are allowed to dress and, before leaving the ship, are given a guided tour around it. Some researchers have found that this tour includes a visit to alien-human hybrid children, which the abductee may have fathered or borne. It may also include screenings of scenes that are sometimes taken to be views of Earth's future, and sometimes of the aliens' home planet.

Some abductees try to remove an item of the craft's equipment as physical proof of their experience, but the aliens prevent them. Others, however, are given gifts by the aliens, and sometimes words of wisdom or a 'message for mankind' as well. Finally, the abductee is 'transferred' directly from the craft or 'floated' back to where the aliens first took him or her captive; this stage of the proceedings, like the entering of the craft, is usually very vague. The UFO then leaves at high speed.

¤ THE MYTH TAKES ROOT

The reality, or otherwise, of UFO abductions became a major issue among ufologists in the 1980s, and excited massive public attention as well. Budd Hopkins, a successful New York artist, became renowned for the new element in the cases he had investigated using hypnosis: men reported having devices applied to them that relieved them of their sperm. A still greater number of women, notably one named Kathie Davis, told stories under hypnosis that suggested to Hopkins that aliens were conducting a deliberate, sustained programme of genetic sampling and possibly even manipulation among the human race.

According to Kathie Davis, aliens first visited her when she was a child, and had implanted a device in her head so that they could keep track of her. (She and other members of her family had similar, mysterious scars on their legs, which Hopkins attributed to cell-sampling by the aliens, noting that other alleged abductees bore similar marks.) As a teenager, Kathie allegedly became pregnant, but the pregnancy ended suddenly and mysteriously. Under hypnosis, she recalled that before her pregnancy aliens had visited her, performed an 'uncomfortable' and intimate procedure, and left. Some months into her pregnancy, they returned and removed her foetus. Years later, after she had married and had two children, the aliens returned again and briefly presented her with a little girl who 'looked like an elf or an... angel'. This was, apparently, her extra-terrestrially induced daughter. Kathie Davis was not the only woman whom Hopkins believed had been impregnated by ufonauts.

Controversy surrounds all these claims, largely because of the investigators' dependence on regressive hypnosis. Doubters point to the experiments of Dr Alvin Lawson and others in the late 1970s, in which people with no interest in or acquaintance with UFO lore produced, under hypnosis, almost startlingly similar accounts of 'alien abductions' as did 'genuine' abductees.

On the other hand, when in 1987 folklorist Dr Ed Bullard analysed 270 abduction cases from all over the world, he found such a consistency among the reports, from the look of the aliens to the idiosyncrasies of their demands, that he concluded that they could not have had a common source (as, he believed, a folk story would). And the more he weeded out likely hoaxes and delusions, the more alike the stories became. Essentially the same thing seemed to be happening to people of entirely different occupations, backgrounds and nationalities.

Cynics might say that, like reading Dickens' description of the death of Little Nell, accounts of so-called 'alien abductions' should reduce strong men to uncontrollable tears of laughter. But the very oddities and absurdities in the abductees' accounts ought to alert us to the possibility that these stories are taken seriously by the abductees themselves and by many 'ordinary' people exactly because they signify something much more profound than what is offered by their bald narrative surfaces. We shall return to and expand on this point. Meanwhile, we have to deal with the misfortune that those who have dictated the focus of the debate on abductions for most of the 1990s, particularly Budd Hopkins, David Jacobs and John Mack, have simply taken the accounts they have been given at face value. Unfortunately, this shows more than simple lack of imagination. Their 'witness statements' and evidence don't stand up very well under rigorous analysis.

¤ LOST IN THE REMEMBERING

One of the aliens' many amazing talents is the power to cover their tracks by altering the memories of their victims. Allegedly, the aliens insert memories of innocuous events into abductees' minds, in order to shield 'real' memories of abductions and prevent victims from remembering the truth and revealing the aliens' activities. These implanted 'screen memories' are, however, surprisingly fragile. When suitably besieged under hypnosis they soon shatter, to reveal the nasty 'truth'. David Jacobs, for example, describes a man who under hypnosis at first recalled a raven-headed, 'beautiful young woman... coming over to him for... a sexual liaison'. His response is revealing:

Through meticulous questioning about the minute details of her actions and her appearance ('If her head is on your upper chest, can you see the top of her head?'), the false memories fell away and the abductee independently [sic] realized that it was her black eyes that he had been describing and not her hair. In fact, she had no hair at all.

This is presumably an example, and the result, of asking 'proper' questions, which earlier abduction investigators, Jacobs says, did not know how to do:

> Even when competent hypnotists were called in on cases, they were not well versed enough in abduction research to ask the proper questions. They could not tell if the subject was 'filling in' with false information.... And because investigators did not know exactly what happened during an abduction, they could not identify false memories purposely placed in the victims' minds.

Where proper questions end and leading ones begin, Dr Jacobs does not say, any more than he offers any justification for adopting the profoundly unscientific principle that one should not undertake any investigation unless one knows what one is going to find.

The notion of screen memories was first conceived by the founder of psychoanalysis, Sigmund Freud (1856–1939). He published his first paper on them in 1899. In Freud's opinion, they were usually very vivid, inexplicably haunting memories of something strangely trivial, which covered up genuine but repressed memories of either distasteful or unbearable events. But, he noted, the screen memory is a transformation of the original event and always left symbolic clues to the 'repressed material' it camouflaged. Significantly, the abductionists transfer the power of repression and substitution from the human mind to the omnipotent aliens. Yet, if screen memories exist at all, there is no need to call in the aliens to impose them. Everyone agrees abduction is a traumatic experience, whose memory one may well want to shut out as thoroughly as possible. Why, then, do abductionists attribute the screening to the aliens?

Because it makes the aliens seem more powerful, more Otherworldly, and more frightening. John Whitmore has identified the strategy:

> In standard captivity narratives victims are often rescued by a morally perfect hero who destroys the victim's tormentors; in abduction tales the hero is the researcher-hypnotist, who alone knows the chilling agenda behind the victim's capture.

In order to be a hero, you have to acquire something suitably distressing to confront and overcome. The dark side of this knightly derring-do is a certain prurience, and a persistent casting of women, in particular, in humiliating roles that they come to believe are genuine and continuing.

One wonders how many abductionists have actually read Freud. Dr Bob Hinshelwood, clinical director of the Riverside Mental Health Service in Richmond, Surrey, told us:

> In principle... a Freudian would tend to regard the [abduction] phenomenon as a visitation from the patient's inner world, his unknown inner world, his unconscious in Freud's terms. ...His reporting a visitation from outer space would seem likely to be a disguised (dream-like) externalization of the 'return of the repressed'.

In other words, if Freud was right, an abduction memory may itself be a species of screening event! But many psychologists have questioned the reality of repressed and screen memories, since a number of innocent people have been jailed for child abuse they did not commit. Their victims' recall of these grotesque alleged events emerged more often than not under hypnosis calculated to dislodge screened and repressed memories. But Harvard psychiatrists Drs Harrison Pope and James Hudson, for example, have made a massive search of the literature for evidence of genuinely repressed memories of childhood sexual abuse – and found none. The concept of screen memories is rarely called on even by Freudians today. And real memories are, according to the best current research, emphatically not graven indelibly on the brain (from where hypnosis can extract them in all their pristine detail), but are malleable, mutable and reconstructed, sometimes out of third-party accounts.

¤ THE MIND'S DRIVE-IN

Whatever they may mean, where does the imagery – the furniture – of the abduction narrative come from? Martin Kottmeyer, Nigel Watson and Bertrand Méheust have unearthed many images and episodes from the silver screen, comic books and TV that have found their way into abductees' narratives. Most telling, when it comes to specific elements in abduction scenarios, is the way sci-fi movies have consistently been the first to air themes that later cropped up in allegedly genuine abduction narratives. One such is the underlying pedal-note of birth and rebirth (not excluding reincarnation) that runs through abductees' accounts. In Chapter 3 we mentioned the woman giving birth to an extra-terrestrial child in the 1974 TV movie The Stranger Within, and God Told Me To (1976), in which the protagonist is the product of alien intercourse that occurred when his mother was abducted by a UFO. These ideas did not make their way into the ufological literature until the 1980s.

Martin Kottmeyer has also shown how abductees borrow motifs and images from one other. Some of the details used in these borrowings include mummy-like entities and a tendency for the aliens to remove and then replace (but not improve) their captives' brains, and are so outlandish even by the standards of abduction lore that looting (perhaps through cryptomnesia) seems the only reasonable explanation for people having such images in their possession.

Peter Rogerson's sedulous bibliographical research turned up the intriguing fact that the first full-blown account of an abduction as we know abductions today appeared not in Brazil, or in a story told by some unfortunate from Disparunia, Arkansas, but in a work of fiction – *The Terror Above Us* by Malcolm Kent – published in 1967, just a year after the Betty and Barney Hill story was made public. This novel was the first work to describe the 'Oz factor', 'doorway amnesia' and the alien in disguise (i.e. the screen memory), and bring them together with the 'medical examination' beloved of the aliens. (The 'Oz factor' is a sense of entering an alternate reality or 'cone of silence' that precedes close encounters and abductions.)

Since such major audience-pullers on TV as *The UFO Incident* (1975) portraying the Hills' 1961 abduction, the

spacenapping of Fallon in *The Colbys* (1987), the miniseries *The Intruders* (1992), based on Budd Hopkins' book of that title, and the long-running and enormously popular *The X-Files* series, let alone the books and films of Whitley Strieber's *Communion* and of Travis Walton's 1975 experience in *Fire In The Sky* (1993), there can hardly be a citizen left in the West who does not now have some idea of what is supposed to happen next if, one dark and lonely night, they see a little gray figure hovering by their bedside or flagging down their pick-up on a lonely blacktop in the boonies. (See Chapter 3 for a detailed discussion of TV and film representations of alien abductions.)

The prior existence of raw materials in the public domain, or even in a specific abductee's mind, doesn't account for the seeming consistency of details in abduction accounts – but these stories were far more varied in almost all respects before Hopkins, Jacobs, Mack and in particular Whitley Strieber began publishing their findings. These researchers make no secret of the fact that they know one another, indeed inspired one another, have discussed cases together, and generally collaborate – if not necessarily on a conscious level. One of the most telling passages in Jim Schnabel's *Dark White* runs:

> *In the spring of 1993, Budd Hopkins hypnotized Calvin Parker, Charles Hickson's companion during the [1973] Pascagoula incident. Under hypnosis... Parker remembered that as he had entered the spacecraft... he had been curled up in the... tuck [i.e. foetal] position.... Hopkins told Jacobs about it, and suddenly Jacobs began to find that a lot of his abductees were being taken into spacecraft while in the tuck position.*

¤ ON THE COUCH

This brings us back to the vexed question of what really happens when abductee candidates present themselves to an abduction researcher and put themselves on the hypnotists' casting-couch. Jacobs calls hypnosis 'an indispensable [*sic*] tool in unlocking memories of an abduction.' All are extraordinarily convinced by the emotional reactions of subjects as they recount horrific events suffered at the hands of the 'aliens'. To the naive literalist, this indicates the genuineness of the memories being relived – 'this intensity of recovered emotion... lends inescapable authenticity to the phenomenon,' writes John Mack.

There was, perhaps still is, in Cardiff, Wales, a lady named Janet Jones, better known to the world as Jane

The village where 'Jordeye', David Howard's alien abductor, guide and friend lives on the planet Dut. Howard describes the architecture as 'oddly prehistoric', although the interior of the dwellings is very high tech. The creature in the foreground is called a 'scrowats' and is domesticated to keep down local vermin. *Dr Sue Blackmore*

Evans. In the late 1970s she was regressed by hypnotist Arnold Bloxham and produced detailed accounts of past lives – one as a member of a wealthy seventeenth-century French household, one as a Roman living in England, and one as a Jewess living in York in the late twelfth century and witnessing the massacre of the city's Jewish population at Clifford's Tower in 1190 – an event of which there is no doubt. While describing her experience of this event under hypnosis, she became progressively 'very agitated', 'very distressed', 'full of stress', 'panicky', 'hysterical' and finally, as her children were murdered in front of her, 'almost incoherent with terror'. As well she might. But two researchers, Melvin Harris and Ian Wilson, established that details Jane Evans gave of Jewish life in York at the time were so wildly wide of the historical mark that the rest of her story had to be fabrication. Melvin Harris tracked down the romantic novels that almost certainly served as the inspiration for her 'former lives' in seventeenth-century France and in Roman Britain. Jane Evans was dramatizing. It really was as simple as that.

Finally, on this point, consider Patrick Harpur's slant on what, in essence, abductees say happens to them. They are typically in their beds at night, somewhere between sleep and waking or, what is (as we all know) often much the same thing, they have been driving for hours at night on empty roads. They see a bright light, and then find themselves in the presence of aliens who waft them aboard a UFO, lay them helpless on a table, read their minds, probe their innermost secrets, intimately but impersonally examine their bodies, reassure them vaguely, and then let them go. After this experience, the victim finds that he, or more often she, cannot recall anything unusual but that an hour or two has gone by in what, subjectively, feels like seconds or a few minutes at most.

What happens at the hypnotist's? You enter a state – hypnotic trance – somewhere between sleep and waking, in another reality, where anything is possible. You lie submissively on a couch, your mind is read by a powerful being, and you give up sometimes embarrassing intimate details about your physical history, habits or proclivities, all in the interests of disinterested, dispassionate investigation. You are reassured by the hypnotist that all is well really. He lets you go, and you find that although it seems only a few minutes have passed, you have been in a trance for a couple of hours.

To be under hypnosis is to be in a condition of extreme suggestibility. Being hypnotized is itself an experience of being led. The people who arrive at the literalists'

'In this extremely desolate area of Dut,' writes David Howard, 'Jordeye and Gowrrodwehn [his associate] show me engraved slabs among the ruins of a university which they claimed to be over one million Earth years old. They seemed to have a particular sadness or perhaps reverence about them, somewhat as we do when we go into a church and talk in whispers.' *Dr. Sue Blackmore*

doorsteps must, in the nature of things, already be set up to expect, even hope for, the revelation that they have been 'abducted'. They can hardly be surprised when they pour forth confirmatory 'evidence' under hypnosis.

Naturally, abductionists deny this and harp on the horror and dismay with which their subjects greet the news that they are victims of aliens. 'I thought this only happened to white people,' one Afro-American lady remarked ruefully to one researcher when being assured that what she had remembered was literally true. Another subject implied he would rather have been told he was mad than have to accept the idea that his 'hypnotically refreshed' memory was a factual record of events. But note that the insistence on the actuality of the accounts is coming from the investigators – not from the 'victims', who seem instinctively to recognize the inherent absurdity of what they have said. But insistence, more hypnosis, and reinforcement through contact with other abductees will soon turn created memories into apparently real ones – and skepticism into distressed belief. The creation of belief is consistent with the findings of those who believe in ritual satanic abuse (RSA) and universal sexual abuse of children – and those who have questioned those findings.

John Mack's attempts to dismiss the astonishing parallels noted by journalist Lawrence Wright between RSA narratives and abduction stories focus on anything but the point that Wright actually makes, which is that these tales are produced in exactly the same way, have common motifs, and serve similar psychological purposes. Wright shows that there are exactly parallel motifs in satanic ritual abuse and abduction accounts. Victimization, mind control, 'little people', witches coming in through windows who later transmute into adult male abusers – all these images were produced by one alleged RSA 'survivor' who was, in effect, being bullied in a trance-like state. It is clear that had this subject been questioned in the presumption that an abduction sequence had occurred, he could have produced the appropriate 'memories' with only a slight shift of imagery. In due course he retracted his 'evidence' and refused to testify against his father and others accused with him.

Mack goes several dimensions beyond other leading abductionists in abandoning any application of Occam's razor to the material he so willingly laps up – but then he constantly reminds the reader of his view that Western logic and science are inadequate and useless for dealing with it. At any rate, he is probably unique among abduc-tionists in managing to roll alien encounters, alien-human reincarnation (four of his 13 subjects produced accounts of past lives involving alien contact) and alien-human hybrids into one alleged phenomenon. He is surely the best living indicator that the investigator, not the subject, determines the content of abduction narratives.

Nonetheless, many do believe that alien abductions really happen. In a scientist culture like ours, we are soon obliged to scrabble for some physical evidence to back up the beliefs we want to promote, no matter how bizarre. The literalists offer a variety of such 'exhibits' to support their case.

¤ ALIEN STIGMATA

Abductees display scars that 'prove' they have been phys-ically assaulted by aliens. In some cases, mysterious bleed-ings (nosebleeds are a favourite) and discharges from a person's private portions are cited in evidence. In no such cited case known to us do the investigators suggest that they have attempted to find a simpler medical cause for the symptoms they describe. Nor do they admit to having consulted or co-operated with their subjects' medical doctors. Why not?

Virtually everyone can find a scar somewhere on their body and not be able to remember how it got there. Besides, as any doctor will confirm, any symptom, and sometimes a whole set of symptoms, has a range of possible, and absolutely prosaic, causes. One slash of Occam's razor removes aliens – whose presence demands a massive elaboration of hypotheses – from the list.

There is another possible cause of allegedly alien-induced scars, bleedings and other minor traumata. The literalists seem not to have studied the phenomenon of religious, overwhelmingly Roman Catholic Christian, stigmata. According to one expert on the subject, British broadcaster Ted Harrison, it is possible that stigmatics initially produce their wounds by savaging their own flesh, but it remains an open question as to whether the infliction was conscious – that is, calculated and fraudu-lent – or committed in the heat of the visionary moment. But Harrison also cites the findings of Italian psycho-therapist Dr Marco Margnielli, who videotaped one

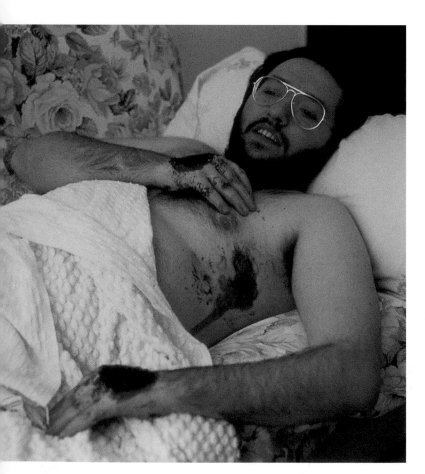

The wounds of Italian stigmatic Giorgio Bongiovanni bleed five times a day. Bongiovanni is unusual among stigmatics in combining orthodox religious visions with UFO experiences: according to him, Jesus and Mary descend from UFOs to earth, and some ETs are angels. He has also met traditional 'gray' aliens, who, he says, are ETs about a century ahead of Earth in technology. *Fortean Picture Library*

stigmatic, Domenico Lo Bianco, as she produced – without any external stimulus – the marks of the cross and the rosary on her left arm.

So, it is by no means impossible that – perhaps as a result of auto-suggestion, perhaps as an outcome of prior belief, predisposition or false memories induced by hypnosis – that the physical scars and symptoms of 'abductees' are either unconsciously self-inflicted or are psychosomatically induced. And in some cases, plain fraud is possible, too. People in need of attention will go to extraordinary lengths to acquire it, as cases of Munchausen's Syndrome so eloquently demonstrate.

¤ SONGS OF MISSING PERSONS

Abductionists refer time and again to cases in which abductees have been noticed to be missing during abductions. Unfortunately, they offer only vague descriptions of instances, without names, dates or other details. In one, cited by Mack, two teenage girls vanish late one evening from their bedroom, are 'returned' by 6am, and are greeted by parental uproar. Egregiously, Mack omits to say how they accounted for this at the time, and shows no sign of having asked the girls' parents for their accounts. At the age of 24, however, one of the pair explains this episode as an abduction. Teenagers have plenty of reasons for going missing at night that they would not want to admit to their parents, or even to a professor of psychiatry, especially when they think an abduction story is what he really wants to hear.

Jacobs makes an outrageously bloated claim in this respect. 'Never,' he writes in *Secret Life*, 'has an abductee claimed to be abducted and later been physically accounted for during that exact time.' Those only half-acquainted with the subject on which Dr Jacobs is considered a world expert remember the date 22 February 1973 with clarity and even with some affection. On that day, Mrs Maureen Puddy made history by being 'abducted' from her car in front of two witnesses. As we noted in Chapter 7, Mrs Puddy's body never left the driver's seat.

Mrs Maureen Puddy at the spot south-east of Melbourne, Australia, where on 25 July 1972 she had her first abduction experience. Seven months later she was abducted again in front of witnesses, although that story has a special twist. *Fortean Picture Library*

¤ SECOND OPINION

Then there are those endlessly repeated stories of alien-induced pregnancies and stolen progeny. Let us be quite clear about this. No abductionist has ever produced any material evidence of an alien-induced pregnancy. Where are the medical records, the results of pregnancy tests? Have the investigators ever asked for them, or asked the victims to acquire them? Or are they merely taking their subjects' assertions as truth and proof? If these 'virgin' pregnancies were appearing, they would surely be deemed more than sufficiently intriguing to be written up in medical journals by the doctors involved. But there are no such cases in the literature.

On being asked her expert opinion, Dr Barbara L. Skew, formerly of the Royal United Hospital, Bath, and at the time of writing staff gynaecologist at Southmead Hospital, Bristol, both in the west of England, dealt bluntly with 'abductees' who are alleged to be pregnant and then found not to be:

This is clearly a failure of proper diagnosis. It is perfectly possible for false positive pregnancy tests on urine to occur. Bimanual palpation (vaginal examination) of the uterus is unreliable even in experienced hands, especially for pregnancies of fewer than eight weeks. The only truly reliable method of diagnosis is ultrasound scanning, in which [if a pregnancy exists] an intrauterine sac can be seen and photographed. This has been freely available for 20 years at least, is cheap, non-invasive and absolutely diagnostic. Without [such] photographic evidence... I would be very sceptical that a pregnancy was there in the first place.

There is nothing unusual or otherworldly about 'unreal' pregnancies. Said Dr Skew:

Amenorrhea (lack of 'periods') may be confused with pregnancy. Most gynaecologists have seen at least one woman who maintained she was pregnant and was proved not to have been. The more suggestible the patient the more easily she will convince herself she is pregnant.

Dr Skew pointed out that in any form of artificial insemination, the crucial issue is the menstrual cycle. Fertilization has to take place within 48 hours of ovulation. The abductionists show no sign of having checked even this fundamental datum with their subjects. Worse, Jacobs has indulged in at least one spectacular exercise of dissimulation in an attempt to counter criticism. Peter Brookesmith sat next to him in July 1994 as he told an audience of hundreds that 'skeptics' and gynaecologists 'explain away' these temporary, 'alien' pregnancies by referring to what he miscalled 'absorption' of the foetus back into the womb. But, he said, 'There's no real evidence for that; gynaecologists don't really know if it happens.' There is indeed no real evidence for what gynaecologists actually call resorption of singleton foetuses in humans. But then gynaecologists have never claimed that it has ever happened. No case has ever been reported in the medical literature. In four-legged mammals, with several progeny in a long, tube-like uterus, resorption (for whatever immediate cause) is a biologically efficient means of disposing of necrotic material. But women suffer a miscarriage or an abortion – a summary ejection of the dead foetus from the short, squat human uterus.

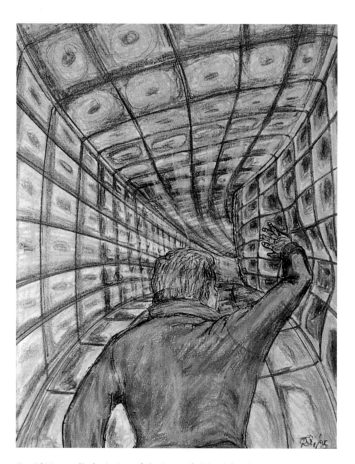

David Howard's depiction of the 'tunnel vision' that is common to near-death experiences, UFO abductions and other altered states of consciousness. Researcher Alvin Lawson suggested abductions were memories of being born; certainly themes of birth, rebirth and even reincarnation run right through abduction accounts. David Howard calls the tunnel 'a form of transport used by the Dutions, in which one floats. If one tries to touch the sides, they just stretch away from you.' *Dr Sue Blackmore*

Once more we find ourselves in a land of delusions, of abductee claimant and investigator alike. Jacobs made his statement two years after attending a Study Conference on Alien Abductions at Massachusetts Institute of Technology. There, one speaker, John Miller, berated his colleagues for treating the missing-foetus legend as fact, having found no evidence for it whatever. David Jacobs is also the man who wrote: 'No significant body of thought exists that presents strong evidence that anything else is happening other than what the abductees have stated.'

¤ WILL THE CIRCLE BE UNBROKEN?

In *Intruders*, Budd Hopkins says he considers Kathie Davis' abduction 'one of the most important' because of the 'landing trace marks' found in the garden of her parents' house. To Hopkins, this was the Grail: physical evidence of a UFO landing. However, even Hopkins admits that none of the Davis family had ever claimed that the 8ft (2.5m) circle of dead grass in question was a landing trace, or had ever seen anything resembling a UFO land in the garden. Having received soil samples from both the circle and the surrounding area, Hopkins waited two years before sending them to Mobay Chemicals' Inorganic Chemicals Division. (Why he did not send them sooner, and to a soil – i.e. organic, biochemical – laboratory remains a mystery.) Hopkins says, 'crystallographic and spectrographic analysis showed no apparent difference between the two samples.'

Veteran skeptic Philip J. Klass is underwhelmed by what Hopkins makes of this. In *UFO Abductions: A Dangerous Game*, he points out drily that Hopkins 'often refers to the dead-grass area as "burned", when in reality the grass itself showed absolutely no evidence of intense heat.' Further, Klass considers the 'dead area' soil – dry, hard and lightish gray-brown in colour – to be strangely like that typically found in a fungus-infested 'fairy ring'. In light of the literalists' disdain for any connection between fairy lore and abductions, this is most deliciously ironic.

Abduction promoters often refer in their books to independently witnessed UFO sightings, contemporaneous with abductions, as if they were a species of corroboration of space-nappings, too. Unfortunately, they give no details of these sightings, remaining particularly tight-lipped as to whether equally independent investigators have actually confirmed that genuine 'unknowns' were seen.

Just how little regard the literalists have for such conscientious research may be gauged from an interview

¤ THE ALIEN BOOGER MYSTERY ¤

No doubt, there have been X-rays and CAT scans of apparently anomalous lumps, bumps, nodes and odd objects in people's heads or up their noses. In the pictures, they look like metal swarfs or even toenail clippings.

Photographed they may be, but they just keep vanishing, like those books of cosmic wisdom that the aliens give to some abductees. In a 1988 interview, David Jacobs said ingenuously, and no doubt a trifle sadly, that such objects had 'so far been lost or thrown away' – which is worse than misfortune: it smacks of carelessness. In 1994, in Pensacola, Budd Hopkins said:

If [implants] ever do show up on an X-ray or CAT scan, within a day or two – before there is any ability to try to recover them – they disappear. The aliens seem to have a little alarm bell that goes off in the sky, and they come and remove the object.

Assiduous research has shown that there is no good reason to suppose that the MRI and other scanned images of 'implants' passing around in ufological circles are anything but artefacts of the imaging process itself, and there is nothing to indicate that the genuinely mysterious-seeming objects that have popped out of people's bodies are not the by-product of natural, if not particularly common, events. One no more needs aliens in the mix of explanations than one does in accounting for a limp.

with David Jacobs printed in *UFO Magazine* (Quest UK, November/December 1995). Here, Jacobs reveals his belief that the abduction phenomenon 'begins with great airship sightings in the US in 1897'. But there are no CE-III or CE-IV reports from the 1896–7 US airship wave that have not been shown to be jokes or hoaxes.

But the abduction syndrome is based on something. The question is, what?

¤ MYTHS ARE NOT FOR MOCKING

It is possible to see the meaning of UFO myths as centred on the inner life – not the world of the mind, but the realm of the soul, and the relations between everyday kitchen-sink reality and the need, seemingly a human universal, to discern a meaning in life and to acquire a language in which to express, celebrate and refine the life of the spirit. From this point of view, aliens may be seen as godlings, reconciling religious and scientific responses to both timeless and immediate, contemporary human dilemmas. Peter Rogerson has written:

It seems to me totally obvious that the ufonauts do not represent aliens, but are perceived as non-human (or at least non-humane) aspects of ourselves and our society. The 'grays' are surely personifications of 'little gray men' — that stock term of abuse for petty, colourless, hidebound bureaucrats — an apt image of 'only doing my job' cosmic social workers. I would go further, and say that there is being made here an identification between the impersonal forces of mass society and the impersonal forces of wild nature.

¤ ENOUGH ROPER TO HANG THEMSELVES ¤

Ever since the findings of the famous Roper Organization poll of 1991 became known, Hopkins and his associates have touted them as an indication of the vast scale of alien abductions in the US. In particular, they have done so through a pamphlet titled *Unusual Personal Experiences*, published in 1992, with an introduction by John Mack. The interpretation, by Hopkins, Jacobs and Ron Westrum (HJ&W), of the survey's results is 100 per cent mistaken.

The presumption behind their reading of the figures was that a person had possibly been abducted if he or she answered 'Yes' to five key questions and 'No' to a 'lie detector' question.

Out of 5947 respondents, Roper found precisely 18 people who fulfilled this criterion. This represents 0.3 per cent of the sample. It does not represent 0.3 per cent of the US population or (using HJ&W's figures) 555,000 people. This is because the margin of error in the poll is ±1.4 per cent. Any number below that might, statistically, just as well be zero. To find out if this number is representative, you would need to question at least five times as many people as Roper did, and probably many more, in order to overcome a law of diminishing returns.

All the Roper research tells us is that in this particular sample there were 18 people who had had five experiences that, according to HJ&W, indicate they have been abducted. It is even possible, statistically, that they are the only 18 such people in the US. It shouldn't, then, be hard to speculate why HJ&W decided that if a person gave positive answers to only four of the five questions it would show, in their words, 'there is a strong possibility [that] that individual is a UFO abductee.' Not surprisingly, this relaxation of standards gave a rather more startling result – HJ&W concluded that 119 people in the sample, representing 2 per cent of the population or 3.7 million people in the continental US, were abductee candidates. Taking the margin of error into account (which they don't), this could actually mean that as 'few' as 1.11 million or as many as 6.29 million adult Americans may have been abducted.

The trouble is that no known system of logic will support any such conclusion at all. In the words of veteran market researcher James R. Adams:

What they are saying is, if abduction, then all these other symptoms. All these other symptoms (or some of them, even), therefore abduction. This does not follow; the logic has what is known as an 'undistributed middle'. If it is raining, the pavements are wet. But, the fact that the pavements are wet does not mean that it is raining.

In other words, HJ&W are offering a classic false syllogism, of the kind that amuses schoolboys, as 'fact': 'A dog has four legs; a table has four legs; therefore tables enjoy marrowbones, chase cats, and bark.'

Whatever else the Roper results may tell us – and they tell us much about the incidence of anomalous experiences – they reveal absolutely nothing about the incidence or reality of abductions by aliens in the US.

And Paul Devereux has said:

My guess is that the extra-terrestrial is the image of our own estrangement from our inner selves and from nature itself. ...The machine is within the modern soul. And the ET robot or alien could be the very image of our estrangement.

It is not surprising that, in the twentieth century, in which both God and humanism have so egregiously failed to save humanity from its own incomprehensible capacity for cruelty, a frustrated craving for the transcendental has elaborated on technologically otherworldly elements in contemporary culture and combined them with motifs from traditional Western religion to reflect, explain or redeem the human predicament. Of the literalists, John Mack is the most honest about this aspect of the phenomenon – not as an analyst, but as a potential believer. Possibly it arises from his known concerns about nuclear arms and 'the environment' – which, by a mysterious coincidence, his subjects' aliens seem to share and echo:

Is it possible that... an effort is being made to place the planet under a kind of receivership? This would... arrest the destruction of life and make possible the evolution of consciousness or whatever the anima mundi has in store. ...I would merely suggest that if we could allow ourselves to reintroduce the possibility of a higher intelligence into the universe, and experience the numinous mystery of creation, this scenario is consistent with the facts of the abduction phenomenon.

Mack's 'facts' may not be the facts of the mundane world. But it is certainly not hard to detect apocalyptic elements in the imagery of abductees' 'visions', and not difficult either to discern in them parallels with many aspects of Western, that is Semitic, religious traditions. And which, in the end, is more likely – that 'scientifically advanced' aliens are using the crudest possible methods in a probably impossible programme of interbreeding with humanity, and indulging in the occasional spot of amateur reincarnation at the same time, or that the abduction scenario is just that: a shared drama that reveals us to ourselves?

We don't need real, live aliens to explain accounts of abductions; but we may need the stories of aliens in ways, and at levels, that we are only just beginning to understand (an issue taken up in more detail in the Epilogue). The literalists have at least revealed the

David Howard and Jordeye visit a forest near the alien's village. 'To describe Jordeye is very difficult',' says Howard. 'In some ways he is quite like us. But in a God like way. In my dreams I talk and communicate with him, I feel as though I physically touch him, I see him, I smell him. At times he has even come into my normal life.' *Dr Sue Blackmore*

landscape through which we must travel if we are to understand the abduction narrative as a social construction – and they have shown how tenaciously attractive is this most revealing, and revelatory, myth of our times.

But in saying that, we are not dismissing abduction experiences, or relegating them to the level of delusions, 'all in the mind' of people who by implication are not quite normal. Far from it.

¤ FIELDS OF DREAMS

If it is true that many 'abductees' self-generate their experiences psychologically because of personal, medical or social tensions or problems, it might also be true that there is an objective component in a limited number of cases. It could be that the otherworldly, nightmarish experiences are triggered by close contact with an energetic object such as an earth light.

In 1983, Michael Persinger described a number of possible effects on the body, brain and mind of a witness dependent on distance from a light phenomenon, based on clinical observations of the effects of electromagnetism on human physiology.

At a range beyond the influence of the energy fields associated with an earth light, a person will simply see a strange light. Closer in, the observer will notice details of the light form: colours, shape, internal fluctuations and so on. As the light moves closer, or is approached, the witness enters the presumed electromagnetic fields associated with the phenomenon. The first effects to be noticed would include tingling sensations, goose bumps, hair raising, and an oppressive feeling on the chest. Deeper into the field, closer to the light phenomenon, the observer is likely to experience altered states of consciousness as brain function is increasingly affected. Hallucinatory material is released into waking awareness. As the encounter becomes closer, the witness will experience deeper modifications of consciousness, vision and memory. Emotional states such as terror, or, conversely, religious awe might appear. If electrical aspects of the field dominate, then localized effects on the neck and thighs would occur, whereas if magnetic components were predominant, then the waist and genital regions would be especially affected. Sensations in these parts of the body would readily be incorporated into the mental states being created at the same time within the witness by the ambient energy fields. (We have all experienced this in more mundane circumstances. In a deep sleep, for instance, external sounds such as door banging or an alarm bell going off, or bodily discomfort such as thirst or a stomach ache, can become woven into the content of a dream. Thirst, for instance, might encourage a dream of wandering through a desert, or a dream of cascading waterfalls might indicate a message from the bladder!) As the witness and the light draw even closer together, the person will risk unconsciousness. On awakening, there may be partial or complete amnesia. Even closer contact could result in burning, hair loss and radiation sickness (all these effects have been found on some claimed close encounter witnesses). An extreme close encounter could result in death by electrocution or, as Persinger chillingly puts it, by 'carbonization'.

It is interesting to recall (see Chapter 1) that some traditional peoples, such as the Wintu of California and the inhabitants of the Darjeeling area of northern India, have lore which states that close encounter with strange lights can result in illness or death ('spirit eating' in the Wintu phrase).

The parts of the brain most likely to be affected by electromagnetic fields are the temporal lobes and amygdala, as they are particularly electrically sensitive, and that is why seizures are most often associated with them. All human brains fall on a scale of temporal lobe sensitivity. Those at the one extreme, 'temporal lobe sensitives', are the most likely to experience transpersonal – mystical or otherworldly – experiences, as well as to suffer epileptic seizures. Beneath the temporal cortex are the hippocampus and the amygdala. Alterations in the function of the hippocampus can change or modify memory and release dreams into the waking state. The amygdala is associated with emotional feelings. Temporal lobe epilepsy occurs because of the chronic occurrence of tiny electrical seizures within the temporal cortex. A sufferer will report dreamy states, the hearing of voices, the seeing of apparitions and the feeling of compulsions. When small currents are induced in the tissues of the hippocampus and amygdala during clinical experimentation, subjects report scenes or apparitions, and experience alterations in time and space, out-of-body experiences, feelings of unreality, *déjà vu* and memory blanks. Meaningful auditory messages may seem to emanate from the subject's environment. Even brief stimulation can cause hours of alteration in the brain's information processing.

The biochemical and electrical alterations in these sensitive brain tissues can be caused by a number of circumstances, such as electrochemical effects within the brain itself resulting from a person's medical condition, behaviour patterns (including regular psycho-spiritual exercises) or experiences, the taking of certain drugs, or exposure to external electromagnetic fields, both geophysical such as earth lights, and artificial such as around high-tension cables.

When electrical disturbance within the temporal cortex has happened once or a few times, cells within the tissues can become effectively primed. This is known as 'kindling'. People who have experienced this become prone to entering altered mind states with only the minimum of stimulation from whatever external or internal source.

Since the late 1980s, Persinger has been running a series of experiments to test in practice the effects of magnetic fields on the temporal cortex. The subject is placed in a sound-proofed chamber and is fitted with a helmet containing computer-controlled electrodes that direct magnetic 'vortices' to the temporal lobes with great precision. Some people see visions – of, say, a religious figure in accord with their beliefs (a person's expectations and beliefs have a profound effect on the content of visionary material, however caused), or, occasionally, ghosts or demons. But most simply have a powerful feeling of a presence. One person was of the opinion that the acoustic chamber ought to be exorcised as it was haunted by the Devil himself!

'After several sessions,' Persinger told journalist Ian Cotton, 'it took little to trigger the mystical state of mind.' Cotton decided to try the experiment for himself, and had a range of interesting experiences (see panel).

In the early days of the experiments, Persinger formed two groups of subjects who had never experienced a close encounter with a UFO. One group used the magic magnetic helmet, while the other group, acting as a control, did not. Both groups were told to imagine that they were emerging from woods and could see a light in the sky. Persinger set up a pulsing electric light in the laboratory. He asked them to free-associate. Those who were having their brains magnetically massaged disgorged images full of standard UFO abduction scenes – 'from gray-skinned, slit-mouthed aliens to blue beams of light to horrific reports of medical probes', ufologist and journalist Dennis Stacy learned. Such imagery was far richer in those exposed to the magnetic field than in those who were not.

But what about the real thing? Is there any evidence that this sort of brain effect could be occurring during some actual UFO sightings?

¤ LIGHT FANTASTIC

As a matter of fact, there is. The Yakima outbreak (see Chapter 10) provides some good examples. As well as hearing poltergeist-like gravel-crunching around their remote lookout posts, fire wardens on the reservation also reported 'happy little voices singing', a woman screaming, someone 'hollering'. There were no mundane explanations for any of these. In addition, there were reports of strong, repulsive odours (olfactory hallucinations can occur as well as visual and auditory ones), and in one case the fleeting appearance of a wild-looking humanoid, 7ft (2m) tall. And there was an interesting reported close encounter case with an earth light, involving a group of

¤ INTO ANOTHER REALITY ¤

Journalist Ian Cotton experienced two sessions with Persinger's magnetic helmet. He sat in total darkness, and heard 'little prickling noises' which he took to be the electric charges going in. He drifted into a kind of lucid dream state, in which his consciousness became like a video camera looking at scenes from his early childhood. (Childood and infantile memories are quite common experiences in disturbed temporal-lobe states.) He saw the pattern on the wallpaper in his bedroom, the design of red roses on a table cover, and other long-forgotten, intricate details. After a short break, Cotton underwent a second session, and this time Eastern bell music was played in the background. This sounded to the journalist like Tibetan bells, and this gradually grew into a conviction. Suddenly, 'with a kind of booster rocket of realism' he was in a temple, observing rows of brown-cowled monks and listening to loud temple bells. When a voice over the intercom called him back to normal consciousness, the other reality somehow carried on for a while 'in tandem, entwined together' with his normal waking state.

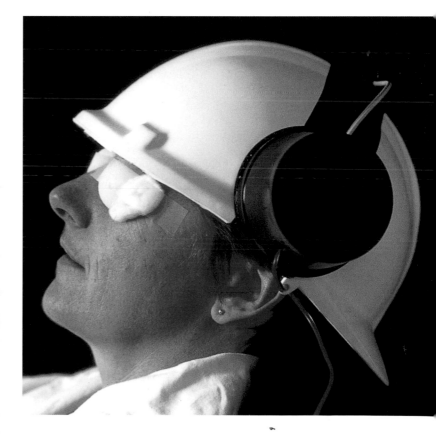

Dr Sue Blackmore in a helmet modelled on the device created by Professor Michael Persinger to test the effects of magnetic fields on the brains' temporal lobes. *Dr Sue Blackmore*

people travelling across the reservation one night in the midst of the wave of sightings. Their car broke down and they saw a light in the distance. The light got closer. No one recalls what happened next – they were all suffering from amnesia when they later recovered. However, one man in the group did recall a sensation of floating out of his body and glimpsing the others standing stock-still, as if in trance.

Evidence of a mind-altering experience resulting from an earth lights encounter is even detectable in one of the classic abduction cases, cited by Budd Hopkins in *Intruders*: namely, one of his earlier cases, involving the pseudonymous Kathie Davis, whose story we touched on earlier in this chapter. Kathie had contacted Hopkins on account of his earlier book, *Missing Time*, which dealt with UFO abductions and which she felt resonated with her confused feelings.

The basic story of this Indiana woman's encounter is that she saw a ball of light in her backyard. When Kathie went outside to check a short while later, there was no lightball to be seen and everything seemed in order. She then went off and visited a neighbour. During her absence, however, Kathie's mother, who was inside the house, saw a light alongside the pool house. It was translucent, for she could see the bird feeder through it. The basketball-sized light was curious – 'there wasn't any beam'. Then it 'sort of faded out, all at once'. She called the neighbour's house where Kathy was visiting, and Kathie returned to investigate. This was at 9.30pm. She recalls being outside for only ten minutes and finding nothing unusual. She then went to a friend's house to suggest a moonlight swim in the pool, as it was a hot, humid night. She should have arrived at her friend's place no later than 10pm if only ten minutes had elapsed in the garden, yet it was 11pm when she got there. Kathie, her friend and another companion returned to the Davis' home and entered the swimming pool. They all began to experience odd sensations such as inexplicable coldness, and either a fogging of vision or a highly localized haze condition, as a halo could be seen around the electric lights. All three swimmers felt nauseous at about the same time.

Hopkins discovered that the Davis's closest neighbours had noticed some unusual occurrences that evening. They had seen a brief flash of light in the direction of the Davis' house and had felt a low, vibrating sound. Their own house shook and a chandelier moved slightly. The TV set displayed interference, the house lights dimmed, and the digital clocks in the house had to be reset. The neighbours felt that there had been a small earth tremor.

The next morning, the Davis' lawn showed a burnt circle with a long line leading up to it.

Every single aspect of this incident is consistent with the appearance of an earth light, which left physical damage and had mental effects on witnesses, preceding a minor, local tectonic event. Yet Hopkins was insistent on interpreting it within the context of his overweening belief in the literal reality of UFO abductions. This was the context he offered Kathie Davis, and she underwent hypnotic regressions in which, mosaic like, a story of abduction by extra-terrestrials was constructed. According to the hypnotically induced memories, Kathie was subjected to highly invasive medical examinations in some unfamiliar environment, and was inseminated. From this (as noted above), a half-human, half-alien child resulted.

So the aliens and the spaceships appeared only in hypnotically derived imagery. If Kathie's brain functions had been affected by energy fields associated with the ball of light, then such confabulation, let alone partial amnesia, would be a typical consequence. The hypnotic regression merely probed the period of amnesia and the peripheral periods of disturbed memory, and because of the set and setting in which the sessions were conducted, could well have actually implanted imagery into Kathie's mind. Cognitive science now understands that memory is not like some video library or photo album from which objective, stored snapshots of the past are retrieved, but is mediated by electrical configurations of brain cells which reconstruct memorial images. While these memories are real to the person involved, they need not necessarily be of anything that objectively happened. (The whole issue of false memory is a fraught matter with important legal implications in some circumstances.)

In Kathie's case, we see a hybrid of traditional fairy changeling themes amalgamated with modern UFO folklore, perhaps spiced with psychological imagery relating to the woman's response to living in a modern, technological society with all its pressures, fears and alienating aspects. The extra-terrestrial abduction context had been powerfully supplied by Hopkins himself. In another culture or time, Kathie's memories may have been biased towards demons and spirits. (Talking with abductees in both Britain and the US, Paul Devereux has found a preparedness on their part to entertain an 'altered-states' context for their experiences. As one said to him: 'The UFO abduction explanation was the only one I knew about.')

¤ FIRE FROM THE SKY

One of ufology's most famous (or infamous) abduction cases, that of Travis Walton in 1975, is also amenable to an interpretation along the lines of the Persinger model. Walton was a member of a wood-cutting crew returning home in the darkness of a November evening from the Arizona forest where they had been working. Before their pick-up truck had cleared the trees, the men saw a glowing disc about 20ft (6m) wide and 8ft (2.5m) high, hovering in a clearing. There seemed to be panel-like geometric forms on the smooth, glowing surface of the object. The crew responded with mixed emotions, mostly fear, but Walton was excited and leapt from the truck even before the driver had brought it to a swerving halt, and then ran towards the object. He stopped at the edge of the circle of light that the disc was casting onto the ground. The object was giving off a strange beeping and soft rumbling sounds. When it commenced a wobbling action, Walton's curiosity could not prevent a wave of fear, and he turned to run back to the truck. He heard a crackling or popping sound, then felt 'a numbing shock... like a high voltage electrocution' that particularly affected his head and chest. His workmates saw him being struck by a blue-green bolt of light that lifted him, spread-eagled, into the air. He was thrown backwards some 10ft (3m), hit the hard ground right shoulder first, and lay still. The crew viewing from the truck were overcome with terror, and left the scene in panic. Over-hasty driving soon led the truck into a pile of dirt and a crunching halt.

Gathering what little was left of their wits, the men decided they had to go back for Walton. They had some difficulty locating the specific clearing, and when they did they saw no sign of Walton, nor anything out of order. They drove down to the community of Heber, and in a highly emotional state told the police there what had happened. There was a somewhat patchy and unsatisfactory search, which did not involve trained dogs.

The police began to suspect that Travis Walton may have been murdered, and became increasingly unhappy with the UFO story. But after five days, Travis phoned his brother-in-law, purportedly from a phone booth in the Heber gas station, saying he was basically okay and asking to be picked up.

Walton stated that he recalled recovering consciousness and finding himself in a hospital-like room which was diffusely lit,

Travis Walton is zapped by an alien light beam – as depicted in the film *Fire in the Sky. Robert Grant Archive*

with a metallic taste in his mouth. He was thirsty, his vision was blurred, his body ached and he had some difficulty breathing. As his eyesight came into focus, he saw three non-human figures in the room. They were under 5ft (1.5m) tall and had large, domed, 'foetus-like' bald heads with enormous eyes 'almost all brown, without much white in them'. They had soft, marshmallowy skin. Walton struggled to his feet and lunged at the figures, who backed off and left the room. Travis himself ran out of the room and down a curving corridor. He entered another domed room which had just an empty, high-backed pedestal chair in its centre, with a panel of control buttons on its right armrest. Whenever Travis approached the chair, the light in the room faded and the walls became transparent, revealing an encompassing, star-spangled blackness. When he sat in the chair he felt as if he were floating in the starry void of space. He was interrupted by what appeared to be a particularly well-formed human being. The Caucasian man, who had strange, bright hazel-coloured eyes, wordlessly led Walton out of the craft and into a hangar-like space. Light glowed from some of the panels forming the walls. The craft he had left looked like the disc seen in the woods only larger, and other craft were parked nearby. He was taken into a room where there were more good-looking humanoids. Silently and smilingly, they lifted Travis onto a table. He began to struggle but they forced him down and put something like an oxygen mask on his face. He awoke to find himself lying face up on a highway near Heber, 10 miles (16km) from the scene of the original encounter. He claimed to glimpse momentarily a round light in the distance.

The subsquent investigation had many unfortunate aspects that confused the nature of the experience Travis Walton claimed to have had, but there is not the space here to go into the details. Walton failed one lie-detector test, but passed another. Each of his workmates also passed polygraph tests – all except one, and there were special reasons why he failed. There were inconsistencies in the overall story that have never been explained, such as the fact that Walton showed no bruising from his impact with the ground when he was struck (or electrocuted) by the light beam, why analysis of the urine sample he provided (no one knows for sure if it was his) did not reveal certain chemicals that should have been present if he had not eaten for five days, and why his fingerprints were not on any of the telephones in the Heber gas station. There were yet more difficulties than these, and overall the case remains inconclusive. To this day, opinion is divided between those who feel sure Walton

really was abducted by aliens and those who think the whole thing was a hoax. In 1993, a feature film about the incident, *Fire in the Sky*, based on Walton's own book of his experiences, was released.

American ufologist Jerome Clark has assembled a most comprehensive account of the Walton case. He points out that some of the inconsistencies can be explained, and against them there is a mountain of supporting circumstantial evidence. He feels that if it was fabrication, then it was remarkably skilful and intricate in execution, and if not, then the event holds vital implications for us all.

It could be that the real answer exists between the extremes: neither hoax nor literal UFO abduction. What is described about the encounter itself is consistent with electric shock caused by close proximity to a glowing plasma, causing an initial brief mental blackout and seizures within Walton's temporal cortex with concomitant hallucinations, partial amnesia, mental confusion and further blackout periods. As one of the reporters at the time was later to suggest: 'He had seen something out there in the woods, some kind of an eerie light that had triggered a powerful hallucination that might recur at any time.' Could Travis Walton have wandered about disoriented for five days in the woods, alternately hallucinating and lapsing into unconsciousness, oblivious to night-time cold and hunger? Lack of food isn't a problem, but he would have had to have been able to huddle in survivable warmth overnight, and to have taken water in some form – dew off leaves, a stream, or whatever. Could anyone have maintained such an instinctive behaviour pattern while in traumatized, confused, trance and semi-trance states? The answer is essentially yes: it is known that people can perform quite complex tasks such as driving a vehicle for quite long periods while in a unconscious, entranced state. But what exactly happened in Travis Walton's case must remain an open question.

Jerome Clark lays emphasis on the fact that Travis Walton described entities that were later to dominate the accounts of claimed abductees. This does not necessarily imply some form of physical objectivity in Walton'sabduction account, nor that foetus-like extraterrestrials took a fancy to our planet as from the mid-1970s. The recurring image of the alien with large head and enormous black eyes might well be a product of deeply ingrained psychic factors, as discussed in Chapter 7. For instance, stimulation of the temporal cortex seems to evoke infantile memories, and perhaps encourages the foetal imagery of Alvin Lawson's Birth Trauma Hypothesis (see Chapter 7). Alternatively, or in addition, the image of the alien may be a visual metaphor offered to the conscious mind by the subconscious for very deep and obscure mental realities revealed only recently to the modern gaze by experiments with drugs like DMT – a vitally important new factor discussed further in the Epilogue.

¤ ELECTRIC NIGHTMARES

Altered mind states can be also occasioned by artificial energy fields as already indicated. This is suggested in the recent work of British researcher Albert Budden who has looked closely at a range of close encounter cases from a particular angle. He wrote in 1994:

> Such high-strangeness encounters occur in locations where the environmental electromagnetic fields are elevated.... The encounters can take the form of vivid hallucinatory visions induced by the effects of electrical fields on the brain and are 'symptoms' of a syndrome called 'Electrical Hypersensitivity and Multiple Allergy' [EHMA]. This condition, which is the subject of university and clinical research, is caused by prolonged exposure to electromagnetic fields induced by such environmental hotspot sources as radio/TV transmitting antennae, radar, radio-cab offices, telecommunications towers, electrical sub-stations, pylons, etc.
>
> My own research has shown that individuals who experience these bizarre high-strangeness encounters have usually had a major electrical event in their formative years which acts as an initiation for electrical hypersensitivity in later life This event may have been proximity to a lightning strike, ball lightning, geological light phenomena ('earth lights'), major electrocution, and so on.

In other words, Budden is suggesting that the close encounter witness is typically one who has had a 'kindling' experience that has sensitized his or her temporal cortex, and tends therefore to be prone to entering altered states of consciousness under relatively mild stimulus, of either a psychological or physically external nature. (Budden might have added that some people are in any case 'temporal lobe sensitives' simply by dint of their neurophysiological make-up.)

One of the many cases Budden has been revisiting is known in the British ufological literature as 'The Quantock Horror'. In 1988, the witness, Tony Burfield, was taking photographs on the Quantock hills in Somerset when he saw an object flying towards him. It flew directly over him and was huge, blocking out the light of the sun. It was a very complex object with 'bat-like' wings. He took several photographs, including a shot of an entity standing on the rim of the craft. (Budden saw one of Burfield's photographs, and it showed a black dot that the investigator felt looked like a hang glider.)

Burfield had an allergic sensitivity to aspects of his home environment, and used to go for walks on the Quantocks just to feel better. But after his encounter he developed serious symptoms, such as an inability to eat solid foods, extreme sensitivity to electrical equipment, and a metallic taste in his mouth. His allergic reactions to his environment have become so strong that even walking on the hills makes him feel ill. He is oversensitive to light, so that even car headlights at night can cause him pain and blind him with after-images. He suffers memory loss, and food and substance allergies. He also saw fleeting hallucinations of 'little men' in his house. These often shot at him with painful rays.

Budden considered that the man was suffering from EHMA. He discovered that Burfield lived close to a row of high-tension electricity pylons, and suggested that his hallucinatory imagery was actually his subconscious self-articulating the effects of the strong electromagnetic fields in his home environment. Budden further pointed out that the metallic taste Burfield complained of was typically caused by the effect of an electrical field on the mercury-tin amalgam of the witness's tooth fillings.

It also transpired that the encounter itself took place between two rows of intersecting pylons carrying high-tension cables. In answer to Budden's questions, Burfield revealed that he had had 'a big electrical accident' in the past. Budden concluded that the witness had been rendered liable to electrical hypersensitivity with multiple allergies as a result of his initial accident and subsequent highly charged home environment, and that his experiences were, in effect, symptoms of his condition. These had perhaps been brought to a crisis by the location of the 'encounter'.

Encounters with Ourselves?

After joining forces to act as guides through the pageant that is ufology, we now offer our concluding comments separately. Readers will know, by now, where we stand together in our view of the remarkable history of ufology: now we expand on our individual perspectives.

¤ PAUL DEVEREUX

It is surely difficult for anyone who has studied this overview of ufology – that penumbra of fact and fiction, genuine research and gullible belief, that surrounds strange lights in the sky – to conclude that there has been one single line of human enquiry into extra-terrestrial craft and visitation for the past 50 years. Gullibility, personal agendas, profound naivety, downright chicanery, misinformation and confused thinking mark the course of ufology. As for the UFOs themselves, most credible ufologists would agree that the great majority of all reported sightings result from misperception of mundane objects, hoax, mirage effects, confabulation of unfamiliar sights or other psychological aberrations caused by psychosocial stress, and so on. This goes almost without saying. The crucial concern is whether or not there are some genuinely unknown phenomena that are also being occasionally seen and reported – signals within the noise, if you like. Those of the extra-terrestrial persuasion are sure that there are such sightings, and that they are caused by alien craft. Some others, and I am one of them, are also convinced that there is 'signal in the noise', but I have maintained for many years now that one aspect at least can be identified as 'earth lights' – those exotic forms of natural energy originating from the Earth itself, described in Chapter 10.

But it seems to me that a deep, virtually unconscious and barely noticed conceptual split has occurred within ufology. On the one hand, there is the focus on unidentified objects seen primarily in the skies, which are perceived – 'identified', as it were – by most mainstream ufologists as extra-terrestrial craft. On the other hand, there is the fascination with UFO 'abductions'. These are seen by many ufological traditionalists as being human interactions with the occupants of the extra-terrestrial craft that are seen in our skies. In 'standard ufology', therefore, it is considered that it is one and the same problem that is involved. 'The UFO phenomenon is the abduction phenomenon.... The meaning of what was happening inside the UFOs eluded researchers until the importance of abductions became apparent,' writes Dr David Jacobs, professor of history at Temple University, who has somehow allowed himself to be seduced into literalist intepretations of abductions (see Chapter 11).

I beg to differ. I suggest that these two trains of ufological concern are running on separate tracks that most people within standard ufology are mistaken in considering to be the same line. 'Abductions' run on an inner track, that of human consciousness, while the things-seen-in-the-sky (when not misperception, hoax, mirage, psychosocial aberration or whatever) run on the outer track of little-understood aspects of environmental nature.

Let us consider that 'inner track'. As indicated in Chapter 7, there could well be a real 'alien' in our psyche, but right now it is hovering just beyond the reach of our imagination. It may be far more weird, in fact, than the current 50-year-old ufological idea of the extra-terrestrial, which has become so familiar and conceptually invasive as to hinder the intellectual life of ufology. The notion of the extra-terrestrial visitor was an important one to have had at an early stage – it set an important process in motion – but it is now well past its shelf life. The 'alien' I shall hint at in these final pages will have at least as great an impact on us as would a meeting with extra-terrestrial life, because, however exciting and traumatic that would be, it would nevertheless come within the compass of what we currently think we understand about ourselves and the universe. The alien we are about to catch a glimpse of here requires us to go beyond that compass.

The literalist interpretation of the abduction phenomenon lacks the 'hard' evidence that is so often claimed but that somehow evaporates over time and with due analysis. The more meaningful intepretation is likely to lie in the mysteries of the mind – that alien within we know so little about – for there are other states of consciousness which are very peculiar indeed. Our culture actually shuns the study of such states, and we tend to dismiss them as 'not real' and so think they could not account for experiences such as those described by the abductees. This attitude is simply not correct. Other, older cultures than our own have mapped such alternate mental states in much greater detail than we have, and hold a drastically different world view as a consequence. Where we

talk about aliens, they may speak of spirits, or ancestors. They have mental and social procedures for organizing encounters with such entities, whereas we have encounters we do not understand and couch in literalist and mechanistic terms, resulting in a kind of pathology.

One altered state of consciousness highly relevant to the abduction phenomenon is the so-called 'lucid dream' state, briefly mentioned in Chapter 7. This mental condition is one in which a person is physiologically asleep but their mind is still consciously active. It was first confirmed scientifically in 1975 by English sleep researcher Keith Hearne. In such a state, dream consciousness appears completely 'real': there is the experience of three-dimensional space, and all five senses can appear to be functioning. One can seemingly move around – walk, fly, run, glide – with total realism. It is not merely a vivid dream, and it is unfortunate that the term 'dream' has come to be involved with its description, which is due simply to historical accident. If one is unaware of the situation, if one knows nothing about such states, experiences had during lucid dreaming are virtually undetectable from those in normal waking consciousness (except for their bizarre aspects). Therefore, the abduction experience can be real (and thus recoverable by regression hypnosis), even if the literalist interpretation of being kidnapped by space beings is not. The fact that so many abductions occur when the person is near sleep at home – and often in the bedroom – or driving at night in a car is what makes this altered state worthy of special attention. Lucid dreaming is particularly likely to happen in those half-sleep states which occur just before and after sleeping or a brief nap – the hypnogogic and hypnopompic states respectively – and is a well-known hazard of long-distance driving: most truck drivers, for instance, can cite instances of 'missing time'.

The mind-change view of abductions is further supported by some psychological studies of the abduction phenomenon. The work of psychologist Kenneth Ring, to take just one example, provides some evidence to indicate that abductees as a group tend to have suffered a higher than average background of child abuse. The significance of this, we noted earlier (see Chapter 7), is that children suffering abuse tend to develop a psychological defence mechanism known as 'dissociation', in which they compartmentalize their consciousness so that they can escape from the appalling physical realities that surround them into vivid levels of other mental realities. Later in life, because of this learned mental reflex, they can be unusually prone to entering alternate states of consciousness, given the appropriate psychological, social or geophysical stimulus. (There are of course many other factors leading to such susceptibility than just a history of child abuse.)

This ability to dissociate, to move swiftly and effectively into other mental realities, was a highly prized skill in many earlier and traditional societies, where its prime form was shamanism. The shaman, the 'walker between the worlds' of everyday living and the spiritual Otherworld, interceded with the spirits on behalf of the tribe for healing, divinatory or other purposes. The person who became a shaman might have had a visionary experience in childhood as the result of, perhaps, a severe illness; more often, or as well, the individual would undergo initiatory procedures of a profoundly stressful physical or mental nature. This was to achieve that very ability of dissociation involuntarily developed by many child abuse victims, and sufferers of other kinds of trauma. In the tribal society, however, there was a spiritual and social context for that ability: there was recognition of it and social and religious 'road maps' for its use.

As consciousness researcher Jim DeKorne has written: 'The UFO contact is now seen by many investigators to be an interface between inner and outer dimensions, analogous to a kind of involuntary shamanic encounter.' The hard fact is that tribal societies had one technology we still lack – the technology of consciousness. In that regard, it is we who are the primitives. People within our 'tribe' of Westernized societies are undergoing their involuntary mind-change experiences in a cultural context where mechanization, isolation and depersonalization is greater than in any society previously. Added to that is the dearth of experiential spiritual life on a culture-wide level: there are only rote religions and insufficiently integrated drug and ritual experiences. There is no longer a consensual cultural niche for such states of consciousness other than the 'abduction' scenario. That this experience should be interpreted as being caused by alien machines and extra-terrestrial entities says much about our culture and our times.

One of the techniques employed by traditional shamanism to access the spirit worlds – what we would call other, or dissociated, mental states – was (and still is in some cases) the use of hallucinogenic plants. As mentioned in Chapter 7, there is a growing body of literature and expertise on psychoactive substances to which ufologists of virtually all persuasions are currently paying insufficient attention. This is partly because of a chaotic social and political attitude regarding 'drugs'. This amounts to ignorance and lack of discrimination between potentially useful, informative and non-addictive psychoactive substances and harmful, physically addictive ones, and has severely hampered bona fide scientific research on mind-changing substances for decades (although this is now changing slowly). Yet despite the unfounded prejudices that abound, there is much to be learned in a ufological sense from this body of knowledge.

Consider this account:

I got a glimpse of several entities moving in front of a giant, complex control panel.... The creatures were bipedal and roughly human size. I had direct awareness of an overwhelmingly powerful and knowledgeable presence! It was neither frightening, nor encouraging. It was just there.... A gaggle of elf-like creatures in standard-issue Irish costume were playing with objects that looked like hybrids of crystals and machines.

Or this:

I found myself approaching a 'Space Station' (a long, beige-coloured, triangular-shaped 'landing platform') which was below and to my right. There were at least two entities (one on either side of me), guiding me to the platform... I was aware of many other beings inside the space station – automatons: android-like creatures... like a cross between crash dummies and the Empire troops from Star Wars, *except they were living beings, not robots. They were doing some kind of routine technological work and paid no attention to me.*

These could have come from any abductee's account – but they didn't. They came from people experiencing the profound altered states of consciousness induced by the powerful hallucinogen DMT, or N,N-Dimethyl-tryptamine. (The first account is by Gracie and Zarkov, in *Psychedelic Illuminations* 6; the second by Jim DeKorne, 1994). As DeKorne writes, 'The UFO contact/abductee phenomenon manifests too many themes analogous to psychedelic states and shamanic initiation to be regarded as unrelated.'

DMT is one of the key chemical constituents of some of the botanical hallucinogens used by tribal peoples, and also occurs naturally in human beings and other mammals (our dreams, lucid and otherwise, may result from the action of such natural, endogenous hallucinogens). It was originally synthesized in Hungary from Amazonian hallucinogenic snuffs 30 or so years ago, and is an extraordinarily powerful and quick-acting hallucinogen (trance is entered within seconds of taking a dose of DMT and can be over in five minutes). It is not widely known and so is a 'relatively obscure drug of abuse', informs Federally approved American DMT researcher Dr Rick Strassman. He further acknowledges that many people who have undergone DMT trance tell of 'encounters with... "alien" intelligences'.

Terence McKenna, another major authority on hallucinogens, is one of the few to have written descriptively about the effects of DMT. In his *The Archaic Revival*, a collection of his interviews and papers, he has important observations to share with regard to this 'meeting with the alien' so often encountered in the DMT trance. In this most intense of altered mind states, one enters a 'somehow insulated' place that is fully, vividly real albeit exceedingly weird. One 'meets entities'. McKenna describes these variously as 'self-transforming machine elves', 'dynamically contorting topological modules', 'tryptamine munchkins' and 'fractal elves.'

'These beings,' writes McKenna, 'are like fractal reflections of some previously hidden and suddenly autonomous part of one's own psyche.' What shocked McKenna after his first DMT experience was the feeling that 'right here and now, one quanta away, there is raging a universe of active intelligence that is transhuman, hyperdimensional, and extremely alien.'

This sense of contact with alien entities is not the mere subjective experiences related by one or two present-day experimenters – many of them do so. And in the past, also. The Haitians, for instance, took it (in the form of *Piptadenia peregrina* seeds) to communicate with their gods. In presenting numerous reports of DMT subjects who claimed contact with some kind of alien entity during their sessions, researcher Peter Meyer states that 'the phenomenon of apparent alien contact is so impressive' in the DMT experience that the matter 'deserves serious investigation'.

McKenna cites another tryptamine variation of DMT, psilocybin (4-phosphoryloxy-DMT), found in the 'magic mushrooms' of pre-Hispanic Mexican Indians, to whom the mushroom was *teonanacatl* – the 'flesh of the gods'. The experience of psilocybin can be similar to DMT, but takes longer to act and lasts longer. 'UFO contact is perhaps the motif most frequently mentioned by people who take psilocybin.... There is the same confrontation with an alien intelligence,' McKenna informs.

The nature of this tryptamine entity experience is open for interpretation. Meyer has suggested that the tryptamine aliens may be inter-dimensional beings or intelligences, time-travellers or discarnate spirits, all of which can only communicate to humans in the appropriate frequency of consciousness. McKenna is likewise open to possibilities. Shamans call the entities 'spirits', but McKenna observes that that may be like a quantum scientist talking of 'charm', both terms being 'a technical gloss for a very complicated concept'. McKenna has written perceptively:

I've recently come to suspect... that the human soul is so alienated from us in our present culture that we treat it as an extra-terrestrial. ...Aliens Hollywood-style could arrive on earth tomorrow and the DMT trance would remain more weird and continue to hold more promise for useful information for the human future.

I feel that ufology in its multifarious forms is potentially valuable because it might not only inadvertently encourage the discovery of new geophysical phenomena, but it also provides us with a window on ourselves, on our complex, surprising, infuriating and occasionally inspiring human nature. This window covers views of sociological and psychological phenomena on both individual and mass levels, as well as the deep experience of the 'Other' within the psyche that I suggest is at the heart of the abduction experience. In short, whether taken at mundane or profound levels, ufology represents an encounter with ourselves. While the possibility of extra-terrestrial visitation cannot be ruled out, and I remain open to it, I see nowhere in the passing parade of ufology any totally convincing evidence that that is what is involved.

We will have to wait another 50 years, perhaps, to see if ufology grows up into a scholarly, multi-disciplinary study of the human condition, or regresses ever deeper into an absurd swamp of lies, deception and self-deception, gullibility and escapist fantasy. Right now, it seems to me, it is on the cusp, and could go either way.

¤ PETER BROOKESMITH

To observe that human knowledge and understanding are neither static nor absolute is hardly to reveal a great new truth to the world. Informed and reasonable people will always welcome new ideas, new solutions to old problems, and more effective ways of getting a job done. Nonetheless, in any disciplined body of thinkers or doers there is disagreement; that is the way people are, of course, but urbane debate is also the way in which thought is refined, decisions are made, and our grasp on reality is made more sure.

Take a simple example. Engineers will contend over what is the best technical solution to bridging a river. Military strategists, from section commanders to marshals of armies, will have opinions on the best means of attacking or defending that bridge. In due course, historians will dispute the exact economic and social effects of its presence. Poets may praise or scorn its aesthetic worth, and literary critics in turn will argue over the merits of their verses. Physicists will discuss the fundamental nature of the steel from which the bridge (and the ink of the poets) is made.

Anyone familiar with the history of ideas, or of scientific research or technological innovation, knows that debates of this kind can be remarkably heated. At the same time, they take place among people who agree on a number of fundamental assumptions, lessons from history and even laws of nature that their disciplines take for granted. Within their respective fields, conservative defenders of those assumptions represent the current, working wisdom – the standard against which new ideas have to prove themselves. Ufology is different from 'conventional' academic and practical disciplines in that, taken as a whole, one can discern little agreement on basic laws, the nature of acceptable evidence, or even rules of thumb. Even the fundamental laws of physics, without which nothing in the world we know would actually function and which are proven every second because the world does work, are often regarded as mutable or surpassable. To no one's surprise, the upshot is chaos.

The nearest manifestation in ufology to the conservatism of established disciplines are 'the skeptics', who persist in reminding 'the believers' of obstacles such as the laws of physics. What ufological skeptics do not do is provide the kind of benchmark within ufology itself that cautious historians, soldiers, engineers, scientists – and even poets – represent among their own peers. Among themselves the skeptics may agree, but they challenge the basic intellectual idleness of ufology, and have done almost since the first flying saucers were reported. For the many who will take outraged exception to the notion that ufologists are intellectual layabouts, I would politely point to the almost complete lack of interest that 'conventional' scientists show in UFOs, and their exasperation with ufology – often expressed privately, but lately made quite public in dealing with the plethora of far-fetched claims concerning comet Hale-Bopp (see Chapter 8). And there is a continuous rumbling in scientific publications countering ufologists' strange ideas about magnetism, gravity waves, the origins of the transistor and other notions.

Apart from the inherent difficulties involved in subjecting UFOs to the usual forms of scientific investigation

(as one skeptic never tires of repeating, 'There are no UFOs, only reports of UFOs'), there is no agreement among the ufological factions as to what UFOs and ufology actually are – as the preceding chapters surely make plain. Ufologists spend more than half their time attacking each other rather than reporting actual research, according to one recent survey of Internet traffic. Calls for peer-group review of ufological findings sound fine, until one wonders who the 'peers' actually might be who would be acceptable to all parties. The leading researchers into the Roswell incident are barely civil to one another, for example (and cannot even agree where the alleged aliens finally crashed), while abduction researchers range from the highly conservative neuropsychologist Ronald K. Siegel (see Chapter 7) to New Age tailgaters like John Mack ('Now, really, we can stop fussing over whether we have got something real here') and Whitley Strieber, whose pronouncements are increasingly milleniarist (see Chapter 11). The only peer-reviewed journal in the field has no skeptics on its board, and the organization that publishes it includes not even the mildest skeptical material in the list of recommended reading on its Website. Devotees of the paranormal in general and ufology in particular are quick to complain of the conservatism and intolerance of science, yet inoculate themselves far more thoroughly against caution than do 'conventional' scientists.

The key point in the present context is that within ufology itself, skeptics are not seen (as they would be among a body of engineers, or even scholars of history) as setting or reiterating time-honoured standards of enquiry, investigation and theorizing. They are seen as nothing less than a threat, attacking the 'reality' of UFOs like a mindless, destructive virus. Indeed, ufology sees them as beyond its pale. This makes the fascination they seem to exert upon ufologists all the more intriguing.

Yet skeptics are 'ufologists' – insofar as they comment on and interpret UFO reports, and make judgements on general trends in ufology. And, although relatively few in number, they gain a remarkable amount of attention from ufologists of all persuasions, while among believers in ufology's more exotic doctrines they generate a degree of ire that is out of all proportion to their apparent ability to sway ufological (let alone public) opinion. In view of the attention these non-ufological ufologists attract, one cannot help but wonder if their shameless presence is in some way a necessity for those who call themselves, and one another, ufologists. This began to make sense to me when I stopped thinking of ufology as a formative (or wannabee) science knocking vainly, or prematurely, at the establishment's door, and began looking at it as a cultural excrescence, in an age of uncertainty in the West – in which scientific thinking is regarded as normative, yet the power of science itself is suspect, and there is little trust in God.

Demonizing the opposition is not an activity that is exclusive to religion, or to the religions deriving from Judaism, but it is buried in the very foundations of Christianity, which defined itself in terms of its enemies, and increasingly identified those enemies with the Devil and the forces of darkness and evil. Christian cultures and civilizations inevitably took over the habit of thought, without thought or reflection, so fundamental was it. Any new symbolism to satisfy the religious impulse that is no longer served by Christianity but is born within a post Christian culture, would be almost doomed to inherit (or adopt) that basic emotional structure. That, I think, is what has happened in ufology – by which I mean the 'extra-terrestrial' interpretation of UFOs and aliens, which includes all those speculations about time travel, parallel universes and the like, as well as plain vanilla off-worlders from our own or other galaxies. Whether it is a substitute for religion, or a parallel religion, or an emerging new religion, it is too soon to say with much certainty. It may turn out to be no more than an experimental dead end.

To the extent that ufology embraces at one extreme people who maintain that aliens can make themselves and their craft selectively invisible, and that crop circles are messages from visitors from Sirius, and at the other extreme hard-headed scholars and statisticians and scientists looking for natural explanations for UFO reports, many schisms can be expected before a theology, or theodicy, becomes a coherent 'true church'. Perhaps the nearest parallel in modern times of a possible future development is the devotion that Marxism demanded and extracted from its cohorts. While the cults described in Chapter 6 show how vulnerable ufology is to religious decoration, the embarrassment that the cults evoke in mainstream ufology indicates that the theistic, teleological and eschatological drives within 'UFO belief' are unlikely to become overt, especially in our scientistic culture. That is to say, the dynamics of ufology will probably always nest within ufology's masquerade as science, just as Marxism claims to be scientific but serves other purposes (including religious ones).

As with most cultural analyses, the proposition that ufology is at bottom a religious quest is not amenable to hard-and-fast proof. But there are some cogent indications that the language and imagery of UFO lore are borrowed (even looted) from the storehouse of religious concepts. To begin with, there is the linguistic tic with which committed and uncommitted alike refer to 'believing in' UFOs and/or aliens. There is a recognition that a degree of faith is involved here. One also notes the extremity of the rhetoric with which believers defend their faith and vilify those who expose its logical and scientific flaws. One could point, too, to the conviction that ufology is, or must be, 'scientific', which is one of the few ways knowledge can claim respectability in our culture. (The direct parallel is Jesus of Nazareth's insistence that his teaching was consistent with Jewish law.) There are unconscious puns ('lexi-links' in Fortean terms) on other worlds and Otherworlds, the heavens and outer space, and the descent and ascension of the aliens to and from Earth.

Gods have always been alien and unknowable, and none more so than the Judaic and Christian God. The aliens of ufology, too, are inscrutable and very strange. Despite the febrile insistences of relatively recent abduction researchers who consistently find their subjects' mental landscapes are populated by diminutive 'grays', the whole historical spectrum of CE-IIIs and CE-IVs shows that aliens come in all shapes and sizes, all of them essentially non-human, if largely of humanoid or primatial configuration. Some are robotic, some monstrous; some are quite angelic – the so-called 'Nordics'. David Jacobs has suggested that the Nordics are alien-human hybrids, but this only confirms their equivalence to angels: both are midway between gods and men, and prettier than most of the latter.

Nonetheless, the little gray fellows have been reported more often of late by abductees, mainly from North America, but from elsewhere too. One can, I think, safely grant both the extreme unlikelihood that these are actual organic creatures, and the strong probability that they are visionary beings. To that extent, they are projections, and in meeting them we symbolically encounter ourselves – specifically, those parts of ourselves that we find incomprehensible, uncontrollable, all-powerful and dangerous, and from which we are alienated. In other words, the aliens' peculiar behaviour and singular appearance speak to the condition of those who encounter them, and perhaps to our general condition as well. The truth is less 'out there' than 'in here'. It doesn't matter whether the sources of the imagery in the 'alien' synthesis are cultural, pharmacological, neurological, imaginal or imaginative, or anything else. We can take it that the 'gray' alien type (and its activities) seems to be marginalizing the others because *that is how people want aliens to be* – this is what best embodies their idea of alien-ness. And I suspect, too, that the 'grays' have become so fashionable because they are incarnations of all the god-like powers and properties that have been attributed to spacefaring Otherworldlings down the years, and we have projected our longings, fears and conflicts onto them.

We have touched on this theme in previous chapters. Here, I'd like to tease out some specific reported qualities of the 'grays' to illustrate how they stand in a line-up of other god-like attributes. Physically, the gray aliens have:

• *Huge heads*: these plainly symbolize superhuman brains and intellects.
• *Bizarre eyes*: with which they gaze into abductees' souls, read their minds, control their actions, and bind them psychologically and emotionally. For their captives, the aliens hold 'the final way of escape, the most intimate of all places', as the great Christian theologian Paul Tillich said of God. Gods always see too much. Pagan gods dating to 2500BCE and consisting almost entirely of eyes have been found as far apart as Iraq, Spain and Syria.
• *Attenuated bodies*: this suggests that the aliens have no physical warmth or emotional sympathy, no earthy distractions of digestion and dirt; the implications are of frigid intellect and passionless asceticism. The Houyhnhnm-like gutlessness is the corollary of the huge heads: the creatures seem to embody unfeeling, super-rational intellectuals – they are certainly not large, warm, comforting Earth Mothers! Reports that autopsies on aliens reveal a chlorophyll-based metabolism that depends on photosynthesis reinforce the image of emotional incapacity. The entities have as much visceral feeling as an aspidistra.
• *No naughty bits*: they go straight round like my teddy bear, or like an angel, or like Satan in William Blake's illustrations of Job, in which Satan was not the Devil of the New Testament, but a companion (i.e. angel) of God. Once more, the aliens' passionless nature is emphasized. There is also a powerful suggestion of purity in this. Sex is 'the chief obstacle to spirituality in Gnostic thought, and the source of all evil in medieval Christian thought' remarks Professor Harold Bloom in his *The American Religion*, and so it is in what passes for thought among fundamentalist Christians today, too. Lacking genitalia, the aliens can know no original sin, a dubious privilege of ignorance otherwise accorded only to God, his angels and the Nazarene. Uproar always greets any suggestion that Jesus of Nazareth had a sex life, and Protestant cultures are notorious not just for disapproving of sex, but for sexual repressiveness.

And what do the aliens do?

• *Aliens physically invade their victims*: they poke, probe, bugger, impregnate, dismember, even de-brain their captives. This last was notably reported by Sandy Larson, who on 26 August 1975 had her brain taken out and a fresh (if not noticeably improved) one inserted in its stead.

These casually inflicted horrors underscore the aliens' indifference and Otherness, but also their ability to *remake* humanity: as gods can. At the same time, like rape in the real world, they are a display of power that humiliates and degrades the abductee. On the one hand, the imagery directly echoes shamanic accounts of symbolic death and rebirth: what else can one make of Ms Larson's traded-in brain? On the other hand, the emotional content relates directly to traditions of self-abasement, flagellation and self-degradation in some Semitic religions – most notably Christianity, which has made a cult of martyrdom. An apparent paradox is that, once they have submitted to the noxious embraces of the aliens, the victims proceed to do their owners' bidding. On the secular level, however, I'm reminded of the Stockholm Syndrome – the tendency of hostages to begin to identify with the aims of their captors. And it also parallels the psychopathology of the victim in Christianity, and the doctrine of absolute predestination in Islam.

Apropos the medical and sexual components of abductions: I am extremely glad for the personal safety of the ancient-astronaut brigade that none of them seems to have studied Islam, and that when their effusions were fashionable the abduction syndrome was not. There is a startling story in the earliest biography of the Prophet, written in the eighth century CE by Ibn Ishaq (AH 85–151, 707–773CE). As a child, Mohammed had a wetnurse; as she told it, one day

> his milk-brother came running to me and his father, saying, 'Two men dressed in white garments have taken hold of my brother [Mohammed], and have thrown him on the ground. They ripped open his belly, and are stirring it up!' We hastened out and found [the boy] standing apparently unharmed but with his countenance quite altered.

It is surely significant that later biographers put this incident in Mohammed's adult life, immediately before his ascension to heaven; in any case, the parallels with the abduction syndrome are glaringly apparent here.

• *Aliens choose their victims*: the abduction syndrome is at once very democratic, and yet elitist. Just as anyone may be washed in the blood of the Lamb or be received into the bosom of Allah, anyone can be abducted (or see a UFO, or have a close encounter of the third kind). But once in the fold, you are someone special. The aliens reinforce this 'chosenness' by using implants to track abductees wherever they go, but most especially by passing on messages or 'wisdom' for the rest (the 'gentiles') of humanity. In other words:

• *Aliens grant revelation*: the messages either concern human destiny, which the aliens at least partly control, through genetic manipulation, for example (peace on Earth and mercy mild – God and Darwin reconciled!), or divulge particulars of the aliens themselves. These revelations fall into four general categories:

(1) apocalyptic warnings (nuclear or, since approximately 31 December 1989 and the collapse of the Soviet empire, ecological disaster);

(2) moral injunctions;

(3) messianic appointments (the abductee becomes the aliens' messenger to humanity, a role sometimes shared by the abduction researcher); and

(4) the identity and purpose of the aliens.

All these messages, in one form or another, echo the fundamentals of all religions anywhere. More or less explicitly, they suggest the means to human redemption, and they explain the purpose of life.

The fourth of those alien revelations also bears interesting comparison with a religious theme. The aliens' own accounts of their origins have shifted over the decades from the near and impossible to the distant and no less unlikely – Mars, Venus, Saturn to begin with, then the Pleiades and Zeta Reticuli and the like. Intermingled with these have been still more exotic, fabulous places such as Clarion, Zircon, Martarus, the galaxy of Guentatori-Elfi, and so on. But all said they were extra-terrestrial, and that they lived in utopian societies (i.e. Paradise) free from money, meat-eating, politicians, war, and so on. Lately, they have become distinctly furtive about the locations of their home worlds. Abductees who ask get shifty answers: 'That is not for you to know', 'It doesn't matter', and so on.

'Thou canst not see my face,' God told Moses in the tabernacle at Mount Horeb (although he did offer to show him his back parts, which has always intrigued me: perhaps their tricksterish place in the alien pantheon is taken by those strange locations like Guentatori-Elfi). Jorge Louis Borges in his writings makes repeated reference to the 99 names of God, and the hundredth which is unknowable and unspeakable; among Jews, the Tetragrammaton (YHWH) is never pronounced, but signalled by the utterance 'Adonai' when reading the *Tanach* aloud. Apart from this magic of naming, but

related to it, Semitic religion and alien encounters share another version of the secret that cannot be told. Saul of Tarsus, after his conversion, reported of himself that

> *(whether in the body, or out of the body, I cannot tell: God knoweth;) How that he was caught up into paradise, and heard unspeakable words, which it is not lawful for man to utter.*

Herb Schirmer, a seminal experient who was more contactee than abductee, also said that he had been given information he was not permitted to repeat; some abductees are vouchsafed great truths that they must forget, but that will be restored to memory at a later time. Another form of this motif is the 'book of wisdom' (of a blue hue, in abductee Betty Andreasson's case) presented to abductees, that is retained by the aliens at the last minute or mysteriously misplaced later.

To the percipients, the close encounter phenomenon can be revelatory in another, more radical and manifest fashion. For many (I do not know what proportion) the experience changes their priorities, and they change their way of life. This is true of those who undergo revelation in a more overtly religious context, too, of course; the examples from the Bible alone are legion.

Abduction as revelation; ufology as secular religion: these ideas do not go down well among nuts-and-bolts ufologists and abduction researchers, but they are not unknown among sociologists and students of religion. That doesn't make them right, but it does indicate how lacking in self-awareness ufology is – and that is another quality this amorphous field shares with religious devotees.

To me, the irony in all this is that buried somewhere in the ufological noise – among the extraordinary reports and the astonishing claims – there may be a true account of just one alien, extra-terrestrial visit to Earth. And no one knows which report is the real nugget. And so I find it fascinating that a belief system of such proportions, and with such deep and tenacious roots, has grown up regardless of the solidity of the evidence or the likelihood of the event. It will probably take another 50 years for those beliefs to wither away, or to become – as all successful religions do, however informal they may be – a political force. The latter prospect is not a happy one: and I say that as one awed, time and again, by the achievement and creativity of science. But then I know, as all true scientists do, that neither science nor religion is a universal panacea for the pain of being human – of being, in Alexander Pope's lines, 'Sole judge of truth, and in endless error hurl'd; The glory, jest, and riddle of the World!'

Bibliography

INTRODUCTION

Lammer, Helmut. 'Atmospheric Mass Loss on Mars and the Consequences for the Cydonian Hypothesis and Early Martian Life Forms' in *Journal of Scientific Exploration*, Vol 10, No 3, 1996.

CHAPTER 1

Aldrich, Jan. 'Project 1947: An Inquiry into the Beginning of the UFO Era' in *International UFO Reporter*, Vol 21, No 2, 1996.

Arnold, Kenneth. 'How It All Began' in *Proceedings of the First International UFO Congress* (1977; Warner Books, 1980).

—, and Palmer, Ray. *The Coming of the Saucers* (1952).

Bach, Egon W. *'UFOs' From the Volcanoes* (Hermitage Publishers, 1993).

Brookesmith, Peter. *UFO: The Complete Sightings Catalogue* (Blandford Press, UK/Barnes & Noble, US, 1995).

Bullard, Thomas E. 'The Mechanization of UFOs' in *International UFO Reporter*, Vol 13, No 1, 1988.

Clark, Jerome. 'The Salvation Myth' in *International UFO Reporter*, Vol 21, No 4, 1996.

—, and Truzzi, Marcello. *UFO Encounters: Sightings, Visitations, and Investigations* (Publications International, 1992).

Clarke, David, and Oldroyd, Granville. *Spooklights – A British Survey* (Private, 1985).

Constable, Trevor James. *The Cosmic Pulse of Life* (Spearman, 1976).

Devereux, Paul. *Earth Lights Revelation* (Blandford Press, 1989).

Evans, Hilary, with Spencer, John (eds). *UFOs 1947–1987: The 40-Year Search for an Explanation* (Fortean Tomes, 1987).

Jung, C.G. *Flying Saucers – A Modern Myth of Things Seen in the Sky* (1959; Routledge & Kegan Paul edition, 1977).

Knight, David C. *UFOs – A Pictorial History* (McGraw-Hill, 1979).

Kottmeyer, Martin. 'A Universe of Spies' in *Magonia*, No 39, 1991.

Laon, Herman of. *De Miraculis Sanctae Mariae Laudunensis*, translated from the Latin by Jeremy Harte (Private, 1985).

Roerich, Nicholas. *Altai-Himalaya* (1929; Arun Press edition, 1983).

Sanderson, Ivan T. *Uninvited Visitors* (1969; Tandem edition, 1974).

Steiger, Brad (ed). *Project Blue Book* (1976; Ballantine edition, 1987).

Urton, Gary. *At the Crossroads of the Earth and the Sky* (University of Texas Press, 1981).

CHAPTER 2

Adamski, George, and Leslie, Desmond. *Flying Saucers Have Landed* (Werner Laurie, 1953).

Bord, Janet and Colin, *Life Beyond Planet Earth?* (Grafton, 1992).

Bowen, Charles (ed). *The Humanoids* (Futura, 1974).

— *Encounter Cases from Flying Saucer Review* (Signet, 1977).

Brookesmith, Peter. *UFO: The Complete Sightings Catalogue* (Blandford Press UK/ Barnes & Noble US, 1995).

— *UFO: The Government Files* (Blandford Press UK/ Barnes & Noble US, 1996).

Clark, Jerome. *The UFO Encyclopedia Vol 2* (Omnigraphics Inc, 1992).

Heard, Gerald. *The Riddle of the Flying Saucers* (Carrol & Nicholson, 1950).

Keel, John. *Operation Trojan Horse* (Abacus, 1973).

Keyhoe, Donald. *The Flying Saucers Are Real* (Fawcett, 1950).

CHAPTER 3

Conrad, Dean. *Star Wars: The Genesis of a Legend* (Valis Books, 1996).

Slade, Darren, and Watson, Nigel. *Supernatural Spielberg* (Valis Books, 1992).

Watson, Nigel. 'The Day the Flying Saucers Invaded the Cinema' in *UFOs 1947–1987: The 40-Year Search for an Explanation*, ed Hilary Evans with John Spencer (Fortean Tomes, 1987).

CHAPTER 4

Aldrich, Jan. 'Project 1947: An Inquiry into the Beginning of the UFO Era' in *International UFO Reporter*, Vol 21, No 2.

Brookesmith, Peter. *UFO: The Complete Sightings Catalogue* (Blandford Press UK/ Barnes & Noble, US, 1995).

Bullard, Thomas E. 'Waves' in Clark, 1996.

Chapman, Robert. *Unidentified Flying Objects* (1969; Mayflower edition, 1970).

Clark, Jerome. *The UFO Encyclopedia Vol 3* (Omnigraphics Inc, 1996).

— and Truzzi, Marcello. *UFO Encounters: Sightings, Visitations, and Investigations* (Publications International, 1992).

Devereux, Paul. *Earth Lights* (Turnstone Press, 1982).

— *Earth Lights Revelation* (Blandford Press, 1989).

Forshufvud, Ragnar. 'Unidentified Flying Objects – A Physical Phenomenon' in *Pursuit*, Vol 13, No 2, 1980.

Fort, Charles. *The Books of Charles Fort* (compendium).

Hendry, Allan. *The UFO Handbook* (1979; Sphere Books edition, 1980).

Hynek, J. Allen. *The UFO Experience* (1972; Corgi Books edition, 1974).

Keel, John A. *The 'Flap' Phenomenon in the United States*, reprinted from *Flying Saucer Review*, No 2, June 1969 (1969; New York Fortean Society edition, 1989).

— *Operation Trojan Horse* (1970, Abacus edition, 1973).

Persinger, Michael A. 'Geophysical Variables and Behaviour III. Prediction of UFO Reports by Geomagnetic and Seismic Activity' in *Perceptual and Motor Skills*, No 53, 1981.

Petrakis, Perry. '40 Years of French Ufology' in *UFO Brigantia*, No 46, 1990.

Sotomayor, Hector Escobar. 'The Mexican Euforia' in *UFO Times*, No 41, May–June, 1996.

Vallée, Jacques and Janine. *Challenge to Science* (1966; Neville Spearman, 1967).

Watson, Nigel. 'Phantom Aerial Flaps and Waves' in *Magonia*, 1987.

CHAPTER 5

Aveni, Anthony F. (ed). *The Lines of Nazca* (American Philosophical Society, 1990).

Daniken, Erich von. *In Search of Ancient Gods* (1973; Corgi edition, 1976).

— *Return to the Stars* (1968; Souvenir Press edition, 1970).

Devereux, Paul. *Shamanism and the Mystery Lines* (Quantum/Foulsham, 1992; Llewellyn, 1993).

— 'Acculturated Topographical Effects of Shamanic Trance Consciousness in Archaic and Medieval Sacred Landscapes' in *Journal of Scientific Exploration*, Vol 7, No 1, 1993.

Dobkin de Rios, Marlene. 'Plant Hallucinogens, Out-of-Body Experiences and New World Monumental Earthworks' in *Drugs, Rituals and Altered States of Consciousness*, (ed) Du Toit, Brian M. (A.A. Balkema, 1977).

Freidel, David, Schele, Linda, and Parker, Joy. *Maya Cosmos* (William Morrow, 1993).

Halifax, Joan. *Shaman – The Wounded Healer* (Crossroads, 1982).

Keen, Montague. 'Keen on Crop Circles' in *The Anomalist*, No 4, 1996.

Leslie, Desmond, and Adamski, George. *Flying Saucers Have Landed* (British Book Centre edition, 1953).

Lewis-Williams, David, and Dowson, Thomas. *Images of Power* (Southern Book Publishers, 1989).

Michell, John. *The Flying Saucer Vision* (Sidgwick and Jackson, 1967).

Pennick, Nigel, and Devereux, Paul. *Lines on the Landscape* (Robert Hale, 1989).

Reiche, Maria. *Mystery on the Desert* (1968; private edition, 1976).

Schnabel, Jim. *Round In Circles* (Hamish Hamilton, 1993).

Schultes, Richard Evans, and Hofmann, Albert. *Plants of the Gods* (1979; Healing Arts Press Edition, 1992).

— and Raffauf, Robert F. *Vine of the Soul* (Synergetic Press, 1992).

Trombold, C.D. (ed). *Ancient Road Networks and Settlement Hierarchies in the New World* (Cambridge University Press, 1991).

Watkins, Alfred. *The Old Straight Track* (1925; Garnstone Press edition, 1970).

Wedd, Tony. *Skyways and Landmarks* (1961; private edition, 1972).

Whitley, David S. 'By the Hunter, for the Gatherer: Art, Social Relations, and Subsistence Change in the Prehistoric Great Basin' in *World Archaeology*, Vol 25, No 3, February 1994.

CHAPTER 6

Clark, Jerome. *The UFO Encyclopedia Vol 2* (Omnigraphics Inc, 1992).

— *The UFO Encyclopedia Vol 3* (Omnigraphics Inc, 1996).

Jung, C.G. *Flying Saucers – A Modern Myth of Things Seen in the Sky* (1959; Routledge & Kegan Paul edition, 1977).

Keel, John A. *Operation Trojan Horse* (1970; Abacus edition, 1973).

King, George. *The Nine Freedoms* (Aetherius Society, 1963)

Korff, Karl. *Spaceships from the Pleiades* (Prometheus, 1996).

Lewis, James (ed). *The Gods Have Landed* (State University of New York, 1995).

CHAPTER 7

Baker, Robert. 'Alien Dreamtime' in *The Anomalist*, No 2, 1995.

Basterfield, Keith, Godic, Vladimir and Pony, 'The Abduction Phenomenon in Australia' in *International UFO Reporter*, Vol 14, No 4, 1989.

Brookesmith, Peter. *UFO: The Complete Sightings Catalogue* (Blandford Press, UK/ Barnes & Noble, US, 1995).

Bullard, Thomas E. 'America Strikes Back' in *Magonia*, No 37, 1990.

— 'The American Way: Truth, Justice and Abduction' in *Magonia*, No 34, 1989.

— 'In the Light of Experience' in *Magonia*, No 44, 1992.

Clark, Jerome. 'Two Cheers for American Ufology' in *International UFO Reporter*, Vol 14, No 2, 1989.

Clarke, David, and Roberts, Andy. *Phantoms of the Sky* (Robert Hale, 1990).

Devereux, Paul. *Earth Lights* (Turnstone Press, 1982).

— *Earth Lights Revelation* (Blandford Press, 1989).

Evans, Hilary. 'Folklore Rules, OK?' in *Magonia*, No 42, 1992.

— 'Abductions Are Really Something' in *UFO Brigantia*, No 51, 1992.

Grof, Stanislav. *Realms of the Human Unconscious* (1975; Condor/Souvenir Press edition, 1979).

Howarth, R., Mantle, P., and Roberts, A. 'A Soapy Abduction' in *UFO Brigantia*, No 32, 1988.

Jaynes, Julian. *The Origin of Consciousness in the Breakdown of the Bicameral Mind* (Houghton Mifflin, 1976).

Jung, C.G. *Flying Saucers – A Modern Myth of Things Seen in the Sky* (1959; Routledge & Kegan Paul edition, 1977).

Kottmeyer, Martin. 'Abduction: The Boundary Deficit Hypothesis' in *Magonia*, No 32, 1989.

— 'Entirely Unpredisposed' in *Magonia*, No 35, 1990.

— 'Eye-Yi-Yi' in *Magonia*, No 41, 1991.

Lawson, Alvin H. 'The Abduction Experience – A Testable Hypothesis' in *Magonia*, No 10, 1982.

Méheust, Bertrand. 'UFO Abductions As Religious Folklore' in *UFOs 1947–1987: The 40-Year Search for an Explanation* ed Hilary Evans with John Spencer (Fortean Tomes, 1987).

Olsen, Geoff. 'The Eyes Have It' in *International UFO Reporter*, Vol 19, No 6, 1994.

Rogerson, Peter, 'Blood, Vision and Brimstone' in *Magonia*, No 53, 1995.

Russo, Edoardo, and Grassino, Gian Paolo. 'Ufology in Europe: or, What is America Coming To?' in *International UFO Reporter*, Vol 14, No 2, 1989.

Siegel, Ronald K. *Fire in the Brain* (1992; Plume edition, 1993).

Stacy, Dennis. 'Alien Abortions, Avenging Angels' in *Magonia*, No 44, 1992.

Stillings, Dennis. '"The American Way": A Cock and Bullard Story' in *Magonia*, No 35, 1990.

Vallée, Jacques. *Passport to Magonia* (1970; Tandem edition, 1975).

CHAPTER 8

Brookesmith, Peter. *Future Plagues* (Blandford Press UK/ Barnes & Noble US, 1997).

— *UFO: The Government Files* (Blandford Press, 1996).

Clark, Jerome. *The UFO Encyclopedia Vol 3* (Omnigraphics Inc, 1996).

Cooper, William M. *Behold a Pale Horse* (Light Technology, 1991).

Garrett, Laurie. *The Coming Plague* (Penguin, 1995).

Gilmore, Daniel S. (ed). *Scientific Study of Unidentified Flying Objects* (Bantam, 1969). (Generally known as 'The Condon Report'.)

Keyhoe, Donald. *The Flying Saucers Are Real* (Fawcett, 1950).

Klass, Philip J. (ed). *Skeptics UFO Newsletter*, No 43, January 1997.

Lorenzen, Jim and Coral. *Encounters with UFO Occupants* (Berkley, 1976).

Mack, Arien (ed). *In Time of Plague* (New York University Press, 1991).

Menzel, Donald H., and Taves, E. *The UFO Enigma* (Doubleday, 1977).

Norman, Eric. *Gods, Demons and UFOs* (Lancer, 1970).

Peebles, Curtis. *Watch the Skies!* (Berkley, 1995).

Quintanilla, Colonel Hector J. 'Project Blue Book's Last Years' in *The Anomalist*, No 4, 1996.

CHAPTER 9

Allen, Christopher D. 'The Roswell Non-incident: How to Make a Spaceship out of Sticks, Tinfoil and Rumor' (unpublished, 1990).

— 'Stretching Credibility' in *Magonia*, No 45, 1993.

Berlitz, Charles, and Moore, William L. *The Roswell Incident* (Berkley, 1988).

Campbell, Joseph. *The Masks of God: Creative Mythology* (Viking, 1968).

Clark, Jerome. *The UFO Encyclopedia Vol 2* (Omnigraphics Inc, 1992).

Eberhart, George (ed). *The Plains of San Agustin Controversy, July 1947* (CUFOS and FUFOR, 1992).

Friedman, Stanton T. *The Roswell Incident, the USAF and the New York Times* (UFORI, 1994).

— *Roswell Revisited* (UFORI and MUFON, 1995).

— *Top Secret/Magic* (Marlowe 1997)

— and Berliner, Don. *Crash at Corona* (Marlowe, 1992).

General Accounting Office. *Report on the Roswell Incident* (US Government Printing Office, 1994).

Harney, John. 'Roswell: the Search for the "Real" UFO' in *Magonia*, No 41, 1991.

Klass, Philip J. *Skeptics' UFO Newsletter*, 1987–1996 (passim).

McCarthy, Paul. 'The Case of the Vanishing Nurses' in *Omni*, Vol 17, No 8, 1995.

Peebles, Curtis. *Watch the Skies!* (Berkley, 1995).

Pflock, Karl T. 'Star Witness' in *Omni*, Vol 17, No 8, 1995.

Randle, Kevin D. *A History of UFO Crashes* (Avon, 1995).

— *Roswell UFO Crash Update* (Global Communications, 1995).

— *UFO Crash at Roswell* (Avon, 1991).

— and Schmitt, Donald R. *The Truth About the UFO Crash at Roswell* (Avon, 1994).

Sobell, Dave, 'The Truth About Roswell' in *Omni*, Vol 17, No 8, 1995.

Todd, Robert G. 'Major Jesse Marcel: Folk Hero or Mythomaniac?' in *The KowPflop Quarterly*, Vol 1, No 3, 1995.

Weaver, Richard L., and McAndrew, James. *The Roswell Report: Fact Versus Fiction in the New Mexico Desert* (Headquarters US Air Force, 1995). (Includes photographs, interviews, affidavits, and a comprehensive collection of relevant government documents and contemporary press clippings.)

E-mail exchanges concerning the MJ-12 papers, Area 51 and the 'alien autopsy' footage can be found archived on the World Wide Web at: http://www.ufomind.com/ufo/updates

CHAPTER 10

Brady, Brian T., and Rowell, Glen A. 'The Laboratory Investigation of the Electrodynamics of Rock Fracture' in *Nature*, 29 May 1986.

Clarke, David, and Oldroyd, Granville. *Spooklights – A British Survey* (Private, 1985).

Derr, J.S. 'Luminous Phenomena and Earthquakes in Southern Washington' in *Experientia*, No 42, 1986.

— 'Luminous Phenomena and their Relationship to Rock Fracture' in *Nature*, 29 May 1986.

— and Persinger, Michael A. 'Quasi-Experimental Evidence of the Tectonic Strain Theory of Luminous Phenomena: The Derby, Colorado Earthquakes' in *Perceptual and Motor Skills*, No 71, 1990.

Devereux, Paul. *Earth Lights* (Turnstone Press, 1982).

— *Earth Lights Revelation* (Blandford Press, 1989).

— McCartney, Paul, and Robins, Don. 'Bringing UFOs Down to Earth' in *New Scientist*, 1 September 1983.

— and York, Andrew. 'Portrait of a Fault Area', Parts 1 and 2, in *The News* (now *Fortean Times*), Nos 11 and 12, 1975.

Forshufvud, Ragnar. 'Unidentified Flying Objects – A Physical Phenomenon', in *Pursuit*, Vol 13, No 2, 1980.

Fort, Charles. *The Books of Charles Fort* (compendium).

Gearhart, Livingston, and Persinger, Michael A. 'Onsets of Historical and Contemporary Poltergeist Episodes Occurred with Sudden Increases in Geomagnetic Activity' in *Perceptual and Motor Skills*, No 62, 1986.

Hameroff, Stuart. 'Quantum Coherence in Microtubules: A Neural Basis for Emergent Consciousness?' in *Journal of Consciousness Study*, Vol 1, No 1, 1994.

Keel, John A. 'Is the "EM" Effect a Myth?' in *Flying Saucer Review*, Vol 14, No 6, 1968.

— *The 'Flap' Phenomenon in the United States*, reprinted from *Flying Saucer Review*, No 2, June 1969 (1969; New York Fortean Society edition, 1989).

Lagarde, F. *Flying Saucer Review*, Vol 14, No 4, 1968.

McClure, Kevin and Sue. *Stars And Rumours of Stars* (Private, 1980).

Ouellet, Marcel. 'Earthquake Lights and Seismicity' in *Nature*, 6 December 1990.

Persinger, Michael A. 'Geomagnetic Variation as Possible Enhancement Stimuli for UFO Reports Preceding Earth Tremors' in *Perceptual and Motor Skills*, No 60, 1985.

— 'The Tectonic Strain Theory as an Explanation for UFO Phenomena: A Non-Technical Review of the Research, 1970–1990' in *Journal of UFO Studies*, New Series, Vol 2, 1990.

— and Derr, J.S. 'UFO Reports in Carman Manitoba and the 1975 Minnesota Quake: Evidence of Triggering by Increased Volume of the Red River' in *Perceptual and Motor Skills*, No 71, 1990.

— and Lafrenière, Gyslaine F. *Space-Time Transients and Unusual Events* (Nelson-Hall, 1977).

Randles, Jenny. *Pennine UFO Mystery* (Granada, 1983).

Rutledge, Harley D. *Project Identification* (Prentice-Hall, 1981).

Salisbury, Frank B. *The Utah UFO Display* (Devin-Adair, 1974).

CHAPTER 11

Brookesmith, Peter. 'Do Aliens Dream of Jacobs' Sheep?' and 'Pregnant with Meaning' *Fortean Times*, Nos 88 and 90.

Budden, Albert. 'The "Quantock Horror" Revisited' in *The Ley Hunter*, No 122, 1994.

— *UFOs – Psychic Close Encounters* (Blandford Press, 1995).

Clark, Jerome. *The UFO Encyclopedia, Vol 3* (Omnigraphics Inc, 1996).

Cotton, Ian. 'Dr Persinger's God Machine' in the *Independent on Sunday*, 2 July 1996.

Devereux, Paul. *Earth Lights Revelation* (Blandford Press, 1989).

Harpur, Patrick. Letter to *Magonia*, No 41, 1991.

Harris, Melvin. 'Past-life Regression: The Grand Illusion' in Basil, Robert (ed) *Not Necessarily The New Age* (Prometheus Books, 1991).

Hopkins, Budd. *Intruders* (Random House, 1987).

Jacobs, David M. *Secret Life* (Simon & Schuster, 1992; published in the UK as *Alien Encounters*, Virgin, 1994).

Kottmeyer, Martin S. 'Alienating Fancies' in *Magonia*, No 49.

— 'The Curse of the Space Mummies' in *Promises and Disappointments 2, 1996*.

Mack, John E. *Abduction* (Simon & Schuster, 1994).

Méheust, Bertrand. *Science-Fiction et Soucoupes Volantes* (Mercure de France, 1978).

— *Soucoupes Volantes et Folklore* (Mercure de France, 1985).

Persinger, Michael A. 'Expected Clinical Consequences of Close Proximity to UFO-Related Luminosities' in *Perceptual and Motor Skills*, No 56, 1983.

Pritchard, A., Pritchard, D., Mack, J.E., Kasey, P., and Yapp, C. (eds). *Alien Discussions: Proceedings of the Abduction Study Conference* (North Cambridge Press, 1994).

Rimmer, John. *The Evidence for Alien Abductions* (Aquarian Press, 1984).

Rogerson, Peter. 'Northern Echoes' in *Magonia*, No 35, 1990.

Schnabel, Jim. *Dark White* (Hamish Hamilton, 1994).

Stacy, Dennis. 'Transcending Science', in *Omni*, December 1988.

Whitmore, John. 'Religious Dimensions of the UFO Abduction Experience' in Lewis, James R. (ed) *The Gods Have Landed* (State University of New York, 1995).

Wright, Lawrence. *Remembering Satan* (Serpent's Tail, 1994).

EPILOGUE

Paul Devereux

Baker, Robert. 'Alien Dreamtime' in *The Anomalist*, No 2, 1995.

DeKorne, Jim. *Psychedelic Shamanism* (Loompanics Unlimited, 1994).

Devereux, Paul. 'Meeting with the Alien' in *New Ufologist*, Vol 1, No 1, 1994.

— *The Long Trip – A Prehistory of Psychedelia* (Penguin Arkana, 1997).

Hearne, Keith. *The Dream Machine* (Aquarian Press, 1990).

LaBerge, Stephen. *Lucid Dreaming* (Ballantine, 1985).

McKenna, Terence. *The Archaic Revival* (Harper San Francisco, 1991).

Meyer, Peter. 'Apparent Communication with Discarnate Entities Induced by DMT' in *Yearbook for Ethnomedicine and the Study of Consciousness* (VWB, 1992).

Ring, Kenneth. *The Omega Project* (William Morrow, 1992).

Strassman, Richard. 'DMT Research' in *The Scientific and Medical Network Newsletter*, No 51, April 1993.

— 'The Pineal Gland: Current Evidence for its Role in Consciousness' in *Psychedelic Monographs & Essays*, Vol 5, 1990.

Szara, Stephen. 'Hallucinogenic Effects and Metabolism of Tryptamine Derivatives in Man' in *Federation Proceedings*, No 20, 1961 (cited in Meyer, 1992).

Peter Brookesmith
Armstrong, Karen. *A History of God* (Ballantine, 1993).
Bloom, Harold. *The American Religion* (Simon & Schuster, 1992).

Brookesmith, Peter. 'Holy Violence' and 'The Godlings Descend' *Magonia*, Nos 55 and 57, 1996.
Maccoby, Hyam. *Judas Iscariot and the Myth of Jewish Evil* (Free Press, 1992).
Pagels, Elaine. *The Origin of Satan* (Allen Lane, 1995).

Selected Recommended Journals

International UFO Reporter (IUR)

The bi-monthly organ of the Center for UFO Studies. Although IUR essentially supports an extra-terrestrial view of the UFO phenomenon, the editorial content is sane, scholarly, informative, and wide-ranging. All views are published. Available from: CUFOS, 2457 West Petersen Avenue, Chicago, Illinois 60659, USA.

Journal of UFO Studies

An annual, book-length journal exploring ufological themes in considerable depth. Also available from: CUFOS, 2457 West Petersen Avenue, Chicago, Illinois 60659, USA.

Magonia

A leading journal of the 'psychosocial' persuasion. Scholarly, highly informative and thought-provoking. Essential reading even for those who do not share the psychosocial approach. It publishes articles from international authors and experts, and acts as a vehicle for debate, especially on such matters as UFO 'abductions'. Like IUR, it does not shrink from publishing a wide range of views. Quarterly. Available from: John Rimmer, John Dee Cottage, 5 James Terrace, London SW14 8HB, UK.

The Anomalist

Published twice a year, this paperback-length journal is a treasure-trove of articles and information on anomalous phenomena, altered mind states and many mysteries of science, history and nature. Everything from UFOs to abductions to crop circles to sleep disorders to strange creatures. Has highly-informed international contributors. From: Fenner Reed and Jackson, PO Box 754, Manhassett, NY 1030, USA

The Ley Hunter (TLH)

This quarterly journal is *the* source for updated news on earth lights research. In addition, it carries numerous articles and items dealing with ancient traditions of altered mind states and the 'spirit' worldviews that resulted from that (all of which can have significant bearing on the mind states involved in UFO 'abductions'). TLH's overt focus on ancient sites, landscapes and knowledge actually covers for a wide-ranging, cross-disciplinary forum that for the alert and intelligent reader can put the anthropology and ethnopsychology into ufology. In the UK and Europe available from: TLH, PO Box 258, Cheltenham, GL53 OHR. In North America: Dept. TLH, PO Box 940, Beacon, NY 12508, USA.

Fortean Times (FT)

The premier journal on anomalous phenomena and events. FT has been running in one form or another for decades, and is now monthly. Its founding editor, Bob Rickard, and his editorial colleagues are the best-informed in the business. Along with news of latest events, FT carries articles ranging from UFOs, earth lights and abductions to studies in false memory syndrome, conspiracies, and the full range of associated subject matter. Available from any good news-stand, or for subscription enquiries phone 01454 202515 (from outside the UK that would be +44 1454 202515).

¤ Index ¤

hollow Earth belief 58–9
hypnosis 87, 94–5, 162–3, 164–5

iatrogenesis 99–100
ideologies in ufology 92–7
Independence Day 6, 38–9, 43
Indiana 18
International Consciousness Research
    Laboratories (ICRL) 151, 152
Irving, Robert 74, 75

Japan 16
Johannis, Rapuzzi 33–4
Jones, Janet (Jane Evans) 164–5
Jung, Carl 76, 87

Keel, John 53–4, 83, 84–5
Keyhoe, Donald 24, 27, 32, 106–7
Kimberley lights 152–4
King, George 78–80
Klarer, Elizabeth 30–1
Klass, Philip J. 109
Korff, Kal 82–3
Kottmeyer, Martin 93–4
Kraspedon, Dino 30

Lear Document 111–12
Leslie, Desmond 60
Levelland, Texas 50
Levengood, Dr W.C. 68–9, 72–3
ley lines 63–6
light phenomena 54, 138–59
    body and mind effects of 171–4
    Burton Dassett 146, 148
    and earthquakes 53, 139–40, 143, 157
    Egryn Lights 147
    Hessdalen 143–5
    history of 148
    Kimberley 152–4
    Marfa lights 150–2
    Mount Popocatapetl 155–6
    piezo-electrical effect 141
    and poltergeists 158
    Quebec 159
    scientific research 149–50
    Tectonic Strain Theory (TST) 141
    Yakima 141–2
lightning 156–7
linear markings
    ley lines 63–6
    Nazca lines 62–3
Lyons, Jim 75

Majority 12 committee 112–13, 120,
    122–5
Maldekians 79
Mansfield, Ohio 51
Marcel, Major Jesse 122, 126–8
Marfa lights 150–2
Mars 6–10
Mayan Kukulcan 59
media influences 36–43

on abductions 42–3, 96, 163–4
    on waves 55, 57
medieval accounts of UFOs 15–17
Meier, Eduard 'Billy' 81–3
Menger, Howard 31
Metonites 30–1
Mexican wave 56–7
Michell, John 65–6
MJ12 112–13, 120, 122–5
Mochras Fault 148

National Security Agency (NSA) 108–9
Nazca lines 62–3
Nebraska 18
Nelson, Buck 65
Norman, Ruth and Ernest 80–1
NSA (National Security Agency) 108–9
Nuremberg 16

Opus Dei 71

Philip experiment 75
photographs 46–7, 49
piezo-electrical effects 141
Pleiadians 81
poltergeists 51–2, 158
Popocatapetl, Mount 155–6
Project Blue Book 88–9
Project Grudge 106
Project Hessdalen 143–5, 150, 158
Project Sign 24, 26, 106
Protocols of the Elders of Zion 113
psychosocial ufology 86, 90, 95–103, 138
Puddy, Maureen 92, 167
Purdy, Ken W. 106

'Quantock Horror' 177
Quebec lights 159

reincarnation 80
religion 40, 85, 183, 185
ritual satanic abuse (RSA) 165–6
Robertson panel 107
rock art 60–1
Roper Organization Poll 170
Roswell Incident 38, 120–34
Russian wave 34–5

Sandby, Thomas 12–13, 14
Scandinavian ghost rockets 20–1
Schnabel, Jim 70–1
science fiction
    films 37–43
    publications 22
screen memories 163
Scully, Frank 26–7
'Shamanic Mandala' 70
Socorro case 50
solarization 60
Sorenson, Peter 74
'Space Brothers' 30
'Space People' 31, 64, 65

Spielberg, Steven 37, 41
Star Trek 37
Star Wars 37
stone circles 65
Stonehenge 65
Strieber, Whitley 97
sunspots 51
Swedenborg, Emanuel 27
Swedish ghost rockets 21
Symmes, John Cleves 58

Tashkent earthquake 53
Tectonic Strain Theory (TST) 141
Teed, Cyrus Reed 58
telepathy 78
television influences 37, 43, 96
    see also media influences
Terran civilization 79
TST (Tectonic Strain Theory) 141

UFOCAT 46
Unarius 80–1
United States Air Force
    Project Blue Book 88–9
    Project Grudge 106
    Project Sign 24, 26, 106
    see also conspiracy theories

Val Camonica 60
Valensole 50–1
Vallée, Jacques 87
Venusians 29
von Daniken, Erich 60–3
vorton particles 157–8

Walton, Travis 175–6
'war nerves' 36
Warminster 49, 146
Watkins, Alfred 63–4
wave phenomena 18–19, 44–56
    of 1957 55
    of 1964–8 49–51
    chronology 47
    French wave 35, 47–8, 52–3
    and the media 55, 57
    Mexican wave 56–7
    patterns in 46
    reasons for 51–3
    Russian wave 34–5
    and social conditions 57
Wedd, Tony 64–5
Williamson, George Hunt 113
Wilson, Jack 90–2
windows 46, 53–4
Windsor object 12–13, 14–15
witnesses *see* contactees
Wolffart, Conrad 15, 16
wraparound eyes 103

Yakima Indian Reservation 141–2

Zamora, Lonnie 50